W9-BCI-839

Austria
a country study

Federal Research Division
Library of Congress
Edited by
Eric Solsten and
David E. McClave
Research Completed
December 1993

On the cover: Coat of arms of the Republic of Austria

Second Edition, First Printing, 1994.

Library of Congress Cataloging-in-Publication Data

Austria : a country study / Federal Research Division, Library of Congress ; edited by Eric Solsten and David E. McClave. — 2nd ed.
    p. cm. — (Area handbook series, ISSN 1057-5294)
(DA pam ; 550-176)
    "Supersedes the 1976 edition of Area handbook for Austria, coauthored by Eugene K. Keefe et al."—T.p. verso.
    "Research completed December 1993."
    Includes bibliographical references (pp. 273-286) and index.
    ISBN 0-8444-0829-8
    1. Austria. I. Solsten, Eric, 1943- . II. McClave, David E., 1947- . III. Library of Congress. Federal Research Division.
IV. Area handbook for Austria. V. Series. VI. Series: DA pam ; 550-176.
DB17.A8 1994   94-21665
943—dc20   CIP

Headquarters, Department of the Army
DA Pam 550-176

For sale by the Superintendent of Documents, U.S. Government Printing Office
Washington, D.C. 20402

Foreword

This volume is one in a continuing series of books prepared by the Federal Research Division of the Library of Congress under the Country Studies/Area Handbook Program sponsored by the Department of the Army. The last two pages of this book list the other published studies.

Most books in the series deal with a particular foreign country, describing and analyzing its political, economic, social, and national security systems and institutions, and examining the interrelationships of those systems and the ways they are shaped by cultural factors. Each study is written by a multidisciplinary team of social scientists. The authors seek to provide a basic understanding of the observed society, striving for a dynamic rather than a static portrayal. Particular attention is devoted to the people who make up the society, their origins, dominant beliefs and values, their common interests and the issues on which they are divided, the nature and extent of their involvement with national institutions, and their attitudes toward each other and toward their social system and political order.

The books represent the analysis of the authors and should not be construed as an expression of an official United States government position, policy, or decision. The authors have sought to adhere to accepted standards of scholarly objectivity. Corrections, additions, and suggestions for changes from readers will be welcomed for use in future editions.

Louis R. Mortimer
Chief
Federal Research Division
Library of Congress
Washington, DC 20540–5220

Acknowledgments

This edition supersedes the *Area Handbook for Austria,* published in 1976. The authors wish to acknowledge their use of portions of that edition in the preparation of the current book.

The authors also are grateful to individuals in various United States government agencies who gave their time and special knowledge to provide information and perspective. These individuals include Ralph K. Benesch, who oversees the Country Studies/ Area Handbook Program for the Department of the Army. Frank J. LaScala reviewed portions of the manuscript and provided military photographs. In addition, the authors wish to thank various members of the staff of the Embassy of Austria in Washington, especially Hedwig Sommer, and of the Austrian National Tourist Office in New York for their assistance.

Various members of the staff of the Federal Research Division of the Library of Congress assisted in the preparation of the book. Sandra W. Meditz made helpful suggestions during her review of all parts of the book, as did Andrea M. Savada. Tim L. Merrill assisted in the preparation of some of the maps, checked the content of all the maps, and reviewed the sections on geography and telecommunications. Thanks also go to David P. Cabitto, who provided graphics support; Wayne Horn, who designed the cover and chapter art; Marilyn L. Majeska, who managed editing and edited portions of the manuscript; Laura C. Wells, who helped prepare the Country Profile, tables, and Bibliography; Andrea T. Merrill, who managed production; and Barbara Edgerton, Alberta Jones King, and Izella Watson, who did the word processing.

Others who contributed were Harriett R. Blood and the firm of Greenhorne and O'Mara, who assisted in the preparation of maps and charts; Martha E. Hopkins, who edited portions of the manuscript; Sheila L. Ross, who performed the final prepublication editorial review; and Joan C. Cook, who prepared the Index. Linda Peterson of the Library of Congress Composing Unit prepared camera-ready copy under the direction of Peggy Pixley. The inclusion of photographs was made possible by the generosity of various public and private agencies.

Contents

	Page
Foreword	iii
Acknowledgments	v
Preface	xiii
Country Profile	xv
Introduction	xxi
Chapter 1. Historical Setting	1

Steven R. Harper

THE ALPINE-DANUBIAN REGION BEFORE THE
HABSBURG DYNASTY 4
    The Celtic and Roman Eras 4
    The Early Medieval Era 5
    The Holy Roman Empire and the Duchy of Austria . 6
RISE OF THE HABSBURG EMPIRE 7
    The Habsburg Dynasty in the Late Medieval Era . . . 7
    Territorial Expansion, Division, and Consolidation . . 8
    The Protestant Reformation in the Habsburg Lands . . 9
    The Turkish Threat 10
THE COUNTER-REFORMATION AND THE THIRTY
YEARS' WAR 11
    Division and Rebellion 11
    The Thirty Years' War, 1618–48 11
    The Peace of Westphalia 12
THE BAROQUE ERA 13
    Political and Religious Consolidation under Leopold . . 13
    The Turkish Wars and the Siege of Vienna 14
    The War of the Spanish Succession 14
    The Pragmatic Sanction and the War of the Austrian
    Succession, 1740–48 15
THE REFORMS OF MARIA THERESA AND
JOSEPH II 16
    Baroque Absolutism and Enlightened Despotism 16
    The Strategic Impact of the Reform Era 17
THE HABSBURG EMPIRE AND THE FRENCH
REVOLUTION 18
    The Napoleonic Wars 18
    The Congress of Vienna 19

AUSTRIA IN THE AGE OF METTERNICH 21
    International Developments, 1815–48 21
    Domestic Policies 21
THE REVOLUTION OF 1848 AND NEOABSOLUTISM .. 22
    Revolutionary Rise and Fall 22
    The Failure of Neoabsolutism 24
    Loss of Leadership in Germany 25
AUSTRIA-HUNGARY TO THE EARLY 1900s 26
    The Founding of the Dual Monarchy 26
    Final Defeat in Germany and Reconciliation
       with Prussia 27
    The Eastern Question 29
    Internal Developments in Austria 30
THE FINAL YEARS OF THE EMPIRE AND WORLD
    WAR I 33
    The Crisis over Bosnia and Hercegovina 33
    World War I 33
    The End of the Habsburg Empire and the Birth
       of the Austrian Republic 35
THE FIRST REPUBLIC 35
    Overview of the Political Camps 35
    The Foundation of the First Republic 38
    Political Life of the 1920s and Early 1930s 39
    The End of Constitutional Rule 41
    Growing German Pressure on Austria 43
THE ANSCHLUSS AND WORLD WAR II 44
    Absorption of Austria into the Third Reich 44
    Nazi Economic and Social Policies 45
    Repression and Compliance 47
    World War II and the Defeat of Nazi Germany 47
RESTORED INDEPENDENCE UNDER ALLIED
    OCCUPATION 48
    Foundation of the Second Republic 48
    Four Power Occupation and Recognition of the
       Provisional Government 50
    The 1945 Election and Consolidation of the
       Austrian Government 51
    Consolidation of Democracy 52
    Austria's Integration with the West 54
    The 1955 State Treaty and Austrian Neutrality 55
THE GRAND COALITION AND THE AUSTRIAN
    PEOPLE'S PARTY CODA, 1955–70 56
    Foreign Policy in the Late 1950s and the 1960s 56
    Elections and Parties 58

Domestic Tranquillity under the Grand Coalition 59
THE KREISKY YEARS, 1970–83 60
Electoral Politics in the Kreisky Era 60
Domestic Issues 61
Foreign Policy 62
End of the Kreisky Era 63

Chapter 2. The Society and Its Environment 65
Lonnie Johnson

GEOGRAPHY 69
Landform Regions 70
Human Geography 73
Climate 75
Ecological Concerns 76
AUSTRIAN NATIONAL IDENTITY 78
DEMOGRAPHY 80
Demographic Development 80
Immigration 83
Emigration 86
SOCIAL MINORITIES 86
Official Minority Groups 87
Other Minorities 89
Attitudes Toward Minorities 93
SOCIAL STRUCTURE 94
FAMILY LIFE 96
Family Developments after the 1960s 96
Status of Women 99
RELIGION 101
EDUCATION 104
SOCIAL SECURITY 109
Employment, Unemployment, and Pension
Benefits 110
Health and Health Insurance 111
Family Benefits 113
HOUSING 114

Chapter 3. The Economy 117
W.R. Smyser

ECONOMIC GROWTH AND GOVERNMENT
POLICY 121
Historical Background 121
Developments During the 1970s and 1980s 126
The New Policies 127

The Magic Pentagon 130
The Subsidy Policy 130
Foreign Workers in Austria 132
PRINCIPAL ECONOMIC INTEREST GROUPS 133
The Chambers of Commerce 134
The Chambers of Agriculture 134
The Chambers of Labor 135
The Professions 135
The Austrian Trade Union Federation 136
Works Councils 137
The Federation of Austrian Industrialists 137
SOCIAL PARTNERSHIP 138
STRUCTURE OF THE ECONOMY 140
The Agricultural Sector 143
The Industrial Sector 146
Energy 149
The Services Sector 150
FOREIGN ECONOMIC RELATIONS 159
Foreign Trade and the Balance of Payments 159
Austria and European Integration 160
Openings Toward the East 162

Chapter 4. Government and Politics 165
John F. Schaettler

CONSTITUTIONAL FRAMEWORK 168
GOVERNMENT INSTITUTIONS 171
The Federal President 172
Chancellor and Cabinet 174
Nationalrat 175
Bundesrat 179
Bundesversammlung 179
Judicial System 180
Civil Service 183
Provincial Government 184
Local Government 185
Electoral System 186
POLITICAL DYNAMICS 188
The Social Democratic Party of Austria 190
The Austrian People's Party 194
The Freedom Party of Austria 197
The Green Parties 200
Political Developments since 1983 202

MASS MEDIA 210
    Newspapers and Periodicals 210
    Radio and Television 212
FOREIGN RELATIONS 213
    Foreign Policy During the Kreisky Era 213
    New Focus on Europe 216
    Regional Issues 219

Chapter 5. National Security 221
                  Jean R. Tartter

HISTORICAL BACKGROUND 224
    The Habsburg Military 224
    Two World Wars, 1914–18 and 1939–45 226
STRATEGIC CONCEPTS AND MISSIONS OF THE
  AUSTRIAN ARMED FORCES 228
NEUTRALITY AND THE ARMED FORCES 232
NATIONAL DEFENSE 233
    Army 235
    Personnel, Conscription, Training, and Reserves 237
    Army Equipment 241
    Air Force 242
    Uniforms, Ranks, and Insignia 244
    Military Justice 245
    The Defense Budget 247
    Domestic and Foreign Sources of Military
      Equipment 248
INTERNAL SECURITY 249
    Penal Codes 252
    Criminal Court Proceedings 253
    Police 253
    Incidence of Crime 257
    Penal System 257

Appendix. Tables 261

Bibliography 273

Glossary 287

Index 291

Contributors 311

List of Figures
1 Administrative Divisions of Austria, 1993 xx
2 Europe in the Sixteenth Century 10

3   Austrian Empire, 1815   20
4   Austria-Hungary, 1867–1918   28
5   Topography and Drainage   72
6   Population by Age and Gender, 1990   82
7   Population by Age and Gender, Projected 2020   84
8   Structure of the Education System, 1993 108
9   Economic Activity, 1993 148
10   Transportation System, 1993 154
11   Structure of Government, 1993 172
12   Organization of National Defense, Planned 1995 236
13   Major Military Installations, Planned 1995 238
14   Military Ranks and Insignia, 1993 246

Preface

Like its predecessor, this study attempts to review the history and treat in a concise and objective manner the dominant social, political, economic, and military aspects of Austria. Sources of information included books, scholarly journals, foreign and domestic newspapers, official reports of government and international organizations, and numerous periodicals on Austrian and international affairs. Chapter bibliographies appear at the end of the book, and brief comments on some of the more valuable sources recommended for further reading appear at the end of each chapter. A glossary also is included.

Spellings of place-names used in the book are in most cases those approved by the United States Board on Geographic Names. Exceptions are the use of Vienna rather than Wien, Danube rather than Donau, Lake Constance rather than Bodensee, and the English names of four Austrian provinces rather than their German names: Carinthia rather than Kärnten, Lower Austria rather than Niederösterreich, Styria rather than Steiermark, and Upper Austria rather than Oberösterreich.

Measurements are given in the metric system. A conversion table is provided to assist readers unfamiliar with metric measures (see table 1, Appendix).

The body of the text reflects information available as of December 31, 1993. Certain other portions of the text, however, have been updated. The Introduction discusses significant events that have occurred since the completion of the research, the Country Profile and Glossary include updated information as available, and the Bibliography lists recently published sources thought to be particularly helpful to the reader.

Country Profile

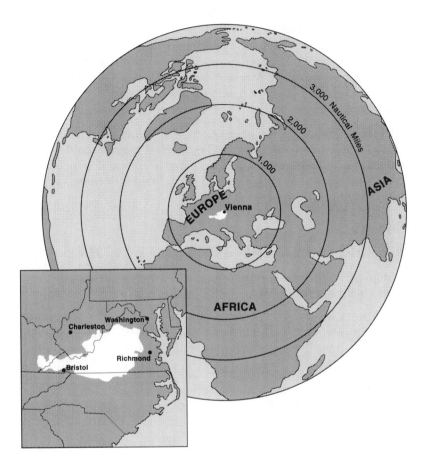

Country

Formal Name: Republic of Austria.

Short Form: Austria.

Term for Citizens: Austrian(s).

Capital: Vienna.

NOTE—The Country Profile contains updated information as available.

Geography

Size: Approximately 83,859 square kilometers.

Topography: Most of country Alpine or sub-Alpine; heavily wooded mountains and hills cut by valleys of fast-flowing rivers. Plains around Vienna and Danube Valley in northeast only lowland areas and contain most of population. Danube, flowing east through northern provinces and Vienna, principal river. Of total area, 20 percent arable land, 29 percent pasture, 44 percent forest, and 7 percent barren.

Climate: Continental weather systems predominate; temperatures and rainfall vary with altitude. Temperate, cloudy, cold winters with frequent rain in lowlands and snow in mountains; cool summers with occasional showers. Humidity highest in wetter western regions, diminishing toward east.

Society

Population: In May 1991 census, population 7,795,786.

Language: Of native-born population, 99 percent German-speaking with small minorities speaking Serbo-Croatian or Slovenian.

Religion: Of native-born and foreign-born population combined, about 78 percent Roman Catholic, 5 percent Protestant, 8 percent other (includes Jewish, Muslim, and Orthodox), and 9 percent no denomination.

Education: Public elementary, secondary, and higher education free; nine years compulsory. By ninth year, students usually in preuniversity academic schools or vocational education. Literacy 99 percent for population over age fifteen.

Health and Welfare: Social insurance covers all wage-earners and salaried employees, self-employed workers, and dependents. Coverage compulsory. State-required health insurance covers 99 percent of population. In 1990 average life expectancy almost seventy-six years (seventy-two for males and seventy-nine for females).

Economy

Gross National Product (GNP): US$174.8 billion in 1992 with 2 percent growth rate; US$22,110 per capita with 2.4 percent growth rate.

Agriculture and Forestry: Agriculture and forestry accounted for 2.8 percent of gross domestic product (GDP) and 7.4 percent of labor force in 1991. Principal crops: grains, fruit, potatoes, sugar beets, sawn wood, cattle, pigs, and poultry. About 80 to 90 percent self-sufficient in food.

Industry: Major sector with 36.3 percent of GDP and 36.9 percent of employment in 1991.

Services: Services accounted for 60.9 percent of GDP and 55.8 percent of employment in 1991. Largest growth sector; 10 percent growth in share of GDP and 14 percent growth in share of labor force since 1970.

Major Trading Partners: Most trade with European Union (EU). Germany largest single trading partner (in 1993 accounted for 38.9 percent of exports and 41.5 percent of imports), followed by Italy and Switzerland.

Imports: US$48.6 billion in 1993. Major imports: machinery and equipment, manufacturing products, chemical products, fuels and energy, and foodstuffs.

Exports: US$40.2 billion in 1993. Major exports: machinery and equipment, paper and paper products, transport equipment, metal manufactures, and textiles and clothing.

Balance of Payments: Current account deficit US$900 million in 1993. Persistent trade deficit. Per capita income from tourism highest in world; helps balance deficit.

General Economic Conditions: Stable economy with generally good rates of growth; high living standards, comparable with other countries of Western Europe. In 1992 real GDP growth 1.6 percent, inflation 4.1 percent, and unemployment 5.9 percent; in 1993 real GDP growth – 0.3 percent, inflation 3.6 percent, and unemployment 6.8 percent.

Currency and Exchange Rate: Schilling. In March 1994, exchange rate US$1 = S12.1.

Transportation and Communications

Railroads: 6,028 kilometers total (94 percent standard-gauge 1.435 meter and 6 percent 0.760 meter), of which about 5,388 kilometers state owned and 640 kilometers privately owned.

Highways: As of December 1992, 108,000 kilometers of roads, of which about 1,800 kilometers major highways, 9,900 kilometers main roads, and 25,900 kilometers secondary roads.

Inland Waterways: More than 350 kilometers, carrying approximately one-fifth of total trade. Danube River only navigable waterway with barges carrying up to 1,800 tons; important connection with North Sea, Germany, and Black Sea.

Ports: Vienna major river port.

Civil Airports: Fifty-five total; twenty with permanent-surface runways. Main international airport at Vienna-Schwechat, southeast of Vienna; international flights also from Graz, Innsbruck, Klagenfurt, Linz, and Salzburg.

Telecommunications: Highly developed and efficient system with 4 million telephones, twenty-seven radio stations, forty-seven television stations, and four satellite ground stations.

Government and Politics

Government: Federal republic with nine provinces, each with own assembly and government. 1920 constitution, revised 1929, forms constitutional basis of government. Government consists of executive, legislative, and judicial branches. President head of state, elected every six years by popular vote. Executive headed by chancellor (prime minister) and cabinet, which reflect party composition of parliament. Legislative power vested in bicameral parliament consisting of Nationalrat (National Council) and Bundesrat (Federal Council). Nationalrat primary legislative power, with 183 popularly elected members; Bundesrat represents the provinces with sixty-three members elected by provincial assemblies. Independent judiciary.

Legal System: Supreme Court for civil and criminal cases, Administrative Court for cases involving administrative agencies, and Constitutional Court for constitutional cases. Four higher provincial courts, seventeen provincial and district courts, and numerous local courts.

Politics: Dominated by Social Democratic Party of Austria (Sozialdemokratische Partei Österreichs—SPÖ) and Austrian People's Party (Österreichs Volkspartei—ÖVP); government coalition of these two parties since 1987. Freedom Party of Austria (Freiheitliche Partei Österreichs—FPÖ) gaining strength despite split in early 1993 with formation of The Liberal Forum (Das Liberale Forum). Environmentalists also represented in parliament.

Foreign Relations: Founding member of European Free Trade Association (EFTA) and member of United Nations (UN) and European Economic Area (EEA). Admission into European Union (EU) expected in January 1995.

National Security

Armed Forces: In 1994 defense forces consisted of 51,250 troops, of which 44,000 were in Bundesheer (Federal Army; including 19,500 conscripts) and 7,250 in air force (including 2,400 conscripts). No women serve in armed forces.

Treaty Commitments: State Treaty of 1955 prohibits union with Germany. Constitutional Law of October 26, 1955, declares permanent neutrality, rejects participation in any military alliance, and prohibits establishment of any foreign military base on territory.

Conscription and Reserves: Males obliged to perform total of six months of active duty and two months of reserve training (or eight months of active duty with no reserve training). Ready reserves (ready within seventy-two hours) 119,000 in 1994. Each year 66,000 receive refresher training. Additional 960,000 under age fifty with reserve training (all ranks).

Standing Forces: According to *The Military Balance, 1994–1995,* army consists of three corps (one organized as mechanized division consisting of three armored infantry brigades) and one provincial military command. Air force (part of Bundesheer) has one air division headquarters, three air regiments, and three air defense battalions. Reorganization of Bundesheer under New Army Structure to be completed in 1995.

Troops Abroad: In 1994 Austrian military troops serving in UN peacekeeping forces included deployment in Cyprus, Golan Heights, Iraq-Kuwait border, and Rwanda.

Sources of Equipment: Heavily dependent on foreign suppliers: United States, 29 percent; Western Europe, excluding Germany, 67 percent. State Treaty precludes arms imports from Germany. Sweden primary source of aircraft and missiles.

Defense Expenditures: In 1993 defense budget US$1.63 billion, lowest proportion of GNP (1 to 2 percent) in Europe, except for Luxembourg.

Internal Security: Most important law enforcement agencies part of national government and organized by Ministry for Interior. Federal Police, oriented to urban areas; Gendarmerie, responsible for rural areas and towns without federal or local contingent; State Police, concerned with counterterrorism and counterintelligence.

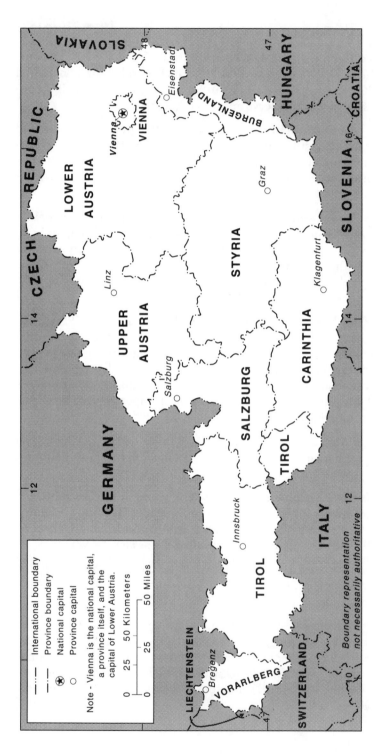

Figure 1. Administrative Divisions of Austria, 1993

Introduction

THE AUSTRIAN PEOPLE ENDURED a series of political, social, and economic upheavals between the outbreak of World War I and the division of Europe into two hostile blocs shortly after World War II. In the next few decades, however, they succeeded in establishing a prosperous and stable democracy. Indeed, they were so successful that by the 1970s Austria had come to be widely characterized as "an island of the blessed" because of the material well-being of its people and the virtual absence of social conflict.

Devised in the first decade after War World II, the system of governing—the social partnership—that made this achievement possible gave each of Austria's main social groups a decisive say in the management of the country's affairs. In marked contrast to the social tensions of the interwar period, which culminated in a brief civil war in 1934, in the postwar era the representatives of agriculture, commerce, and labor were able to work together harmoniously for the benefit of all. By the 1990s, the decades of prosperity engineered through the system of social partnership had given Austrians one of the world's highest living standards. Sustained prosperity and social peace yielded yet another achievement, the creation of a viable nation supported by the overwhelming majority of its citizens. Thus, the Austrian state assembled out of the ruins of the Habsburg Empire at the end of World War I— said by many to be "the state no one wanted"—was replaced by one that gradually won the allegiance of its citizens by providing them with a long period of uninterrupted peace and prosperity.

At the beginning of the twentieth century, the territory occupied by present-day Austria had been ruled by the Habsburg Dynasty for more than 600 years. This territory was the core of an empire that at its height in the sixteenth century included Spain and its colonies in the New World, and much of Italy and the Low Countries. Although a military defeat at the hands of Prussia in 1866 had weakened Emperor Franz Joseph I (r. 1848–1916) and had obliged him to make such significant concessions to his Hungarian subjects the following year that the lands he ruled came to be known as Austria-Hungary (also seen as the Austro-Hungarian Empire), his empire remained one of Europe's great powers. In the last decades of the nineteenth century, it allied itself with Germany and Italy and in the years leading up to World War I actively pursued an aggressive foreign policy to extend Habsburg influence farther south in the Balkans.

The Habsburg Empire was supranational in nature. Many ethnic groups lived within its boundaries, including Germans, Czechs, Slovaks, Poles, Hungarians, Slovenes, Croats, Serbs, and Romanians. Most of the empire's German-speaking subjects lived in the territory that makes up present-day Austria, but significant numbers also lived in Bohemia, Moravia, and Silesia, and smaller numbers were found throughout the empire. Although the Hungarians had been granted the right to govern themselves and to have a significant say in determining the empire's affairs, German speakers remained dominant within the empire. Their dominance had gone on for centuries, although they made up only one-fourth of the population. Perhaps owing to their privileged status, the German speakers were more loyal to the empire than any other ethnic group. They did not see themselves as Austrian, however, but instead felt a strong local patriotism for their native provinces. They also thought of themselves as belonging to the German cultural community, a community found not only in Austria but also in Germany and Switzerland, and anywhere else German was spoken.

Germany's unification in 1871 under Prussian leadership after many centuries of division was only the most notable result of the powerful force of nationalism that appeared in many areas of Europe in the nineteenth century. Just to the south of the Habsburg Empire, for example, the many small states of the Italian peninsula had come together to form a united Italy. The nationalist ideal also came to touch with an ever-growing strength many of the peoples living within the Habsburg Empire. It was an ideal completely at variance with the supranational foundations of the empire and would in the end lead to its destruction. As nationalism gained in influence, growing numbers of the empire's inhabitants came to believe that they more rightly owed allegiance to their own ethnic group than to a ruling elite speaking a different language.

In response to the nationalist movements emerging within Austria-Hungary, the empire's German speakers formed their own political groups, often described as German nationalist-liberal, to protect their rights. Because the German-speaking community remained loyal to Emperor Franz Joseph, few of its members wished to see the areas in which they lived secede from the empire and become part of the newly united and powerful Germany. Their aims were to maintain their privileged position within the empire and to ensure that the German language did not lose ground to the empire's other languages.

In addition to the German nationalist-liberal parties active in the late nineteenth century, German speakers created political parties that had other goals. The Social Democratic Workers' Party and the Christian Social Party were the most important political parties. The former sought to establish a socialist society based on Marxist principles. The latter sought to improve society, particularly (but not exclusively) rural society, by emphasizing Christian values and traditions. Because the memberships of both parties were largely German speaking, they had some sympathy with the aims of the empire's German nationalists. Their main concerns, however, were elsewhere.

World War I was set off by the June 1914 assassination of Archduke Franz Ferdinand, heir to the Habsburg throne, by Serbian nationalists. Within weeks, a system of interlocking alliances set the Great Powers of Europe against one another. By the war's end in November 1918, the Habsburg Empire had ceased to exist. Some of the empire's ethnic groups formed new nations. A German Austrian state was established on October 21, 1918. On November 12, 1918, one day after the war ended, the new state was declared a republic.

The new Austrian state was only one-fourth as large as the empire. In the eyes of many of its citizens, it was a mere "rump state" and was neither economically nor socially viable. Many argued that it logically should be part of Germany. The war's victors—the United States, Britain, and France—feared such a union would strengthen Germany, and they prohibited it. They also required that the new state be called the Republic of Austria rather than the German Austrian Republic. Despite the Allied prohibition, desire for union with Germany remained strong in Austria, particularly among German nationalist-liberals and socialists.

Shorn of many of the traditional economic connections it had had within the empire, Austria was poorly positioned to prosper. Its struggling economy was also hurt by the European economic slump of the early 1920s. The new republic's economic troubles diminished the support it needed from its citizens to survive. Rather than joining together to build a nation, Austrians sought social and economic security by withdrawing into the three large social groups, or camps (*Lager*), that predated the war: German nationalist-liberal, socialist, and Christian Social. Austrians usually gave their loyalty to the *Lager* in which they were born rather than to the country as a whole. Each *Lager* maintained a network of organizations such as credit unions, sports clubs, home mortgage funds, and the like that ministered to the economic and social needs of its members. Thus, contact among Austrians of different social backgrounds was lessened.

The hostility the groups felt for one another increased their inner cohesion. Socialist plans to establish a society founded on

Marxist principles frightened the right-wing German nationalist-liberals and Christian Socials and heightened their determination to defend their property. Socialist and German nationalist-liberal anticlericalism caused Christian Socials to be more resolute in defending their religious values. German nationalist-liberal and Christian Social anti-Semitism caused many Austrian Jews to become active in the socialist movement. This in turn meant that many on the right came to hate socialism even more because they saw it as a Jewish-controlled conspiracy to subvert all cherished values.

In response to the animosity the *Lager* felt for one other, armed militias were soon formed. The right-wing militia joined at times with state forces to oppose the socialists. Organized violence became frequent as the Christian Socials combined with the German nationalist-liberals to exclude socialists from the national government. Socialists governed only in Vienna. The many leftist social measures they enacted in "Red Vienna" further hardened conservative opposition.

A failed uprising in February 1934, in which the socialists sought to stand up to the central authorities, marked the definitive end of Austrian parliamentary democracy, already partially suspended the previous year. The Christian Social Engelbert Dollfuss established a right-wing authoritarian regime that attempted to govern Austria according to Christian principles. Austrian National Socialists, or Nazis, who desired to unite Austria with Germany, then ruled by Adolf Hitler, assassinated Dollfuss in July 1934. They were not strong enough to seize power, however, and the Dollfuss regime continued under the leadership of Kurt von Schuschnigg.

Despite the failed Nazi coup d'état, agitation for annexation, or Anschluss, of Austria by Germany continued. Schuschnigg resisted Hitler's demands for Anschluss for a time, but in March 1938 German troops occupied Austria. Because most Austrians felt little loyalty to their country, its seizure by Germany was widely supported, even by many socialists.

Austria was quickly and thoroughly absorbed by Nazi Germany. The country's new rulers attempted to expunge all traces of an independent Austria by ruthless personnel and administrative practices. Even the name *Austria* was replaced by a new designation—*Ostmark*. Austrians were drafted into the German army, the Wehrmacht, and when World War II began, they fought until Germany's unconditional surrender in May 1945.

Austria's human and material losses from the war were great. Furthermore, the country was divided into four zones, each occupied by one of the victorious Allies: the United States, Britain,

France, and the Soviet Union. Under the watchful eyes of the occupation powers, Austrians reestablished a government based on the constitution of 1920, as amended in 1929. This second attempt of Austrians to govern themselves in a parliamentary democracy proved eminently successful. In what came to be called the Second Republic, Austrians enjoyed a long period of social peace and prosperity.

A key reason for the success of the Second Republic was the manifest failure of the First Republic (1918–38). Confronted with a defeat of this magnitude, Austrian politicians vowed not to repeat the mistakes of the earlier period. Leaders of opposing parties imprisoned together in Nazi concentration camps discussed what was needed to rebuild their country and agreed to play down the ideological differences that had made interwar politics so bitter. In addition, Nazi barbarities gave them good reason to emphasize what distinguished Austria from Germany.

External forces also contributed to the eventual success of the Second Republic. The occupation of Austria by foreign troops and the need to resist their demands encouraged a new Austrian unity, as opposed to the lethal divisiveness of the First Republic. Furthermore, the gradual extinguishing of political freedom in Eastern Europe in the first years after World War II made the principles of parliamentary democracy more attractive than they had been in the interwar period. The Soviet Union's practices in its occupation zone were a daily affront to Austrians and discredited political groups not committed to parliamentary democracy. In the interwar period, in contrast, no political party had fully supported this form of government, and several had been actively opposed to it.

In addition to failing to establish a working democracy during the First Republic, Austrians also had failed to put in place a nation supported by most of its citizens. During the Second Republic—likewise born in defeat at the end of a world war—a stable, prosperous society was created that with time engendered in its members a sense of pride in their Austrian identity. This feeling of a national identity was new. As late as 1956, only 49 percent of Austrians believed that they constituted a nation, whereas 46 percent saw themselves as Germans. Several decades of success as a nation altered the views of most Austrians on this matter. An opinion poll in 1989, for example, found that 78 percent of Austrians agreed that they constituted a nation, and only 9 percent held that they did not.

After World War I, Austria's economy floundered for a time, improved in the second half of the 1920s, then collapsed with the onset of the Great Depression. In contrast to this failure, after World War II an initial period of hardship was followed by decades of economic growth, which has continued into the 1990s.

In the first years after World War II, Austrians nationalized a large portion of their economy to protect it from foreign seizure, particularly by the Soviet Union. They also worked out mechanisms to involve the main participants in the economy—agriculture, commerce, and labor—in determining democratically how the economy was to be managed. During the 1950s and 1960s, further bargaining institutions were created, most notably the Parity Commission for Prices and Wages, that involved economic interest groups and the government in major economic decisions. The resulting system, the social partnership, is responsible for the extremely low incidence of strikes in Austria and the sustained stability crucial for economic growth.

The economy fostered by the social partnership has grown steadily in the postwar period, often at growth rates above the Organisation for Economic Co-operation and Development (OECD—see Glossary) average. Between 1955 and 1990, the economy increased in size by two-and-one-half times. In step with the rest of Western Europe, the Austrian economy modernized quickly. Agriculture, still a significant part of the economy in the 1950s, by the early 1990s provided only about one-twentieth of the work force with employment and accounted for an even smaller share of the gross domestic product (GDP—see Glossary). In 1970 the industrial sector and the services sector accounted for roughly equal shares of GDP; by the 1990s the latter had become twice the size of the former and provided jobs for more than half the work force.

Although Austrian industry has a smaller place in the overall economy than it did earlier in the postwar period, it has become more specialized and produces high-quality goods that are competitive on the world market. Despite its small size, Austria is an active participant in the global economy, and foreign trade, two-thirds of it with the European Union (EU—see Glossary), accounts for two-fifths of GDP. A persistent trade deficit is largely offset by high earnings from tourism. Austria's place in the global economy has made imperative its membership in international economic organizations, such as the European Free Trade Association (EFTA—see Glossary) and the European Economic Area (EEA—see Glossary). Austria is scheduled to become a member of the EU on January 1, 1995.

The expanding economy has brought higher living standards for nearly all Austrians. Automobile ownership and travel abroad are commonplace, and an ever-widening range of state-supervised social benefits has made material want a thing of the past for ordinary Austrians. Sustained prosperity and a modernizing economy have permitted many Austrians to find better employment than did their parents. White-collar salaried employees now outnumber blue-collar workers. Much of the menial work is done by foreigners, who first began to arrive in significant numbers in the early 1960s and who at times have made up nearly 10 percent of the work force.

The great increase in white-collar employment permitted a tenfold increase in the number of Austrians enrolled at institutions of higher learning between the mid-1950s and the early 1990s. The upgrading of education at lower levels, such as specialized vocational training, is also impressive. As a result, many Austrians who themselves attended only elementary school have seen their children receive an education that results in well-paid skilled employment.

Social mobility has eroded the interwar division of Austria into *Lager*. The farming sector has dwindled into insignificance. The traditional blue-collar working class has diminished both in size and in cohesion as workers have become more middle class in their habits and expectations because of improvements in their housing, working conditions, and general standard of living. Many of their children have entered the ever-expanding middle class, which is no longer closed to outsiders. Younger Austrians, growing up in a more prosperous and egalitarian society than their parents, not only earn their livelihood in new ways but also have different social and political attitudes than the older generation.

In the decades after World War II, Austrian society has become more secularized. Regular church attendance has declined sharply, although the number of Austrians who have officially withdrawn from the Roman Catholic Church in this overwhelmingly Roman Catholic country has increased only slightly. The church itself has changed, withdrawing from the active and polarizing role it played in the interwar period. It speaks out only on issues it regards as within its legitimate sphere of interest. One such issue has been abortion. In the early 1970s, the church waged an ultimately unsuccessful campaign against the legalization of abortion.

The role of women also has changed in this new social environment. The so-called three Ks of *Kinder, Kirche,* and *Küche* (children, church, and kitchen) no longer dominate women's lives to the extent they did in the past. Marriage is no longer seen as the only socially acceptable goal of a woman's life. Families are smaller, and by the 1990s the birthrate was below that needed for the population to increase. Divorce is more frequent, as is cohabitation by unmarried couples. The number of illegitimate births also has risen, although most of these children are subsequently legitimized by marriage.

Women now work outside the home in greater numbers than in the past. Although as of the first half of the 1990s women still earned less than men at all levels of employment, more women than ever before hold responsible positions. Some of the country's foremost politicians are women, and the number of seats held by women in the nation's lower house of parliament, the Nationalrat (National Council), increased from eleven in 1970 to thirty-nine in 1994. Laws have been passed to improve women's position in society. The Equal Treatment Law of 1979 mandates equal pay for equal work, and the Women's Omnibus Law of 1993 aims at increasing the employment of women in government agencies.

The economic and social changes Austria underwent in the postwar era began to affect the country's political life only in the second half of the 1980s. It was during this period that the dominance of political life by two large parties—a dominance that began immediately after World War II—began to be threatened by several smaller parties. Representing two of the country's three traditional social camps, the two parties are the Socialist Party of Austria, known since 1991 as the Social Democratic Party of Austria (Sozialdemokratische Partei Österreichs—SPÖ), the successor to the Social Democratic Workers' Party, and the Austrian People's Party (Österreichische Volkspartei—ÖVP), descended from the Christian Social Party.

The SPÖ and ÖVP have governed Austria since 1945, often together in coalition governments. The latest of these so-called grand coalitions was formed in November 1994. Until 1970 the ÖVP was generally the stronger of the two parties. In that year, however, the SPÖ was led to power by the able and extremely popular Bruno Kreisky, who remained chancellor until 1983. In 1986 another effective leader, Franz Vranitzky, took over the SPÖ and through his personal popularity has been able keep the party in power, even though the party's share of the vote has declined steadily.

However strong their political rivalry may be, both parties are committed to democracy, and they have adopted less ideological positions than did their predecessors in the interwar period. Decades of governing together have reduced the ideological differences between the two parties, and both support maintaining Austria's mixed economy and social welfare state. They have also been bound together by the elaborate patronage system of dividing between them the right to fill many positions in government agencies, in the extensive social welfare system, in the numerous bodies that make up the social partnership system, and in the large state-owned business enterprises. Because appointments to these positions often depend more on party membership than on qualifications, there have been instances of corruption and incompetence.

As an indication of the overall success of the SPÖ and ÖVP in governing Austria in the postwar era, only in 1990 did their joint share of the vote in a national election drop below 80 percent. In fact, in many national elections their joint share had been over 90 percent. Beginning in 1986, however, their support began to fall steadily. In the national election of October 1994, they received only 62.6 percent of the vote. The decline stems in part from the slow breakup of the *Lager,* which had loyal voting habits, and the emergence of a sizable pool of "floating voters," no longer invariably tied to the SPÖ or to the ÖVP.

The decline of the large parties also stems from voter dissatisfaction with the inefficiency and corruption of traditional political practices of governing the country and the emergence of new issues in a rapidly changing economy and society. The most serious challenger to the two main parties is a right-wing populist party formed in 1956, the Freedom Party of Austria (Freiheitliche Partei Österreichs—FPÖ), descended from prewar German nationalist-liberal groups. The party had seemed doomed to extinction until a young politician, Jörg Haider, seized control of it in 1986 and through his dynamic leadership increased its share of the vote to 9.7 percent in that year's national election. The FPÖ nearly doubled its share in the national election of 1990 and won 22.5 percent of the vote in the national election of October 1994. This last victory occurred despite a split within the FPÖ in early 1993, when some of its members left to form a new party, The Liberal Forum (Das Liberale Forum). These members disagreed with Haider's position on foreigners in Austria and his departure from classic positions of European liberalism.

A superbly gifted politician, Haider has campaigned as a conservative populist, speaking out against the SPÖ–ÖVP decades-long stewardship of the country's affairs. He has exploited the anger of many voters at the pervasive cronyism and corruption of the SPÖ–ÖVP coalition and promised to end its system of patronage. Despite his clearly expressed hostility to socialism and the role of government in general, he has been able to successfully court many blue-collar SPÖ voters worried by the challenges posed to their country's small economy by a united Europe. With what many regard as demagogy, he has won votes by addressing that portion of the electorate who are concerned about the foreign presence in Austria and who fear *Überfremdung,* that is, Austria's submersion in a flood of foreign immigrants fleeing the social and economic chaos of Eastern Europe.

Traditional politics has also been challenged by the emergence of an environmentalist movement. Widespread economic security has freed young Austrians from immediate practical concerns and has allowed them to become concerned with longer-term issues such as protection of the environment. Galvanized by the construction of a large SPÖ-sponsored nuclear power plant in 1978, citizen groups focusing on the environment were formed; shortly thereafter, several environmentalist parties were established. In 1986 environmentalists were first elected to the Nationalrat; they have increased their share of the vote in each national election since. In the national election of 1994, the largest environmentalist party, The Greens (Die Grünen), won thirteen seats.

The European trend toward unification has also altered Austrian politics. In the first half of the 1990s, Austria's possible membership in the EU was likely the issue of greatest significance for the country's future. In 1989 Austria applied for admission to the European Community (EC—see Glossary), the predecessor of the EU. An interim step before admission was the January 1994 entry into the EEA. After years of negotiations with EC officials, in which the central points were protection of the environment, foreign ownership of real estate property, and farm subsidies, the SPÖ-ÖVP government called for a June 1994 referendum about EU membership.

The referendum was hotly contested. Although 66.4 percent of the electorate voted in favor of EU membership, the outcome of the vote was uncertain until the end. In addition to the SPÖ-ÖVP coalition, The Liberal Forum also supported membership. The most eloquent spokesman for this position was the minister for foreign affairs, Alois Mock, who had conducted the difficult negotiations concerning the conditions under which Austria would join the EU. In the late 1980s, Mock had persuaded his party, the ÖVP, that it should advocate Austria's becoming part of a united Europe. The SPÖ gradually came to the same view, even though EU membership would conflict with Austria's traditional neutrality. The EU has as a long-term goal not only economic unity but also a common foreign and security policy, which would by its nature preclude neutrality. Proponents of EU membership argued that it would bring economic benefits and contribute to the nation's security in a new and rapidly changing world.

Opponents of EU membership included many Austrian intellectuals, environmentalists, and the FPÖ, which had reversed its previously positive stance. Opponents argued that membership would bring a loss of Austrian sovereignty and that bureaucrats in Brussels would come to exert a suffocating control over the country's affairs. They feared that Austria's national identity might gradually be lost in a united Europe, given the country's small size. Haider justified his party's change of opinion by saying that it still desired European unity, but not one in which Austrian liberty was so restricted.

The overwhelming support voters gave to EU membership was a win for the coalition, but support came from many sectors of society, not just from traditional SPÖ and ÖVP voters. In fact, some members of the SPÖ and ÖVP opposed their parties' position because they feared the social and economic consequences of membership. This drop in support can be seen by comparing the two-thirds majority the two parties received in the referendum with the three-quarters majority the coalition received in the 1990 national election.

The national election of October 9, 1994, was a resounding setback for the coalition. Both parties suffered significant losses in this election, which had an 82 percent voter turnout. The SPÖ remained the largest party in the Nationalrat. However, its share of the vote fell from 42.8 percent in the 1990 election to 34.9 percent, and its number of seats in the 183-member body fell from eighty to sixty-five. The ÖVP fared nearly as badly. Its share of the vote dropped from 32.1 percent in 1990 to 27.7 percent in 1994, and its share of seats fell from sixty to fifty-two. The FPÖ continued its upward trend by increasing its share of the vote, going from 16.6 percent in 1990 to 22.5 percent in 1994, and by winning forty-two seats, compared with thirty-three seats four years earlier. The largest of the environmentalist parties, The Greens, increased its share of the vote from 4.8 percent to 7.3 percent and the number of its seats from ten to thirteen. The Liberal Forum, in its first national election, won 6.0 percent of the vote and gained eleven seats.

The election showed that the political trends that had been under way through the 1980s had continued. The SPÖ-ÖVP share of the vote continued to drop precipitously, amounting to only 62.6 percent in 1994. As a result of these losses, the SPÖ-ÖVP coalition government formed in late November 1994 with Vranitzky as chancellor will not have the two-thirds majority needed to pass some legislation.

The election was a triumph for Haider, who throughout its course had determined the issues on which the election was fought: the alleged threat of foreign immigration to the welfare of ordinary Austrians; and the incompetence and corruption of the pervasive system of governmental, party, and economic interest organizations that the SPÖ and ÖVP coalition had devised and that supposedly was suffocating the country's social and economic life. Haider saw his victory as merely another step toward becoming chancellor in 1998. To reach this goal, he has begun transforming his party into a political movement similar to that headed by Ross Perot in the United States. Whether or not Haider achieves his goal, he is likely to remain one of Austria's foremost politicians because of his skill in raising issues that have become central concerns to voters facing the challenges of the new Europe emerging after the end of the Cold War.

The end of the Cold War and the breakup not only of the Warsaw Pact but also of some of the countries that belonged to it have ended the decades of relative stability in Central Europe. In addition, in the early 1990s Yugoslavia, Austria's neighbor to the south, also broke into a number of separate states, some of which were soon at war. Large numbers of refugees have fled to Austria and other Western countries, seeking temporary or permanent asylum. As a result of these events, Austria, once securely tucked away in one corner of Western Europe and sheltered from the East by the Iron Curtain, has come to occupy a more exposed and less secure position in Central Europe.

In the postwar era, Austria has pursued a neutral and active foreign policy. The State Treaty of 1955 ended the country's occupation by foreign troops and restored its sovereignty. As a condition for winning its independence, Austria pledged itself to permanent neutrality and promised never to join a military alliance or to allow foreign troops to be stationed on its territory. Lying between the two military alliances of the Cold War, Austria became an intermediary between the two blocs. Vienna became the home to international organizations and the site of important international meetings. An Austrian diplomat, Kurt Waldheim, was secretary general of the United Nations (1971–81), and Austrian military forces regularly participated in that organization's multinational peacekeeping missions around the world.

In the post-Cold War environment, however, Austria's active neutrality is seen by many as no longer relevant. Hence, policy makers are searching for a security policy better adapted to Austria's newly exposed position. Entry into the EU will reduce Austria's foreign policy independence and its traditional neutrality. Austria is expected to apply for observer status in the Western European Union (WEU—see Glossary) after it joins the EU and is likely to eventually become a member of this security organization. Austria's foreign policy makers contend that there is no conflict between being a member of the WEU and maintaining the constitutional pledge of permanent neutrality, stating that it is Austria's right to interpret its neutrality. Whatever new security agreements are entered into later in the 1990s, however, Austria's policy of permanent and active neutrality, at least as it has so far been practiced, is probably nearing an end.

The likely extension of EU membership early in the next century to East European nations with free-market economies and parliamentary democracy will also reduce Austria's postwar role as an intermediary between East and West. As a result of the new Europe forming after the political and economic revolutions beginning in 1989, Austria is faced with abandoning the foreign policies that have served it so well in the postwar era. However, Austria will meet this new international environment not as a small poor nation surrounded by more powerful neighbors, as it did twice in the twentieth century after defeats in world wars, but as a prosperous and stable society and an integral part of a united Europe.

December 5, 1994   Eric Solsten

Chapter 1. Historical Setting

Coat of arms of the province of Styria

GERMANIC TRIBES WERE not the first peoples to occupy the eastern Alpine-Danubian region, but the history and culture of these tribes, especially the Bavarians and Swabians, are the foundation of Austria's modern identity. Austria thus shares in the broader history and culture of the Germanic peoples of Europe. The territories that constitute modern Austria were, for most of their history, constituent parts of the German nation and were linked to one another only insofar as they were all feudal possessions of one of the leading dynasties in Europe, the Habsburgs.

Surrounded by German, Hungarian, Slavic, Italian, and Turkish nations, the German lands of the Habsburgs became the core of their empire, reaching across German national and cultural borders. This multicultural empire was held together by the Habsburgs' dynastic claims and by the cultural and religious values of the Roman Catholic Counter-Reformation that the Habsburgs cultivated to provide a unifying identity to the region. But this cultural-religious identity was ultimately unable to compete with the rising importance of nationalism in European politics, and the nineteenth century saw growing ethnic conflict within the Habsburg Empire. The German population of the Habsburg Empire directed its nationalist aspirations toward the German nation, over which the Habsburgs had long enjoyed titular leadership. Prussia's successful bid for power in Germany in the nineteenth century—culminating in the formation in 1871 of a German empire under Prussian leadership that excluded the Habsburgs' German lands—was thus a severe political shock to the German population of the Habsburg Empire.

When the Habsburg Empire collapsed in 1918 at the end of World War I, its territories that were dominated by non-German ethnic groups established their own independent nation-states. The German-speaking lands of the empire sought to become part of the new German republic, but European fears of an enlarged Germany forced them to form an independent Austrian state. The new country's economic weakness and lack of national consciousness contributed to political instability and polarization throughout the 1920s and 1930s and facilitated the annexation (Anschluss) of Austria by Nazi Germany in 1938.

As part of Germany, Austria came under Nazi totalitarian rule and suffered military defeat in World War II. To escape this Nazi German legacy, Austrians began to seek refuge in a national identity

3

that emphasized their cultural and historical differences with Germans even before the end of the war. Thus, the population welcomed the 1945 decision of the victorious Allied powers to restore an independent Austria.

The bitter experience of the Anschluss and World War II enabled Austrians to overcome the extreme political polarization of the interwar years through a common commitment to parliamentary democracy and integration with the West. The close cooperation of the two major parties, the Socialist Party of Austria (Sozialistische Partei Österreichs—SPÖ) and the Austrian People's Party (Österreichische Volkspartei—ÖVP), helped Austria frustrate Soviet efforts after World War II that might have seen the country's absorption into the Soviet bloc or division into communist and noncommunist halves. The signing of the State Treaty in 1955 ended Allied occupation of Austria and any immediate danger of communist dictatorship and/or partition. But the occupation era and the continuing Cold War shaped the country's identity and self-understanding as it positioned itself as a neutral country bridging East and West.

This new Austrian cultural, political, and international identity laid the foundation for a stable democracy, a strong economy tied to the West, and neutrality between communist and democratic Europe. At the same time, however, it discouraged close examination of the role played individually and collectively by Austrians in Nazi aggression and war crimes. Revelations about the wartime record of Kurt Waldheim during the presidential election in 1985 thus initiated a painful reassessment of Austria's Nazi past. Moreover, the end of the Cold War has undercut Austria's self-appointed mission as a bridge between East and West. A redefinition of Austrian nationalism and its international role thus seems likely in the 1990s.

The Alpine-Danubian Region Before the Habsburg Dynasty

The Celtic and Roman Eras

Around 400 B.C., Celtic peoples from Western Europe settled in the eastern Alps. A Celtic state, Noricum, developed around the region's ironworks in the second century B.C. The Romans occupied Noricum without resistance in 9 B.C. and made the Danube River the effective northern frontier of their empire.

North of the Danube, various German tribes were already extending their territory. By the latter half of the second century A.D., they were making devastating incursions into Roman territories.

Nevertheless, Roman arms and diplomacy maintained relative stability until the late fourth century, when other Germanic tribes, including the Ostrogoths, Visigoths, and Vandals, were able to establish settlements in Roman territory south of the Danube. The Roman province gradually became indefensible, and much of the Christian, Romanized population evacuated the region in 488. In 493 the Ostrogoths invaded Italy, seized control of what remained of the western half of the Roman Empire, and brought the Roman era in the eastern Alps to an end.

The Early Medieval Era

Various Germanic and Slavic tribes vied for control of the eastern Alpine-Danubian region following the withdrawal and collapse of Roman authority. Among the Germanic tribes, Alemanni (later known as Swabians) and Bavarians were the most notable. The Alemanni had arrived during the Roman era and by 500 were permanently established in most of modern-day Switzerland and the Austrian province of Vorarlberg. The early history of the Bavarians is not clear, but by the mid-500s they were established alongside remnants of earlier, Romanized peoples in areas north and south of the present-day border between Austria and Germany. Both Swabians and Bavarians were subject to another Germanic tribe, the Franks, but effective Frankish control did not occur until the time of Emperor Charlemagne in the late 700s.

Slavic peoples, including Slovenes, Croats, Czechs, and Slovaks, settled in the region as subject peoples of the Avars, a nomadic tribe, and gradually absorbed their nomadic overlords. During the Carolingian era (eighth and ninth centuries), the areas of Slavic settlement, like those of the Swabians and Bavarians, became subject to the Franks.

Under Frankish patronage, Irish monks, most notably Saint Columban and Saint Gall, pioneered the Christian evangelization of the region in the seventh and eighth centuries. Their work gave rise to important monasteries whose agricultural activities on the frontiers of the Carolingian Empire helped open the region's primeval forests to wider settlement. Eventually integrated into the feudal political structure, the abbots of these monasteries vied with bishops and secular lords for religious and political influence well into the modern era. Bishoprics were established in four major Bavarian towns in the 730s. Salzburg, the only one of these to lie within modern Austria, was raised to the status of an archbishopric in 798 and was given jurisdiction over the other bishoprics. Salzburg became the center of the Christian evangelization efforts in the Slavic territories, which were instrumental in spreading the political reach of the Carolingian Empire.

The Holy Roman Empire and the Duchy of Austria

The gradual eastward extension of the Carolingian Empire was stopped by the arrival of the Magyars—a Finno-Ugric people who form the ethnic core of the Hungarian nation—in the Danubian region in 862. Within fifty years, the Magyars had seized the Hungarian Plain, conquered Moravia and the eastern Danubian marches of the Carolingian Empire, and raided deep into Frankish territory. A reorganization of the German portion of the Carolingian Empire in the first half of the tenth century enabled the Germans to rally their forces and defeat a Magyar invasion force at the Battle of Lechfeld in 955. This new and essentially German empire became known as the Holy Roman Empire and eventually regained much of the territory lost to the Magyars. Nevertheless, the Magyars' continuing military strength and their conversion to Christianity during the reign of King Stephen (r. 997–1038) enabled Hungary to become a legitimate member of Christian Europe and check German expansion to the east.

Under the Holy Roman Empire, the territories that constitute modern Austria were a complex feudal patchwork under the sway of numerous secular and ecclesiastical lords. Most of the territories originally fell within the boundaries of the Duchy of Bavaria. Over the years, various territories were effectively detached from Bavaria, either becoming part of the newly established duchies of Carinthia (976) and Styria (1180) or, like Salzburg and Tirol, falling under the jurisdiction of powerful bishops. In the final years of the reign of Emperor Otto the Great (r. 936–73), a small margravate roughly corresponding to the present-day province of Lower Austria was formed within Bavaria. This margravate became known as Ostarrichi (literally, Eastern Realm), from which the modern name *Austria* (Österreich) ultimately derives. The Margravate of Austria was detached from Bavaria and became a separate duchy in 1156.

Between 976 and 1246, the Duchy of Austria was one of extensive feudal possessions of the Babenberg family. Through their ties of blood and marriage to two successive German imperial dynasties, the Babenbergs gradually acquired lands roughly corresponding to the modern provinces of Upper Austria, Lower Austria, Styria, and Carinthia. When the Babenberg line died out in 1246, their lands passed to the ambitious king of Bohemia, Otakar II. As king of Bohemia, Otakar was one of the small circle of "elector-princes" who were entitled to participate in the election of the Holy Roman

Emperor Maximilian I,
Holy Roman Emperor
from 1493 to 1519,
greatly expanded
Habsburg territory.
Courtesy Austrian
National Tourist
Office, New York

Emperor. When Otakar failed to be elected emperor in 1273, he contested the election of the new emperor, Rudolf von Habsburg. The Bohemian king met his defeat and death in battle in 1278, and the former Babenberg lands passed to the Habsburgs, who added them to their already extensive lands in present-day Switzerland, southwestern Germany, and eastern France.

Rise of the Habsburg Empire

The Habsburg Dynasty in the Late Medieval Era

Although the Duchy of Austria was just one of the duchies and lands that the Habsburgs eventually acquired in the eastern Alpine-Danubian region, the Habsburgs became known as the House of Austria after the Swiss peasantry ousted them from their original family seat in Habichtsburg in the Swiss canton of Aargau in 1386. The name *Austria* subsequently became an informal way to refer to all the lands possessed by the House of Austria, even though it also remained the proper, formal name of a specific region. Thus, through the legacy of common rule by the House of Austria, the lands that constitute the modern state of Austria indirectly adopted the name of one region of the country as the formal national name in the early twentieth century.

Because the elector-princes of the Holy Roman Empire generally preferred a weak, dependent emperor, the powerful Habsburg

Dynasty only occasionally held the imperial title in the 150 years after Rudolf's death in 1291. After the election of Frederick III in 1452 (r. 1452-93), however, the dynasty came to enjoy such a dominant position among the German nobility that only one non-Habsburg was elected emperor in the remaining 354-year history of the Holy Roman Empire.

The Habsburgs' near monopoly of the imperial title, however, did not make the Habsburg Empire and the Holy Roman Empire synonymous. The Habsburg Empire was a supranational collection of territories united only through the accident of common rule by the Habsburgs, and many of the territories were not part of the Holy Roman Empire. In contrast, the Holy Roman Empire was a defined political and territorial entity that became identified with the German nation as the nation-state assumed greater importance in European politics.

Although the succession of Holy Roman Emperors from the Habsburg line gave the House of Austria great prestige in Germany and Europe, the family's real power base was the lands in its possession, that is, the Habsburg Empire. This was because the Holy Roman Empire was a loosely organized feudal state in which the power of the emperor was counterbalanced by the rights and privileges of the empire's other princes, lords, and institutions, both secular and ecclesiastical.

Habsburg power was significantly enhanced in 1453, when Emperor Frederick III confirmed a set of rights and privileges, dubiously claimed by the Habsburgs, that paralleled those of the elector-princes, in whose ranks the family did not yet sit. In addition, the lands the Habsburgs possessed in 1453 were made inheritable through both the male and the female line. Because feudal holdings usually reverted to the emperor to dispose of as he wished when the holder of the fief died, the right of inheritable succession measurably strengthened the Habsburgs. The lands they held in 1453 became known collectively as the Hereditary Lands, and—with the exception of territories possessed by the archbishops of Salzburg and Brixen—encompassed most of modern Austria and portions of Germany, France, Italy, Croatia, and Slovenia.

Territorial Expansion, Division, and Consolidation

The Habsburgs also increased their influence and power through strategic alliances ratified by marriages. Owing to premature deaths and/or childless marriages within the Burgundian and Spanish dynasties into which his grandfather, Maximilian I (r. 1493–1519), and his father had married, Emperor Charles V (r. 1519–56) inherited not only the Hereditary Lands but also the Franche-Comté and the Netherlands (both of which were French fiefs) and Spain and its empire in the Americas.

Challenged on his western borders by France and on his eastern borders by the Turkish Ottoman Empire, Charles V divided his realm geographically in 1522 to achieve more effective rule. Retaining the western half under his direct control, he entrusted the eastern half, the Hereditary Lands, to his brother, Ferdinand (r. 1522–64). Although Ferdinand did not become Holy Roman Emperor until 1556 when Charles V abdicated, this territorial division effectively created two branches of the Habsburg Dynasty: the Spanish Habsburgs, descended through Charles V, and the Austrian Habsburgs, descended through Ferdinand (see fig. 2).

In addition to the lands he received from his brother, Ferdinand also increased his territorial reach by marrying into the Jagiellon family, the royal family of Hungary and Bohemia. When his brother-in-law, King Louis, died fighting the Turks at the Battle of Mohács in 1526, Ferdinand claimed the right of succession. Although the diets representing the nobility of Bohemia (and its dependencies of Moravia and Silesia) did not acknowledge Ferdinand's hereditary rights, they formally elected him king of Bohemia. As king of Bohemia, he also became an elector-prince of the Holy Roman Empire. In Hungary and in the subordinate Kingdom of Croatia-Slavonia-Dalmatia, however, Ferdinand faced the rival claim of a Hungarian nobleman and the reality of the Turkish conquest of the country. He was able to assert authority only over the northern and western edges of the country, which became known as Royal Hungary. His Hungarian rival became a vassal of the Turks, ruling over Transylvania in eastern Hungary. The rest of Hungary became part of the Ottoman Empire in 1603.

Although Ferdinand undertook various administrative reforms in order to centralize authority and increase his power, no meaningful integration of the Hereditary Lands and the two newly acquired kingdoms occurred. In contrast to the authority of kings of Western Europe, where feudal structures were already in decline, Ferdinand's authority continued to rest on the consent of the nobles as expressed in the local diets, which successfully resisted administrative centralization.

The Protestant Reformation in the Habsburg Lands

From the beginning of the Protestant Reformation in the 1520s, Protestant doctrines were welcomed by the people living in the areas under Habsburg domination. By the middle of the sixteenth century, most inhabitants were Protestant. Lutherans predominated in German-speaking areas, except in Tirol, where the Anabaptists

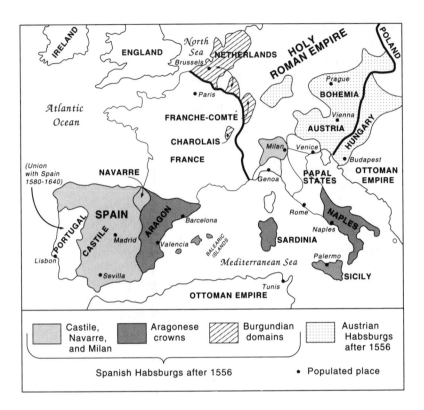

Figure 2. Europe in the Sixteenth Century

were influential. Nevertheless, the Roman Catholic Church retained the support of the Habsburg Dynasty and was able to maintain a strong presence throughout the area.

Religious violence and serious persecution were rare after the 1520s, and an uneasy coexistence and external tolerance prevailed for most of the sixteenth century. Ferdinand pressed Rome for concessions that would bridge the positions of moderate reformers and Catholics, but at the Council of Trent (1545–63), the Catholic Church chose instead a vigorous restatement of Catholic doctrine combined with internal reforms. The council thus hardened lines of division between Catholicism and Protestantism and laid the foundation for the Counter-Reformation, which the Habsburgs would pursue aggressively in the 1600s.

The Turkish Threat

After the Turkish siege of Vienna in 1529, Ferdinand recognized that defense of the Habsburg lands required that Hungary form a bulwark against the Turks. Although Turkey's ultimate objective was the conquest of Europe, Western Europe did not see the Turks as a threat and was unwilling to aid Ferdinand in the defense of the continent's eastern borders. He thus signed a peace agreement with the Turks in 1562 that formalized the stalemated status quo in Hungary.

The Counter-Reformation and the Thirty Years' War
Division and Rebellion

Ferdinand I died in 1564, and Habsburg territories in Central Europe were divided among his three sons, with the eldest, Maximilian III (r. 1564–76), becoming Holy Roman Emperor. Although Maximilian's sympathetic policies toward the Protestants contrasted with his brothers' efforts to reestablish Catholicism as the sole religion in their lands, military policy, not religious doctrine, was to divide the dynasty in the final years of the sixteenth century and open the door to the religious wars of the seventeenth century.

Maximilian's son, Rudolf II (r. 1576–1612), succeeded his father as both king of Hungary and Holy Roman Emperor. After the Turks reopened the war in Hungary in 1593, Rudolf was blamed for the rebellion among Protestant nobles in Royal Hungary caused by his brutal conduct of the war. Backed by junior members of the dynasty, Rudolf's younger brother, Matthias (r. 1612–19), confiscated Rudolf's lands, restored order, and, after Rudolf's death, became Holy Roman Emperor. But the religious and political concessions that the two brothers had made to the nobility to win their support in this dynastic feud created new dangers for the Habsburgs.

The childless Matthias chose his cousin Ferdinand as his successor. To facilitate Ferdinand's eventual election as Holy Roman Emperor, Matthias secured his election as king of Bohemia in 1617. Before accepting Ferdinand as king, however, the Protestant nobility of Bohemia had required this strong proponent of the Catholic Counter-Reformation to confirm the religious charter granted them by Rudolf II. A dispute over the charter in 1618 triggered a rebellion by the Protestant nobles. Hopes for an arbitrated settlement were dashed when Matthias died in March 1619, and other areas under Habsburg control rebelled against Habsburg rule.

The Thirty Years' War, 1618–48

The anti-Habsburg rebellions reflected the rising tensions between Catholics and Protestants in the early 1600s. Proponents of

11

the Counter-Reformation, often operating under Habsburg protection, were reaping the fruits of a generation of work: monastic life was reviving, Catholic intellectual life was regaining confidence, and prominent figures were returning to the Catholic Church. As a result, Protestants were increasingly on the defensive. The German princes split into two military camps based on religious affiliation: the Evangelical Union and the Catholic League.

In August 1619, a Bohemian diet elected as king the Protestant elector-prince of the Palatinate, Frederick V, and the conclave of elector-princes elected Ferdinand II (r. 1619–37) Holy Roman Emperor. On November 8, 1620, a force combining troops from the Catholic League and the imperial army decisively defeated Frederick V's largely mercenary force at the Battle of White Mountain. Throughout the 1620s, the combined imperial and Catholic forces maintained the offensive in Germany, enabling Ferdinand to establish his authority in the Hereditary Lands, Bohemia, and Hungary.

Equating Protestantism with disloyalty, Ferdinand imposed religious restrictions throughout the Hereditary Lands. In 1627 he implemented a long-planned decree to make Bohemia a one-confession state: Protestants were given six months to convert or leave the country. In the face of a strong Hungarian nationalist movement headed by the Calvinist prince of Transylvania, however, Ferdinand could maintain his hold on Royal Hungary only by confirming guarantees of religious freedom.

Foreign intervention by Denmark, Sweden, and France kept Ferdinand from bringing the war to a conclusion through military power and also frustrated his efforts in the mid-1630s to reach a compromise with the Protestant German princes. The subsequent military campaigns of the Thirty Years' War, however, only marginally affected those portions of the Habsburg territories that are part of modern Austria.

The Peace of Westphalia

The Thirty Years' War was finally ended in 1648 by the Peace of Westphalia. The treaty guaranteed the religious and political constitution of the Holy Roman Empire, giving the German princes the sovereign right to settle the religious question in their respective territories. France also achieved its main war aim because the costly war and the concessions to the princes effectively stopped the Habsburgs from transforming the Holy Roman Empire into an absolutist state under their direction. Nonetheless, in their own lands, the Habsburgs enjoyed greater political and religious control than before the war: they had gained loyal new followers from among the nobles by redistributing estates confiscated from rebels, and they were free to enforce religious conformity, which they did based on the model applied earlier in Bohemia.

The Baroque Era

Political and Religious Consolidation under Leopold

Reconstruction of the social, political, and economic infrastructure destroyed by the Thirty Years' War began during the reign of Ferdinand III (r. 1637–57) and continued through the reign of his son, Leopold I (r. 1658–1705). Central to the restoration of the Habsburgs' social and political base was the reestablishment of the Roman Catholic Church. But the Habsburgs did not seek to make the church an independent force within society. They found no contradiction between personal piety and use of religion as a political tool and defended and advanced their sovereign rights over and against the institutional church.

The Habsburg effort to establish religious conformity was based on the model already implemented in Bohemia. Closure of Protestant churches, expulsions, and Catholic appointments to vacated positions eliminated centers of Protestant power. Reform commissions made up of clergy and representatives of local diets appointed missionaries to Protestant areas. After a period of instruction, the populace was given a choice between conversion and emigration— an estimated 40,000 people emigrated between 1647 and 1652.

The reestablishment of Catholic intellectual life and religious orders and monasteries was a key component of Habsburg Counter-Reformation policies. The Jesuits led this effort, and their influence was broadly disseminated throughout Central European society, owing to their excellent schools, near monopoly over higher education, and emphasis on lay organizations, which provided a channel for popular devotional piety. Benedictine, Cistercian, and Augustinian monastic foundations were also revitalized through the careful management of their estates, and their schools rivaled those of the Jesuits.

Through the court's patronage of the arts and religious orders and through public celebrations, both secular and religious, the dynasty transmitted a worldview based on the values of the Counter-Reformation. These values, rather than common governmental institutions and laws, gave the Heridatary Lands a sense of unity and identity that compensated for the continued weakness of administrative bodies at the center of Habsburg rule.

The Turkish Wars and the Siege of Vienna

In 1663 rivalries between the Ottomans and the Habsburgs in Transylvania triggered renewed fighting between the Ottoman Empire and the Habsburg Empire. The Turkish threat, which included a prolonged but unsuccessful siege of Vienna in 1683, prompted Poland, Venice, and Russia to join the Habsburg Empire in repelling the Turks. In 1686 Habsburg forces moved into central Hungary and captured Buda. By 1687 the Ottoman Empire had been eliminated as a power in central Hungary. In the late 1690s, command of the imperial forces was entrusted to Prince Eugene of Savoy. Under his leadership, Habsburg forces won control of all but a small portion of Hungary by 1699.

The War of the Spanish Succession

In 1700 the death of Charles II of Spain ended the Spanish Habsburg line. Spain's steady decline throughout the seventeenth century had already led to minor armed conflicts aimed at a realignment of power among European countries, and these rivalries blossomed into the War of the Spanish Succession (1701–14). Both Leopold I and King Louis XIV of France, Charles's two nearest relatives, hoped to establish a junior branch of his own dynasty in Spain. But neither was willing to rule out the possibility that a single heir might someday inherit the lands of both the principal line and its Spanish offshoot. The strong central government and political institutions of France made the possible union of Spain and France a far greater threat to other European countries than the possible union of Spain and the Habsburg lands in Central Europe. Thus, when the dying Spanish king named as his heir Louis's son, Philip, England and a number of other European countries rallied to the Habsburg cause.

Despite early victories by the Austro-English alliance, the allies were unable to install the Austrian Archduke Charles on the Spanish throne. As the war dragged on, the alliance began to unravel, especially when, after the death of Leopold's elder son, Charles became Holy Roman Emperor in 1711. The actual unification of the Habsburg lines in Charles VI (r. 1711–40) posed a greater threat to other European powers than did the possible union of war-weakened France and Spain. Austria's allies made peace with France in 1713 and signed the Treaty of Utrecht. Because his former allies negotiated a treaty to protect their own interests, the settlement Charles received when he finally abandoned the war in 1714 was meager: the Spanish Netherlands (present-day Belgium) and various Italian territories.

The Pragmatic Sanction and the War of the Austrian Succession, 1740-48

Although the Habsburg Empire continued to expand in the east at Turkish expense, Charles VI recognized that defense of Austria's position in Europe required greater economic and political centralization to foster the development of a stronger economic base. Because he lacked a male heir, however, the continued unity of the Habsburg Empire was jeopardized. In 1713 Charles promulgated the Pragmatic Sanction to establish the legal basis for transmission of the Habsburg lands to his daughter Maria Theresa (r. 1740-80). The price extracted by local diets and rival European powers for approval of the Pragmatic Sanction, however, was abandonment of many centralizing reforms.

Nonetheless, Charles's concessions did not prevent the War of the Austrian Succession (1740-48) from breaking out on his death in 1740. Prussia occupied Bohemia's Silesian duchies that same year. Late in 1741, the elector-prince of Bavaria, Charles Albert, occupied Prague, the capital of Bohemia, with the aid of Saxon and French troops and was crowned king of Bohemia. This paved the way for his election as Holy Roman Emperor in 1742, thus breaking the Habsburgs' three-hundred-year hold on the imperial crown.

The Austrians, however, retook Prague, and Maria Theresa was crowned queen of Bohemia in the spring of 1743. Aided by a British diplomatic campaign, Austria also made important military gains in Central Europe. Thus, when Charles Albert unexpectedly died in January 1745, his son made peace with Austria and agreed to support the Habsburg candidate for emperor. This enabled Maria Theresa's husband, Franz (r. 1745-65), to be elected Holy Roman emperor in October 1745. In the west, the war with France and Spain gradually settled into a military stalemate, and negotiations finally led to the Peace of Aix-la-Chapelle in 1748.

Although Maria Theresa emerged with most of her empire intact—owing largely to the early support she received from Hungarian nobles—Austria was obliged to permanently cede Silesia, its most economically advanced territory, to Prussia. Recognizing that the costly war with France had done more to promote British colonial interests in North America than its own interests in Central Europe, Austria abandoned its partnership with Britain in favor of closer ties with France. This reversal of alliances was sealed by the marriage of Maria Theresa's youngest daughter, Marie Antoinette, to the future Louis XVI of France.

The Reforms of Maria Theresa and Joseph II

Baroque Absolutism and Enlightened Despotism

Although her husband was emperor, Maria Theresa ruled the Habsburg lands. However, when her son Joseph became Holy Roman Emperor after the death of her husband in 1765, she made her son coregent. Following Maria Theresa's death in 1780, Joseph II reigned in his own right until his death in 1790. The Counter-Reformation's political and religious goals had largely been accomplished by the time Maria Theresa came to the throne, but maintaining Austria's great-power status urgently required broad internal reform and restructuring to strengthen the central authority of the monarchy and curtail the power of the nobility.

Maria Theresa began administrative and economic reforms in 1749, drawing on mercantilist theory and examples provided by Prussian and French reforms. In addition, she undertook reforms in the social, legal, and religious spheres. During the coregency and after Maria Theresa's death, Joseph continued the reforms along the lines pursued by his mother. But mother and son had sharply different motivations. Maria Theresa was a pious Catholic empress working within the structure of a paternalistic, baroque absolutism and was unsympathetic to the Enlightenment. Joseph, in contrast, gave the reforms an ideological edge reflecting the utilitarian theories of the Enlightenment. Because his reforms were more ideologically driven and thus less flexible and pragmatic, they frequently were also less successful and disrupted the stability of the Habsburg Empire.

Although the statist religious policy that evolved in this era became known as Josephism, Joseph's policy was largely an extension of his mother's, whose piety did not exempt the church from reforms designed to strengthen state authority and power. Joseph's utilitarianism, however, contributed to two important divergences from Maria Theresa's policy: greater religious toleration and suppression of religious institutions and customs deemed contrary to utilitarian principles. The Edict of Tolerance, issued in 1781, granted Protestants almost equal status with Catholics; other decrees lifted restrictions on Jews and opened up communities, trades, and educational opportunities previously barred to them. The utilitarian principles behind religious toleration, however, also inspired Joseph to dissolve Catholic monasteries that were dedicated solely to contemplative religious life and to suppress various traditional Jewish customs he viewed as detrimental to society and a hinderance to the Germanization of the Jewish population.

16

Maria Theresa (r. 1740–80)
reformed and united
Habsburg holdings.
Courtesy Embassy of Austria,
Washington

The reforms created an administrative, fiscal, and judicial bureaucracy directly responsible to the monarch. As the seat of the new centralized institutions, Vienna grew from merely being the sovereign's place of residence to a true political and administrative capital. Hungary, however, was not included in these centralizing administrative reforms. In appreciation for the support Austria had received from the Hungarian nobles during the War of the Austrian Succession, Maria Theresa never extended her reforms to that kingdom.

The Strategic Impact of the Reform Era

Although the reforms improved Austrian military preparedness, they fell short of their original goal of enabling Austria to defend its interests in Europe. Hopes of regaining Silesia and partitioning Prussia were abandoned after only limited military success in the Austro-Prussian Seven Years' War (1756–63). Efforts to check Russian expansion yielded mixed results. Unable to prevent Russian and Prussian ambitions against Poland, Austria reluctantly joined them in the First Partition of Poland in 1772 and gained the province of Galicia. Five years later, Austria intervened between Russia and Turkey to prevent Russian gains at Turkish expense and in the process acquired Bukovina, a territory adjacent to Galicia and Transylvania. Because the new territories were economically backward, their acquisition served mainly to shift the

17

ethnic balance of the Habsburg Empire through the addition of a large Slavic population (Poles and Ruthenians), a sizable Jewish minority (which accounted for 60 percent of the empire's total Jewish population), and a lesser number of Romanians.

The ideological rigidity with which Joseph II carried out his reforms also weakened the Habsburg Dynasty by provoking social unrest and, in Hungary and Belgium, rebellion. When Joseph died in 1790, his brother, Leopold II (r. 1790–92), had to reverse many of the reforms and offer new concessions to restore order. To get Prussian support for the military action that reestablished Habsburg authority in Belgium in 1790, Leopold foreswore further Austrian territorial gains at Turkish expense. He also confirmed Hungary's right not to be absorbed into a centralized empire, but to be ruled by him as king of Hungary according to its own administration and laws. In exchange, the Hungarian nobility ended their rebellion.

The Habsburg Empire and the French Revolution

The Napoleonic Wars

What began as a retrenchment in Austria's reform program ground to a complete halt when the international crisis caused by the French Revolution engulfed Europe in a generation of war. Meeting in Potsdam in 1791, Leopold II and the king of Prussia jointly declared that the revolutionary situation in France was a common concern of all sovereigns. Although the declaration did not become the framework for European military intervention in France as its authors had hoped, it set Austria and the French Revolution on an ideological collision course. In April 1792, revolutionary France declared war on Austria.

The first war lasted for five years until Austria, abandoned by its allies, was forced to make peace on unfavorable terms. Austria renewed the war against France in 1799 and again in 1805 but was swiftly defeated both times. In the otherwise unfavorable settlement after the defeat in 1805, however, Austria did receive Salzburg, a territory formerly ruled by an archbishop, in compensation for the loss of various Italian and German possessions.

Because French domination of Germany raised the possibility that Napoleon Bonaparte or one of his subordinates could be elected Holy Roman Emperor, Leopold's son, Franz II (r. 1792–1835), took two steps to protect Habsburg interests. First, to guarantee his family's continued imperial status, he adopted a new, hereditary title, Emperor of Austria, in 1804, thus becoming Franz I of Austria. Second, to preclude completely the possibility of

Napoleon's election, in 1806 he renounced the title of Holy Roman Emperor and dissolved the Holy Roman Empire.

In the final years of the decade, the German Habsburg area was swept with anti-French nationalist fervor. Erroneously believing that similar nationalist fervor throughout Germany would produce a victory, Austria declared war on France in April 1809. In the Tirol, then under Bavarian rule, the peasants, led by Andreas Hofer, rebelled and scored surprising victories before being subdued by Napoleon's forces. Elsewhere in Germany, however, nationalist feeling had little effect. Austria's defeat was swift, and significant territorial losses followed.

In the wake of this defeat, Franz appointed a new foreign minister, Clemens von Metternich, who sought reconciliation with France. He accomplished this by arranging a marriage between Franz's daughter, Marie Louise, and Napoleon, who was eager for the prestige of marriage into one of the principal dynasties of Europe and the creation of an heir. The marriage took place in the spring of 1810 but yielded little immediate return for Austria.

In 1813 Napoleon's position began to weaken. His invasion of Russia had failed, and Britain was scoring victories in the Iberian Peninsula. Both sides of the conflict began bidding for Austria's support. In August of that year, Austria broke its alliance with France and declared war. Despite generous subsidies from Britain, the final campaigns against Napoleon in 1814 and 1815 strained Austria's financial and human resources. Thus, Austria emerged as a victor from the war but in a severely weakened state.

The Congress of Vienna

From September 1814 to June 1815, representatives of the European powers met in Vienna. Guided by Metternich, the Congress of Vienna redrew the map of Europe and laid the foundation for a long period of European peace. The Habsburg Empire emerged with boundaries both more extensive and compact than it had had for several centuries. Belgium and the Habsburg lands in southwest Germany were lost, but Austria regained all other possessions that it had held in 1792 and virtually all of those it had obtained during the long years of war, including Salzburg (see fig. 3). The Holy Roman Empire was not resurrected but was replaced with a German Confederation composed of thirty-five sovereign princes and four free cities. Austria held the permanent presidency of the confederation and probably had more real influence in Germany than it had had under the Holy Roman Empire. Austria also enjoyed the dominant position on the Italian peninsula, where it possessed the northern territories of Lombardy and Venetia.

Figure 3. Austrian Empire, 1815

The wartime allies—Austria, Britain, Russia, and Prussia—concluded the Congress of Vienna by signing the Quadruple Alliance, which pledged them to uphold the peace settlement. In a secondary document, the European monarchs agreed to conduct their policies in accordance with the Christian principles of charity, peace, and love. This "Holy Alliance," proposed by the Russian tsar, Alexander I, was of little practical import, but it gave its name to the cooperative efforts of Austria, Russia, and Prussia to maintain conservative governments in Europe.

Although Austria emerged from the Congress of Vienna as one of the great powers in Europe, throughout the nineteenth century its status and territorial integrity depended on the support of at least one of the other great powers. As long as the allies were willing to cooperate in the "Congress System" to maintain the peace, order, and stability of Europe, Austrian interests were protected. But the other great powers, which were better able to defend their interests by force, did not always share Austria's devotion to Metternich's creation.

Austria in the Age of Metternich
International Developments, 1815–48

Clemens von Metternich was initially successful in maintaining a European consensus favorable to Austrian interests. He used the example of liberal revolutions in Spain and Naples and revolutionary activity in Germany to demonstrate the universal menace posed by liberalism and thus won Austria the support of Prussia and Russia. Britain also supported Austria because the two countries had common interests favoring a strong Austrian presence in Germany, limited French influence in Italy, and the maintenance of the Ottoman Empire to prevent Russian advances in the Balkans.

The support from the other great powers dissipated, however, in the mid- and late 1820s. Russia became more assertive in the Balkans, and British policy increasingly reflected that nation's liberal popular opinion. But Metternich was able to regain Russian and Prussian support in the early 1830s, following another round of liberal uprisings in Europe. Even Britain returned to close cooperation with the other powers to block French interests in Egypt. Nevertheless, Metternich failed to respond effectively to Prussia's formation of a German customs union in 1834. The customs union excluded Austria and promoted the economic integration of the other German states, thus facilitating German political unification under Prussian leadership later in the century.

Domestic Policies

Despite Metternich's high profile, it was the emperor's conservative outlook and hostility toward the values and ideas of the French Revolution that set the parameters for Austrian policy. This was especially true of domestic policy, which Franz I retained under his direct personal control until his death in 1835. The composition of the state council that Franz selected to rule in the name of his mentally incompetent son Ferdinand I ensured the continuance of his policies until revolution shook the foundations of Habsburg rule in 1848.

Franz's aim was to provide his subjects with good laws and material well-being. To accomplish the first, he issued a new penal code in 1803 and a new civil code in 1811. He expected that the second—material well-being—would evolve naturally with the reestablishment of peace, and he considered additional measures unnecessary. Political and cultural life was kept under careful scrutiny, however, to prevent the spread of nationalism and liberalism. These two movements were a common threat to Franz's conservative regime because his political opponents looked to the establishment of a unified German nation-state incorporating Austria as a means for realizing the liberal reforms impossible in the framework of the Habsburg state.

Political stagnation, however, did not prevent broader socioeconomic changes in the empire. By 1843 the population had risen to 37.5 million, an increase of 40 percent from 1792. The urban population was rising quickly, and Vienna counted nearly 400,000 inhabitants. Economically, a degree of stability was reached, and the massive wartime deficits gave way to almost balanced budgets. This was made possible by cutting state expenditures to a level near actual revenues, and not by instituting fiscal reforms to increase tax revenues. Austria's ability to protect its interests abroad or carry out domestic programs thus continued to be severely restrained by lack of revenue.

The Revolution of 1848 and Neoabsolutism
Revolutionary Rise and Fall

In 1848 liberal and nationalist ideologies sparked revolutions across Europe. In late February, the proclamation of the revolutionary Second Republic in France shook conservative Austria. Popular expectations of war caused a financial panic in the Habsburg Empire that worked to the advantage of the revolutionaries. By early March, events throughout the empire were accelerating faster than the government could control them. As a symbol of conservative government, Metternich was an early casualty of the revolution. His resignation and flight in mid-March only led to greater demands. By mid-April the court had sanctioned sweeping liberal reforms passed by the Hungarian diet. In May the government was forced to announce plans for a popularly elected constituent assembly for the Habsburg lands. This assembly, the first parliament in Austrian history, opened in July 1848.

As part of the German Confederation, the German-speaking Habsburg lands were also caught up in the revolutionary events in Germany. German nationalists and liberals convened an assembly in Frankfurt in May 1848 that suspended the diet of the German Confederation and took tentative steps toward German unification. However, the close association of nationalism and liberalism in Germany belied the growing conflict between these two ideologies. Although ethnic Germans from Bohemia were participating in the Frankfurt assembly, Czech nationalists and liberals rejected

Clemens von Metternich (1773–1859) restored Habsburg power after the defeat of Napoleon. Courtesy Embassy of Austria, Washington

Bohemian participation in the German nation being born in Frankfurt. They envisioned a reconstituted Habsburg Empire in which the Slavic nations of central and southern Europe would assume equality with the German and Hungarian components of the empire and avoid absorption by either Germany or Russia. The government gave concessions that appeared to endorse this plan, and the Czechs convened an Austro-Slavic congress in Prague in June as a counterpart to the Frankfurt assembly.

As conservative political authority gave way before the revolutionary forces, two bold military commanders began to reassert control over the situation, often ignoring or contravening timid orders from the court. General Alfred Windischgrätz routed the revolutionaries from Prague and Vienna and reestablished order by military force. South of the Alps, General Joseph Radetzky reestablished Austrian control of Lombardy-Venetia by August.

Although only Hungary remained in the hands of the revolutionaries, the Austrian government began to reorganize in the fall of 1848. A team of ministers associated with constitutionalism was presented to the constituent assembly in November. The minister-president not only committed the government to popular liberties and constitutional institutions but also to the unity of the empire. To cap the reorganization, the mentally incompetent Ferdinand formally abdicated on December 2, 1848, and his eighteen-year-old nephew was crowned Emperor Franz Joseph I (r. 1848–1916). The young emperor faced three pressing tasks: establishing effective political authority in the empire, crushing the rebellion in Hungary, and reasserting Austrian leadership in Germany.

To accomplish the first, the government promulgated a secretly prepared constitution in March 1849, thus undercutting the constituent assembly. This constitution contained guarantees of individual liberties and equality under the law, but its greatest significance lay in provisions that established a centralized government based on unitary political, legal, and economic institutions for the entire empire.

The new constitution exacerbated the revolutionary situation in Hungary. The Hungarian diet deposed the Habsburg Dynasty and declared Hungarian independence. Although Austria could have eventually restored order on its own, the need to deal simultaneously with events in Germany prompted Emperor Franz Joseph to ask for and get Russian military assistance, thus accomplishing his second objective. The rebellion was effectively, if brutally, ended by September 1849.

Austria's decision to organize itself as a unitary state also set the terms for dealing with the German nationalists and liberals sitting in Frankfurt: Austria would enter a unified Germany with all of its territories, not merely the German and Bohemian portions. This contradicted an earlier decision of the assembly, so the assembly turned from the *grossdeutsch* (large German) model of a united Germany that included Austria to the *kleindeutsch* (small German) model that excluded Austria. The assembly offered a hereditary crown of a united Germany to the Prussian king. The conditions under which the offer was made, however, caused the Prussian king to decline in early April 1849. Combined with the withdrawal of the Austrian representatives, his rejection effectively ended the Frankfurt assembly. The German Confederation was restored, and Franz Joseph's tasks were completed. However, Austria and Prussia continued to jockey for influence and leadership in Germany.

The Failure of Neoabsolutism

Initially, the new Austrian government apparently intended to implement the constitutional political structures promised in March 1849. But on December 31, 1851, Franz Joseph formally revoked the constitution, leaving in place only those provisions that established the equality of citizens before the law and the emancipation of the peasants. Popular representation was eliminated from all government institutions. In order to solidify a political base supporting neoabsolutist rule, the government also eliminated the

Josephist religious regulations that had been the source of continuing conflict with the church. In 1855 the government signed a concordat with the Vatican that recognized the institutional church as an autonomous and active participant in public life. The agreement signaled a new era of cooperation between throne and altar.

Neoabsolutism, with its aim of creating a unified, supranational state, however, ran counter to the prevailing European trend. The empire's peoples could not be isolated from the larger nationalist struggles of the German, Italian, and Slavic peoples. In Hungary active resistance to the Austrian government declined, but passive resistance grew. During the Crimean War (1853–56), the situation in Hungary made Austria vulnerable to economic and political pressure from Britain and France, the allies of Turkey against Russia. Thus, when Russia asked for Austria's support, Austria initially sought to mediate the conflict but then joined the western allies against Russia. By failing to repay Russia for its help in Hungary in 1849, Austria lost critical Russian support for its position in Germany and Italy.

France took advantage of the estrangement between Austria and Russia to set up a military confrontation between Austrian and Italian nationalist forces. This opened the door to French military intervention in support of the Italians in 1859. Because Franz Joseph was unwilling to make the concessions that were Prussia's price for assistance from the German Confederation and because he feared the French might stir up trouble in Hungary, Franz Joseph surrendered Lombardy in July 1859.

These failures did not bode well for the anticipated conflict with Prussia over German unification, so the emperor began to abandon absolutism and create a more viable political base. He experimented with various arrangements designed to attract the support of the military, the Roman Catholic Church, German liberals, Hungarians, Slavs, and Jews, who were assuming a strong presence in the economic and political life of the empire. Urgently needing to resolve the tensions with the Hungarians, the government opened secret negotiations with them in 1862. The outline of a dual monarchy was already taking shape by 1865, but negotiations were deadlocked on the eve of the war with Prussia.

Loss of Leadership in Germany

Through the early 1860s, Austria maintained hope of retaining leadership in Germany because the smaller states preferred weak Austrian leadership to Prussian domination. Nonetheless, by mid-1864 Franz Joseph realized that war was inevitable if Austrian leadership were to be preserved.

25

The immediate cause of the Seven Weeks' War between Austria and Prussia in 1866 was Prussia's desire to annex the Duchy of Holstein. Austria and Prussia had together fought a brief war against Denmark in 1864 to secure the predominantly German duchies of Schleswig and Holstein for Germany. Pending final decision on their future, Prussia took control of Schleswig, and Austria took control of Holstein. In April 1866, however, Prussia plotted with Italy to wage a two-front war against Austria that would enable Prussia to gain Holstein and Italy to gain Venetia. Although Austria tried to keep Italy out of the war through a last-minute offer to surrender Venetia to it, Italy joined the war with Prussia. Austria won key victories over Italy but lost the decisive Battle of Königgrätz (Hradec Králové in the present-day Czech Republic) to Prussia in July 1866 (see The Habsburg Military, ch. 5).

Defeated, Austria agreed to the dissolution of the German Confederation and accepted the formation of a Prussian-dominated North German Confederation, which became the basis of the German Empire in 1871. The south German states—Bavaria, Baden, Württemberg, and Hesse-Darmstadt—were accorded an "independent international existence" and, in theory, could have gravitated toward Austria. Nevertheless, their military and commercial ties to Prussia militated against such an outcome. The province of Venetia, Austria's last Italian possession, was transferred to Italy.

Austria-Hungary to the Early 1900s
The Founding of the Dual Monarchy

Defeat in the Seven Weeks' War demonstrated that Austria was no longer a great power. Looking to the future, Franz Joseph set three foreign policy objectives designed to restore Austrian leadership in Germany: regain great-power status; counter Prussian moves in southern Germany; and avoid going to war for the foreseeable future. Because reconciliation with Hungary was a precondition for regaining great-power status, the new foreign minister, Friedrich Ferdinand von Beust, became a strong advocate of bringing the stalemated negotiations with the Hungarians to a successful conclusion. By the spring of 1867, a compromise had been reached and was enacted into law by the Hungarian Diet.

The Compromise (Ausgleich) of 1867 divided the Habsburg Empire into two separate states with equal rights under a common ruler, hence the term "Dual Monarchy." Officially, these states were Hungary and the "Kingdoms and Lands represented in the Parliament," the latter being an awkward designation necessitated by the lack of a historical name encompassing all non-Hungarian lands (see fig. 4). Unofficially, the western half was called either Austria or Cis-Leithania, after the Leitha River, which separated the two states. The officially accepted name of the Dual Monarchy was Austria-Hungary, also seen as the Austro-Hungarian Empire.

The two national governments and their legislatures in Vienna and Budapest shared a common government consisting of a monarch with almost unlimited powers in the conduct of foreign and military affairs, a ministry of foreign affairs, a ministry of defense, and a finance ministry for diplomatic and military establishments. In the absence of a shared parliament, discussion of the empire's common affairs was conducted by parallel meetings of delegates from the two national legislatures communicating with each other through written notes. A key topic of these meetings was the common commercial policy and customs union that had to be renegotiated every ten years.

The Austrian parliament passed legislation implementing the Ausgleich in late 1867. This "December Constitution" was the product of German-speaking Liberals, who were able to dominate parliament because of a boycott by Czech delegates. The December Constitution closely followed the constitution of 1849 and placed no significant restrictions on the emperor with regard to foreign and military affairs but did add a list of fundamental rights enjoyed by Austrians. The lower house of the Austrian parliament was elected through a highly restricted franchise (about 6 percent of the male population). Seats were apportioned both by province and by curiae, that is, four socioeconomic groups representing the great landowners, towns, chambers of commerce, and peasant communities.

By building on the two dominant nationalities in the empire, German and Hungarian, dualism enabled Austria-Hungary to achieve relative financial and political stability. It did not, however, provide a framework for other nationalities, in particular the Slavs, to achieve equivalent political stature. Indeed, the Hungarian state used its power to preclude such an outcome. Hungary interpreted provisions in the Ausgleich as requiring Austria to retain its basic constitutional structure as a unitary state, so that any federalist accommodation with the Czechs would invalidate the Ausgleich and dissolve the Dual Monarchy.

Final Defeat in Germany and Reconciliation with Prussia

Because Russia was aligned with Prussia and because Britain had retreated into isolationism, Austria-Hungary turned to France as an ally in its bid to regain leadership in Germany. France wanted

Figure 4. Austria-Hungary, 1867–1918

gains in Germany at Prussia's expense and was receptive to an alliance. Open cooperation with French expansionist ambitions, however, was inconsistent with Austria-Hungary's efforts to be the leader and defender of the German nation. The success of the alliance thus depended on France's position as the defender of the south German states against Prussia—which France failed to do.

France declared war on Prussia and invaded German territory in July 1870. The south German states rallied to Prussia's side in the Franco-Prussian War, and Beust's patient effort to detach those states from Prussia lay in ruins. Austria watched helplessly as Prussia, the presumed underdog, quickly and soundly defeated France. In January 1871, Prussia founded the Second German Empire, uniting the German states without Austria.

Unable to undo what Prussian military prowess had wrought in Germany, Austria-Hungary trimmed its sails accordingly. Count

Gyula Andrássy, a Hungarian, replaced Beust as foreign minister, and the empire's foreign policy began to reflect the anti-Russian sentiments of the Hungarians. Before 1871 ended, Austria-Hungary and Germany were working toward a united foreign policy.

This diplomatic cooperation with Prussian-dominated Germany contributed to the internal political stability of Austria-Hungary. Exclusion from a united Germany was a psychological shock for German Austrians because their claim to leadership in the Habsburg Empire had rested in part on their leadership of the German nation. Cut off from Germany, they became just one of many national groups in the Habsburg Empire and constituted only slightly more than one-third of Austria's population. Had Prussia remained hostile, Austria-Hungary's German population might have been the excuse for Prussian territorial ambitions similar to those harbored by the other nation-states that surrounded Austria-Hungary. Aligned with Austria-Hungary, however, Prussia distanced itself from German nationalists in Austria-Hungary, and the annexation movement remained politically insignificant. But, because German Austrians no longer had their majority status guaranteed by participation in the larger German nation, many felt increasingly vulnerable and threatened. German Austrians thus became open to a nationalism based on ethnic fear and hostility that contrasted with the self-confident Liberal nationalism of earlier decades.

The Eastern Question

Having reconciled itself to exclusion from Germany and Italy, Austria-Hungary turned to the east, where declining Turkish power made the Balkans the focus of international rivalries. Foreign Minister Andrássy was opposed to any annexation of Balkan territories because that would have increased the empire's Slavic population. Ideally, he favored maintenance of Turkish authority in order to check the expansion of Russian influence. This option, however, was not viable. To prevent either Russia from replacing Turkey as the dominant power in the region or the already independent Balkan states (Serbia, Montenegro, Greece, and Romania) from dividing up the remaining Turkish territory, Austria-Hungary was forced to seek a partition of the Balkans with Russia.

Because Germany was aligned with both Russia and Austria-Hungary, it acted as a moderating force on Russia to prevent war between its partners in the 1870s. So successful was Germany at limiting Russian gains after the costly Russo-Turkish War (1877–78), that Russia's relations with Germany cooled considerably. With Germany's support, Austria-Hungary acquired Bosnia and Hercegovina as part of the settlement to that war. Andrássy, however, did not directly annex Bosnia and Hercegovina but obtained the right of an Austro-Hungarian occupation, while Turkey retained sovereignty.

With relations strained between Russia and Germany, Austria-Hungary exploited Germany's need to strengthen its position against France and obtained an anti-Russian alliance. Under the resulting Dual Alliance, Austria-Hungary and Germany pledged to help defend the other against an attack by Russia. In the event of war between Germany and France, however, Austria-Hungary promised nothing more than neutrality unless Russia were also involved. As favorable as the Dual Alliance appeared, it drew Austria-Hungary into Otto von Bismarck's web of alliances and diplomatic maneuverings. Austria-Hungary thus became party to conflicts with France and Britain, countries with which it had no directly conflicting interests. The Triple Alliance signed by Germany, Italy, and Austria-Hungary in 1882, for example, mainly protected Italian and German interests against France and did nothing to resolve outstanding issues between Austria-Hungary and Italy.

Great-power tensions in the Balkans eased in the 1890s, as Africa and the colonial territories in the Far East became the focus of competition among European powers. Although Austria-Hungary was not involved in this colonial competition, Russia was. Its interests in the Far East paved the way for an accommodation with Austria-Hungary to maintain the status quo in the Balkans. In 1903, however, Serbia, a Balkan country that European powers had assigned to the Austro-Hungarian sphere of influence, launched an expansionistic program directed against Austria-Hungary. Without Russian support, however, Serbia's threat was not a major concern.

Internal Developments in Austria

The Czech boycott of the Austrian parliament enabled the German Austrian Liberals to dominate the government of Austria until the late 1870s. They used their position to block concessions to Czechs and Poles in the early days of the Dual Monarchy, and they further protected their interests in 1873 by altering the franchise law to increase the representation in parliament of their constituency—the urban, ethnically German population and assimilated Jews. The Liberals' legislative program focused on anticlerical measures, but conflict over foreign policy issues, not religious ones, caused the Liberals' fall from power in 1879. The Liberals opposed the annexation of Bosnia and Hercegovina—which was favored by the emperor—and claimed certain powers in the conduct of foreign policy that Franz Joseph saw as an infringement on his sovereign authority.

After the fall of the Liberals, a nonparty government known as the Iron Ring was formed under Eduard Taaffe. Intended to encircle and limit the influence of the Liberals, the Iron Ring represented court interests and enjoyed broad support from clerical parties, German Austrian conservatives, Poles, and Czech representatives, who had decided to end their boycott. Backed by this comfortable parliamentary majority, the executive branch was able to operate smoothly. Although the concessions given the Czechs in return for their support were linguistic and cultural rather than political, the concessions raised sensitive issues because the expanded use of the Czech language in Bohemian public life weighed heavily on the ethnic German minority.

The major legislative initiative of the Taaffe government was the 1883 franchise reform. This measure broadened the socioeconomic base of the electorate and thus weakened the support of the Liberals while strengthening the conservatives. An even broader franchise reform was proposed in 1893 after the election of 1891, which had been conducted in an atmosphere of heightened ethnic tensions in Bohemia. The proposed reform would have given the vote to all male citizens over the age of twenty-five and thus diluted still further the middle-class urban vote that the court associated with fervid nationalism. The bill, however, was widely rejected by the conservative backers of the Iron Ring, and Taaffe resigned.

Ethnic tensions, however, did not subside, even though a modified version of the franchise legislation proposed in 1893 was ultimately enacted. With the parliament highly fragmented both nationally and politically, Minister-President Count Kasimir Badeni offered new concessions to the Czechs in 1897 to forge the majority coalition he needed to conduct customs and trade policy negotiations with the Hungarians. These concessions, which dealt with the use of the Czech language by the bureaucracy, inflamed German-speaking Austrians. Violent rioting on a near-revolutionary scale erupted not only in Bohemia but also in Vienna and Graz. The Badeni government fell. Because no effective majority could be assembled in the polarized parliament, the government increasingly used emergency provisions that allowed the emperor to enact laws when parliament was not in session.

The political stalemate in parliament was a reflection of socioeconomic changes in the empire that were heightening tensions among social classes and nationalities. Although the economic and psychological impact of the economic crash of 1873 endured for some time, Austria experienced steady industrialization and urbanization in the late nineteenth century. By 1890 Austria stood midway between the rural societies that bordered it on the east and south and the industrially advanced societies of Western Europe.

The German-speaking middle class, including assimilated Jews, had been the first group to translate growing numerical and economic power into political leverage. Even after the 1879 fall of the Liberal government, which had represented this group's interests, the government had to consider the concerns of the German-speaking middle class in order to maintain political stability.

In contrast to that of the middle class, the positions of the aristocracy and the Roman Catholic Church weakened. Individual aristocrats played prominent roles in the government, but the bureaucracy was assuming many functions once played by the aristocracy as a whole. For the church, the 1855 concordat between the empire and the Vatican had been a high-water mark for its formal role in political life. The Liberals' anticlerical legislation and abrogation of the concordat in 1870 curtailed the church's public presence and influence. Nonetheless, popular support for the church remained strong, and a new form of Catholic political participation was beginning to take shape based on a socially progressive platform endorsed by the 1891 papal encyclical *Rerum Novarum*. This largely urban movement coalesced into the Christian Social Party (Christlichsoziale Partei—CSP). Papal support was not sufficient to win the new party the approval of the conservative Austrian bishops, who continued to work through the older clerical-oriented parties.

Initially, the CSP found strong support in Vienna and controlled the city administration at the turn of the century. Nonetheless, the party was unable to hold its desired base among industrial workers in the face of competition from the Social Democratic Workers' Party (Sozialdemokratische Arbeiterpartei—SDAP). Founded in 1889 at a unity conference of moderate and radical socialists, the SDAP adhered to a revisionist Marxist program. The SDAP became a political home for many Austrian Jews uncomfortable with the growing anti-Semitism of the German nationalist movement, the other major political current of the time.

Rising ethnic tensions made it difficult for political parties to ignore the influence of German nationalism in the closing decades of the nineteenth century. The Liberal movement faded, largely because of its resistance to becoming a specifically German party, and dissatisfied Liberals were key figures in the formation of new nationalist movements and parties. Even though the CSP and SDAP were based on political ideologies that transcended national identity, they too were obliged to make concessions in their program to German nationalism. In the late 1890s, all German-oriented parties, with the exception of the SDAP and the Catholic People's Party, united in the German Front. The specific demands of the German Front were modest, but by calling for recognition of a special position for Germans in light of their historic role in the empire, German Austrians were on a collision course with other national groups.

The Final Years of the Empire and World War I
The Crisis over Bosnia and Hercegovina

Around 1906 the Balkans again became the focus of great-power rivalry, as Russia renewed its interest in the Balkans and became Serbia's great-power patron. A crisis erupted in 1908, when Turkey began to be reorganized as a constitutional state. Bosnia and Hercegovina, which was Turkish territory under Austro-Hungarian administration, was invited to send delegates to the new Turkish parliament. Austria-Hungary responded by formally annexing Bosnia and Hercegovina in violation of various international agreements. It quelled Turkey's objections with financial compensation. But by alienating Russia and Italy, the annexation was a costly diplomatic victory for Austria-Hungary at a time when the military alliance system of Europe was moving against it. Britain had resolved colonial rivalries with both France and Russia, paving the way for the cooperation of the three countries in the Triple Entente.

Following the crisis over Bosnia and Hercegovina, Russia encouraged the independent Balkan states to form what was intended to be an anti-Austro-Hungarian coalition. But the new coalition, called the Balkan League, was more interested in partitioning the remaining Turkish territories in the Balkans, and it defeated Turkey in the First Balkan War in 1912. The Balkan allies turned on each other in 1913 in a war over the division of the former Turkish territories. In this Second Balkan War, Serbia doubled both its territory and its population.

World War I

Austria-Hungary considered the newly enlarged and Russian-backed Serbia to be the principal threat to its security because Serbian military intelligence supported anti-Habsburg groups and activities in Bosnia and Hercegovina. Thus, when the heir to the Habsburg crown, Franz Ferdinand, and his wife were assassinated in Sarajevo by Bosnian nationalists on June 28, 1914, the presumption of Serbian complicity was strong. The idea of a preemptive war against Serbia was not new in Vienna, and, despite the weak pretext, Germany indicated a willingness to back its ally.

On July 23, Austria-Hungary presented Serbia with an ultimatum designed to be rejected. The key demands were that Serbia suppress anti-Habsburg activities, organizations, and propaganda and that Habsburg officials be permitted to join in the Serbian investigation of the assassination. Serbia responded negatively but appeared conciliatory. Nonetheless, Austria-Hungary declared war on Serbia on July 28 without further consultations with Germany.

Russia's decision to mobilize on July 30 escalated the war beyond a regional conflict by bringing into play the system of European alliances. Because German war strategy depended on avoiding a two-front war, Germany had to defeat France before Russia could fully mobilize. Thus, Germany responded to Russia's mobilization by immediately declaring war on France and Russia. On August 4, Britain declared war on Germany. On August 6, Austria-Hungary declared war on Russia. Finally, on August 12, France and Britain declared war on Austria-Hungary.

Once the major powers were engaged, they sought to enlist the support of the smaller powers. Despite its partnership with Austria-Hungary and Germany in the Triple Alliance, Italy was not bound by that treaty to join the war, and it declared its neutrality. Germany pressed Austria-Hungary unsuccessfully to cede to Italy Austrian territories it desired, in order to win Italian support. Because the Triple Entente powers readily promised transfer of the territories in the event of victory, Italy entered the war on their side in April 1915.

Although German and Austro-Hungarian military victories in the east during the spring of 1915 overcame the military disasters that Austria-Hungary experienced early in the war, the empire's internal economic situation steadily grew more precarious. Austria-Hungary was not prepared for a long and costly war.

The death of Emperor Franz Joseph on November 21, 1916, deprived Austria-Hungary of his symbolic unifying presence. His twenty-nine-year-old grandnephew, Karl (r. 1916–18), was unprepared for his role as emperor. But by this time, the future of the monarchy no longer depended on what the emperor did; rather, its fate hinged on the outcome of the war. Despite revolutionary Russia's withdrawal from the war, military success in the east could not counter events in the west. The United States had entered the war on the side of the Allies in April 1917, and with the failure of its military offensive in the spring of 1918, Germany was no longer capable of continuing the war.

The End of the Habsburg Empire and the Birth of the Austrian Republic

The dismantling of the Habsburg Empire had not been an objective of the Allies. Following the collapse of the tsarist government in Russia, however, the Allies increasingly portrayed the war as pitting freedom and democracy against oppression and autocracy. This strategy benefited the representatives of Czech, Slovak, Hungarian, and other nationalist committees-in-exile, which skillfully played on the theme of self-determination expressed in United States president Woodrow Wilson's Fourteen Points. Austria-Hungary was unable to put forward a meaningful program of reform while still preserving the monarchy and so could not successfully resist the centrifugal forces pulling it apart. By mid-1918 the Allies began recognizing the national committees-in-exile and made plans for an independent Poland and Czechoslovakia. By October 1918, when the Austro-Hungarian government was seeking an armistice, control of the empire's constituent lands was passing to national committees, including one representing German Austrians.

On October 21, German Austrian delegates to the Austrian parliament voted to establish an Austrian state incorporating all districts inhabited by ethnic Germans. At the end of the month, the delegates established a coalition provisional government. On November 3, imperial authorities signed an armistice, bringing Austro-Hungarian participation in World War I to an official end. On November 11, Karl renounced any role in the new Austrian state, and the next day the provisional government issued a constitution for the German Austrian Republic.

The First Republic

Overview of the Political Camps

Conditioned to view themselves as the ruling elite of a supranational empire by virtue of what they regarded as their superior German culture, German Austrians (including assimilated Jews and Slavs) were the national group least prepared for a post-Habsburg state. The provisional government formed at the end of the war included representatives from three political groups: the Nationalists/ Liberals, the Christian Social Party (Christlichsoziale Partei—CSP), and the Social Democratic Workers' Party (Sozialdemokratische Arbeiterpartei—SDAP). These three groups dominated political life in interwar Austria and reflected the split of Austrian society into three camps (*Lager*): pan-German nationalists, Catholics and Christian Socials, and Marxists and Social Democrats, respectively.

The parliamentary bloc represented by the Nationalists/Liberals was the smallest and most internally divided. Seventeen nationalist groups were unified in the Greater German People's Party (Grossdeutsche Volkspartei), commonly called the Nationals, which described itself as a "national-anti-Semitic, social libertarian party." The political heirs of the Liberals, the Nationals drew their support from the urban middle class and retained liberalism's strong anticlerical views. Unification (Anschluss) with Germany was the Nationals' key objective, and they were cool, if not openly hostile, toward restoration of the Habsburg Dynasty to rule in Austria. In rural Austria, another party, the Agrarian League (Landbund), endorsed a nationalist program in conjunction with a corporatist and anti-Semitic platform. Radical nationalists were few in number, and some, Adolf Hitler, for example, had emigrated to Germany. The National Socialist German Workers' Party (National-Sozialistische Deutsche Arbeiterpartei—NSDAP, or Nazi Party) represented this segment of the nationalist movement but was numerically insignificant during the 1920s.

The NSDAP originated in prewar Bohemia, where the German Workers' Party (Deutsche Arbeiterpartei) drew on a virulently racist movement headed by Georg von Schönerer to put together an anti-Semitic, anti-Slav nationalist program hostile toward capitalism, liberalism, Marxism, and clericalism. In 1918 the party changed its name to the National Socialist German Workers' Party. After World War I, the party split into two wings, one in Czechoslovakia among Sudeten Germans (German Austrians of Bohemia, Moravia, and Silesia), and one in Austria. A similar party was founded in Germany and eventually came under the leadership of Hitler. Although the Austrian party leader favored parliamentary participation and internal party democracy in contrast to Hitler's antiparliamentarianism and emphasis on the "leadership principle," the Austrian and German parties united in 1926 but maintained separate national organizations.

The original Christian Social Party (Christlichsoziale Partei—CSP) had merged with one of the rural-based clerical parties in 1907 and had become more conservative in outlook. Because the church had lost the political protection of the Habsburg Dynasty with the collapse of the monarchy in 1918, the church was increasingly reliant on the political power of the CSP to protect its interests. Nevertheless, the church hierarchy, which was distrustful of parliamentary democracy, remained cool toward the CSP.

During the 1920s and early 1930s, the CSP was dominated by Ignaz Seipel, a priest and theologian who had served in the last imperial ministry. The party was well disposed toward the Habsburg

Vienna's Karlsplatz art nouveau subway stop with baroque
Karlskirche in the background
Courtesy Austrian National Tourist Office, New York

Dynasty and inclined toward its restoration under a conservative, constitutional monarchy. The CSP gave only conditional support for unification with Germany and emphasized Austria's distinct mission as a Christian German nation. In light of public opinion favoring unification, however, the party was circumspect in voicing its doubts. The CSP inherited an anti-Semitic strain from its association with the prewar nationalist movement. In addition, the close identification of Jews with both liberalism and socialism, which were the ideological foes of the CSP, made anti-Semitism an easy way to cultivate a political base.

The Social Democratic Workers' Party (Sozialdemokratische Arbeiterpartei—SDAP) endorsed a revisionist Marxist program. Although it spoke of the dictatorship of the proletariat, it sought to gain power through the ballot box, not through revolution. Karl Renner, who headed the provisional government, was the chief spokesman for this revisionist program after the war, but leadership of the party was held by Otto Bauer, who vocally supported a more radical, left-wing position. Bauer's rhetoric helped the party outflank the Communist Party of Austria (Kommunistische Partei Österreichs—KPÖ). But because CSP leader Seipel was given to similarly strong rhetoric, the two contributed to the polarization of Austrian society. The Social Democrats (members of the SDAP), were strong supporters of unification with Germany, their fervor declining only with the rise of the Nazi regime in the early 1930s.

The Foundation of the First Republic

Although the SDAP was the smallest of the three parliamentary blocs, it received a preeminent role in the postwar provisional government because it was perceived as best able to maintain public order in the face of the revolutionary situation created by economic collapse and military defeat. With Bauer's Marxist rhetoric and the party's strong ties to organized labor, the SDAP was able to outmaneuver the KPÖ for control and direction of workers' and soldiers' councils that sprang up in imitation of the revolutionary government in Russia. The SDAP suppressed the old imperial army and founded a new military force, the Volkswehr (People's Defense), under SDAP control, to contain revolutionary agitation and guard against bourgeois counterrevolution.

When parliamentary elections were held in February 1919, the SDAP won 40.8 percent of the vote, compared with 35.9 percent for the CSP and 20.8 percent for the Nationals. As a result, the Nationals withdrew from the coalition and left a SDAP–CSP government headed by Renner to negotiate a settlement to the war and write a constitution. At the peace talks in the Paris suburb of St. Germain, however, the Allies allowed no meaningful negotiations because Austria-Hungary had surrendered unconditionally. The Allies had decided that Austria was a successor state to Austria-Hungary, so the treaty contained a war-guilt and war-reparations clause and limitations on the size of Austria's military. Although the provisional government had declared the Austrian state to be a constituent state of the German republic, the treaty barred Austria from joining Germany without the consent of the League of Nations and compelled the new state to call itself the Republic of Austria rather than the German Austrian Republic. After Austria's parliament approved these unexpectedly harsh terms, the Treaty of St. Germain was signed on September 10, 1919.

In setting the territorial boundaries of the Austrian state, sometimes referred to as the First Republic, the Allies were faced with the basic problem of carving a nation-state out of an empire in which ethnic groups did not live within compact and distinct boundaries. Austria received the contiguous German or German-dominated territories of Upper Austria, Lower Austria, Styria, Carinthia, Tirol (north of the Brenner Pass), Salzburg, and Vorarlberg, as well as a slice of western Hungary that became the province of Burgenland. Under the empire, however, no specifically "Austrian" identity or nationalism had ever developed among these provinces. Thus, despite a common language and historical ties through the Habsburg Dynasty, pressure from the Allies was necessary to keep even these contiguous areas together.

Although geographically contiguous and ethnically German, South Tirol was transferred to Italy as promised by the Allies when Italy joined the war. The Sudeten Germans were not geographically contiguous and could not be included in the new Austrian state. As a result, the Sudeten Germans were incorporated in the new Czechoslovakia. Austria's population numbered 6.5 million, as against Czechoslovakia's 11.8 million, of whom 3.1 million were ethnic Germans.

The constitution of 1920 established a bicameral parliament, with a lower house, the Nationalrat (National Council) elected directly by universal adult suffrage, and an upper house, the Bundesrat (Federal Council) elected indirectly by the provincial assemblies (see Government Institutions, ch. 4). In accordance with the SDAP desire for a centralized state, real political power was concentrated in the Nationalrat. Significantly, however, none of the three major parties was truly committed to the state and institutions established by the constitution. The SDAP goal was an Austria united with a socialist Germany, and the party's inflammatory Marxist rhetoric caused the other parties to fear that the SDAP could not be trusted to maintain democratic institutions if it ever achieved a parliamentary majority. Although the CSP under Seipel came closest to accepting the idea of an independent Austria, it preferred a monarchy over a republic. Seipel himself voiced increasingly antidemocratic sentiments as the decade advanced. The Nationals were fundamentally opposed to the existence of an independent Austrian state and desired unification with Germany.

Political Life of the 1920s and Early 1930s

With traditional sources of food and coal located across new national borders, Austria suffered extreme economic dislocation, and the country's economic viability was in doubt. Moreover, having settled the immediate questions of the peace treaty and constitution, the SDAP and CSP found it increasingly difficult to cooperate.

Unfortunately, the October 1920 parliamentary elections did not provide the basis for a stable government. The CSP increased its share of the vote to 41.8 percent, while the SDAP declined to 36.0 percent and the Nationals to 17.2 percent. Seipel tried to form an antisocialist coalition with the Nationals, but that party was not yet prepared to set aside its own ideological differences with the CSP. Weak, neutral governments guided the country for the next two years.

In 1922 Seipel assumed the office of chancellor (prime minister). By adroitly manipulating the European political situation and accepting renewed prohibitions on union with Germany, he managed to obtain foreign loans to launch an economic stabilization plan. Although the plan stabilized the currency and set state finances on a sound course, it provided no solution to the underlying economic problems and dislocation, and it extracted a high social cost by cutting government social programs and raising taxes.

Otto Bauer, leader of the SDAP, kept the party in self-imposed isolation after the collapse of the initial SDAP–CSP coalition in the belief that the natural role for a socialist party in a bourgeois democracy was opposition. Thus, Seipel remained the key public figure in Austrian national politics throughout the 1920s, even though he did not continuously serve as chancellor. Nevertheless, the CSP was not able to win an outright majority in the Nationalrat, and the SDAP registered steady gains among voters, polling 41 percent of the vote in 1927 against 55 percent of the CSP-National coalition. Vienna, which was given the status of a province under the 1920 constitution, was the SDAP stronghold. Vienna's city government of Social Democrats purposely sought to make health and housing programs and socialist-inspired "workers'culture"of "Red Vienna"a model for the rest of Austria.

Although the CSP had secured the suppression of the SDAP-controlled Volkswehr in 1922 when a more traditional army was established, the SDAP responded by forming the Republikanischer Schutzbund (Republican Defense League). Well armed and well trained, it numbered some 80,000 members by the early 1930s. Of even greater political significance, however, were the provincial-based homeland militias, variously called the Heimwehr (Home Guard) and the Heimatschutz (Homeland Defense). Independently organized, these militias initially lacked any overarching political ideology except anti-Marxism. Until 1927 they were not an effective political force and were viewed by many, including Seipel, as a military reserve supplementing inadequate military and police forces. In the late 1920s, however, the Heimwehr gained greater ideological coherence from contact with Italian fascism. But with the exception of the Styrian branch, the Heimwehr was unable to bridge differences with Austrian Nazis. For this reason, the Heimwehr leader, Prince Ernst Rüdiger von Starhemberg, founded a Heimwehr political wing, the Heimatbloc (Homeland Bloc), in 1930.

In the parliamentary election of 1930, the CSP experienced a severe setback, winning only sixty-six seats to the SDAP's seventy-two. The Heimatbloc picked up the seven seats lost by the CSP. Although the CSP-National coalition had broken down in the late 1920s, a new government was formed that combined the CSP with the Nationals and the peasant-based Landbund. Eager for a political success to bolster its popular support, the government began negotiations with Germany for a customs union in March 1931. When France learned of the negotiations, however, it immediately denounced the proposal as a violation of the international ban on Austrian-German unification. Under severe diplomatic pressure, Austria and Germany were forced to drop their plans, but not before France's economic retaliation had led to the collapse of Austria's largest bank, the Creditanstalt, in June 1931.

In the wake of this foreign policy and economic disaster, Seipel sought a new coalition between the CSP and the SDAP but was rebuffed. With no other alternative, Seipel resurrected the CSP-National coalition. The growing political strength of the Nazis in Germany and the worsening economic conditions marked by the rise in unemployment from about 280,000 in 1929 to nearly 600,000 in 1933, however, were effecting a political realignment in Austria. In the spring of 1932, the Austrian branch of the Nazi Party registered important gains in local elections. Although the CSP lost important segments of its constituency to the Nazis, the parties in the nationalist camp suffered greater defections, especially after Nazi triumphs in Germany in early 1933. Austrian elections were increasingly three-way contests among the CSP, the SDAP, and the Nazi Party.

The End of Constitutional Rule

In May 1932, a new cabinet was formed under the leadership of Engelbert Dollfuss, a CSP member. Dollfuss's coalition, composed of the CSP, the Landbund, and the Heimatbloc, had a one-vote majority. Both the SDAP and the Nazi Party pressed for new elections, but Dollfuss refused, fearing defeat. Instead, he sought support from fascist Italy and the Heimwehr and increasingly relied on authoritarian measures to maintain his government.

In early March 1933, parliamentary maneuvering by the SDAP, which was trying to block government action against a pro-Nazi labor union, created a procedural crisis in the Nationalrat. Urged on by the Italian dictator, Benito Mussolini, Dollfuss exploited the confusion in the Nationalrat to end parliamentary government and began governing on the basis of a 1917 emergency law. Dollfuss outlawed the Nazi Party, the politically insignificant KPÖ, and the Republikanischer Schutzbund. All, however, continued to exist underground.

Seeking a firmer political footing than that offered by Italy and the coercive power of the police, military, and Heimwehr, Dollfuss formed the Fatherland Front (Vaterländische Front) in May 1933. The front was intended to displace the existing political parties and rally broad public support for Dollfuss's vision of a specifically Austrian nationalism closely tied to the country's Catholic identity. Dollfuss rejected union with Germany, preferring instead to see Austria resume its historical role as the Central European bulwark of Christian German culture against Nazism and communism. In September 1933, Dollfuss announced plans to organize Austria constitutionally as a Catholic, German, corporatist state.

The opportunity to put the corporatist constitution in place came after a failed socialist uprising in February 1934 triggered by a police search for Schutzbund weapons in Linz. An unsuccessful general strike followed, along with artillery attacks by the army on a Vienna housing project. Within four days, the socialist rebellion was crushed. Both the SDAP and its affiliated trade unions were banned, and key leaders were arrested or fled the country. Dollfuss's constitution was promulgated in May 1934, and the Fatherland Front became the only legal political organization. Austrian society, however, remained divided into three camps: the nationalist bloc that was associated with the Heimwehr and the bloc represented by the CSP struggled for control of the Fatherland Front; the socialist bloc fell back on passive resistance; and the nationalist bloc dominated by the Nazis boldly conspired against the state with support from Germany.

Although a variety of political labels have been applied to the Dollfuss regime, it eludes simple classification. Its ideology harked back to early religious and romantic political critiques of liberal democracy and socialism. The regime incorporated many elements of European fascism, but it lacked two features widely viewed as essential to fascism: adherence to the "leadership principle," and a mass political base. In any event, the complex corporatist structures of the 1934 constitution, in which citizens participated in society on the basis of occupation and not as individuals, were never fully implemented. And the regime's relations with the Roman Catholic Church were never as straightforward as the regime's ideology suggested. Although the incorporation of a new concordat with the Vatican in the 1934 constitution bespoke harmony between church and state, in practice the concordat became the bulwark on which the church claimed its autonomous rights. Longstanding rivalries between church and state actually intensified as state-affiliated organizations intruded on what the church viewed as its interests in youth, family, and educational policies and organizations.

Growing German Pressure on Austria

In June 1934, Hitler and Mussolini had their first meeting. Mussolini defended his support of Dollfuss, while Hitler denied any intent to annex Austria but made clear his desire to see Austria in Germany's sphere of influence. Austrian Nazis, however, were embarked on a more radical course. They conspired to seize top government officials and force the appointment of a Nazi-dominated government.

The Dollfuss government learned of these plans before the putsch began on July 25 but did not make adequate preparations. Although the army and the Heimwehr remained loyal and the coup failed, Dollfuss was killed. Strong international indignation over the putsch forced Hitler to rein in the Austrian Nazis, but Hitler's goal remained the eventual annexation (Anschluss) of Austria.

Dollfuss was succeeded as chancellor by Kurt von Schuschnigg, another of Seipel's CSP protégés. Schuschnigg's political survival directly depended on Italian support for an independent Austria, but by 1935 Mussolini was already moving toward accommodation with Hitler and began to advise Schuschnigg to do the same. Schuschnigg was in fact prepared to make concessions to Germany, if Hitler in turn would make a clear statement recognizing Austrian independence.

Schuschnigg, however, did not understand the degree to which even moderate nationalists, whose support he needed, were already operating as fronts for Hitler and the Nazis. Thus, in the agreement signed with Germany on July 11, 1936, Hitler gave Austria essentially worthless pledges of Austrian independence and sovereignty, while Schuschnigg agreed to bring into his government members of the "National Opposition," who, unbeknownst to him, were taking their orders from Berlin.

The 1936 agreement furthered Germany's desire to isolate Austria diplomatically and encouraged other European countries to view Austrian-German relations as a purely internal affair of the German people. Bereft of external support and in no position to resist German pressure, Schuschnigg agreed to meet Hitler in

Berchtesgaden on February 12, 1938. Hitler used the meeting to intimidate the Austrians with an implicit threat of military invasion, and Schuschnigg accepted a list of demands designed to strengthen the political position of the Austrian Nazis. Although the list did not include the legalization of Austria's Nazi Party, the Nazis and their sympathizers began to come into the open.

On his return to Vienna, Schuschnigg began secret plans for one last desperate bid to preserve Austrian sovereignty: a plebiscite designed to secure a yes vote "for a free and German, independent and social, for a Christian and united Austria, for peace and work and equality of all who declare themselves for Nation and Fatherland." Representatives of the SDAP agreed to call a plebiscite in exchange for various concessions.

Hitler recognized that the plebiscite would be a new obstacle to Anschluss and a symbolic defeat for Nazi Germany, so he quickly moved against it. The German army began preparing for an invasion on March 10, and Nazi sympathizers in the Austrian cabinet demanded that the plebiscite be postponed. Schuschnigg agreed to cancel it altogether and then acceded to demands for his resignation. Nonetheless, on March 12, Hitler sent the German army into Austria.

The Anschluss and World War II

Absorption of Austria into the Third Reich

Most Austrian proponents of the Anschluss had foreseen a gradual coordination and merger of the two German states that would preserve some semblance of Austrian identity. But, influenced by the tumultuous welcome he received on his arrival, Hitler made an impromptu decision for quick and total absorption of Austria into the Third Reich.

The Anschluss violated various international agreements, but the European powers offered only perfunctory opposition. Italy had acquiesced to the invasion beforehand, and in return Hitler later agreed to allow Italy to retain the South Tirol despite his aggressive policies elsewhere to bring all German populations into the Third Reich. Britain was following a policy of appeasement in 1938 and was unwilling to risk war over Austria's independence, while France, traditionally the strongest foe of German unification, was incapable of unilateral military action.

To provide a legal facade for the Anschluss, Hitler arranged a plebiscite for April 10, 1938. The Nazis portrayed the plebiscite as a vote on pan-Germanism and claimed a 99.7 percent vote in favor of the Anschluss. Although the outcome was undoubtedly influenced by Nazi intimidation, the Anschluss enjoyed broad popular support. Nevertheless, the positive vote reflected the Austrians' desire for change far more than it did widespread support for Hitler and Nazism. Unification offered a way out of the political turmoil of the First Republic, and ties with the larger German economy promised economic revitalization. Many Austrians probably also harbored unrealistic notions of Austria's position within the Third Reich, expecting an arrangement similar to the Dual Monarchy in which Austria and Germany would be equal partners. And the full dimensions of Nazi barbarism were not yet apparent. Underlying these factors, however, was the widespread appeal of pan-Germanism that cut across political lines. Austrians had traditionally thought of themselves as Germans, and the Austrian nationalism cultivated by Dollfuss and Schuschnigg had not taken root. Although the SDAP had moderated its long-standing support for unification when Hitler came to power in Germany, Karl Renner urged a yes vote in the Nazi-organized plebiscite. Once unification was a fact, other Socialist leaders felt that the Nazi regime was not sufficient reason to reject the fulfillment of what they viewed as a progressive goal of German nationalism.

Hitler moved quickly to suppress what little independent identity and national unity Austria had. The name *Austria* was banned, provinces were freed of central administration from Vienna, and provincial loyalty and identification were cultivated. In addition, Austrian Nazis and Nazi sympathizers who might have become effective national leaders were transferred to relatively unimportant jobs in the administration of the Third Reich or, after World War II began, were sent to administer the occupied territories. Thus, a disproportionate number of Austrians came to be in charge of the bureaucracy overseeing the implementation of the Nazis' extermination of the Jews and other peoples and groups deemed undesirable.

Nazi Economic and Social Policies

Between 1938 and mid-1940, the Nazi administration in Austria focused on stimulating the economy and relieving social distress in order to win popular support, woo the working class away from socialism, and enable Austria to contribute to the German war machine. By early 1939, the Austrian economy was recovering, and unemployment was falling rapidly.

Policies designed to speed economic efficiency and integration with Germany led to the rise of large firms and to the relocation of industry from the east to the Austria-Germany border in the west. Although these changes brought much of the Austrian economy under the control of the Third Reich, the economy was modernized and diversified. Thus, in spite of the wartime damage done to the Austrian economy and economic infrastructure, the Anschluss years helped overcome the belief that Austria was economically inviable and laid the foundation for the mixed economy of the postwar years.

These economic advances, however, came hand-in-hand with the Nazis' political repression and barbaric racial policies, of which the Jews were the principal victims. Unification with Nazi Germany legitimized the full venting of Austria's anti-Semitic political heritage in which the pronounced Jewish presence in key areas of economic, political, and cultural life—especially in Vienna—had associated Jews with many developments in Austrian society that were opposed by the country's conservative, rural, and Catholic population.

The Jewish population of Austria—almost all of whom lived in Vienna—numbered around 220,000 in 1938. In general, Nazi anti-Semitic legislation and policies were imposed more quickly and more comprehensively in Austria than in Germany, and Austria became the testing ground for the political acceptability of policies later adopted in Germany. After allowing a wave of violent popular anti-Semitism in the weeks immediately after the Anschluss, the Nazis systematized anti-Semitic harassment. Laws and regulations were implemented to drive Jews from the economic sector, and out of Austria in general, in an orderly manner to ensure that the transition did not disrupt the economy or cause the loss of economically valuable assets. Initially, Jews were encouraged to emigrate—after they had been stripped of money and assets—and the Central Office for Jewish Emigration (Zentralamt jüdischer Auswanderung—ZjA) was set up in Vienna to streamline the emigration process. In 1938 about 80,000 Jews left Austria, legally and illegally, and ultimately some 150,000 fled. In October 1941, however, Germany's policy of encouraging emigration, already made difficult by the war, was replaced with policies to exterminate the Jews. The ZjA, which had been expanded to the occupied countries, organized the registration and transportation of Jews to death camps to implement the so-called Final Solution. About one-third of Austria's Jewish population is estimated to have died in the Holocaust. In addition to the Jews, there were other victims of murderous German nationalism. Austrian Slavic minorities, such as the Czechs, Slovaks, Slovenes, and Croats, for example, were targeted for assimilation, deportation, or extermination (see Social Minorities, ch. 2).

Repression and Compliance

In comparison with non-German minorities, the political repression suffered by German Austrians was lenient but still effective in preventing significant organized resistance. The left had already been the target of political repression before the Anschluss, but as early as March 1938, conservative political leaders associated with the Dollfuss-Schuschnigg regime were also subject to arrest and detention. Some 20,000 people were arrested in the early days of the Anschluss. Most were quickly released, but some, like Schuschnigg, were held at the Dachau concentration camp throughout the Nazi era. During the entire 1938–45 period, some 100,000 Austrians were arrested on political charges. About 34,000 of these died in prisons or concentration camps, and some 2,700 were executed.

Prior to the Anschluss plebiscite, the Nazis courted and received the support of the Roman Catholic hierarchy for annexation. After the plebiscite, the church desired to maintain loyal cooperation with what was perceived as legitimate state authority, but the Nazis were just as eager to eliminate the church's influence in society on both the institutional and the ideological level. In July 1938, the government declared the 1934 concordat void and closed Catholic education institutions, dissolved some 6,000 church-affiliated associations, and took control of the Catholic press. In August relations between the church hierarchy and the state were broken off. Although it did not see its role as supporting open resistance to the Nazi state, the Catholic Church, as the only legal entity propagating an ideology intrinsically hostile to Nazism, was a focus of opposition to the regime and was closely watched by the state. The persecution of the church over the next several years was designed to gradually wear it down by depriving it of resources and institutional unity. These measures, which evoked popular resentment, were eased in late 1941 because of the need to maintain public support of the regime during the war. Nevertheless, by detaching the church from the state, the policies had the effect of increasing the church's legitimacy and credibility and helped lay the groundwork for a more positive redefinition of the church's role in society after the war.

World War II and the Defeat of Nazi Germany

In a strict sense, Austria was not a participant in World War II because it did not formally exist when the war began with the invasion of Poland in September 1939. On an individual level, however, some 800,000 Austrians were drafted into the army (the German Wehrmacht), and another 150,000 served in the Waffen

SS, an elite Nazi military unit. Austrians were integrated into German units, and no specifically Austrian military brigades were formed.

Austrians loyally supported Germany through the early years of World War II. The early German military victories and Austria's geographic location beyond the reach of Allied bombers shielded the Austrian population from the full impact of the war. Only after the German defeat at the Battle of Stalingrad in early 1943, when the course of the war increasingly turned against Germany, did popular support for the war and for the Anschluss begin to erode.

More important for Austria's future, however, was the evolution in the Allies' position on Austria. In November 1943, the foreign ministers of the Soviet Union, Britain, and the United States met and issued the Moscow Declaration. In contrast to the earlier Allied acceptance of the Anschluss, the declaration described Austria as "the first victim of Hitlerite aggression" and called for the reestablishment of an independent Austria. At the same time, however, the declaration also held Austria liable for its participation in the war, effectively giving it the status of an enemy state.

Allied advances in Italy in 1943 enabled bombers regularly to attack Austrian industrial and transportation centers. The winter of 1944–45 saw an intensification of the air campaign and steady advances toward Austria by the Soviet Union's Red Army. On March 30, 1945, the Red Army entered Austrian territory and captured Vienna on April 13. Although the Germans resisted the Soviet advances into eastern Austria, the Western Allies—the United States, Britain, and France—met minimal resistance as they advanced into the country. United States forces began entering Austria on April 30, and French and British troops soon followed. On May 8, 1945, Germany surrendered unconditionally.

Restored Independence under Allied Occupation
Foundation of the Second Republic

As the Soviet troops advanced on Vienna, they occupied the town where Socialist leader Karl Renner lived in retirement. Despite his anti-Soviet reputation, Renner was chosen by the Soviet leaders to form and head a provisional government, apparently believing the aging politician would be an easily manipulated figurehead. Renner, however, established authority based on his leadership role in the last freely elected parliament, not on the backing of the Soviet Union. Conditions did not permit the members of the old parliament to be summoned, as had been done in 1918, so Renner turned

St. Stephen's Cathedral, Vienna
Courtesy Embassy of Austria, Washington

to the leaders of the three nonfascist parties that the Soviet leaders had already allowed to become active and established a provisional city administration in Vienna in early April. The three parties consisted of the Socialist Party of Austria (Sozialistische Partei Österreichs—SPÖ), a reorganization of the SDAP; the Austrian People's Party (Österreichische Volkspartei—ÖVP), a reorganization of the CSP; and the Communist Party of Austria (Kommunistische Partei Österreichs—KPÖ).

Renner apportioned ministries in the provisional government's cabinet roughly based on the political balance of the pre-1934 era, but the nationalist bloc was excluded and Communist representation increased. The SPÖ held ten ministries; the ÖVP, nine; and the KPÖ, only three, but these included the important ministries of interior, which controlled the police, and of education. Three additional ministries were held by members without party affiliation. Because of widespread distrust of the Communists, Renner created undersecretary positions for the two other parties in the Communist-headed ministries.

On April 27, 1945, the provisional government issued a decree nullifying the Anschluss and reestablishing an independent, democratic Republic of Austria under the 1920 constitution as amended in 1929. Germany had yet to surrender, however, and the formation of a provisional government in Soviet-occupied Austria surprised the Western Allies, who had yet to enter Austria. The Western Allies feared that the provisional government was a puppet of the Soviet Union and declined to recognize it. This decision left the Renner government dependent on the Soviet Union but forced it to allow the provisional government the means to establish reasonable credibility so Western acceptance could be won. Thus, as pre-1938 political figures became active in the areas occupied by United States, British, and French troops, the Renner government was allowed to establish contact with them despite initial Soviet plans to seal off its occupation zone.

Four Power Occupation and Recognition of the Provisional Government

The four Allied powers had not agreed to any firm plans for Austria prior to the war's end, and only in early July 1945 were the borders dividing the country into four occupation zones finally set. Vienna's city center was placed under Four Power control, while the rest of the city was divided into specific occupation zones. Supreme authority in Austria was wielded by the Allied Council, in which the Four Powers were represented by their zonal commanders. Each of the four Allies held veto power over the decisions of the council.

The Allied Council held its first meeting in early September, but the Western Allies still declined to recognize the Renner government. Soon thereafter the provisional government held a meeting in Vienna attended by representatives from parties from all the occupation zones. Unlike the situation after World War I, the provinces displayed no separatist tendencies—the experience of the Anschluss and World War II had forged an appreciation of a common Austrian identity. The provisional government was expanded to accommodate national representation, and the representatives agreed to national elections. Because of these developments, the Allied Council recognized the provisional government on October 20, 1945.

The 1945 Election and Consolidation of the Austrian Government

The first national election since 1930 was held on November 25, 1945. Nazi Party members were barred from participation. This exclusion sharply limited electoral participation by the nationalist camp, and no party was formed to represent its viewpoint. The ÖVP was thus able to monopolize the entire anti-left vote. Voters gave overwhelming support to the two democratic parties: the ÖVP received nearly 50 percent of the vote and eighty-five seats in the Nationalrat, and the SPÖ received 45 percent of the vote and seventy-six seats. The KPÖ received only 5 percent—well below its anticipated 25 percent—and four seats.

Although the ÖVP thus held an absolute majority in parliament, the government, headed by Chancellor Leopold Figl of the ÖVP, preserved the three-party coalition. The distribution of cabinet seats was adjusted, however, with the KPÖ receiving only a specially created and unimportant Ministry for Electrification. In December parliament elected Renner to the largely ceremonial position of president of the republic. With the Austrian government clearly evolving along democratic lines, the Western Allies grew more supportive, and the Soviet Union grew increasingly hostile.

In 1946, however, the Soviet Union agreed to changes in the Four Power Control Agreement that governed the relationship between the Four Powers and the Austrian government, thus weakening their influence. Originally, Austrian legislation had to be unanimously approved by the Allied Council, effectively giving each of the Allies veto power. In light of the Austrian government's democratic bent, the Western Allies favored allowing laws passed by the government to take effect unless the Allied Council unanimously rejected them. Although the Soviet Union was generally opposed to surrendering its veto power, it hoped to extract an agreement from the Austrians that would give the Soviet Union effective control over Austrian petroleum resources and thus did not want the other Allies to be able to veto any eventual agreement. In June 1946, the Allied powers agreed to a compromise. Agreements between one of the occupying powers and Austria would not be subject to a veto. "Constitutional laws" would require the approval of the Allied Council and thus remain subject to vetoes by the individual Allies, but all other laws would take effect in thirty-one days unless rejected by the council.

The Soviet Union only realized the implications of the new Control Agreement when a dispute arose over German assets in Austria. In early July 1946, the Soviet Union confiscated German assets in its occupation zone as war reparations—mines, industrial facilities, agricultural land, and the entire Austrian oil production industry. To protect the Austrian economy from such Soviet seizures, the Austrian government nationalized German assets. The Soviet Union attempted to veto the nationalization law but was rebuffed by the other Allies, who made it clear that the Austrian government had wide latitude in determining whether a particular law was a constitutional law or not. Although the Soviet Union was able to prevent implementation of the nationalization law in its occupation zone, the 1946 Control Agreement significantly enhanced the power of the Austrian government. By 1953 more than 550 laws had been implemented over the objection of the Soviet Union.

Consolidation of Democracy

The experience of the Anschluss and Nazi rule—which for many Austrian politicians had included imprisonment at Dachau—deepened the commitment of the ÖVP and SPÖ to parliamentary democracy and Austrian statehood. The electorate remained divided into three political camps—socialist/Marxist, Catholic, and nationalist/liberal—but cooperation replaced extreme political polarization.

The SPÖ ratified the moderate social democratic and anticommunist outlook of Renner, while downplaying the legacy of Austro-Marxism associated with Otto Bauer, the party's leader after World War I. Over the objections of the left wing, the party rejected an alliance with the KPÖ, endorsed cooperation with the ÖVP, and sanctioned the rebuilding of a capitalist economy tied to the West. It also decided to seek broad support beyond its working-class base.

The ÖVP underwent a similar transformation. Many of its postwar leaders, drawn largely from people associated with the prewar CSP trade unions and peasant organizations, had developed personal relationships with socialist leaders during their time at Dachau. After the war, they advanced a program emphasizing freedom and social welfare. Although essentially a Christian democratic party, the ÖVP sought to broaden its constituency and downplayed its confessional identification. No formal organizational ties were established with the Roman Catholic Church, and clerics were barred from running for office on the party's ticket.

Denazification posed a special problem for the emerging democratic society, often referred to as the Second Republic. Favorable Allied treatment of Austria was based in part on the premise that it was a liberated victim of Nazi aggression and not a Nazi ally. Thus, the government wanted to avoid any suggestion of collective guilt while at the same time prosecuting individual Nazis. The party and its affiliates were banned, and ex-members were required to register. Approximately 536,000 did so by September 1946. The government attempted to draw a distinction between committed Nazis and those who had joined because of economic, social, or personal coercion. Thus, the presumably more committed pre-1938 Nazis were dismissed from the civil service and a variety of other professions. Special tribunals were created to try war crimes.

Following the 1945 parliamentary election, the Allies sought more extensive denazification. In February 1947, the Figl government enacted the National Socialist Act. The law distinguished between "more implicated" persons, such as high party officials, and "less implicated" persons, such as simple party members. Individuals in both categories were subject to fines and employment restrictions, but with different levels of severity. By 1948, however, political and popular support for what was perceived as indiscriminate denazification was waning. Ex-Nazis and their families accounted for nearly one-third of the population, and both major parties feared that the stability of Austrian political and civil society would be undermined if they were not eventually reintegrated. In June 1948, the government promulgated the Amnesty Act, which restored full citizenship rights to the less implicated ex-Nazis before the 1949 election. Some 42,000 people, however, those categorized as more implicated, remained excluded from full participation in the nation's life.

Both the SPÖ and the ÖVP actively solicited the electoral support of ex-Nazis, but this new bloc of voters also enabled the formation of a successor party to the prewar parties in the nationalist-liberal camp. The SPÖ encouraged the formation of the new party, known as the League of Independents (Verband der Unabhängigen—VdU), expecting that it would split the antisocialist vote and thus weaken the ÖVP. In the October 1949 parliamentary election, however, the SPÖ lost nine seats, compared with the eight lost by the ÖVP. The VdU, with nearly 12 percent of the vote, won sixteen of these seventeen seats. The KPÖ, with 5 percent of the vote, increased its representation from four to five seats. Although the ÖVP thus lost its absolute majority in the Nationalrat, it was still the largest party, with seventy-seven seats and 44 percent of the vote. The SPÖ held sixty-seven seats, having won nearly 39 percent of the vote. The ÖVP and the SPÖ formed another coalition government with Figl as chancellor, continuing what was to become known as the "grand coalition."

To limit conflict between themselves, the coalition partners devised a system to divide not only cabinet ministries but also the entire range of political patronage jobs in the government and nationalized industries based upon each party's electoral strength. This proportional division of jobs, called the *Proporz* system, became an enduring feature of coalition governments.

Austria's Integration with the West

Early Soviet expectations for domination of Austria were pinned on a serious misreading of the KPÖ's electoral strength, and reality forced the Austrian Communists and their Soviet backers to turn to extraparliamentary means. With the Soviet Union occupying Austria's industrial heartland, the KPÖ hoped first to gain control of the labor movement and then to exploit popular discontent with the difficult postwar economic situation to bring mass pressure to bear on the government. As part of its overall strategy, the KPÖ sought to weaken the SPÖ by encouraging party factionalism and to undermine the cooperation between the two major parties. Similar tactics successfully brought Communists to power in neighboring East European countries in the late 1940s. But in Austria, Socialists united around Renner's social democratic approach and managed to outflank the Communists for worker support, as they had done after World War I.

In 1947 and 1948, the Soviet Union attempted to block Austria's participation in United States-sponsored aid programs, including the European Recovery Program (known as the Marshall Plan), and in the fall of 1947 the KPÖ pulled out of the coalition government over this issue. Ironically, the provisions that the Soviet Union itself had sought in the 1946 Control Agreement enabled Austria to freely sign the aid agreements and join the Organisation for European Economic Co-operation (OEEC), the body charged with planning how to use the Marshall Plan. Membership in the OEEC facilitated Austria's economic integration with

The State Treaty of 1955, which ended Austria's occupation and restored the country's sovereignty, is displayed by its signatories in Vienna.
Courtesy Embassy of Austria, Washington

the West and provided the economic basis for a stable parliamentary democracy in the postwar period.

The 1955 State Treaty and Austrian Neutrality

A key objective of post-1945 Austrian governments was ending the Four Power occupation and preventing the permanent division of Austria. The Allies' greater preoccupation with Germany delayed formal treaty negotiations with Austria until January 1947. By then, however, the larger strategic issues of the Cold War overshadowed the negotiations. The Soviet Union dropped its support for Yugoslav territorial claims against Austria in 1948 when Yugoslavia broke with the Soviet Union, but new issues arose to block progress toward ending the occupation: the Berlin blockade of 1948; the founding of the North Atlantic Treaty Organization (NATO) and the division of Germany into two rival states in 1949; and the start of the Korean War in 1950.

Following Soviet leader Joseph Stalin's death in March 1953, the Austrian government, headed by the newly elected chancellor, Julius Raab, sought to break the stalemate by proposing that Austria promise not to join any military bloc. The Indian ambassador to Moscow, acting as intermediary for the Austrians, went further and suggested permanent neutrality as the basis for a treaty. The Western Allies did not favor this proposal, and the Soviet Union continued to insist on the priority of a settlement in Germany.

In late 1954 and early 1955, however, the Western Allies and the Soviet Union feared that the other side was preparing to incorporate its respective occupation zones into its military bloc. In February the Soviet Union unexpectedly signaled its willingness to settle the Austrian question. In April a delegation composed of Raab, Figl, Adolf Schärf, and Bruno Kreisky went to Moscow. Four days of intense negotiations produced a draft treaty premised on permanent Austrian neutrality. The Western Allies only grudgingly accepted the draft for fear that it would be a model for German neutrality. They particularly objected to a proposed Four Power guarantee of Austrian neutrality, believing that it would provide an opportunity for Soviet intervention in Austria. Under strong Western opposition, the Soviet Union dropped the proposal.

On May 15, 1955, the State Treaty was signed. The treaty forbade unification with Germany or restoration of the Habsburgs and provided safeguards for Austria's Croat and Slovene minorities. Austrian neutrality and a ban on foreign military bases in Austria were later incorporated into the Austrian constitution by the Law of October 26, 1955. The 40,000 Soviet troops in Austria were withdrawn by late September. The small number of Western troops that remained were withdrawn by late October.

The Grand Coalition and the Austrian People's Party Coda, 1955–70

Foreign Policy in the Late 1950s and the 1960s

After the signing of the State Treaty, Austria's foreign policy concerns focused on three issues: South Tirol, European economic integration, and the meaning of neutrality. The status of the ethnically German province of South Tirol had been an Austrian concern ever since the province's transfer to Italy after World War I. Austria hoped that Italy's participation on the losing side of World War II might open the door to the Allied powers' awarding of the disputed territory to Austria. But the strategic interests of the Western Allies after the war forced Austria to settle for a 1946 agreement in which Italy promised South Tirol autonomous rights.

In 1948, however, Italy undercut the autonomy of the South Tiroleans by expanding the autonomous region to include the entire province of Trentino, the total population of which was two-thirds ethnically Italian. The South Tiroleans appealed to Austria for assistance. The General Assembly of the United Nations (UN) adopted a resolution in 1960 instructing Italy and Austria to enter into negotiations on the issue. Austria's right to intervene on behalf of the South Tiroleans was thus affirmed but brought no results until 1969. In the intervening years, South Tirolean activists undertook a terrorist bombing campaign, which, Italy alleged, Austria facilitated through lax border controls. The 1969 agreement affirmed South Tirol's autonomous rights, including the use of German as the official language. The International Court of Justice in The Hague was given the right to judge disputes over implementation of the pact, and Austria waived its rights to intervene.

Although the OEEC continued to function as a coordinating body for European economic integration after the end of the Marshall Plan in 1952, six of its members sought closer economic integration. In 1957 they formed the European Economic Community (EEC—see Glossary). Because Austria's main trading partners, the Federal Republic of Germany (West Germany) and Italy, belonged to the EEC, Austria would have liked to join that organization. But provisions in the EEC agreement imposed obligations in time of war, which were viewed as inconsistent with Austrian neutrality. Further, EEC membership also raised questions regarding unification with Germany, which was forbidden by the State Treaty. Austria thus joined six other countries in a looser, strictly economic association, the European Free Trade Association (EFTA—see Glossary), established in 1960. This was not an entirely satisfactory solution, and in 1961 Austria sought limited, associated membership in the EEC.

The Soviet Union objected to Austria's association with the EEC as a violation of Austria's neutrality. Austria responded that because its neutrality was a matter of Austrian law, Austria alone had the right to judge what were or were not violations. Nonetheless, Austria proceeded cautiously to avoid needlessly provoking the Soviet Union. EEC members also questioned Austria's membership. Italy blocked Austria's application to the EEC in 1967 because of the dispute over South Tirol. French president Charles de Gaulle was cool toward Austrian membership, both because of his desire to maintain relations with the Soviet Union and because of his concern that it might strengthen West Germany's position to the detriment of that of France. Austria's persistence, the resolution of South Tirol's status, and de Gaulle's retirement, however, paved the way for an agreement between Austria and the EEC in 1972 (see Austria and European Integration, ch. 3).

When Austria adopted a policy of neutrality in 1955, its leaders made it clear that political neutrality did not mean moral neutrality.

Austrian sympathies clearly lay with the Western democracies, an attitude that was reinforced by its opposition to the Soviet invasion of Hungary in 1956 and of Czechoslovakia in 1968. Nonetheless, Austria attempted to cultivate good relations with the Soviet bloc countries, which accounted for about one-sixth of Austrian exports in the mid-1960s. Austria thus benefited when détente eased relations between East and West in the late 1960s and early 1970s. Austria's efforts to make itself a bridge between East and West— an idea the Austrians had proposed as early as 1945—however, remained a largely unfulfilled ambition.

Elections and Parties

The outcome of the four parliamentary elections between 1955 and 1970 hinged on relatively small changes in the division of the votes. The ÖVP consistently held the largest number of seats in the Nationalrat and thus leadership of the ÖVP–SPÖ coalition, the so-called grand coalition, even though in the 1959 election it polled fewer votes than the SPÖ. Prior to the 1966 election, the share of the vote received by the ÖVP fluctuated between 44 and 46 percent. By achieving an increase to 48 percent in 1966, the party was able to win eighty-five parliamentary seats, an absolute majority. Julius Raab served as chancellor between 1953 and 1961, when he was replaced by Alphons Gorbach. Gorbach brought some younger politicians into the party's leadership, where they began to press for reforms. One of these younger men, Josef Klaus, replaced Gorbach as chancellor in 1964 and headed the ÖVP government between 1966 and 1970. His rise, coming about the same time as the deaths of Raab and Figl, marked the passing of party leadership to a younger generation that had not experienced the trauma of the 1930s.

The SPÖ saw its share of the vote fluctuate between 42 and 45 percent over the course of the four elections. Although the SPÖ held the position of junior partner in the coalition, the electorate consistently gave the presidency of the republic to the SPÖ following reinstitution of direct elections for that post in 1951. Theodor Körner, who had succeeded Renner in 1951, died in office prior to the 1957 presidential election. Schärf, who had been chairman of the SPÖ since 1945, handily won the 1957 election and was reelected in 1963. When he died in 1965, he was succeeded by the Socialist mayor of Vienna, Franz Jonas.

The VdU was reorganized in 1956 as the Freedom Party of Austria (Freiheitliche Partei Österreichs—FPÖ). Its share of the vote ranged from about 5 percent to 8 percent. The party drew on a diverse base of voters that included liberals, anticlerical conservatives, monarchists, and former Nazis.

The KPÖ was hurt by its association with the Soviet Union and by events in Eastern Europe, particularly the Soviet invasion of Hungary. The party's already small share of the vote continued to decline, from about 4.5 percent in 1956 to just over 3 percent in 1962. After 1959 the KPÖ held no seats in the Nationalrat.

Domestic Tranquillity under the Grand Coalition

The pattern of political cooperation established during the occupation years and the economic reconstruction that took place through the Marshall Plan laid the foundation for eleven years of political tranquillity and economic prosperity. In 1957 the government informally established the Parity Commission for Prices and Wages. This commission soon far exceeded its intended function of setting prices and wages and effectively established the country's basic economic policy. By bringing together the representatives of the major economic interest groups—the social partners—and requiring unanimous decisions, the commission became a powerful stabilizing force in Austrian society.

The effort of the SPÖ to broaden its electoral base helped resolve long-standing questions about the status and role of the Roman Catholic Church. The party realized that its inheritance of liberal anticlericalism and Marxist hostility toward religion stood in the way of attracting supporters who were devout Roman Catholics. As the SPÖ moved away from Marxist rhetoric, party leaders began to bridge the gulf between the SPÖ and Roman Catholics. In this eased atmosphere, the coalition partners were able to put the divisive issue of the 1934 concordat behind them. A new agreement with the Vatican was signed in 1960.

The overall effect of the ÖVP–SPÖ grand coalition and the social partnership represented by the Parity Commission, which brought together major economic groups, was to limit parliament's power. Most major economic and social decisions were made outside parliamentary channels and simply ratified by the Nationalrat, usually unanimously. Because no major policy differences were at stake, elections mainly served to determine the proportion of the patronage positions that would be accorded to the coalition partners. As the country progressed from the trauma of World War II and the occupation, members of both major parties began to express dissatisfaction with the coalition and the toleration of mismanagement and abuse of public office that the system appeared to condone. In the 1966 electoral campaign, ÖVP leader Klaus called for an end to the grand coalition. After winning an absolute majority, however, the ÖVP proposed terms for continuing the coalition, which Kreisky and other SPÖ leaders unsuccessfully urged their party to accept. Despite the breakup of the coalition, the Klaus government introduced no significant breaks with past policy. The ÖVP's four years in office were thus a coda to the grand coalition before the long period of SPÖ domination under Kreisky began in 1970.

The Kreisky Years, 1970–83

Electoral Politics in the Kreisky Era

As the Austrian economy developed in the 1950s and 1960s, the nature of the electorate slowly shifted. The declining economic importance of agriculture and forestry undermined the rural base of the ÖVP. Further, economic growth was occurring primarily in the service sector, not in heavy industry or manufacturing, the traditional base of the SPÖ. By 1970 service-sector employees constituted just under 40 percent of the working population, and both parties sought to position themselves in the middle of the political spectrum in order to attract these voters. Under the leadership of Bruno Kreisky, the SPÖ proved more adept at redefining itself in this new era.

Kreisky's personal popularity played a large part in the success of the SPÖ, and the party capitalized on this by campaigning on slogans like "Kreisky—who else?" and "Austria needs Kreisky." Although Kreisky came from a wealthy Viennese Jewish family, he declared himself an agnostic. Kreisky had been imprisoned in the mid- and late 1930s for political activity, but the Nazi regime eventually allowed him to emigrate to Sweden, where he became acquainted with Swedish socialism and met Willy Brandt, the future leader of the German Social Democrats. Kreisky returned to Austria after the war and by the early 1950s was working in the Ministry for Foreign Affairs and becoming active in party politics.

Kreisky was deeply involved in efforts to broaden SPÖ appeal in the 1950s. As chancellor, he continued to move the party toward the political center, reaching out toward swing voters and Roman Catholic and rural constituencies. Indicative of SPÖ reconciliation with the mainstream of Austrian culture and history was campaign literature in 1979 that featured Kreisky sitting beneath a portrait of Emperor Franz Joseph. As the differences between the two major political parties lessened, the ÖVP found it difficult to enunciate a distinct political identity because Kreisky so successfully occupied the middle ground.

In the election of 1970, the SPÖ emerged as the largest party but lacked a parliamentary majority. An attempt to revive the grand coalition failed. And Kreisky could not lure the FPÖ into a coalition. But the FPÖ did agree to cooperate in passing the SPÖ budget in exchange for electoral reform. Kreisky thus formed a minority government in 1970, and another election was held under a new electoral law in October 1971.

The electoral reform raised the number of seats in the Nationalrat from 165 to 183 and increased the degree of proportionality between a party's percentage of the popular vote and its parliamentary seats, thus boosting the fortunes of small parties. The SPÖ emerged from the election with an absolute majority, winning a bare 50 percent of the vote and ninety-three seats in the enlarged Nationalrat. The ÖVP won only eighty seats and 43 percent of the vote. The FPÖ won 5.5 percent of the vote, the same as in 1970, and held ten seats.

The election of 1975 repeated the 1971 results. But in 1979, the SPÖ increased its share of the vote to 51 percent and won ninety-five seats. The ÖVP declined to just below 42 percent and won only seventy-seven seats. The FPÖ improved its performance slightly, getting 6 percent of the vote and taking eleven seats.

While the electorate had opted for a Socialist chancellor, it also continued to elect a Socialist or Socialist-backed presidential candidate throughout the Kreisky era. Six months before the 1970 parliamentary election, Jonas won reelection, defeating Kurt Waldheim. Jonas died in 1974 and was succeeded by Kreisky's foreign minister, Rudolf Kirchschläger. Although he was not a member of the SPÖ, Kirchschläger, a practicing Catholic and a political independent, was a Kreisky associate, having been brought into Kreisky's cabinet in 1970. His reelection bid was unopposed in 1980.

Domestic Issues

Kreisky's style and tone struck a chord with the Austrian electorate, and his personal popularity was enhanced by the country's economic prosperity in the 1970s. His legislative and economic program was built on the existing political consensus and ratified by the social partners. Many measures continued to pass unanimously in the Nationalrat. Employee benefits were expanded, the workweek was cut to forty hours, and legislation providing for equality for women was passed. The period of mandatory military service was cut from nine months to six months. Three issues, however, divided the country: abortion, nuclear power and environmental damage, and ethnic minority rights.

In 1973 the SPÖ passed a law over the opposition of the ÖVP and the FPÖ that legalized abortion on demand during the first trimester. Popular opposition backed by the Roman Catholic Church manifested itself in a petition drive that helped bring the issue before parliament again in the spring of 1976. The law, however, was upheld.

In the early 1970s, the international energy crisis triggered by the Organization of the Petroleum Exporting Countries (OPEC) oil cartel and the Arab oil embargo exposed Austria's vulnerability to imported energy supplies. To reduce this vulnerability, Kreisky continued the construction of a nuclear power plant at Zwentendorf, sixty kilometers from Vienna, and planned the construction of three other plants. As the Zwentendorf facility neared completion in the late 1970s, however, the public expressed growing concern about the safety of nuclear power. The SPÖ did not want to alienate the environmental movement and its bloc of voters, but it also needed to satisfy its trade union constituency, which favored the project. The issue was settled by means of a national referendum on November 5, 1978. Despite Kreisky's vigorous campaign for the plant, the electorate narrowly rejected opening the plant.

Seeking to implement provisions in the 1955 State Treaty regarding the rights of the country's Croat and Slovene minority communities, parliament enacted a law in 1972 to erect dual-language signs wherever the minority population of a locality was at least 20 percent. Such signs were placed in some 200 of the 2,900 towns and villages in Carinthia. With the support of local officials and police, however, the German-speaking population reacted violently and ripped the signs down, reflecting lingering hostility provoked by Yugoslav efforts to annex the province after World War II. In an effort to resolve the matter, the government took a census in 1976 to determine Carinthia's ethnic make-up. Because the Slovene population had declined greatly since 1914, when it accounted for 25 percent of the total populace, Slovene leaders called for a boycott of the census, and the results were not considered reliable. Dual-language signs were erected in 1977 where the local minority population was believed to be over 25 percent.

Foreign Policy

Under Kreisky's leadership, Austria sought to play an active role in international politics in the 1970s, particularly through the UN. Reflecting the acceptance of Austrian neutrality, Waldheim, the unsuccessful conservative presidential candidate in 1970, was elected UN secretary general in 1971 and reelected to that post in 1976. Austria continued to cast itself as a bridge between East and West, and Vienna was the site for some early rounds of the Strategic Arms Limitation Talks (SALT) between the United States and the Soviet Union. Kreisky became personally involved in issues relating to the Arab-Israeli conflict. Despite general support for maintenance of Israeli security, he criticized Israel for its treatment of the Palestinians. In 1980 Austria gave de facto recognition to the Palestine Liberation Organization (PLO) by accepting an accredited agent of the PLO in Vienna. Throughout the 1970s, however, Austria was also a transit point for Jews leaving the Soviet Union for destinations in Israel and the West.

Austria established a more favorable trading relationship with the EEC in 1972, but the EEC continued to move toward still fuller economic and political integration in Western Europe. Although Kreisky pointed to the possibility of Austria's adopting legislation on its own in coordination with these developments, he stressed that Austria's neutrality would continue to prevent full membership in the EEC unless it were expanded to include all of Europe.

End of the Kreisky Era

During Kreisky's tenure as chancellor, Austria enjoyed unprecedented prosperity, but by the time the April 1983 election approached, the SPÖ had few fresh ideas with which to attract critical swing voters. Its image also suffered from various political and financial scandals (see Political Developments since 1983, ch. 4). Its proposal for a tax hike aimed at upper-income Austrians to finance job creation was countered by the ÖVP with promises of no new taxes and more careful use of existing government tax revenues. Although the ÖVP failed to unseat the SPÖ as the largest party in the Nationalrat, the ÖVP benefited from a significant shift in voter sentiment, and the SPÖ lost its majority, winning ninety seats, which was five seats fewer than in 1979. The ÖVP gained four seats for a total of eighty-one. The FPÖ won an additional seat, for a total of twelve, despite a decline in its share of the vote. Two "green" parties, the United Greens of Austria (Vereinigte Grüne Österreichs—VGÖ) and the Alternative List of Austria (Alternative Liste Österreichs—ALÖ), sought to rally voters on environmental issues. Together they took about 3.3 percent of the vote but won no parliamentary seats.

Kreisky had campaigned strongly for an absolute majority and resigned rather than lead a coalition government. His minister of education, Fred Sinowatz, became chancellor in 1983, heading an SPÖ-FPÖ coalition. Kreisky's departure marked a major turning point in Austria's postwar history, and the Sinowatz government was to be a transitional phase into the contemporary era.

* * *

Given the scope of Austrian history and Austria's complex relationships with the other countries of Central Europe, English-language histories of Austria generally focus on particular segments of Austrian history rather than on an attempt to give equal attention to all centuries. Alexander Wigram Allen Leeper's *A History of Medieval Austria* is a key source for medieval history prior to the Habsburgs. *The Habsburg Empire, 1790-1918* by Carlile Aylmer Macartney is an excellent and inclusive treatment of the late history of the Habsburg Empire, although its level of detail and thoroughness may be more than the casual reader desires. Robert A. Kann's *A History of the Habsburg Empire, 1526-1918* is a more accessible text, focusing on broader themes rather than on the minutiae of history. Robert John Weston Evans's *The Making of the Habsburg Monarchy, 1550-1700* also takes a thematic approach but covers only a portion of the Habsburg centuries. However, it provides a useful examination of the intellectual underpinnings of the Habsburg state.

Barbara Jelavich has written two excellent books covering the post-1815 era: *The Habsburg Empire in European Affairs, 1814-1918* and *Modern Austria: Empire and Republic, 1815-1986.* Their relative brevity and conciseness make them excellent overviews.

The selection of books covering specific topics is growing steadily. Of particular interest and merit are Samuel R. Williamson, Jr.'s *Austria-Hungary and the Origins of the First World War;* Radomir Luza's two books, *Austro-German Relations in the Anschluss Era* and *The Resistance in Austria, 1938-1945;* and Alfred D. Low's *The Anschluss Movement, 1918-1938.*

For those interested in more current history, Melanie A. Sully's *A Contemporary History of Austria* focuses on the post-Kreisky era. (For further information and complete citations, see Bibliography.)

Chapter 2. The Society and Its Environment

Coat of arms of the province of Vorarlberg

AUSTRIA'S SECURITY AND PROSPERITY during the second half of the twentieth century are a striking contrast to the instability and poverty of the first half of the century. Between 1914 and 1950, Austrians had five different forms of government and four different currencies. After enduring much hardship during World War I, they experienced the collapse of Austria-Hungary (also seen as the Austro-Hungarian Empire) and the proclamation of the Republic of Austria. In the early 1920s, they endured hyperinflation and in the 1930s the Great Depression. The end of Austria's fledgling democracy and the establishment of an authoritarian regime in 1934 were followed by the demise of Austria altogether when Nazi Germany occupied the country in 1938. The proclamation of the Second Republic in 1945 began a long period of peace and prosperity. However, the republic's first years were a difficult time of economic and social reconstruction that occurred while Austria was occupied by the Four Powers (Britain, France, the Soviet Union, and the United States). War, inflation, unemployment, poverty, authoritarian and totalitarian rule, and foreign occupation formed the average Austrian's experience during the first half of the twentieth century.

The new state of Austria that emerged out of the chaos of World War I faced such serious structural problems that many of its citizens doubted it could survive. Social and economic relationships that had evolved over centuries either ended or were greatly altered. Moreover, the regions of this small German-speaking "rump state" did not join together well to form a new nation. Austria's rural areas, populated predominantly by peasant-farmers, were underdeveloped, most notably in the Alpine regions of western and central Austria. They did not mesh well with the large urban and industrial centers in eastern Austria, especially Vienna, which had evolved to meet the markets and needs of an entire empire, not a small state. The virtual absence of an Austrian national identity merely aggravated concerns about the state's viability.

The events of the late 1930s and 1940s proved these concerns justified, but by 1955 Austria had regained its independence, laid the foundations for decades of sustained economic growth, and established a system of cooperation among rival political parties, interest groups, and government bodies that brought the country an unprecedented degree of stability. Stability did not bar change, however, and Austrian society changed greatly as a thriving, continuously modernizing economy altered the way Austrians earned their living and the way they lived.

The number of Austrians engaged in agriculture and forestry fell from more than 60 percent at the end of World War II to 7 percent by the beginning of the 1990s. More and more Austrians came to live in urban areas, and over two-thirds of the country's population was concentrated in the valleys and lowlands of eastern Austria. The initial industrial growth was followed by a pronounced shift to the service sector, and peasant-farmers or blue-collar workers, who had frequently lived and worked under abject conditions, increasingly were replaced by white-collar, service-sector employees. By the early 1990s, this sector employed more than 50 percent of the labor force in a society that was predominantly middle class.

The country's population reflects the political and economic traumas that occurred between 1914 and 1945. Austria has been by turns a land of immigration and emigration. After the two world wars and during the Cold War, it was a haven for many refugees from Eastern Europe. Before and during World War II, however, many Austrians fled for racial or political reasons. During the 1960s and later, an increasing number of foreigners from southeastern and Eastern Europe settled in Austria. Their presence offset to some degree the negative growth rate of the country's indigenous population.

The Austrian family has also changed, both in size and in structure. During the last generation, it has became smaller. Traditional family values and life-styles are in a state of rapid transition, as evidenced by the increasing number of people living alone, childless marriages, and steadily increasing rates of divorce and illegitimacy. Although Austria is a predominantly Roman Catholic country, these changes show that religion no longer plays as important a role as in the past.

Social change has led to a much more open, democratic, socially mobile, and prosperous society in which there are few rigid class distinctions. Traditionally disadvantaged groups have had greater access to secondary and university education. Furthermore, Austria has a highly developed welfare state that provides a broad spectrum of social security and health care benefits. As a result, in the early 1990s the quality of life in Austria was rated the world's tenth best by Washington's Population Crisis Committee.

Austrians have also developed a new and unprecedented national consciousness. For the first time, they have come to see themselves as a distinct people separate from their German neighbors. They have also found a new European role as a neutral state between the East and the West. However, the anticipated and unanticipated dynamics of West European and East European development—European economic and political integration and the opening of Eastern Europe—have changed the hopes and expectations Austrians have entertained, as well as the nature of their fears and anxieties.

Geography

Austria is a small, predominantly mountainous country located in south-central Europe. It has a total area of 83,859 square kilometers, about twice the size of Switzerland and slightly smaller than the state of Maine. The landlocked country shares national borders with Switzerland and the tiny principality of Liechtenstein to the west (200 kilometers together), Germany (784 kilometers) and the Czech Republic and Slovakia (568 kilometers together) to the north, Hungary to the east (346 kilometers), and Slovenia (311 kilometers) and Italy (430 kilometers) to the south.

The westernmost third of the somewhat pear-shaped country consists of a narrow corridor between Germany and Italy that is between thirty-two and sixty kilometers wide. The rest of Austria lies to the east and has a maximum north-south width of 280 kilometers. The country measures almost 600 kilometers in length, extending from Lake Constance on the Austrian-Swiss border in the west to the Neusiedler See on the Austrian-Hungarian border in the east. The contrast between these two lakes—one in the Alps and the other a typical steppe lake on the westernmost fringe of the Hungarian Plain—illustrates the diversity of Austria's landscape.

Seven of Austria's nine provinces have long historical traditions predating the establishment of the Republic of Austria in 1918: Upper Austria, Lower Austria, Styria, Carinthia, Salzburg, Tirol, and Vorarlberg (see fig. 1). The provinces of Burgenland and Vienna were established after World War I. Most of Burgenland had been part of the Kingdom of Hungary, but it had a predominantly German-speaking population and hence became Austrian. Administrative and ideological reasons played a role in the establishment of Vienna as an independent province. Vienna, historically the capital of Lower Austria, was a socialist stronghold, whereas Lower Austria was conservative, and both socialists and conservatives wanted to consolidate their influence in their respective provinces. Each province has a provincial capital with the exception of Vienna, which is a province in its own right in addition to being the federal capital. In Vienna, the City Council and the mayor function as a provincial parliament and provincial governor, respectively.

Landform Regions

The two best-known features of the Austrian landscape are the Alps and the Danube River (see fig. 5). The Danube has its source in southwestern Germany and flows through Austria before emptying into the Black Sea. It is the only major European river that flows eastward, and its importance as an inland waterway has been enhanced by the completion in 1992 of the Rhine-Main-Danube Canal in Bavaria, which connects the Rhine and Main rivers with the Danube and makes possible barge traffic from the North Sea to the Black Sea.

The major rivers north of the watershed of the Austrian Alps (the Inn in Tirol, the Salzach in Salzburg, and the Enns in Styria and Upper Austria) are direct tributaries of the Danube and flow north into the Danube Valley, whereas the rivers south of the watershed in central and eastern Austria (the Gail and Drau rivers in Carinthia and the Mürz and Mur rivers in Styria) flow south into the drainage system of the Drau, which eventually empties into the Danube in Serbia. Consequently, central and eastern Austria are geographically oriented away from the watershed of the Alps: the provinces of Upper Austria and Lower Austria toward the Danube and the provinces of Carinthia and Styria toward the Drau.

The Alps cover 62 percent of the country's total area. Three major Alpine ranges—the Northern Alps, Central Alps, and Southern Alps—run west to east through Austria. The Central Alps, which consist largely of a granite base, are the largest and highest ranges in Austria. The Central Alps run from Tirol to approximately the Styria-Lower Austria border and include areas that are permanently glaciated in the Ötzal Alps on the Tirolean-Italian border and the High Tauern in eastern Tirol and Carinthia. The Northern Alps, which run from Vorarlberg through Tirol into Salzburg along the German border and through Upper Austria and Lower Austria toward Vienna, and the Southern Alps, on the Carinthia-Slovenia border, are predominantly limestone and dolomite. At 3,797 meters, Grossglockner in Carinthia is the highest mountain in Austria. As a general rule, the farther east the Northern Alps and Central Alps run, the lower they become. The altitude of the mountains also drops north and south of the central ranges.

As a geographic feature, the Alps literally overshadow other landform regions. Just over 28 percent of Austria is moderately hilly or flat: the Northern Alpine Foreland, which includes the Danube Valley; the lowlands and hilly regions in northeastern and eastern

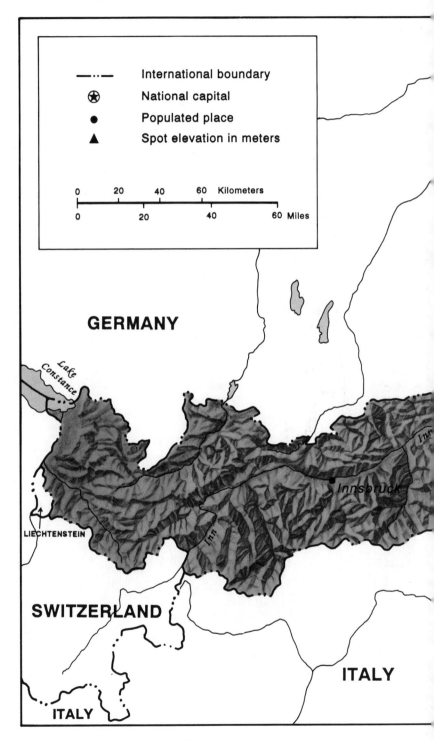

Figure 5. Topography and Drainage

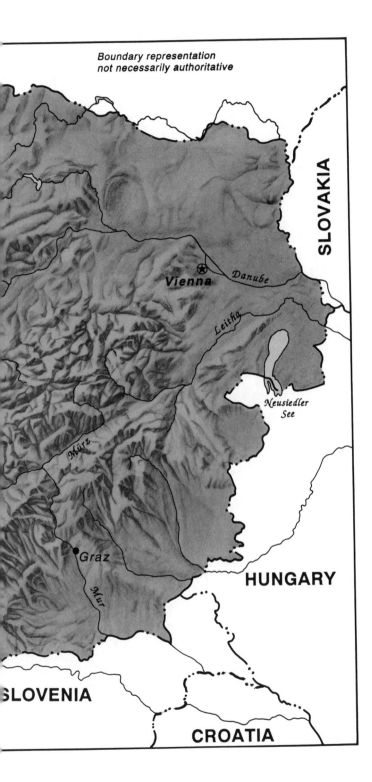

SLOVAKIA

Vienna

Danube

Leitha

Neusiedler
See

Mürz

Graz

Mur

HUNGARY

SLOVENIA

CROATIA

Austria, which include the Danube Basin; and the rolling hills and lowlands of the Southeastern Alpine Foreland. The parts of Austria that are most suitable for settlement—that is, arable and climatically favorable—run north of the Alps through the provinces of Upper Austria and Lower Austria in the Danube Valley and then curve east and south of the Alps through Lower Austria, Vienna, Burgenland, and Styria. Austria's least mountainous landscape is southeast of the low Leitha Range, which forms the southern lip of the Viennese Basin, where the steppe of the Hungarian Plain begins. The Bohemian Granite Massif, a low mountain range with bare and windswept plateaus and a harsh climate, is located north of the Danube Valley and covers the remaining 10 percent of Austria's area.

Human Geography

Land-use patterns in Austria change from Alpine to non-Alpine regions. Approximately one-tenth of Austria is barren or unproductive, that is, extremely Alpine or above the tree line. Just over two-fifths of Austria is covered by forests, the majority of which are in Alpine regions. Less than one-fifth of Austria is arable and suitable for conventional agriculture. The percentage of arable land in Austria increases in the east as the country becomes less Alpine. More than one-fifth of Austria is pastures and meadows located at varying altitudes. Almost one-half of this grassland consists of high-lying Alpine pastures.

Historically, high Alpine pastures have been used during the summer for grazing dairy cattle, thus making space available at lower altitudes for cultivating and harvesting fodder for winter. Many of the high pastures are at altitudes of more than 1,000 meters.

Although agriculture in mountainous areas was at one time economically viable, in recent decades it has survived only with the help of extensive subsidies. A concern of farmers in these mountainous regions is that membership in the European Union (EU— see Glossary) might entail a curtailment of these subsidies and the end of Alpine agriculture. If this occurs, many areas will be reclaimed by nature after centuries of cultivation.

Although the Alps are beautiful, they make many areas of Austria uninhabitable. Austria's so-called areas of permanent settlement—regions that are cultivated, continuously inhabited, and used for transportation, but do not include forests, Alpine pastures, or barren land—cover only four-tenths or 35,000 square kilometers of the country. The great majority of the area of permanent settlement is in the Danube Valley and the lowlands or hilly regions north, east, and south of the Alps, where approximately two-thirds of the population live.

In the country's predominantly Alpine provinces, most of the population live in river valleys: Bregenz on the shores of Lake Constance in Vorarlberg; Innsbruck on the Inn River in Tirol; Salzburg on the Salzach River in Salzburg; and Klagenfurt on the Gail River in Carinthia. The higher the Alps are, the less inhabitable they become in terms of soil, microclimate, and vegetation. Conversely, the lower and broader the Alpine valleys are, the more densely populated they become.

Tirol illustrates most clearly the relationship between Alpine geography and habitation. As the most mountainous province (less than 3 percent of the land is arable), it is the most sparsely inhabited, with an area of permanent settlement of only 15 percent.

Because of the Alps, the country as a whole is one of the least densely populated states of Western and Central Europe. With ninety-three inhabitants per square kilometer, Austria has a population density similar to that of the former Yugoslavia.

Austria's national borders and geography have corresponded very little. Since the fall of the Roman Empire, the Alps and the Danube have not served to mark political boundaries. Even within Austria, provincial borders were only occasionally set by the ranges and ridges of the Alps.

Although the Alps did not mark political boundaries, they often separated groups of people from one another. Because in the past the Alps were impassable, inhabitants isolated in valleys or networks of valleys developed distinct regional subcultures. Consequently, the inhabitants of one valley frequently maintained dialects, native or traditional dress, architectural styles, and folklore that substantially differed from those of the next valley. Differences were great enough that the origins of outsiders could easily be identified. However, mass media, mobility, prosperity, and tourism have eroded the distinctness of Alpine regional subcultures to a great extent by reducing the isolation that gave them their particular character.

Despite the Alps, Austria has historically been a land of transit. The Danube Valley, for centuries Central Europe's aquatic link to the Balkan Peninsula and the "Orient" in the broadest sense of the word, has always been an avenue of east-west transit. However, Europe's division into two opposing economic and military blocs after World War II diminished Austria's importance as a place of transit. Since the opening of Eastern Europe in 1989, the country has begun to reassume its historical role. By the early

1990s, it had already experienced a substantial increase in the number of people and vehicles crossing its eastern frontiers.

Within the Alps, four passes and the roads that run through them are of particular importance for north-south transit. The Semmering Pass on the provincial border of Lower Austria and Styria connects the Viennese Basin with the Mürz and Mur valleys, thus providing northeast-southwest access to Styria and Slovenia, and, via Carinthia, to Italy.

The Phryn Pass, between the provinces of Upper Austria and Styria, and the Tauern Pass, between the High Tauern Range and the Low Tauern Range of the Central Alps in Salzburg, provide access to the Mur Valley in Styria and the Drau Valley in Carinthia, respectively. The highways that run through these passes are important northwest-southeast lines of communication through the Alps. The Phyrn highway has been nicknamed the "foreign workers' route" because millions of "guest workers" in Germany use it to return to their homes in the Balkans and Turkey for vacation. Many Germans and northern Europeans also use it in the summer months to reach the Adriatic coast. After the outbreak of hostilities in Yugoslavia in the summer of 1991, however, a substantial amount of this traffic was rerouted through the Danube Valley and Hungary.

The most important pass in the Austrian Alps is the Brenner Pass, located on the Austrian-Italian border in Tirol. At 1,370 meters, it is one of the lowest Alpine passes. The Inn Valley and the Brenner Pass historically have been an important and convenient route of north-south transit between Germany and Italy, and they provide the most direct route between Europe's two most highly industrialized regions—Germany and northern Italy.

Climate

The Alps serve as a watershed for Europe's three major kinds of weather systems that influence Austrian weather. The Atlantic maritime climate from the northwest is characterized by low-pressure fronts, mild air from the Gulf Stream, and precipitation. It has the greatest influence on the northern slopes of the Alps, the Northern Alpine Foreland, and the Danube Valley. The continental climate is characterized by low-pressure fronts with precipitation in summer and high-pressure systems with cold and dry air in winter. It affects mainly eastern Austria. Mediterranean high-pressure systems from the south are characterized by few clouds and warm air, and they influence the weather of the southern slopes of the Alps and that of the Southeastern Alpine Foreland, making them the most temperate part of Austria.

One peculiarity of the Mediterranean weather systems is the föhn, a warm air mass that originates in the African Sahara and moves north rapidly, periodically raising temperatures up to 10°C in a short period of time. Many people respond to this rapid weather change with headaches, irritability, and circulatory problems. During the winter, the rapid warming that accompanies a föhn can thaw the snow cover in the Alps to such an extent that avalanches occur.

Given the importance of Alpine skiing for the Austrian tourist industry, December is the month during which the weather is watched with the greatest anticipation. As a rule, Atlantic maritime weather systems bring snow, and continental weather systems help keep it. However, a predominance of cold, dry continental systems or warm Mediterranean ones inevitably postpones the beginning of the ski season. In the summer, Mediterranean high-pressure systems bring warm, sunny weather.

Ecological Concerns

Austrians face a number of ecological problems in the 1990s. One of the most pressing is the pollution caused by the staggering increase of traffic through the country. Traffic on the superhighway going through the Brenner Pass has, for example, increased from 600,000 vehicles per year in the early 1970s to over 10 million per year in the early 1990s. One-quarter of the traffic crossing Austria consists of semitrailers used for heavy transport. The opening of Eastern Europe has only exacerbated the problem of transit traffic.

The Alpine valleys through which much of this traffic passes are unusually vulnerable to ecological damage. Narrow valleys are not conducive to dissipation of noise or pollutants caused by motor vehicles. Inversions—cold layers of air that trap warm layers of air or warm layers of air that trap cold layers in the valleys and lowlands—also seasonally contribute to the magnitude of the pollution problem.

Austria has negotiated with the EU to set limits on the amount of commercial transit traffic, especially through Tirol. Work is also under way to develop a "piggy-back" system of loading semitrailers on to flatbed railroad cars in southern Germany and northern Italy, transporting them through Tirol by rail. Environmentalists have pushed for measures that are more far-reaching. They advocate, for example, digging a tunnel from Garmisch-Partenkirchen in southern Germany to Bolzano in northern Italy.

Pollution is also brought by the weather systems that determine the country's climate. Atlantic maritime weather systems carry

*Church at Gargellan in the
province of Vorarlberg
Courtesy Embassy of Austria,
Washington*

pollution into Austria from northwestern Europe. Austria's proximity to industrialized regions of former Communist states, with negligible or no pollution control policies or equipment, combined with the influence of continental weather systems, also has proved to be extremely harmful. Mediterranean weather systems transmit industrial pollutants from northern Italy.

As a result of domestic and foreign pollution, 37 percent of Austria's forests had been damaged by acid rain and/or pollutant emissions by 1991. The damage to forests has had dire consequences, including the decimation of forests that for centuries had protected many Alpine communities from avalanches, erosion, mud slides, or flooding caused by runoff.

The seriousness of the ecological problems confronting the country gave rise in the 1970s to an environmentalist movement. Political parties were formed, and representatives were elected to parliament (see The Green Parties, ch. 4). A referendum in 1978 closed down a newly completed nuclear power plant and turned the country away from the exploitation of nuclear energy. Public opposition in 1984 stopped the planned construction of a hydroelectric power plant in a wetlands region.

The country's long-standing commercial use of the Alps for recreational purposes has also come under examination. Extensive tourism places an inordinate amount of pressure on sensitive Alpine ecosystems. Ski runs damage forests, as do summer sports such as off-trail mountain hiking or mountain biking. Many Alpine villages have also grown greatly because of the tourist industry. In extreme cases, they have up to twenty hotel beds for each inhabitant, a ratio that places a disproportionate seasonal burden on communal infrastructures and the environment. For these reasons, efforts have been made to introduce "green" or "soft" forms of tourism that are more compatible with the Alpine environment.

Part of the solution to Austria's ecological problems is being sought in stricter environmental legislation at the domestic level. Ultimately, however, pan-European and global cooperation in the realm of pollution and emission control will be necessary to protect the country's environment.

Austrian National Identity

The absence of an Austrian national identity was one of the problems confronted when Austria became a country in November 1918 (see The End of the Habsburg Empire and the Birth of the Austrian Republic, ch. 1). Before 1918 there had been no tradition among German-speaking Austrians of striving for national independence as a small German-speaking state separated from Austria-Hungary or separated from Germany. Within the context of the multiethnic and multilinguistic empire, the great majority of the inhabitants of what was to become Austria considered themselves "Germans" insofar as they spoke German and identified with German culture.

Strong provincial identities that stemmed from the provinces' histories as distinct political and administrative entities with their own traditions existed for this reason. Tiroleans, for example, identified more with their province than with the new nation-state. As a result, the idea of an "Austrian nation" as a cultural and political entity greater than the sum total of provinces, yet smaller than the pan-German idea of the unification of all German speakers into one state, virtually did not exist in 1918. The Austrian historian Friedrich Heer described the confusion surrounding Austrians' national identity in the following manner: "Who were these Austrians after 1918? Were they Germans in rump Austria, German-Austrians, Austrian-Germans, Germans in a 'second German state,' or an Austrian nation?"

Furthermore, Austrians had serious doubts about the economic and political viability of a small German-speaking state. Two alternatives were envisioned for Austria: either membership in a confederation of the states formed out of Austria-Hungary or unification with Germany as a legitimate expression of Austrian national self-determination. Neither alternative was realized. Efforts to form a "Danube Confederation" failed, and the Allies prohibited Austria's unification with Germany in the treaties signed after World War I. As a compromise between these alternatives, Austria was a "state which no one wanted."

After 1918 many Austrians identified themselves as being members of a "German nation" based on shared linguistic, cultural, and ethnic characteristics. Since unification with Germany was forbidden, most Austrians regarded their new country as a "second" German state arbitrarily created by the victorious powers. During the troubled interwar period, unification with a democratic Germany was seen by many, not only by those on the political right but across the entire political spectrum, as a solution for Austria's many problems.

Nazi Germany's annexation (Anschluss) of Austria into the Third Reich in March 1938 proved to be an impetus for the development of Austrian national consciousness (see The Anschluss and World War II, ch. 1). Austrians increasingly focused on the historical and cultural differences between Austrian and German traditions—or the uniqueness and singularity of an "Austrian nation"—and on the idea of an independent Austrian state. It is one of those quirks of history that the experience of being "German" in the Third Reich was instrumental in awakening feelings of Austrian nationalism for many Austrians, who, by the end of World War II, wholeheartedly endorsed the idea of Austrian independence from Germany. This idea involved rejecting the concept of one "German linguistic and cultural nation" for the sake of two German-speaking nations: one German and the other Austrian.

The reestablishment of Austrian independence in 1945 set the conditions for the development of a new Austrian national identity (see Restored Independence under Allied Occupation, ch. 1). Allied policy, which formulated the reestablishment of an independent Austrian state as a war objective and distinguished between the treatment of Austrians and Germans and the Allied occupation of Austria from 1945 until 1955 contributed to promoting attitudes of national cohesiveness and a desire for independence. After the State Treaty of 1955 arranged for the end of the Allied occupation and a subsequent proclamation of Austria's permanent neutrality, Austrians increasingly identified themselves with their country and saw it as a state with traditions and a history distinct from those of Germany. Although a persistent right-wing minority in Austria continued to insist on "Germanness" as being one of the attributes of being Austrian, ever more Austrians came to identify with the Austrian nation in the decades after World War II.

Seventy-nine percent did so by 1990, compared with 47 percent in 1966. In this respect, Austria is a "young nation."

Demography

The demographic history of Austria corresponds to the general changes that have taken place in other industrial nations, but with a number of regional and historical differences. An increasing life expectancy, a declining fertility rate (or a lower birth rate), and a greater concentration of population in urban areas are trends Austria shares with other advanced industrial nations. The cataclysmic events of World War I and World War II, the substantial population movements—both forced and voluntary—during the interwar period and after World War II, the influx of foreign workers starting in the 1960s, and the opening of Eastern Europe beginning in the late 1980s all affected the size and structure of Austria's population.

Demographic Development

Between 1900 and 1991, the country's population grew from 6,004,000 to 7,795,800 (see table 2, Appendix). War deaths and birth deficits during each of the world wars and the consequences of the Great Depression profoundly influenced the development of Austria's population. Approximately 190,000 men were killed in action in World War I. Increased mortality among the civilian population as a result of the hardships of war and the immediate postwar period and extremely low birth rates resulted in a population decrease of 100,000 between the censuses of 1910 and 1923. Postwar immigration of German-speaking and Jewish populations from the successor states of Austria-Hungary to the Republic of Austria and emigration from Austria after the war basically offset each other. Economic and political crises in the first half of the 1930s caused 72,000 Austrians to emigrate to non-European countries. The largest contingent of emigrants, 37,000, were from the province of Burgenland and went primarily to the United States, mainly for economic reasons.

After Austria was annexed by Nazi Germany in March 1938, an estimated 130,000 Austrians, the great majority of whom had Jewish origins, emigrated from Austria. More than 65,000 Austrian Jews died in the concentration camps and prisons of the Third Reich; 35,000 non-Jewish Austrians shared a similar fate or were executed after trials. An estimated 250,000 Austrians were killed in action during World War II; 25,000 civilians were killed as a result of bombing or military action in Austria. Some of these losses were offset by Nazi population policies that promoted motherhood and large families for racial reasons.

After the war, Austria became a destination for ethnic Germans, who fled from or were driven out of their homes in Czechoslovakia, Romania, and Yugoslavia. Other refugees and "displaced persons," who were either uprooted by hostilities or victims of the expulsions sanctioned by the Allies and carried out by East European governments immediately after the war, also came to Austria. Between 1945 and 1950, about 400,000 immigrants—ethnic Germans from Eastern Europe and other non-German speaking refugees—settled in Austria and eventually became Austrian citizens.

The increase of birth rates in Austria during the 1950s corresponded with the trends in most other West European countries. Between 1950 and 1992, the infant mortality rate in Austria dropped from over 61.3 per 1,000 live births to 7.5 per 1,000, an indication of improvements Austrian health authorities had made in prenatal and postnatal care. During the 1960s, Austria experienced an unprecedented population growth related to an increase of births over deaths and a large influx of foreign workers. After the mid-1960s, however, there was a substantial and continuous drop in the fertility and birth rates in Austria, generally referred to as the "pill drop-off." In 1974 this trend was further influenced by the legalization of abortion during the first trimester of pregnancy. Since the mid-1970s, Austria—after Italy and the Federal Republic of Germany (West Germany)—has had the third lowest fertility rate in the world: 1.44 children per woman in 1990, a rate substantially lower than the replacement rate of 2.09.

In the early 1980s, some demographers predicted that the population of Austria would decline from 7.5 million to its 1965 level of 7.25 million by 2010. This scenario was substantially revised when in the mid-1980s Austria's population experienced a spurt of dramatic growth. Projections in 1990 anticipated a net growth of Austria's population by 500,000 to 8 million by 2010. An increase in immigration and the higher fertility rate of foreign workers accounted for the greatest part of Austria's net population growth in the early 1990s.

Within Austria there are substantial variations in regional patterns of population growth among the indigenous population, in contrast to the immigrant or foreign population. After World War II, Austria's eastern provinces—Lower Austria, Vienna, and Burgenland—had lower rates of fertility than the other provinces in the country. Throughout the 1960s and the 1970s, there was a clear "east-west watershed" in population growth. The west had

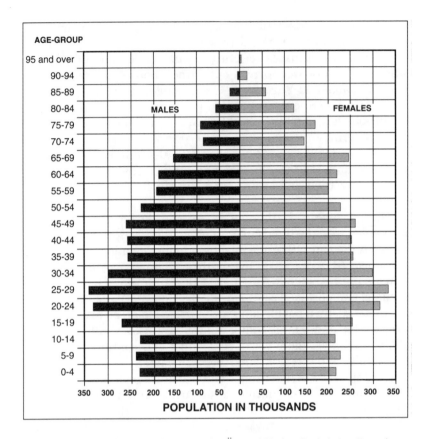

AGE-GROUP

POPULATION IN THOUSANDS

Source: Based on information from Austria, Österreichisches Statistisches Zentralamt, *Statistisches Handbuch für die Republik Österreich, 1991*, Vienna, 1991, 24.

Figure 6. Population by Age and Gender, 1990

higher rates of fertility, while the east's lower rates of fertility led to a stagnating or declining population (see table 3, Appendix). The economic and social reasons for these patterns of development were complex and included the Soviet occupation of eastern Austria from 1945 to 1955 and the depopulation of regions along the Iron Curtain, the traditionally weak economic infrastructure of predominantly rural areas in eastern and southeastern Austria, and the conservatism and deeply rooted Roman Catholicism of western Austria.

In 1970 the average life expectancy was seventy years (sixty for males and seventy-three for females). By 1990 the average life expectancy was almost seventy-six years (seventy-two for males and seventy-nine for females). The increasing life expectancy and the fall in the number of births have meant that Austria's population is aging (see fig. 6; fig. 7). One of the major concerns under these circumstances is the burden placed on the Austrian social security system: to what extent will a constant, or shrinking, labor force be able to maintain an increasing number of pensioners?

The overall decline of fertility among Austria's indigenous population is similar to developments in other advanced industrial nations in Europe. The decline is caused by a complex set of factors, including the increased use of contraception and abortion, and the increased employment of women outside the home, and changing values and attitudes toward marriage, family, and childbearing.

Immigration

Austria's position in Central Europe after World War II—by 1948 about 1,225 kilometers, or 46 percent, of its frontiers were with communist states—and the proclamation of Austrian neutrality in October 1955 made Austria Europe's most important country of east-west transit, transmigration, and the claiming of refugee status. Between 1945 and 1990, approximately 2.6 million people came to Austria as immigrants, transmigrants, or refugees. The great majority of them stayed in Austria only for short periods, and some 550,000 used Austria exclusively as a land of transit. Approximately 1.4 million people were transmigrants who lived in Austria before emigrating to other countries or returning to their countries of origin. About 650,000 people, over half of whom were not ethnic Germans or native German speakers, settled permanently in Austria, the great majority of whom became citizens.

Although Austrians traditionally viewed their country as a neutral land of transit and political asylum, they did not see Austria as a land of immigration like the United States, Canada, or Australia. This perception, however, does not correspond to the fact that more than 10 percent of the country's citizens in 1990 had not been born in Austria and that in the early 1990s more than 500,000 legal foreigners, predominantly guest workers, lived in the country.

Waves of immigration were caused by political events in neighboring countries. After the Hungarian Revolution of 1956, for example, over 250,000 Hungarians fled to Austria, 180,000 of whom eventually applied for asylum. In August 1968, after the Warsaw Pact invasion of Czechoslovakia ended the "Prague Spring," 162,000 Czechs and Slovaks fled to Austria. Although the majority of them eventually returned to Czechoslovakia, 12,000 applied for asylum. In Poland the banning of the Solidarity Movement in December 1981 caused between 120,000 and 150,000 Poles to go to

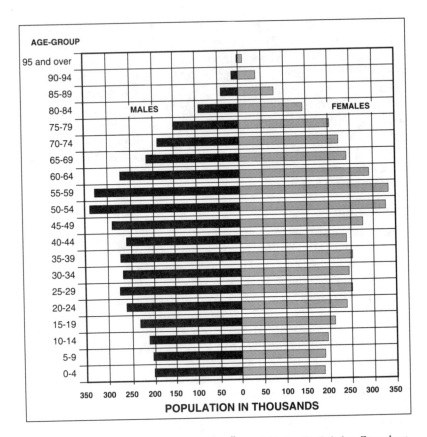

AGE-GROUP

95 and over
90-94
85-89
80-84   MALES   FEMALES
75-79
70-74
65-69
60-64
55-59
50-54
45-49
40-44
35-39
30-34
25-29
20-24
15-19
10-14
5-9
0-4

350 300 250 200 150 100 50   0   50 100 150 200 250 300 350
POPULATION IN THOUSANDS

Source: Based on information from Austria, Österreichisches Statistisches Zentralamt, *Statistisches Handbuch für die Republik Österreich, 1991*, Vienna, 1991, 24.

Figure 7. Population by Age and Gender, Projected 2020

Austria, and 33,000 of them applied for asylum. The opening of Hungary's borders during the summer of 1989 breached the Iron Curtain, and 40,000 East Germans used Austria as a land of transit to emigrate to West Germany.

In addition to European immigrants, since 1972 Austria has accepted contingents of asylum seekers from a number of countries—Chile, Argentina, Uganda, Iran, and Afghanistan—under the auspices of international agreements. Austria was also the main land of transit for 250,000 Jewish emigrants from the Soviet Union beginning in 1976 until the advent of direct Soviet immigration to Israel in 1990.

The number of individuals seeking political asylum in Austria rose from fewer than 5,000 in 1982 to more than 27,000 in 1991.

Before the Iron Curtain fell at the end of 1989, the granting of political asylum in Austria to refugees was relatively liberal. Once democratic governments were established in the former communist states of Eastern Europe and borders were opened, however, Austria began to pursue a more restrictive asylum policy. A distinction came to be made between political refugees and so-called economic refugees, who sought more lucrative employment or better living conditions. As a result, the number of those seeking asylum fell to 16,200 in 1992.

The number of people seeking to immigrate to Austria had increased so greatly by the early 1990s that the nation's army, the Bundesheer (Federal Army), was called in to assist customs and border authorities in patrolling the country's borders. After the fall of communism, these borders were virtually open for a time. By 1992 as many as 100,000 illegal immigrants were in Austria. In addition, for humanitarian reasons, Austria had accepted well over 50,000 refugees from the former Yugoslavia, who had either fled or were expelled from their homes in the course of hostilities that began in 1991. Most of these refugees were Bosnians.

The presence of a large number of foreign workers in Austria also affected population trends. The size of this group fluctuated according to the state of the country's economy. From the mid-1960s through the early 1970s, a period of rapid domestic economic growth, Austria's domestic labor force was not large enough to satisfy the demands of its growing economy, and foreign workers were brought in to meet the labor shortage. Most were unskilled Yugoslavs and Turks who assumed menial jobs with low salaries. As a result of this influx, the number of foreign workers in Austria increased from fewer than 50,000 in 1965 to some 220,000 in 1974. The recession of the second half of the 1970s and early 1980s had reduced their number to 140,000 by 1984. Periods of growth later in the decade raised it to 264,000 by 1991.

Despite these fluctuations, guest workers and their dependents had become a permanent feature of Austria's population and accounted for 80 percent of the 550,000 legally registered foreign inhabitants in Austria in 1991. The remaining 20 percent consisted of asylum seekers and refugees who had fled from the conflict in the former Yugoslavia.

A shrinking population caused by lower birth rates was Austria's greatest demographic concern in the 1970s and early 1980s. Although the low birth rate among Austria's indigenous German-speaking population continues to be an issue, many Austrians are also concerned about the growing number of foreigners in Austria. To offset the low birth rate, Austria needs a projected net annual growth of approximately 25,000 people per year in order to maintain population at a stable level. Most of this growth will come from foreigners living in Austria or from immigrants.

Emigration

In the early 1990s, the number of Austrians living and working abroad—approximately 430,000—was somewhat lower than the number of foreigners in Austria. Since the 1950s, West Germany had been the most frequent destination, and in 1990 about 181,000 Austrians resided there, attracted by prospects of better wages and greater career opportunities. In the same year, 29,000 Austrians lived in Switzerland and 10,000 in Italy. The great majority of the remainder lived outside Europe, predominantly in North America and South America. In contrast to foreign workers in Austria, Austrians working abroad frequently were highly skilled and well educated.

Social Minorities

The ethnic or national backgrounds of many Austrians reflect the multinational heritage of the Habsburg Empire. During the late nineteenth and early twentieth centuries, a substantial amount of migration occurred within Austria-Hungary to the German-speaking provinces of Austria. Austria's western and Alpine provinces were affected much less by migration because their low levels of industrialization and urbanization offered few employment opportunities. Before 1918 Czech and Jewish migration influenced the composition of Austria's population to the greatest extent, although all the empire's peoples participated in it. The migrants to Austria from other parts of the empire were usually assimilated into German-speaking Austrian society in a generation or two. However, traditional religious prejudices and racist doctrines of the late nineteenth century prevented a full acceptance of Jewish migrants.

The post-World War I peace conferences that established the borders of the Republic of Austria created a relatively homogeneous German-speaking state (95.3 percent of the populace) but left German-speaking minorities in Czechoslovakia and Italy. Although the 3 million German-speaking inhabitants of the borderlands of Bohemia and Moravia had been subjects of the Habsburgs for centuries, their national orientation was German, and it would not be accurate to see them as an Austrian minority outside of Austria.

The establishment of the Austrian-Italian frontier at the Brenner Pass involved the dismemberment of the province of Tirol and created an Austrian—or, more specifically, German-speaking Tirolean—minority of 200,000 persons in South Tirol that was incorporated into the Italian region of Trentino-Alto Adige. While Italy was controlled by the Fascists (1922–45), German-speaking South Tiroleans were subjected to Italianization campaigns, and during World War II they were given the "option" of Italianization or emigration as "settlers" to areas occupied by Nazi Germany.

After World War II, a popular movement in South Tirol agitated for the region to be incorporated into Austria, but the Allies did not support these aspirations. An agreement in 1947 between Italy and Austria provided South Tiroleans with a special autonomous status. The realization of this status became a continuing point of contention that sometimes erupted into violence between South Tiroleans and Italians and caused friction between Vienna and Rome. However, in 1992 political representatives of the German-speaking South Tiroleans and the Italian authorities in Rome succeeded in drafting legislation that is likely to satisfy South Tirolean claims for autonomy as an Italian province (see Regional Issues, ch. 4).

Official Minority Groups

Within Austria a distinction is made between "official ethnic groups"—Slovenes, Croats, Hungarians, and Czechs and Slovaks— who are legally defined and recognized as minorities, and other social groups, such as Roma and Sinti (commonly known as Gypsies), Jews, and foreign workers. These other groups do not have a special legal status as "Austrian ethnic groups" but are de facto minorities.

Although Austria was the most homogeneous of the successor states carved out of Austria-Hungary, it had a number of indigenous ethnic and linguistic minorities in the southern and eastern rural borderlands: Slovenes in Carinthia; Croats, Slovaks, and Hungarians in Burgenland. An urban minority of Czechs and Slovaks were also concentrated predominantly in Vienna. These groups accounted for 4.7 percent of Austria's population after World War I.

The Croats represented the largest single official minority in Austria. The Croat enclaves in Burgenland were the result of the Habsburgs' wars with the Ottoman Empire in the sixteenth and seventeenth centuries. The Croats fled north to avoid Turkish subjugation, and after the Habsburgs defeated the Turks, Croats were settled in Burgenland to compensate for the depopulation the wars had caused.

The drafting of the post-World War I frontiers of Burgenland also created Austria's smallest minority. Areas east of the Leitha

River historically had been part of the Kingdom of Hungary, although they were predominantly inhabited by German speakers by 1918. Negotiations of the national frontiers between Austria and Hungary led to Burgenland's becoming a province within Austria. Thus, the province's Hungarian population became an Austrian minority.

The Slovenes of southern Carinthia, Austria's second largest ethnic group, were the descendants of the ancient Slavic population that initially inhabited the southern slopes of the Alps and the Drau River Basin. Beginning in the early Middle Ages, these Slavs were displaced by German speakers. After both World War I and World War II, the newly formed state of Yugoslavia had aspirations of incorporating into it the areas of southern Carinthia inhabited by Slovenes. A Yugoslav invasion of Carinthia in 1918 was followed by a plebiscite in the areas in question in 1920 that resolved territorial claims with a clear vote for Austria. Tensions between the Slovene minority and the German-speaking majority in Carinthia increased during World War II because of Nazi racial policies and the military actions in southern Carinthia of Slovene partisans operating under the directions of Marshal Josip Broz Tito's National Liberation Army.

After World War II, neither the Allies nor the Austrian authorities were willing to meet renewed Yugoslav demands to redraw the Austrian-Yugoslav border. A partial response to Yugoslav demands was Article 8 of the State Treaty of 1955, which granted official minority status to the Slovenes in Carinthia and the Croats in Burgenland. Relations between the Slovenes and the German speakers of Carinthia remained strained in the following decades, more than was the case anywhere else in Austria. One reason for this hostility was the persistence of right-wing and German nationalist attitudes among sections of the German-speaking population.

The Croats and Hungarians of Burgenland and the Slovenes of Carinthia were usually peasant-farmers located in peripheral regions. The Czechs and Slovaks who still spoke their native languages as first languages presented a stark contrast to these groups. This minority descended mainly from migrants who left predominantly rural areas of southern Bohemia, Moravia, and Slovakia in the late nineteenth and early twentieth centuries to settle in industrial centers such as Vienna, Graz, Linz, and Steyr, and in areas in northern Styria. There were so many Czech migrants in Vienna that the imperial capital was said to be the ''second largest Czech city'' after Prague. In these urban and industrial settings, immigrants were soon assimilated.

Austrian censuses use the criterion ''language of everyday communication'' to determine who belongs to one of the official ethnic

Street in Trausdorf an der Wulka in the province of Burgenland
Courtesy Embassy of Austria, Washington

groups. The Ethnic Groups Law of 1976 sought to protect and promote the distinct identities of officially recognized minorities and arranged for bilingual education in their languages. Despite such measures, however, all of Austria's officially recognized minority groups have declined markedly in size. Between 1910 and 1980, the number of Croats and Hungarians who declared themselves as members of their respective ethnic groups dropped by 50 percent, the number of Slovenes by 75 percent, and the number of Czechs and Slovaks by 95 percent (see table 4, Appendix).

The decline of indigenous minority groups in Austria stemmed from a variety of causes. Part of the decline resulted from pressure to assimilate to German-speaking Austrian culture before and after World War II, as well as from Nazi racial policies in Austria, which distinguished between "superior" and "inferior" races. Assimilation, however, was also caused by the modernization of Austria after World War II through an increase in economic and social mobility that drew younger generations away from traditional ethnic and linguistic enclaves, life-styles, and identities.

Other Minorities

Austria contains other minority groups that are not defined as such by law but are perceived as minorities by the general population:

Gypsies, Jews, and foreign workers. Gypsies and Jews have been in Austria for centuries, although a sizable number of Jews came to Vienna during the nineteenth century from other parts of the Habsburg Empire. The presence of a large number of foreign workers dates from the 1960s.

Gypsies

Roma and Sinti, or Gypsies as they are generally called, arrived in Austria in the fourteenth century. An eastern, nomadic people, originally from India, they wore colorful clothes, had their own language and customs, and exchanged goods for survival. Men usually either made pots and other brass objects or were musicians, while women told fortunes or sold handmade goods and fruits from their wagons.

A Gypsy's life centered on the family and the larger group, with individual achievement playing an insignificant role. Marriage with a non-Gypsy typically meant exclusion by the community. Disapproval or punishment by the community was a much more serious reprimand to a Gypsy than any legal action by the state.

The attitude of Gypsies toward work and saving differed from that of the majority group in that they generally aimed at earning enough to meet ''the needs of the day.'' When food or money were needed, the Gypsy code permitted as a last resort stealing from wealthier people. Preferring to feel free and unhindered, Gypsies attached little importance to the accumulation of property, choosing instead a life of wandering and bartering. Only later during their time in Austria did they build semipermanent dwellings. Even so, Gypsies preferred to live among themselves on the outskirts of towns and cities.

Because of these habits and attitudes, Gypsies were mistrusted by the Austrian population. Gypsies were seen as lazy, disorderly, and dirty, and regarded as thieves, criminals, and prostitutes. In the eighteenth century, laws were enacted that banned their migrant way of life and established ''colonies'' for them.

By the late 1930s, an estimated 11,000 Gypsies lived in Austria, predominantly in the province of Burgenland. Because of Nazi racial doctrines, more than half of them were deported to concentration camps during World War II. By the war's end, only an estimated 4,500 Austrian Gypsies survived.

At the beginning of the 1990s, as many as 40,000 Gypsies lived in Austria, mostly centered in the provinces of Vienna and Burgenland. Although they more often speak German than the traditional Romany or Sinti languages, they are by no means assimilated into the larger society. Many Gypsies attend Austrian schools, but their academic performance is below average, and they see schooling as a hindrance to freedom. Young men who have completed apprenticeships are described by their employers as hard-working and honest. They generally do not become long-term employees, however, particularly if they are living away from their families. Young women usually work in factories or as kitchen help.

Jews

Jews have also lived in Austria for centuries, at times enduring hostility and repression. At other times, the Jewish community has flourished and enjoyed a high degree of tolerance. Joseph II (r. 1780-90) lifted restrictions that had barred them from particular trades and education, and despite widespread prejudice against them, Jews achieved positions of eminence in business, the professions, and the arts in the nineteenth and early twentieth centuries. The Jewish community in Austria expanded greatly in the second half of the nineteenth century when Jews from other parts of the empire came to settle there, mostly in Vienna. Most of these so-called Eastern Jews came from the province of Galicia, an area located in southern present-day Poland and in western present-day Ukraine. The province contained about two-thirds of the Habsburg Empire's Jewish population.

After the Anschluss, the Nazis systematically applied their racial policies to the country's Jews. Approximately 100,000 Austrian Jews managed to emigrate from Austria before World War II began, but more than 65,000 Jews died in concentration camps and prisons of the Third Reich. As a result, Austrian Jewry was virtually annihilated. After World War II, few surviving members of Austria's Jewish community returned to Austria, and Austrian authorities made no concerted official efforts to repatriate them.

As of 1990, only a little more than 7,000 Jews were registered with the Jewish Orthodox Religious Community in Vienna. This figure included recent Jewish immigrants from the Soviet Union and Eastern Europe but excluded Jews who did not declare their religious affiliation. Because the only statistical information on the number of Jews in Austria is available on a confessional basis, accurate figures on the number of Austrians with Jewish backgrounds are not available. It is generally assumed that this group is larger than the officially registered one.

Foreign Workers

Foreign workers represent the largest de facto minority in Austria, although they frequently are not perceived as such because they are "foreigners" and "guest workers." Their cultural and linguistic characteristics set them off from the indigenous population, however, and make them a distinct minority. Present in substantial numbers since the 1960s, foreign workers have become a permanent feature of Austrian society.

Initially, many guest workers came to Austria without their families and eventually returned to their countries of origin after having saved some money. In this respect, they were similar to "seasonal" laborers. However, the "rotation" of foreign workers—the return of some to their countries of origin offset by the influx of others to take their jobs—was gradually replaced by the permanent settlement of foreign workers and their families.

Foreign workers who had the required residence visa and work permit were entitled to reside permanently in Austria; their documents were generally renewed. In addition, once foreigners had worked and lived continuously in the country for ten years, they could apply for Austrian citizenship. (Under other conditions, such as political asylum, the waiting period for application could be reduced to four years.) Between 1970 and 1990, over 133,000 foreigners became naturalized Austrian citizens, the majority of whom were long-term foreign workers.

The Employment of Foreigners Law passed in 1991 limited the number of foreign workers who could be employed in Austria to 10 percent of the domestic labor force. The Resident Alien Law of 1993 reduced the number of foreign workers, that is, workers from outside the EU and the European Free Trade Association (EFTA—see Glossary) still further—to 9 percent of the total work force of about 3.5 million. As a result of these laws, approximately 300,000 foreigners can work in Austria. Because many of these workers have dependents, Austrian officials assume foreigners could come to constitute approximately 10 percent of the total population.

Citizens from the former Yugoslavia, predominantly Serbs, account for approximately 50 percent of the foreign workers in Austria. Turks are the second largest group, making up approximately 20 percent of the foreign work force, followed by Germans at 5 percent. Poles, Czechs, Slovaks, Hungarians, and Romanians make up between 3.5 and 4.0 percent each.

Foreigners usually live in urban and industrial centers, most notably Vienna. Although foreigners accounted for just over 6 percent of the total population in 1990, the foreign population of Vienna increased from 7.4 percent in 1981 to 13.2 percent in 1990. Because of the large number of foreigners living in the capital and the low birth rates of indigenous Austrians, at the beginning of the 1990s one-fourth of the children born in Vienna were foreigners.

Despite their essential contribution to the economy and the fact that they are more law-abiding than the indigenous population, foreign workers are generally not held in high esteem. This prejudice is caused by the low pay and social status of their jobs, their lower level of education, and an often limited ability to speak German. Tensions also arise because of their foreign appearance and customs. Some resentment also stems from the social costs their presence entails. For example, the children of these workers are an additional burden for schools, and there are concerns about how well these children are being educated. Determining the national identities of these children is often difficult because they are not familiar with their parents' homeland yet have the status of "foreigners" in Austria.

The degree or quality of assimilation into the larger society is the most serious problem presented by long-term foreign workers. It is not known whether they will remain a minority or gradually come to be seen as Austrian. Generally speaking, workers from the former Yugoslavia show a greater facility for integration or willingness to assimilate—especially in the second generation—than Turks, whose Islamic beliefs tend to make integration more difficult.

Although the arrival of these foreign workers has promoted the upward mobility of Austria's indigenous lower classes by filling the jobs having the lowest pay and social prestige, a new ethnic lower class has been created. The future social mobility and integration of foreign workers will determine to what extent Austria will have an "imported" racial problem in the future.

Attitudes Toward Minorities

Although Austria had a negligible Jewish population by the early 1990s, anti-Semitism remains a prejudice among some segments of the population. Social scientists disagree about the reliability of surveys taken during the 1980s, but the consensus among specialists is that between 7 and 12 percent of the population of Austria holds consistently anti-Semitic attitudes and can be considered "hardcore" anti-Semites. Around 25 percent of the populace is mildly anti-Semitic, and approximately 60 percent is neutral or philo-Semitic. Surveys also reveal that anti-Semitic sentiments are more pronounced among older Austrians than younger ones, increase as one moves from the left to the right of the political spectrum, and tend to be more pronounced in rural areas.

Surveys also reveal that there was a decline of explicitly anti-Semitic sentiments among some sections of the Austrian population during the 1980s. The decline could derive from the worldwide controversy surrounding the nomination and election of Kurt

Waldheim as Austrian president in 1986 and the public discussions of the fiftieth anniversary of the Nazi Anschluss in 1988. Both events caused a critical reevaluation of the role of Austrians in the Third Reich, as well as an open debate about Austrian anti-Semitism.

The opening of Eastern Europe beginning in 1989 and increased immigration to Austria were events that also influenced the structure of Austrian attitudes, anxieties, and prejudices. The special status Austria enjoyed as a neutral state between the two power blocs gave Austrians a sense of security that disappeared after 1989. It was replaced by the widespread concern in the early 1990s that Austria would be overwhelmed by foreigners as a result of open borders. For example, a survey in 1992 found that 38 percent of those polled believed that the greatest threat facing Austria was its being overrun by eastern refugees. The weakest social groups in Austria, the elderly and the retired, and low-income groups—who had the impression that they were competing with foreign workers—tended to feel most threatened by the changes that accompanied Austria's new position in Europe.

The role of immigration became a very sensitive political issue because of the erroneous but common perception that legal immigrants and foreign workers are a burden instead of a demographic and economic benefit. The influx of illegal or ''economic refugees'' from the former communist states of Eastern Europe exacerbated the situation. An increase in crime stemming from illegal refugees who entered Austria as ''tourists'' led to increasingly hostile attitudes toward all foreigners from Eastern Europe, the Balkan Peninsula, and Turkey and the propagation of negative stereotypes. The results of a Gallup poll taken in the fall of 1991 showed strong xenophobic sentiments toward Gypsies, Serbs, Turks, Poles, and Romanians that considerably surpassed anti-Semitic attitudes in Austria. The manner in which Austrians learn to cope with immigration and integration will likely play an important role in domestic politics in the future.

Social Structure

Austrian society was traditionally stratified and had a low degree of social mobility. As a result, social distinctions were clear. Social relations between aristocrats and commoners, masters and servants, large landowners and peasant-farmers, and employers and employees were hierarchical and well defined, and the use of titles as a reflection of rank or social status was important. Austrians born into specific social groups or classes had few opportunities to improve their social and economic standing and identified themselves strongly with their inherited social positions, which were reinforced by education (or the lack thereof), attitudes toward religion, and political convictions.

At the beginning of the nineteenth century, the three predominant social classes in Austria were aristocrats; "citizens" or burghers in towns and cities, who had special charters of rights and privileges; and peasant-farmers—"free farmers" in western Austria who owned and tilled their own land and peasant-serfs in eastern Austria. Reforms had been introduced during the last decades of the eighteenth century to bring about a greater degree of social equality, but legal equality was not established in the Austrian half of Austria-Hungary until the constitution of 1867 was promulgated. Even at the beginning of the twentieth century, society still consisted of a very small upper class composed of an old aristocracy of "blue bloods" and a recently ennobled and new aristocracy of wealth, a small middle and entrepreneurial class (approximately 15 percent), a growing working class (approximately 25 percent), and a class of peasant-farmers (approximately 55 to 60 percent).

During the troubled interwar period, a time of political unrest and economic hardship for most Austrians, the country's main social groups remained rigidly segregated and there was a high degree of identification of specific classes with corresponding political ideologies and worldviews. The resulting *"Lager,"* or *"camp,"* mentality was seen in the embrace of the urban working class of social democracy while the rest of the country became proponents of conservative Roman Catholic Christian politics or, to a much lesser degree, European-style liberalism (see Political Dynamics, ch. 4).

After World War II, however, the structure of Austrian society changed substantially. The white-collar middle class expanded greatly during four decades of unprecedented prosperity. The number of farmers and workers declined as they or their children were able to benefit from the postwar era's social mobility and find better employment. Many low-status jobs were taken by foreign workers from southeastern Europe. An increasingly white-collar service economy reduced the previous social inequalities and blurred traditional class distinctions. Education became the most important vehicle of upward social mobility, and a more open education system made it more available than ever before. Attitudinal barriers to social mobility did not disappear to a corresponding extent, however. Coming from an "established" or older family still played an important role in the social position Austrians were able to assume in society.

The long period of prosperity and social mobility weakened the *Lager* mentality that had characterized the interwar period. Beginning in the 1980s, electoral patterns indicated that the traditional political allegiances of specific classes to corresponding political parties and ideologies had deteriorated. This relaxation of political ties permitted the formation of new political parties that profited from a growing pool of "floating votes."

Family Life

In the late nineteenth century, large sections of the Austrian population were effectively excluded from the institutions of marriage and family because they lacked the property and income necessary to participate in them. In Alpine and rural communities, for example, property ownership was a traditional prerequisite for marriage that neither day-laborers nor household servants of landowning farmers could meet. Among urban and industrial working classes, poverty was so widespread that it made the establishment of independent households and families difficult.

During the course of the twentieth century, however, marriage and family have become increasingly common, especially after World War II, when the "economic miracle" brought prosperity to nearly everyone. For the first time in Austrian history, there was almost uniform access to these basic social institutions. Because of this, the postwar period up through the 1960s represented a "golden age" of the family in Austria. More than 90 percent of the women born between 1935 and 1945 have married—a percentage higher than any generation before or since. The "two-child family" was considered an ideal.

Family Developments after the 1960s

Beginning in the 1970s, a number of trends appeared that represented a dramatic change in attitudes toward the ideals of marriage and family. There was a sharp drop in the birth rate and a decrease in family size, accompanied by a greater prevalence of people who had never married, people who were divorced, single-parent families, cohabiting couples, and marriages without children.

In the early 1990s, fewer Austrian women were bearing children—an estimated 20 to 30 percent will never have a child—and those who have children are bearing fewer. After the end of the "baby boom" of the early 1960s, the Austrian fertility rate dropped steadily from 2.82 to an all-time low of 1.44 in 1989 (then increased marginally to 1.50 by 1991). Family size has shrunk correspondingly. Marriage without children was twice as common in 1990 (32.9 percent) as in the previous generation, and the number of families having three or more children dropped by more than half (to 10.7 percent). Families having one or two children accounted for roughly one-third and one-fourth of families, respectively, in

The Lünersee in the province of Vorarlberg is used to produce electricity.
Courtesy Embassy of Austria, Washington

View of the Danube near Grein in the province of Lower Austria
Courtesy Austrian National Tourist Office, New York

the early 1990s. Large families are most common among farmers, who have a historical and economic tradition of having many children, and among working-class women having little education.

Between 1970 and 1990, the number of single-parent families increased almost five times faster than the traditional two-parent families. In 1990 there were 235,000 single-parent families in Austria, about 15 percent of all families. Nearly 90 percent of single parents were women. Some of these single-parent households resulted from women's conscious choice to bear children without marrying. More often, however, divorce was the cause; more than one-half of single parents were divorced. About one-third of the single parents were unmarried, and about one-tenth were widows or widowers.

One of the consequences of these trends was that the average size of an Austrian household dropped from 2.9 in 1971 to 2.6 persons in 1990 and is expected to drop further. Almost 60 percent of the population lived equally divided between one- and two-person households in 1990. A large number of single-person households result from women's long life expectancy, which causes them to outlive their spouses.

The frequency of marriage has also declined since the 1960s. Of the women born in the late 1930s, only 8 percent remained single, compared with an estimated 25 percent of women born in the 1960s. One reason for the rise in the unmarried population is the increasing number of educated women who have professional and economic alternatives to traditional wife-mother roles. Another reason for the smaller number of marriages is that cohabitation without marriage has become more frequent and socially acceptable.

Austrians are also marrying later. In 1991 the mean age of marriage was 25.6 years for women and 28.0 years for men, an increase over earlier decades. In 1981 about 59 percent of women and 82 percent of men were single between the ages of twenty and twenty-five, compared with 70 percent and almost 90 percent, respectively, at the end of the decade. For those between twenty-five and thirty years of age, the figures showed a similar rise in the numbers of the unmarried—33 percent of women and over 50 percent of men were still single at the end of the decade, compared with 25 percent and 40 percent, respectively, in 1981.

The declining number of marriages is accompanied by an increased frequency of divorce. The divorce rate in Austria increased from 15 percent in the early 1960s to more than 33 percent in the early 1990s. Divorce granted on the basis of "no fault" or mutual consent became legal in Austria in the early 1980s. The divorce rate was highest in Vienna and lowest in Tirol, an indication that traditional and religious values are least binding in urban areas and more persistent in a traditional Alpine setting. Women who are employed outside of the home and have their own sources of income demonstrate a greater readiness to divorce than "traditional wives."

More than one-third of all divorces in Austria occur within the first five years of marriage; thereafter, the frequency of divorce decreases with the length of marriage. In a survey in the early 1990s, more than one-half of people polled identified extramarital sex, selfishness, and inflexibility as the primary causes of divorce.

Illegitimacy has also become more frequent. Beginning in the 1960s, the percentage of illegitimate births increased steadily, from 11.5 percent in 1965 to 25 percent in 1991. For first-born children, the rate was over 33 percent. These figures reflect tolerant attitudes toward illegitimacy in many regions in the Alps where illegitimate children were a traditional aspect of the Alpine agrarian way of life. Wage-laborers and servants within the households of landowning farmers frequently were unable to marry, but their offspring enjoyed a high degree of social acceptance because illegitimacy was common and provided the landowners with the next generation of laborers. Although the traditional agrarian structure of these regions has changed considerably, the tolerance of illegitimacy remains. In other parts of Austria not having comparable traditions, illegitimate birth is not stigmatized to the same extent as it was earlier. More than half of the illegitimate births in Austria are legalized by marriage, and the great majority of second- and third-born children are legitimate. The fact that the social welfare system provides more extensive benefits for single mothers than for married ones also can be interpreted as a financial incentive for initial illegitimacy in some cases.

These changes in Austrian life-style patterns are viewed by some Austrians with great apprehension, and they interpret the increasing rate of illegitimacy, cohabitating, single-parenting, and divorce and the decreasing birth rate as reflections of a crisis for the traditional religious and social values on which the family is based. However, the diversification of life-styles also can be interpreted as an inevitable consequence of the modernization of a traditional society, as well as part of the development of a more pluralistic society within which no particular life-style enjoys a position of predominance.

Status of Women

A patriarchal family structure based on a traditional gender-specific division of labor characterizes attitudes toward marriage and family. By the early 1990s, however, a greater emphasis on marriage as a partnership had become more common among the younger generation, especially among the urban middle class. A 1976 law establishes the principle of equal rights and duties for married men and women, as well as equal rights and responsibilities for caring for children.

The Equal Treatment Law of 1979 makes various forms of discrimination against women illegal. Amended a number of times since it was first passed, the law seeks to establish equal rights for women, especially in the workplace. It posits, for example, the principle of equal pay for equal qualifications and sets up commissions for the arbitration of complaints and violations related to pay, promotion, and sexual discrimination and harassment. The Women's Omnibus Law, which went into effect in 1993, is a further measure to reduce discrimination against women. One of its goals is increasing the employment of women in government agencies in which they make up less than 40 percent of the staff. The law also directs that women who have been denied promotions because of their gender or have suffered sexual harassment receive compensation.

The Austrian concept of "equal treatment" differs substantially from the United States idea of "equal rights." Austrian legislation not only aims at establishing equality in realms where there is discrimination against women, but it also attempts to provide women with additional benefits related to the inequities inherent in the gender-specific division of labor. Thus, it tries to establish benefits to compensate for "unpaid work" in the household, the dual burden of employment and child-rearing many women bear, and single-parenting. In other words, "equal treatment" involves interpreting equality literally in some spheres and attempting to compensate for the gender-specific inequality of burdens in others.

Despite the improvement of the legal position of women in Austria since the mid-1970s, traditional role models prevail. Whether women are employed outside the home or not, many Austrian men consider the great majority of housework and child-rearing tasks to be "women's work." For example, 80 percent of the married women surveyed at the end of the 1980s were solely responsible for laundry, 66 percent for cooking, and 51 percent for cleaning. Almost 20 percent of Austrian men do no household tasks. However, 75 percent of married men assume responsibility for shopping and other activities outside the home, a reflection of the division of labor in the traditional family between work inside and outside the home.

Although education is the primary determinant of income in Austria, a person's gender also plays a role. At the end of the 1980s, the average monthly net income for an employed woman was S12,858 (for value of the schilling—see Glossary), or S11,161 for a blue-collar worker and S14,790 for a white-collar employee. The average monthly net income for an employed man was S19,175, or S17,522 for a blue-collar worker and S24,734 for a white-collar employee. The pay differentials between men and women are lowest for those employed as civil servants (8 percent), compared with the private sector, where a range of 20 to 40 percent for blue-collar workers and white-collar employees prevails. Although sex discrimination is responsible for some of the male-female salary differentials, men traditionally are better trained than women. More women in the labor force are unskilled workers than are men: 38 percent of women versus 25 percent of men. Additional vocational training is much more common among men than among women: 50 percent for men versus 28 percent for women.

Highly educated women are more likely to be employed than those with less education. Around 84 percent of women between the ages of thirty and fifty-five having university degrees are employed, compared with only 53 percent of women who have been in school for only the required nine years. The number of men and women in the labor force who have completed secondary or university educations is approximately the same: 10 and 7 percent, respectively. Nevertheless, equal qualifications among men and women are not a guarantee of equal advancement in professions. For example, at the end of the 1980s only 16 percent of women having university or advanced degrees held leading positions as salaried employees or civil servants. Thus, despite the improvement of the legal status of women, the income differential between men and women has not decreased considerably since the early 1980s, and the implementation of equal rights legislation has proved difficult in practice.

Religion

During the Roman Catholic Counter-Reformation of the sixteenth and seventeenth centuries, the Habsburgs were the leading political representatives of Roman Catholicism in its conflict with the Protestantism of the Protestant Reformation in Central Europe, and ever since then, Austria has been a predominantly Roman Catholic country. Because of its multinational heritage, however, the Habsburg Empire was religiously heterodox and included the ancestors of many of Austria's contemporary smaller denominational groups. The empire's tradition of religious tolerance

101

derived from the enlightened absolutism of the late eighteenth century. Religious freedom was later anchored in Austria-Hungary's constitution of 1867. After the eighteenth century, twelve religious communities came to be officially recognized by the state in Austria: Roman Catholic; Protestant (Lutheran and Calvinist); Greek, Serbian, Romanian, Russian, and Bulgarian Orthodox; Jewish; Muslim; Old Catholic; and, more recently, Methodist and Mormon.

The presence of other communities within the empire did not prevent the relationship between the Austrian imperial state and the Roman Catholic Church—or the "throne and the altar"—from being particularly close before 1918. Because of this closeness, the representatives of secular ideologies—liberals and socialists—sought to reduce the influence of the Roman Catholic Church in such public areas as education.

A relatively complicated series of treaties (or concordats) between the Republic of Austria and the Vatican defined the role and status of the Roman Catholic Church. After 1918 the Roman Catholic Church maintained considerable influence in public life. For example, many members of the church hierarchy explicitly supported the Christian Social Party (Christlichsoziale Partei—CSP). Members of the Social Democratic Workers' Party (Sozialdemokratische Arbeiterpartei—SDAP) responded to this partisanship in the interwar period by being explicitly anticlerical. Some Roman Catholics were committed to a form of "political Catholicism," which was anti-Liberal and anti-SDAP. Because of these sympathies, they supported the authoritarian regime that erected a one-party "Christian Corporatist State" in 1934.

After the Anschluss in 1938, the Roman Catholic Church initially pursued a policy of accommodation with the National Socialist German Workers' Party (National-Sozialistische Deutsche Arbeiterpartei—NSDAP, or Nazi Party), but by 1939 it began to assume an oppositional stance. In the decades after World War II, the Roman Catholic Church abstained from publicly and actively supporting any one political party. An exception to this restraint was the church's involvement in the controversy surrounding the legalization of abortion in Austria in the early 1970s. For its part, the Socialist Party of Austria (Sozialistische Partei Österreichs—SPÖ) developed more accommodating attitudes toward the Roman Catholic Church than were common before World War II.

According to the 1991 census, a majority of Austrians (77.9 percent) belonged to the Roman Catholic Church. This is a decline from the 1971 figure of 87.2 percent. The number of Protestants also declined in the same period. The number of Lutherans, or members of the Augsburg Confession, declined from 5.7 percent in 1971 to 4.8 percent in 1991 according to the census, and Calvinists, or members of the Helvetic Confession, declined from 0.3 percent to 0.2 percent in the same years.

In 1938 the Jewish population of Austria numbered more than 200,000, most of whom lived in Vienna. After the Anschluss, the community was almost wiped out by emigration and the Holocaust. By 1990 the community amounted to about 7,000 and consisted largely of postwar immigrants instead of Austrian-born Jews.

Owing to the influx of foreign workers from Turkey and the former Yugoslavia, the Islamic and Serbian Orthodox communities experienced considerable growth in Austria in the 1970s and the 1980s. However, many of these foreign workers do not officially register with their respective religious organizations, and accurate information about the size of these communities is not available.

The influence of the Roman Catholic Church, although still formidable because of its historical position in Austrian society and network of lay organizations, receded in the postwar period. The form of nominal Roman Catholicism many Austrians practice is called "baptismal certificate Catholicism." In other words, most Roman Catholics observe traditional religious holidays, such as Christmas and Easter, and rely on the church to celebrate rites of passage, such as baptisms, confirmations, weddings, and funerals, but do not participate actively in parish life or follow the teachings of the Roman Catholic Church on central issues. This trend can be seen in the low rate of regular church attendance (less than one-third of Catholics) and the high rates of divorce and abortion in the 1980s and early 1990s.

Within Austria there are regional patterns of religious conviction. Generally, provinces with strong conservative and agricultural traditions, such as Tirol and Vorarlberg, followed by Lower Austria and Burgenland, have higher percentages of Roman Catholics than the national average, and parish churches still fulfill a social function in many smaller communities. Religious affiliation is lower in urban centers, however, and Vienna has the lowest percentage of any Austrian province.

The decline in the number of Austrians professing religious affiliation and the increase in the number who have no religious affiliation—4.3 percent in 1971 and 8.6 percent in 1991—may be interpreted as an increase in the secularization of Austrian society. Renouncing church membership and being without religious affiliation was one of the anticlerical, historical traditions of the SPÖ. In general, Austrians without religious affiliation tend to be associated with the SPÖ, whereas "active" Catholics tend to be connected to conservative parties and hold conservative political views.

The increase in the number of Austrians without religious affiliation should not be interpreted as an exclusively political gesture, however. Recognized religious organizations in Austria finance themselves by "taxing" their members directly with a so-called church tax, which amounts to approximately 1 percent of their income. Austrians who do not actively participate in their religious communities frequently officially withdraw from them in order to avoid paying this tax.

Education

Austria has a free public school system, and nine years of education are mandatory. Schools offer a series of vocational-technical and university preparatory tracks involving one to three additional years of education beyond the minimum mandatory level (see table 5, Appendix). The legal basis for primary and secondary education in Austria is the School Law of 1962. The federal Ministry for Education is responsible for funding and supervising primary and secondary education, which is administered on the provincial level by the authorities of the respective provinces.

The country's university system is also free. The General Law for University Education of 1966 and the University Organization Law of 1975 provide the legal framework for tertiary education, and the federal Ministry for Science and Research funds and oversees education at the university level. Twelve universities and six academies of music and art enjoy a high degree of autonomy and offer a full spectrum of degree programs. Established in 1365, the University of Vienna is Austria's oldest and largest university.

Federal legislation plays a prominent role in the education system, and laws dealing with education effectively have a constitutional status because they can be passed or amended only by a two-thirds majority in parliament. For this reason, agreement between the ÖVP and the SPÖ is needed to pass or amend legislation relating to education.

Private schools that provide primary and secondary education and some teacher training are run mainly by the Roman Catholic Church and account for approximately 10 percent of the 6,800 schools and 120,000 teachers. Roman Catholic schools have a reputation for more discipline and rigor than public institutions, and some are considered elite institutions. Because there is no tradition of private university education in Austria, the state has a virtual monopoly on higher education.

The history of the Austrian education system since World War II may be characterized as an attempt to transform higher education from a traditional entitlement of the upper social classes to an equal opportunity for all social classes. Before the School Law of 1962, Austria had a "two-track" education system. After four years of compulsory primary education from the ages of six to ten in the elementary school, or *Volksschule* (pl., *Volksschulen*), children and their parents had to choose between the compulsory secondary level for eleven- to fourteen-year-olds called the middle school, or *Hauptschule* (pl., *Hauptschulen*), or the first four years of an eight-year university preparatory track at higher schools of general education (*Allgemeinbildende Höhere Schulen*—AHS). AHS is an umbrella term used to describe institutions providing different fields of specialization that grant the diploma (*Reifeprüfung* or *Matura*) needed to enter university.

Before the 1962 reform, the great majority of children—more than 90 percent—attended the compulsory *Hauptschule,* where they were divided according to their performance in elementary school into two groups: an "A group," which was directed toward two- to four-year vocational-technical training schools after graduation from the *Hauptschule;* and a "B group," which was required to complete one additional year of compulsory education before entrance into apprenticeship programs or the work force. The remaining elementary-school graduates—less than 10 percent—enrolled in the AHS at age eleven. Children attending these university-track schools also had to choose a specific course of study.

The rigidity of the two-track system required that the most important educational decision in a child's life—with all of the implications it had for the future—be made at the age of ten. The decision depended to a great extent on the parents' background, income, and social status. Children from agricultural backgrounds or of urban working-class parents generally attended the *Volkschule* and the *Hauptschule* and then entered the work force. Children having lower-middle-class backgrounds frequently received vocational-technical training after the *Hauptschule,* while children from the upper-middle and upper classes, boys in particular, attended the AHS, which gave them access to university-level education.

The early selection process meant that children of the largest segment of the population, farmers and workers, were grossly underrepresented at higher schools and universities, whereas the children of a relatively small segment of the population, those who had attended higher schools or the universities, were overrepresented. Consequently, the education system tended to reproduce or to reinforce traditional social structures instead of being a vehicle of opportunity or social mobility.

The School Law of 1962 and subsequent amendments require that all state-funded schools be open to children regardless of birth, gender, race, status, class, language, or religion. The law also attempts to introduce more flexibility into the traditional two-track system and to provide students with a greater degree of latitude within it so that educational (and hence career) decisions can be made at an older age. Although the primary and secondary school system continues to be fundamentally based on the two-track idea, after a series of reforms in the 1970s and 1980s, ten- to fourteen-year-olds are no longer streamed into A and B groups in the *Hauptschule.* Graduates of this kind of school also have the opportunity to cross over into certain branches of the AHS track at the age of fourteen or to attend a series of different "higher vocational-technical schools" (*Berufsbildende Höhere Schulen* and *Höhere Technische Lehranstalten*), which have five-year programs of specialization (see fig. 8).

Shifts in enrollment patterns reflect these changes in the school system. In the mid-1960s, less than 10 percent of all students finished the university preparatory AHS track, and more than 66 percent of them were male. By the early 1990s, more than 30 percent of all students finished the AHS track and just above 50 percent of them were female. Furthermore, a second educational path was developed that permitted some students without a diploma from the university-track AHS to enroll in a university.

As a general rule, the quality of *Hauptschule* education is high, especially in rural areas and small communities where the schools have maintained their traditional social importance and where attendance at an AHS involves commuting considerable distances, or, for the inhabitants of more remote areas, boarding. In urban centers with a full spectrum of educational opportunities, the *Hauptschule* has become less popular, and parents who earlier would not have enrolled their children in an AHS have begun doing so. The increased enrollments have overburdened the AHS and created a shortage of students at the *Hauptschulen* and at vocational-technical schools (see table 6, Appendix).

In some areas, this trend has been strengthened by the number of children of foreign workers in the compulsory schools. In 1991, for example, almost 30 percent of school-age children in Vienna were the children of foreign workers. In some districts of the city, these children exceeded 70 percent. Although the children of long-term foreign workers frequently speak German well, the numbers of classes in which students with inadequate mastery of German are overrepresented has overburdened the *Hauptschule* system and made it a less desirable alternative than in the past. Therefore, special remedial and intercultural programs are being developed so that the compulsory school system in Austria can continue to fulfill its educational and social roles.

The SPÖ has continued to press for further reforms of the school system. It argued for an abolition of the two-track system for ten- to fourteen-year-olds and for combining the *Hauptschule* and the first four years of the AHS into a new comprehensive middle school. As of 1993, however, because of the resistance of other political parties, this alternative has been limited to a number of experimental schools.

As a result of the reforms since the 1960s, the university system has changed from one serving the elite to one serving the masses. The increasing number of students at Austrian universities reflects the liberalization of educational policy at secondary and higher levels. Between the 1955–56 and 1991–92 academic years, the number of students enrolled in institutions of higher education increased from about 19,000 to more than 200,000 (see table 7, Appendix). The number of students beginning university-level education after having completed the AHS program also increased and amounted to 85 percent in 1990, compared with 60 percent in the mid-1960s.

The reforms have also meant that university education ceased to be a male privilege. Between the 1960–61 and 1991–92 academic years, the number of female students enrolling in universities rose from 23 to 44 percent. Yet, although women account for almost half of the students at university level, only 2 percent of the professors at institutions of higher learning were women in 1990.

Despite the increase in the numbers of university students and the greater presence of women, universities remain primarily the domain of middle- and higher-income groups. The number of students with working-class backgrounds has doubled from 7 to 14 percent, and the number of these with agricultural backgrounds increased from less than 2 percent to more than 4 percent between 1960 and 1990. But children of white-collar workers, civil servants, and the self-employed accounted for more than 80 percent of enrollments at Austrian institutions of higher education in the early 1990s.

Increased accessibility to university-level education has a number of consequences. The dramatic expansion in the number of students has led to overcrowding at many institutions. Some critics maintain that the increasing number of students diminishes the overall quality of university-level education despite increases in federal investment. One obvious problem was that more than 50

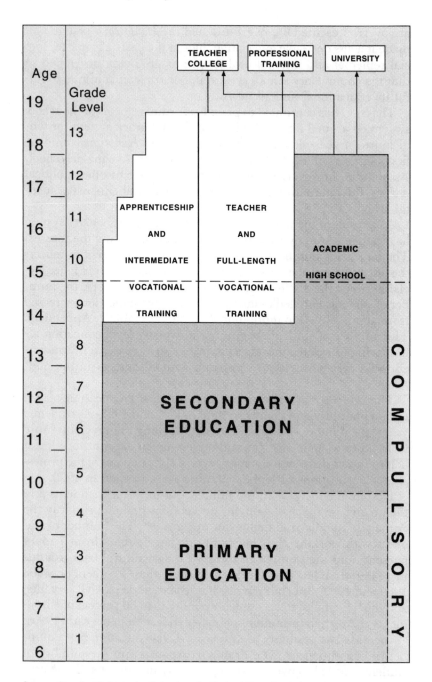

Source: Based on information from Austria, Federal Press Service, *Austria: Facts and Figures*, Vienna, 1990, 119.

Figure 8. Structure of the Education System, 1993

percent of students enrolled at the universities in the 1980s did not successfully complete a degree program. Complex reasons account for this high drop-out rate. Some students enroll simply to acquire student benefits. Others study for the sake of personal enrichment without intending to get a degree. Some are unable to complete their studies for financial reasons. Although a university degree provides students with a substantial amount of social status and better income opportunities, there has been an increase in "academic unemployment," especially among degree-holders in the humanities and social sciences.

Debates about educational policy in Austria frequently are the result of different perspectives related to the strengths and weaknesses of the traditional education system. Proponents of the two-track secondary system, for example, defend it as performance oriented and criticize the leveling of achievement or lowering of standards the introduction of one compulsory middle school would involve. Conversely, opponents of the two-track system criticize its rigidity and inherent absence of equal opportunity. Consequently, such bipolar terms as *performance* and *leveling, elite* and *mass education,* and *achievement* and *equal opportunity* prevail in educational debates. In some respects, Austrians of different political and educational policy persuasions may expect too many different things from one university system. They expect it to provide general education, as do state university systems in the United States, and "Ivy League" performance at the same time.

Social Security

The origins of the contemporary Austrian social security system date back to the end of the nineteenth century, when rudimentary forms of social security were introduced for specific occupational groups. Workers, employees, civil servants, farmers, and the self-employed each paid into a different social security plan. Workers and employees in Vienna, for example, paid into a different social security fund than did civil servants in Vienna or farmers in Tirol. The main thrust in the development of the country's social security system in the twentieth century has been the creation of a unified social insurance policy for all occupational groups.

The organization of the social security system is complex. The General Social Insurance Act of 1955, which has been repeatedly amended, sets social security policy and makes decisions on such matters as the level of social security payments and the kind and extent of benefits. However, tax revenues are collected and benefits are dispersed by individual insurance agencies or "carriers" for specific occupational groups. In this respect, the social security

109

system is a national plan in terms of federal legislation but is not centrally funded or administered.

The extent of social security coverage and the number of benefits increased in Austria steadily from the end of World War II until the early 1980s. As a result, Austria was among the most highly developed welfare states in the world and had a complicated system of direct taxes on employers and employees and indirect taxes that financed a broad spectrum of benefits.

After the early 1980s, social policy entered a phase of consolidation characterized by difficulties related to funding extensive social security programs, growing levels of unemployment, stagnating economic growth, increasing budget deficits, and the demographics of an aging population. However, as of 1993, Austria had managed to maintain its high level of social security without major reductions in benefits.

Employment, Unemployment, and Pension Benefits

As of the early 1990s, the standard work week in Austria was forty hours, although some occupational groups have negotiated a thirty-eight-and-one-half-hour week. Minimum wages and salaries are negotiated by trade unions and the representative bodies of employers, and individual professional groups negotiate increases in wages, salaries, or benefits on the basis of collective bargaining. Salaries are paid fourteen times a year, and two special payments, usually on June 1 and December 1, are taxed at lower rates than regular salaries. In addition, Austrians are entitled to five weeks of paid vacation annually.

All people gainfully employed, employees as well as the self-employed, are subject to compulsory insurance, which includes unemployment, disability, retirement, and provisions for surviving dependents. The right to draw unemployment is contingent on having worked for at least one year. Unemployment benefits range from 50 to 70 percent of the recipient's previous net pay and are limited to a period of seven months. After this period expires, the unemployed can qualify for a series of different support programs depending on need.

As of the early 1990s, the legal retirement age was sixty-five years for men and sixty years for women. However, only 10 percent of men and 50 percent of women actually work until those ages because they may qualify for disability pensions or take advantage of provisions that allow contributors to retire after paying into a pension fund for thirty-five years. Retirement pensions are generally calculated on the basis of the level of income during the last ten years of payment and the overall length of the period of contribution.

For example, if a person's "full working life" is forty-five years, he or she receives a pension equivalent to about 80 percent of his or her previous net income, which is adjusted on a regular basis to compensate for subsequent increases in the cost of living. A widow receives 60 percent of her late husband's pension.

More than two-thirds of the expenditures for pensions are directly covered by payments of employers and employees into pension funds, and the balance is funded by the federal budget. However, given Austria's liberal early retirement practices and demographic trends, the ratio between the active work force and retired persons in Austria is deteriorating and could reach 1:1 by the year 2020. Because of this trend, experts recognize that a reform of the pension system is inevitable, and the financing of social security benefits, which were introduced under fortuitous conditions of economic and demographic growth in the 1960s and 1970s, is becoming an increasingly pressing issue. A reduction of the level of benefits or the introduction of a "flat-rate" pension, which does not take previous salary and contribution differentials into account, are two possible alternatives.

Health and Health Insurance

In the late 1980s and early 1990s, the most common causes of death were cardiovascular diseases, followed by cancer. Accidents were the next most common causes of deaths in males. Respiratory diseases and liver problems were also significant causes of deaths (see table 8, Appendix).

The traditional Austrian diet is high in fats, carbohydrates, and sugar. Smoking is common—20 percent of women and 40 percent of men smoke. Most adults regularly consume alcohol, in particular beer and wine. An estimated 250,000 Austrians are alcoholics, and the incidence of alcoholism is twice as high among men as it is among women. As a result of these unhealthy habits, the incidences of cardiovascular diseases and cirrhosis of the liver are among the highest in Western Europe.

Beginning in the mid-1980s, Austrian health authorities attempted to make the general public more aware of the dangers of cholesterol, smoking, and alcohol. The government introduced a program of preventive check-ups under the auspices of various health insurance plans. As of 1990, however, only negligible inroads had been made into traditional patterns of consumption, which were more pronounced among men than women and contributed to the higher incidence of fatal disease and the lower life expectancy of men in Austria.

Austria ranks behind Hungary and Finland as a country with one of the highest suicide rates in Europe. Although some psychologists attribute the high rate to the national psyche—such as an inability to openly carry out conflicts or the tendency to direct aggression toward oneself—there is no generally accepted explanation for this phenomenon. As elsewhere, men in Austria are almost three times more prone than women to commit suicide.

Public health authorities have had to deal with the spread of acquired immune deficiency syndrome (AIDS) since 1983, when the first cases were noted. As of mid-1993, slightly more than 600 Austrians had died of AIDS. The number of those infected with the human immunodeficiency virus (HIV) was not known at that time, but estimates range between 8,000 and 14,000.

By 1990 state-required health insurance covered 99 percent of the population in Austria. Austrians also are required to pay into compulsory health insurance plans, which are similar to pension plans and are funded by employer and employee groups organized by professions. Foreign workers also are covered by these programs. Active employees and the self-employed, their dependents, the retired, and the socially disadvantaged qualify for medical coverage that includes out-patient treatment, medication, some dental work, surgery, and hospitalization in the so-called general class (general wards as opposed to private rooms). With the exception of minimal flat-rate charges for filling prescriptions and 10 percent of the overall charge for the hospitalization of dependents, out-patient and in-patient treatment is free for individuals covered by the health insurance plans.

Out-patient treatment is almost exclusively handled by physicians who have contracts with specific insurance agencies, and patients are free to seek the physician of their choice provided the physician has a contract with the patients' respective insurance agency. Although many physicians are in private practice, the great majority of them rely on these contracts—which regulate fees for services rendered—to generate the income they need to maintain their practices. This arrangement means that Austrian medicine is not "socialized" in the sense that physicians are employees of the state. However, the system is similar to a national health plan insofar as fees are regulated, and there is an exceptionally high degree of coverage for the population at large. A drawback to this system is that because physicians are free to establish their practices wherever they choose, medical coverage is poorer in rural areas than in urban centers.

Folk dancers in traditional dress
Courtesy Austrian National Tourist Office, New York

Family Benefits

Austria maintains an extensive support scheme for families. For example, it is illegal for pregnant women to work eight weeks before their due date and eight weeks after their delivery, and they receive their full net pay during this period. Parents of newborns can take two years of maternity or paternity leave or split the leave time between both parents. They receive a monthly support payment of S5,100 (S7,500 for single mothers or low-income couples) during that time. Employers also are required to rehire them in positions of equal pay and status after the leave period is over. Special payments totaling S15,000 are made for all children between birth and their fourth birthday. In addition, all mothers receive a monthly child-maintenance allowance of S1,400 for children up to age ten, at which time the allowance is increased to S1,650 for children up to age twenty-one if the child is living at home, in school, or unemployed. These payments increase to S1,950 and are made for children up to age twenty-seven if the child is attending vocational training or enrolled in a university program.

Special provisions exist for single-parent and large low-income families. Single mothers and low-income families having more than two children are most likely to be confronted with severe economic hardship, and benefits for many members of these groups need to be improved to prevent them from slipping below the poverty level. However, the policy of providing higher benefits for unwed mothers is controversial. Because unwed mothers who cohabit with their partners receive the same benefits as single mothers, the higher benefits for single mothers create a financial incentive that can encourage illegitimacy. Married couples with children are eligible for fewer benefits and view themselves as disadvantaged in comparison with unwed, cohabiting parents.

Housing

After World War II, Austria's standard of housing was low, a reflection of the historically low quality of urban and rural housing, the poor economic development of Austria in the interwar period, and the destruction during World War II. Overcrowding was widespread, especially in urban centers and among the working classes, and many living units did not have such modern conveniences as running water, toilets, bathing facilities, or central heating. In 1951, for example, only one-third of the country's living units had running water; less than 31 percent had a toilet on the premises; and only 11 percent had bathing facilities. Stoves using coal, oil, or wood as fuel were the most common forms of heating.

Since then, however, Austrian housing has improved considerably. The number of living units has increased by 53 percent, although the population grew by just over 10 percent, and almost all of the living units built since 1945 have all modern conveniences. Furthermore, improvements have been made in many of the living units built before World War II, although there remains a clear gap between the overall standards of old and new buildings. Seriously substandard housing—living units with running water, but without toilets or bathing facilities on the premises—has been reduced to less than 10 percent of the total. Most of this housing is found in cities. Low-income groups, such as the elderly, unskilled workers, and foreign workers, are the most frequent inhabitants of substandard housing.

As of the early 1990s, just over 55 percent of all Austrians owned their own homes or apartments, either as private individuals or under the auspices of ownership cooperatives. The rate of home ownership is higher in rural areas than in urban areas and higher in western and central Austria than in the east. In urban areas, apartment houses are much more common than single-family dwellings. Renting is more common in cities and in eastern Austria. Renters have considerable legal rights that make the termination of leases difficult and that provide for the regulation of rents. The construction and ownership of apartment buildings by the municipal government are common in cities, such as Vienna, which traditionally have social democratic municipal governments.

By 1990 almost 10 percent of Austrians had a "second residence," used predominantly for recreational purposes. These second homes range from garden plots with huts (*Schrebergarten*), located on the outskirts of the cities, to old houses in rural communities and newly built one-family houses in the country.

At the beginning of the 1990s, around 25 percent of an average Austrian household's expenditures was for housing (mortgage or rent and utilities). Another 25 percent went for food (including alcohol and tobacco), and a further 16 percent was spent on transportation (including automobile payments). About 9 percent was spent on furnishings, 11 percent for clothing, education, or recreation, and the remainder for miscellaneous activities.

*   *   *

No scholarly work in English treats Austrian society as a whole. John Fitzmaurice's *Austrian Politics and Society Today* examines the development and roles of Austria's most important sociopolitical organizations. Although they are somewhat dated, a number of chapters from *Modern Austria,* edited by Kurt Steiner, are good historical and in-depth introductions to various aspects of Austrian society. Specific chapters in *Austria: A Study in Modern Achievement,* edited by Jim Sweeney and Josef Weidenholzer, offer a less detailed but more current analysis of many facets of Austrian society. Lonnie Johnson's *Introducing Austria* provides readers with some general insights into the dynamics of the development of Austrian society as a whole.

The Austrian government is responsible for a range of informative publications. The Federal Press Service's small book *Austria: Facts and Figures* is a good overview of the country's society, economy, and politics. The service also publishes a series of brochures in English and German that deal with specific aspects of Austrian society such as immigration, religion, education, and social security. These publications are available from Austrian embassies, consulates, and cultural institutes around the world. The annually revised *Survey of the Austrian Economy* from the government's Austrian Museum for Economic and Social Affairs in Vienna contains some social data. Scholarly publications in German from the Österreichisches Statistisches Zentralamt contain much information about Austrian society. Particularly valuable are *Sozialstatistische Daten* and *Statistisches Jahrbuch für die Republik Österreich,* both of which appear on a regular basis. (For further information and complete citations, see Bibliography.)

Chapter 3. The Economy

Coat of arms of the province of Carinthia

THE AUSTRIAN ECONOMY MIGHT best be characterized by the old German phrase *klein aber fein,* or—in the loose English equivalent—"small but beautiful." Austria is a small European country in terms of gross domestic product, area, and population. Yet, since the end of World War II, it has achieved a remarkable record of growth, even when international conditions have not been at their most favorable. Austria has done this by concentrating on manufacturing the products of the second industrial revolution— such as high-quality machine tools, chemicals, and other producer goods—and exporting them largely to the countries of Western Europe, especially Germany.

Austria has achieved considerable autonomy in many important economic areas. It is almost self-sufficient in food production, largely through careful development and husbanding of resources and through an extensive program of subsidies. Judiciously planned exploitation of the hydroelectric power-generating capacity of the Alps has lessened the country's dependence on imported fossil fuels. Austria has also been able to train an efficient and dedicated work force, although it has come to rely on foreign workers for some essential tasks.

Austria nonetheless remains fully engaged in the European and global economic environment. It must import fuels—especially oil, coal, and gas—and certain industrial raw materials and as a result has had a consistent trade deficit. But, because the country is one of the most attractive states in Europe to foreign tourists, Austria is generally able to keep its current account in balance.

The Austrian government has long recognized that the country and the economy cannot function without trade and without access to other markets and sources. Therefore, Austria has always wanted to join customs unions and free-trade areas. It was a founding member of the European Free Trade Association (EFTA). Because it could not join the European Community (EC), owing to its pledge of political neutrality, it helped form the European Economic Area, out of the EC and EFTA, in late 1992. In 1989 it had applied to join the EC and is regarded as a prime candidate for admission into the organization, known since late 1993 as the European Union (EU), in 1995.

Austria saw many opportunities opening to the East as the Iron Curtain fell and as the former communist economies turned to the West for trade and guidance. As a result, Austria ranks among

119

the top Western nations in opening joint ventures with East European states and has made a variety of trade agreements with those states as well as with the states that had declared their independence from what was Yugoslavia. Some of the links that Austria established and reestablished antedated World War I and thus offer a potential for the re-creation of historical financial and commercial links.

Since the end of World War II, the Austrian economy has functioned in a comfortable niche among the smaller West European states. It has been sheltered from intense international competition because it is only a small market, although the price of many Austrian goods is higher than international prices. The Austrian system of economic and social consensus, characterized by the term *social partnership,* has functioned effectively to permit a high standard of living for its citizens and especially for its labor force. The chambers of commerce, agriculture, and labor, together with the trade unions, have joined and supported a considerable framework of institutions and regulations that make Austria a model for relations between public and private institutions.

Despite its carefully designed and effectively functioning system, the economy has not been immune to external realities. It was severely shaken by the "oil shocks" of the 1970s and by the sharp global recession at the beginning of the 1980s. The accumulation of public-sector deficits imposed a heavy burden of debt service on the economy. Austria's recovery from that recession did not fully begin until the mid-1980s, although the recovery advanced smoothly after that and accelerated during the late 1980s before the economy suffered another recession beginning in 1990.

With the end of the Cold War and the consolidation of Europe, the economy faces the problems of greater exposure to outside influences and potential outside competition. As this opening occurs, the Austrian economy also must cope with the potential buffeting arising from the EU adoption of the Maastricht Treaty as well as with other pressures resulting from developments since the ending of the division of Europe. The Maastricht Treaty's provision for a common European currency could compel West European countries and central banks to pursue more cautious fiscal policies and more restrictive monetary policies than in the past. Although the Austrian government and the central bank have long pursued such restrictive policies in order to keep the country's currency, the schilling, on a par with the German deutsche mark, the pressures on other currencies could intensify while the deutsche mark establishes itself as the dominant currency of Europe. This could jeopardize Austrian markets in the EU.

Austria's membership in the EU could also open Austrian markets more directly to the competition of large West European companies that not only enjoy economies of scale but also are more able than Austrian companies to withstand the rigors of long-term competition. And, the fall of the Iron Curtain has opened Austria to greater competition from Central and East European states having lower production costs. Conversely, Austrian exporters also have a wider playing field on which to show their wares. Thus, Austrian planners have both many opportunities and many problems to contemplate as they try to maintain and extend the prosperity and economic success that their country has enjoyed in the postwar period.

Economic Growth and Government Policy

Historical Background

After World War I and the breakup of Austria-Hungary (also seen as the Austro-Hungarian Empire), Austria faced serious problems of economic and social adjustment in finding a means of livelihood for its 6.5 million people, one-third of whom lived in Vienna. Without an adequate agricultural and mineral base in the territory left to it and with the old trading relations of the relatively self-sufficient empire and customs union broken, Austria found itself without adequate food supplies for its population and without sufficient coal for its industry. At the same time, its industrial capacity was excessive for the reduced home market. Relief credits grudgingly given by the Allies kept the country from complete chaos for a time, but devastating inflation in the early 1920s brought it close to economic collapse. Finally, in 1922, a League of Nations commission agreed on a program of international financial support that brought currency stabilization and a balanced budget.

Under the austerity program that ensued, considerable progress was made toward economic reconstruction. Because of the austerity, however, it was also a period of high unemployment and political and social unrest (see The First Republic, ch. 1). When the worldwide depression that began in 1929 put an end to this brief period of economic progress, Austria was ripe for the disorders of the 1930s and for the annexation (Anschluss) by Germany in 1938 (see The Anschluss and World War II, ch. 1). This takeover brought an unanticipated measure of economic recovery to Austria as a result of the German buildup of war potential. In order to serve Nazi goals of conquest, most of the existing Austrian industries were expanded and modernized, and several new industrial complexes were established.

Austria emerged from World War II with its economy shattered. The loss of life and the damage to industry and transportation had decreased production to only one-third of its prewar level. Reestablishment of the economy was both hampered and helped by the division of Austria into four Allied occupation zones after the war and by the ensuing ten-year period of foreign occupation. The presence of foreign troops encouraged the Austrian people into a more cooperative attitude toward each other and toward their leaders than that which had prevailed in the interwar period. As a result, the uncompromising divisiveness that had dominated Austrian economic, social, and political life between the wars gave way to a spirit of cooperation that extended well after the occupation ended (see Restored Independence under Allied Occupation, ch. 1).

During the occupation, the primary objective of the Soviet Union seemed to have been the exploitation of the Austrian economy. Although the Western Allies had successfully prevented the exaction of outright reparations from Austria, they agreed to give the Soviet Union "full and unqualified title" to all German assets in eastern Austria, that is, the part of Austria under Soviet occupation. Soviet leaders put the broadest possible interpretation on the term *German assets* and dismantled and removed to the Soviet Union much of the movable industrial equipment. Fixed installations were formally confiscated and put into production to serve Soviet interests. When the occupation ended with the signing of the State Treaty in May 1955, the Soviet Union had under its control some 450 firms with 50,000 employees—about 10 percent of the Austrian industrial labor force. Under the terms of the treaty, Austria agreed to make reparation payments to the Soviet Union in oil, other goods, and cash to compensate for the return of these Soviet-controlled assets. The payments, which were completed in 1963, totaled S7.1 billion (for value of the schilling—see Glossary).

The Western Allies, in contrast, invested considerable effort, money, and material under United States leadership in reconstructing the Austrian economy. The initial effort consisted primarily of relief goods channeled through the United Nations Relief and Rehabilitation Administration (UNRRA). This program, involving over US$300 million from the United States alone, was replaced in 1948 by the European Recovery Program (commonly known as the Marshall Plan). Under the plan, the United States provided US$962 million in aid in the form of consumer goods, raw materials, and capital equipment. The total amount of foreign aid received by Austria between 1945 and early 1955 was US$1.6 billion.

The contrasting policies of the Soviet Union in the eastern zone and those of the Western Allies in the rest of Austria had significant

Vineyard at Retz in the province of Upper Austria
Courtesy Embassy of Austria, Washington

implications for the future of the Austrian economy. In the first place, most United States aid went for economic reconstruction in the Allied occupation zones, rather than in the Soviet areas, to prevent its suffering the fate of capital assets already in Soviet hands. This meant, in turn, the creation of employment opportunities in western Austria that, together with the more relaxed living conditions and political freedoms, stimulated a steady movement of the population westward from Soviet-occupied eastern Austria. Thus, the industrialization of the Austrian hinterland, which had started for military purposes during the Nazi occupation, was further advanced. Finally, the more constructive behavior of the Western Allies encouraged cooperation with Austria's coalition government and created an atmosphere of continuing cooperation, virtually guaranteeing a Western orientation for Austria's economic policies after the occupation.

Within the limited scope of economic matters left for Austrian determination during the occupation, two major developments carried over into the postoccupation period and had significant influence on the future course of the economy. The first was the nationalization of a large segment of Austria's heavy industry. The second was the establishment of a mechanism for coping with inflationary pressures through joint agreements on wages and prices reached by the representatives of business, agriculture, and labor.

The nationalization acts of July 26, 1946, and March 26, 1947, were designed to effect the systematic reconstruction of the basic materials industries after the heavy damages suffered during the war, to channel their output and services toward the reconstruction of other elements of the Austrian economy under impartial government direction, and to maintain some degree of Austrian control over these assets during the occupation. Although the Soviet Union objected to the nationalization laws insofar as they applied to former German properties, the other Allies were able to override Soviet efforts to block these laws. The Soviet Union did prevent their application in the Soviet Zone. As a result, about half the enterprises there, including the entire petroleum industry, were kept from Austrian control until after the occupation ended.

About seventy industrial enterprises and plants were selected for nationalization. The enterprises and plants included the most important lignite mines, the largest iron and steel works, the nonferrous metals mining and smelting works, the most important petroleum extraction and processing installations, a number of firms involved in steel construction and in mechanical engineering, a major chemical concern, and a major shipping company. Outside the manufacturing sector, the three largest credit institutions and the most important electrical energy installations were also nation-alized.

The problem of compensation to the former owners, which had been left undetermined by the original legislation, was covered by laws passed in 1954 and 1959. Under this legislation, compensation was largely covered by issuing federal bonds to the former owners. These bonds, together with the small cash sums paid out, amounted to about S515 million.

The second economic event of fundamental importance was establishing mechanisms to settle wage-price disputes. The initial wage-price agreements were stimulated by unusual inflationary pressures in 1947, which had increased prices nearly threefold since the end of the war. Possibly with the specter of the inflationary period of the early 1920s in mind, four key interest groups—the chambers of commerce, agriculture, and labor and the Austrian Trade Union Federation (Österreichischer Gewerkschaftsbund—ÖGB)—joined forces. They established the Economic Commission, negotiated a schedule of fixed prices for essential goods and services, and adjusted wages and pensions to that schedule. Although the Economic Commission had no legal standing and compliance was voluntary, the first of these agreements, covering the period from August through October 1947, was sufficiently successful to lead to a series of renewals over the next four years. These agreements slowed, but did not stop, the rate of inflation, which averaged 35 percent annually until 1951. Additional stabilization measures were necessary that year, including credit restrictions, an increase in the bank rate, and such fiscal measures as cuts in government spending and increases in taxes. Most important, however, these measures were accompanied by voluntary price reductions and a postponement of wage demands arrived at through the wage-price agreement procedure. This brought a degree of price stability, in marked contrast to the inflationary explosion of the comparable period after World War I.

At the time of the signing of the State Treaty in May 1955, the economy had largely recovered from the effects World War II. The gross domestic product (GDP—see Glossary), in constant prices, had more than doubled since 1946, the first full year of peace, and was 47 percent above that of 1937, the last full year of Austrian independence. Although industrial facilities in the Soviet Zone that had been returned to Austrian control were in poor condition—particularly the oil fields—most of the industrial structure in the Allied occupation zones had been revived and modernized, largely through the application of Marshall Plan funds. Relative price stability had been achieved, and the 1955 unemployment rate of

5.8 percent, although high by subsequent standards, was at least an improvement over the 1953 rate of 8.8 percent and was tending downward. Finally, Austrian independence arrived at a time of growing European prosperity as the full effects of the Marshall Plan were being felt. Thus, Austria was able to take its place in the economy of Western Europe and to share in the prosperity that characterized the postwar period.

Developments During the 1970s and 1980s

After a relatively smooth course throughout the 1960s, Austria was deeply affected by several international developments during the early 1970s. Like the Federal Republic of Germany (West Germany), it revalued its currency upward by 5 percent, but this proved insufficient in light of the weakness of the United States dollar.

In August 1971, when the Bretton Woods system (see Glossary) collapsed and the price of gold was no longer maintained at US$35 per troy ounce, the Austrian government reaffirmed its decision to maintain the stability of the schilling even if it meant a potentially deteriorating competitive position with the dollar. Thus, the schilling remained closely linked to the deutsche mark through the interest rate policies of the Nationalbank (the Austrian central bank).

The Austrian economy could not help being affected, however, by the subsequent turmoil in international trade and finance, the "oil shocks," inflation, and the downturn at the end of the 1970s. By 1975 growth had slowed and inflation had risen because of higher fuel prices. Unemployment had begun to increase and would have risen faster if government-owned industries had not made an effort to maintain employment. The current account, which had remained in balance for most of the postwar period, deteriorated significantly. In addition, the budget deficit rose.

In 1979 and 1980, the Austrian economy began to improve somewhat. Growth resumed and unemployment fell. But exports did not rise as hoped, the budget deficit remained high, and the boom was short-lived. Another downturn appeared, to be overcome only at the expense of considerable fiscal stimulus in 1983 and 1984 when the government budget deficit rose from 4 to 5.5 percent of GDP. After several years of high deficits, the cost of servicing the national debt began to serve as a brake on further expansionary fiscal policies. Although unemployment remained low by the standards of other industrialized states and although the Austrian economy came through the various crises better than most economies, these developments provided little consolation for most Austrians. The only good news was that exports were rising, although the current account remained negative as the strength of the dollar drove energy import costs sharply upward.

It was only in 1985, well after global interest rates had declined from their post-1980 highs, that the economy began moving forward again at an acceptable pace. Even then, growth came more slowly and unevenly than in the 1950s and 1960s, in part because the expense of servicing the accumulated public deficit (which by then had risen to almost one-half of GDP) remained a brake on the economy as a whole. When rapid growth resumed in 1988, it took many observers by surprise. At that point, the rising trend of unemployment experienced since 1981 began to decline, and the volume of investment and exports grew sharply.

The New Policies

In 1987 the government had decided that the Austrian economy needed certain structural reforms if it were to remain competitive in Europe and in the world. The new coalition government, formed by the Socialist Party of Austria (Sozialistische Partei Österreichs—SPÖ) and the Austrian People's Party (Österreichische Volkspartei—ÖVP), was spurred to take action as a result of two significant factors: the passage by the European Community (EC—see Glossary) of the Single European Act, designed to lead to a much closer economic union of EC member states; and Austria's poor growth rate, which lagged behind that of the European members of the Organisation for Economic Co-operation and Development (OECD—see Glossary). Those reforms were aimed principally at fiscal and financial stability for the government sector and at greater efficiency for the private sector. The government later reinforced these measures in order to meet the requirements for establishing the European Economic Area (EEA—see Glossary).

The measures included steps aimed at reducing the fiscal deficit as a share of GDP. The budget deficit began to be brought down to the target level of 2.5 percent of GDP, although somewhat more slowly than the planners had hoped. The government also announced a comprehensive restructuring of the state-owned Austrian Industries, the giant national company that had taken over most of the heavy industry left to Austria by the retreat of the Germans after World War II.

The restructuring efforts moved apace for several years after the government decision of 1987. The single most important area from the standpoint of the government was the reduction of the evergrowing federal share of the economy. A series of measures were implemented to cut the federal share of GDP from 23 to 21 percent and to reduce the provincial and municipal governments' share of GPD from 17.4 to 16.8 percent between 1986 and 1990.

One of the principal objects of reducing the size of the federal government was to control the interest burden of the government sector, a burden that had risen rapidly during the early 1980s. Another was to reduce the government sector's gross indebtedness. The first of these measures had little effect because the interest burden had risen from 18.0 percent of total government tax revenues to 23.5 percent by 1991. The second measure was more successful because the ratio of the new deficit to GDP stabilized at about 2.5 percent, but the government sector's gross indebtedness nonetheless continued to rise, reaching the level of 56.5 percent of GDP by 1991. For a government that contemplated joining the EC and the European Monetary Union (EMU—see Glossary), that level was dangerously high. It was almost as high as the limit of 60 percent that the EC had set in December 1991 as the maximum level acceptable for states that wished to join the EMU.

One reason the government had difficulty managing its own budget was that more than 85 percent of the central government budget expenditures were committed to nondiscretionary items, such as civil service salaries and social security benefits. The government consistently found itself severely constrained in trying to reduce or even to control the remaining discretionary elements.

As for Austrian Industries, some reduction in personnel was accomplished as part of the reform, but the slump in global steel and chemical markets left considerable uncertainty as to whether more restructuring might not be needed. Privatization also made some headway with the sale of the mint to the Nationalbank in 1989 and a reduction in the government's share in Austrian Airlines and several major financial institutions.

While efforts to amend and strengthen the cartel law to increase domestic competition moved slowly at first, certain steps were taken. Among them was the decision to adapt the public monopoly regulation to the standards of the EEA. In November 1991, the last foreign-exchange controls were lifted, thus opening the economy further to foreign competition in financial services and liberalizing cross-border financial transactions. The new Stock Exchange Act of 1989 was designed to increase openness and flexibility.

The most difficult objective of structural reform was reducing government subsidies. Some success was achieved between 1987 and 1990, when federal subsidies as a percentage of GDP fell from 2.2 percent to 1.9 percent and when general government subsidies dropped from 2.9 percent to 2.4 percent. But questions arose as to whether progress of this kind could be continued.

Nonetheless, the government was able to enact a major reform in the tax system in 1989. The reform entailed gross tax reductions of about S45 billion. It lowered personal income tax schedules, reducing the top rate from 62 to 50 percent and the lower rate from 21 to 10 percent, while widening the tax base. The reform also abolished the progressive corporate tax schedule and adopted the earlier 30 percent bottom rate as the standard corporate tax rate (compared with the earlier top rate of 55 percent). The tax reform raised incentives and spurred growth.

European integration played a central role in the drive toward structural reform of the Austrian economy. The EEA treaty's provisions on regulation and liberalization forced far-reaching changes in the form of increased economic opportunities and competition. It also forced the removal of many barriers that had sheltered important sectors from international competition, especially nontariff barriers.

Importantly, unit labor costs—which had almost doubled during the 1970s—held steady throughout much of the 1980s, peaking in 1987 when the new reforms were announced. By the end of the 1980s, lower labor costs had improved the competitive position of Austrian exporters to a level they had not enjoyed for some time. Wages and salaries per unit of output, which had risen steadily from a scale of 100.0 in 1970 to a scale of 205.9 by 1982, rose only gradually to 216.3 in 1987 and then declined to 208.2 in 1990.

Austria's economic environment changed dramatically during the late 1980s and early 1990s with the opening of the Iron Curtain. Many of the trade agreements that Austria had made with formerly communist states behind the Iron Curtain suddenly became null and void, opening new opportunities but also requiring Austrian resources to help invest in those states as well as to offer credit in order to finance exports. In addition, Austria lost some export markets because the German economy registered a sharp decline in the early 1990s as the cost of German unification had to be financed largely by debt and as the German central bank (the Bundesbank) began raising interest rates to reduce the risk of inflation.

The loss of export markets affected Austria adversely, as did the spillover effect of high German interest rates on Austria's own interest rates. GDP growth fell from 4.6 percent in 1990 to a level of only 2.0 percent in 1992 and was expected to decline further. Unemployment rose, especially among foreign workers. Although it appears likely that the recession will not be as long as that of the early 1980s, the slump again shows that Austria remains tied to developments in neighboring countries and cannot rely entirely on its own resources and policies in an uncertain global environment.

The Magic Pentagon

The Austrian government and Austrian economic institutes and analysts have long evaluated the country's economic policies and general economic situation on the basis of five standards, which are termed the *magic pentagon:* keeping the GDP growth rate as high as possible; maintaining the current account balance as high as possible; keeping employment as high as possible; holding down the inflation rate as much as possible; and keeping the government deficit as low as possible. The objective of government policies is to keep some of these measures as high as possible and some as low as possible. Austrian statistics sometimes show the five different objectives as five arrows emanating from a central core, with lines connecting the current statistics on each of those arrows so that they form a pentagon. The purpose of government policy is to make the pentagon as large as possible, recognizing that there might at times be some required trade-offs among the different objectives.

One of the most important elements in the policy mix is a determination to combat inflation—not an easy task, especially given the significant fiscal deficits during parts of the 1970s and 1980s. To fight inflation and keep the schilling strong and stable, the government relies heavily on attaching the schilling to the deutsche mark and following the policies of the German Bundesbank. These practices, on the whole, have kept inflation at acceptable levels. Low inflation has tended to reduce the demands for higher wages. Consumer price increases held steady around the late 1980s but crept up in the early 1990s to 3.3 percent. Producer prices increased at a slower rate, but wages rose even faster. As a result of the government's policy, Austria has had one of the lowest inflation rates in Europe, and the schilling has consistently been one of Europe's strongest currencies.

The Subsidy Policy

Austrian federal subsidies, both direct and indirect, stabilized as a share of GDP during the late 1980s. Direct subsidies were estimated to average about 0.4 percent of GDP, and indirect subsidies were estimated at about 1.3 percent of GDP. The subsidies began changing during the late 1980s from generally defensive subsidies intended to preserve traditional industries to more specifically

The Liebherr plant at Bischofshofen in the province of Salzburg produces
high-quality industrial equipment.
The General Motors plant outside Vienna
Courtesy Luftreportagen Hausmann, Vienna, and ICD Austria, New York

131

targeted programs such as special subsidies for research and development, innovation, and environmental protection. The Innovation and Technology Fund was established, and in 1989 the government conducted a special review to reduce subsidies to certain traditional industries and to tourism.

Agricultural subsidies were well below the EC average during the late 1970s, but they rose during most of the 1980s. By the end of the decade, they had reached a level slightly above the EC average. In addition, the government subsidized investment and debt service for nationalized industries and covered occasional losses for those industries.

To reduce the burden of the nationalized companies on the state budget, the government began a systematic effort to privatize its share in those companies in the late 1980s. Some of the privatization efforts included the sale of the mint to the partially privately owned Nationalbank. The government's share in Austrian Airlines was reduced to a small majority ownership, and 49 percent of the state electricity company was sold. The federal government's share in the Creditanstalt-Bankverein and the Österreichische Länderbank was reduced to 51 percent. In other instances, however, privatization took place through the sale of state assets to other government-owned or government-directed organizations, rather than to the private sector. For this reason, the program did not generate as much income as originally anticipated.

The level of regulation and subsidization, combined with the significant national ownership of major industries, makes production and consumption costs high. On average, consumer prices in Austria are between 10 and 20 percent higher than in European Union (EU—see Glossary) member states. They are even higher than in Germany, which is also noted for its high prices. Direct comparisons indicate that productivity in Austria is lower than in Germany but that markups for consumer retail sales and profit margins in the distribution system are higher.

These figures raise a number of important questions for Austrian economic planners as they prepare for the economic unification of Europe after the collapse of the Soviet Union's satellite system. The competitive pressures against Austrian producers and workers will likely increase in a widened EU, especially if states having low costs, such as those of Eastern Europe, are admitted.

Foreign Workers in Austria

One of the constant factors on the Austrian manufacturing scene since the 1960s has been the employment of foreign workers. Some of them were refugees from Eastern Europe who chose to remain in Austria and were permitted to do so. Others were from Turkey or farther away. In 1973 the number of foreign workers had reached some 227,000, or about 8.7 percent of the work force. After that, as Austria's own boom began to slow after the first "oil shock" and the global slowdown during the mid-1970s, the Austrian government began reducing the number of foreign workers to protect the positions of Austrian workers. In 1978 the number of foreign workers had been reduced to about 177,000. In the 1980s, the number had dropped to approximately 140,000 to 150,000, or about 5 to 6 percent of the labor force. As in other West European countries, foreign workers in Austria performed and continue to perform many tasks not wanted by Austrian workers.

The number of foreign workers began rising rapidly in 1989, as the borders with Eastern Europe became more porous, and almost doubled by 1990. The number of foreign workers actually peaked during the middle of 1991 at about 280,000, or more than 8 percent of the work force. The Austrian government began taking vigorous border-control and administrative measures in order to prevent further entry of these workers into the labor force. The number began dropping during the last several months of 1991, as it had during the 1970s when the government intervened, but there was no certainty that the government would be as successful during the 1990s as it had been during the 1970s because of the more open borders between Eastern and Western Europe. What was more probable was that the rise in Austrian unemployment during the early 1990s, as a result of the Austrian recession, would reduce the number of foreign workers. The unemployment rate among those workers is higher than among native Austrians. Although certain elements of the Austrian economy, especially hotels and restaurants, cannot function without foreign workers, many Austrians resent the employment of foreigners when many Austrians are without work (see Attitudes Toward Minorities, ch. 2).

Principal Economic Interest Groups

The major participants in the Austrian economy are represented in national economic policy determination by a number of official and voluntary organizations. The most important of these are the chambers of commerce, agriculture, and labor. These are public corporations legally responsible for the representation of the interests of their constituent groups. Because of their legal and official status, membership in the chambers is compulsory for all enterprises, farmers, and wage and salary earners. There are also specialized chambers in various professional fields and in some provinces for agricultural workers, although these chambers are not as important in the operation of the economy.

The chambers function as semipublic bodies with broad responsibilities. For example, before the government can present any draft legislation to parliament, the bill must be sent for appraisal by the chambers. The chambers are organized so that they fully represent each of the appropriate professional and other groups involved in their particular sector of the economy. Because of Austria's relatively small size, the chambers constitute instruments for contact and exchange of information at every level of the economy. Therefore, they function not only as pressure groups from the outer reaches of the economy toward the center but also as communication belts that relay the decisions from the center to the regions.

Several other important voluntary organizations also play significant roles in economic policy decisions. These include the Austrian Trade Union Federation (Österreichischer Gewerkschaftsbund— ÖGB), an umbrella organization representing labor; the works councils that represent labor in enterprises; and the Federation of Austrian Industrialists (Vereinigung Österreichischer Industrieller—VÖI), representing management.

The Chambers of Commerce

Originally established under the Habsburg Empire in 1848, the modern chambers of commerce operate under legislation passed in 1946. They serve as the legal representatives of all persons engaged in crafts (small-scale production), industry, commerce, finance (banking, credit, and insurance), transportation, and tourism. Each of these six functional activities is handled by a separate section within the nine provincial chambers and in the parent body, the Federal Chamber of Trade and Commerce, commonly referred to as the Federal Economic Chamber (Bundeswirtschaftskammer). The most important functions of the chambers arise from their authority to interpret laws and regulations affecting the interests of their members and from their right to advise the Nationalrat (National Council) and review draft legislation.

The Chambers of Agriculture

The chambers of agriculture are the principal bodies representing agricultural interests. There is no federal body comparable to the Federal Economic Chamber, but the Conference of Presidents of the Chambers of Agriculture is the de facto representative of the nine provincial chambers in all matters undertaken at the national level. The provincial chambers, in addition to their representational role, function at the local level to modernize and promote agricultural production.

The Chambers of Labor

The chambers of labor, which are public corporations, differ from the labor unions, which are private voluntary organizations, principally in their official character. They were legally established in 1920 to give labor what employers had had since 1848 in the chambers of commerce and thereby to provide labor with a representative voice in the preparation of legislation affecting employees' social, economic, vocational, and cultural interests. The principal governmental function of the chambers is to advise on draft legislation and administrative regulations directly or indirectly affecting labor. Thus, the fields in which they are concerned can include food supply, public health, tariffs and trade, use of leisure time, adult education, employer-employee relations, job safety, social insurance, and the labor market.

Labor, like agriculture, has no chamber at the federal level. The Vienna chamber, however, carries out most of the federal-level functions and maintains a general secretariat for the Chamber of Labor Conference (Arbeitskammertag). This body consists of a large staff of experts having advisory roles in economic policy, statistics, law, and consumer protection.

The Professions

The Regulation of the Professions (Gewerbeordnung) plays as important a role as do the chambers. The term *Gewerbe,* which can theoretically mean any kind of economic activity except large-scale production and services, is a concept that descended to modern Austria from the medieval system of crafts, guilds, and services. The term has no English equivalent but can best be described as the exercise of a particular profession or economic activity.

The Gewerbeordnung is a system of regulations that ensures a profession is exercised in a prescribed manner. The system, which regulates about 220 forms of economic activity, establishes standards covering the following: entry into a profession; operating regulations; methods for limiting price competition; rules governing permissible advertisement; exclusive franchises and licenses; shop-opening and price competition rules; market access controls; capital requirements; and local monopolies. In a variety of instances, the rules also provide for exemption from cartel law regulations (although the cartel law does not prohibit cartels but their abuse). Firms covered by these and similar regulations account for about 40 percent of total value added and investment in Austria and 45

135

percent of total employment. These firms are involved in such matters as professional services, wholesale and retail trade, insurance, banking, capital services, telecommunications, energy, and transportation.

The effect of the rules is to reduce competition in certain fields and to shelter those already admitted in these fields from excessive access as well as predatory practices by others, especially by larger firms. In a small country such as Austria, with many small villages and communities, the system serves largely to preserve the existing structure of economic activity and the position of local service providers who were established first in a community. It also protects consumers and others against fraudulent or unqualified service providers.

The chambers are the principal instruments that obtain protection or other forms of sheltered operation, largely because the chambers participate actively in the political process and are in the best position to make group or sector concerns felt at the national or provincial level. Some of these arrangements, such as sectoral support programs for transportation, mining, cement, or paper, are still in effect, while others, such as those for textiles, clothing, leather, and paper, have been abolished.

The Austrian Trade Union Federation

Although union membership is not compulsory, about three-fifths of employed persons belong to one of the fifteen major labor unions. These fifteen unions constitute the Austrian Trade Union Federation (Österreichischer Gewerkschaftsbund—ÖGB). The total membership of the ÖGB was more than 1.6 million persons at the end of 1991.

The fifteen unions making up the federation represent four major groups: nine unions represent skilled and unskilled workers organized by industry, including farm and forestry workers; four unions represent public employees, including transport and communications workers; one union serves the arts and professions; and another union, the second largest in membership, represents private white-collar salaried employees. Because the latter is the only union not organized on industry lines, all wage earners in an enterprise ordinarily belong to the same union. The smallest union, the Union of Arts, Journalism, and Professions, had 16,310 registered members in 1989. In the same year, the largest union, the Union of Commercial, Clerical, and Technical Employees, had 340,348 registered members.

Works Councils

In addition to the trade unions, and theoretically separate from them, are the works councils, which exist at the plant level as the elected representatives of all plant employees, whether or not they are union members. According to law, the works councils look after the economic, social, health, and cultural interests of employees. This, in practice, means involvement in matters of discipline, safety, sanitation, dismissal, and transfer, as well as the handling of grievances and the implementation of collective bargaining agreements. Works councils in corporations also have a voice in management, electing two members to the corporate board of directors with all the rights and duties of other directors.

Although these various bodies representing labor are theoretically separate, they work closely together, not only because of overlapping interests and responsibilities but also because labor leaders tend to be functionaries of both the unions and the chambers. At higher levels, they are frequently members of parliament as well. At lower levels, the elected members of the works councils in the plants are almost invariably union members and are usually union officials as well.

Despite an apparent superfluity of bodies representing the interests of labor, the division of primary responsibilities between them is fairly clear. The chambers represent a worker's interest on the economic policy level, the works councils are concerned with a worker's everyday interest at the plant level, and the unions serve primarily as collective bargaining agents. In this function, a specific union usually conducts the actual negotiations, and the ÖGB has the ultimate power of approval and reserves for itself the negotiating authority for agreements that pertain to all employed persons.

The Federation of Austrian Industrialists

The principal private-sector organization is the Federation of Austrian Industrialists (Vereinigung Österreichischer Industrieller—VÖI), founded in 1941. In the late 1980s, its membership consisted of about 2,400 firms employing about 420,000 persons. Although the VÖI does not have the legal status of the Federal Economic Chamber, it occupies one of that chamber's two seats on the Social and Economic Affairs Committee of the Parity Commission for Prices and Wages (commonly known as the Parity Commission). Because the VÖI represents the interests of most large-scale private-sector industry, it essentially controls the industry sector of the Federal Economic Chamber. It also deals directly on behalf of its members with the appropriate ministries and committees of the Nationalrat. Like the chambers, the VÖI submits recommendations on proposed legislation. It is also active in handling relations between domestic industries and foreign industrial associations.

Social Partnership

After World War II, the government, as well as industry and the trade unions, realized that the country could not afford to repeat the continuous social, political, and economic conflict that marked the 1920s and 1930s, when the country moved from one crisis to another until Adolf Hitler's Anschluss in 1938. They wanted to avoid ruinous social and industrial conflict, strikes, lockouts, and the kind of persistent social battles that had contributed to the paralysis of the Austrian economy and its body politic during the interwar years.

To find a solution, the government and its political and economic institutions reached back to earlier concepts that also had an influence on Austrian thinking and Austrian history. One was the papal encyclical *Rerum Novarum* of 1891, which had envisaged a working class that would be gradually absorbed into a property-owning class, not through social conflict but through constructive social cooperation. Another was the Austrian tradition of the Labor Advisory Council (Arbeitsbeirat), which had functioned as a section of the Ministry for Commerce from 1898 to the outbreak of World War I and which offered a model for the pragmatic participation of the labor movement in the functions of the state and the general direction of the economy.

After World War II, these concepts coincided with the practical exigencies of the moment to force representatives of social groups to work together to cope with the combination of unemployment, inflation, and widespread poverty and misery. The ÖGB and the reestablished business organizations of the three main economic chambers played central roles in working out a series of wage-price agreements between 1947 and 1951. Those agreements, and the negotiations that led to them, were based on a mutual recognition that no social group could benefit if it imposed its demands at the expense of the collapse of the state and its economy—a collapse that often seemed all too near in the immediate postwar years.

The social partnership system works on the basis of a mutual recognition of three principles. The first is that the three main economic groups—industry, agriculture, and labor—will be properly represented through four mutually recognized organizations—the chambers of commerce, agriculture, and labor, and the ÖGB— that represent their interests and that can take the responsibility for decisions. The second is that economic decisions can be legitimately made outside the ideologically competitive political atmosphere of parliament, thus in effect depoliticizing crucial matters related to the Austrian standard of living. Third, the principle of consensus will function in such a manner that no social group is ignored, and no social group will prolong the struggle once an agreement has been reached.

The core consultative instrument of the social partnership is the Parity Commission. The commission consists of seven members of the government—the chancellor, three ministers, and three state secretaries—and two representatives each from the Federal Chamber of the Economy, the Presidential Conference of the Austrian Chambers of Agriculture, the Council of the Austrian Chambers of Labor, and the ÖGB. This distribution of seats on the commission gives the interest organizations a majority. Experts in various areas attend the meetings in an advisory capacity. The Parity Commission's decisions must be unanimous, because the commission is not based on law, and participation is completely voluntary.

The Parity Commission began its work in 1957 on the basis of an exchange of letters between the president of the Federal Chamber of the Economy and the president of the ÖGB. Its original purpose was to slow down a troubling wage-price spiral, but it later expanded into much broader discussions on the general trends of the European and Austrian economies and what would be the best response to these trends. The commission has subcommittees on wages and prices. In addition, the commission includes the Advisory Committee for Economic and Social Questions, which was established in 1963 to provide the basis for an objective approach to economic policy and to conduct studies required by the Parity Commission.

The Parity Commission, however, only deals with the central questions of the economy. It establishes the general principles for solving economic problems and disagreements. Below it, at the industry level, the interest-group associations of the various chambers or the trade unions negotiate the separate and legally binding agreements governing employers or employees. The agreements are reached on the basis of the broad principles and criteria set by the Parity Commission.

Some forms of social partnership involve little or no participation of government organs. The so-called self-administration associations require the cooperation of interest associations in such structures as social insurance institutions, agricultural boards, labor-market bodies and tribunals, and in other institutions where agreements between potentially conflicting interest groups must be reached. Those institutions more often deal with social than with economic questions, but the participants in the negotiations usually evaluate the broad economic situation and the policies agreed on in the Parity Commission as they negotiate.

Beyond the mechanics of the Parity Commission and the bitter memories of futile class conflict, however, other elements also work to produce an atmosphere of cooperative consciousness. One of these elements is the virtually universal recognition by all Austrians that theirs is a small state and a small economy in a world full of larger and potentially more competitive actors. Austria cannot afford self-indulgence because it would immediately risk its survival.

Another cause for cooperation rather than unbridled competition is the large public and foreign ownership of Austrian firms. At the beginning of the 1990s, state-owned firms constituted a total of 32.8 percent of all Austrian companies, and foreign-owned firms constituted an additional 25.1 percent, leaving only about 35 percent in private hands, with an additional 7 percent in scattered holdings.

The Austrian trade union movement is forced to moderate its demands for wage increases because of the close affiliation between the Austrian schilling and the German deutsche mark. The stability policy of the German Bundesbank thus also has an effect in Austria. Given this fact, the trade unions cannot usually argue that runaway inflation threatens the standard of living of the Austrian worker.

The social partnership has been successful in maintaining a cooperative spirit and in avoiding industrial strife. After World War II, for example, Austria had fewer strike-minutes lost per worker than any major economy. In many years, no strikes have occurred at all. However, there has been debate about whether the social partnership and the work of the Parity Commission and other bodies have impeded progress and if stability could become stagnation. The danger exists that new production and communications systems, as well as progressive organizational structures, will not be introduced quickly and that the social partners will find it convenient to protect established jobs and processes rather than to revise or even revolutionize them.

Structure of the Economy

Like other industrial societies, Austria found its agricultural and industrial sectors declining as the services sector expanded (see table 9, Appendix). The change in the relative importance of the sectors was most pronounced during the 1970s. Changes in the 1980s continued earlier trends. Whereas services and industry had nearly

A railroad car manufactured by Jenbacher Werke
Courtesy Austrian Federal Economic Chamber, Vienna

equal shares of GDP in 1970, by 1990 industry's share was less than half that of services. Agriculture's share has declined steadily, so that by 1990 it was no longer significant economically but still had social importance (see The Agricultural Sector, this ch.).

Employment trends have followed shifts in the relative importance of the three sectors (see table 10, Appendix). Agriculture's share of employment fell by more than half between 1970 and 1990. Industry employed about 47 percent of the work force in the late

1960s and 37 percent in the late 1980s. The services sector employed roughly the same portion of the work force as industry in the late 1960s but by the late 1980s employed nearly 60 percent of the work force.

Despite the increasingly powerful role played by the services sector, however, most of the major firms remain in industrial production. Services, like agriculture, are usually performed locally and by medium- or small-sized firms. Thus, a listing of Austria's twenty largest firms in 1991 showed mainly industrial companies, with the exception of such state-owned firms as railroad and postal agencies and several large retail organizations.

Most Austrian firms are small. An analysis of nonagricultural concerns in 1988 showed that well over half the nonfarm labor force was employed by firms with fewer than 100 employees. About 500,000 Austrians worked in medium-sized firms having between 100 and 499 employees, and only 140 firms had more than 1,000 employees.

The largest single enterprise in Austria is Austrian Industries, a holding company created in 1987 to take over and manage the assets that had been nationalized by the Austrian state after World War II. An enterprise of about 75,000 employees, in 1993 it was divided into four branches that respectively managed the steel, metal, petroleum, and diversified operations of the company. The latter includes mining and the manufacture of various kinds of machinery, as well as other less easily classifiable activities of the holding company. As intended, it has moved vigorously to become a competitive enterprise despite its nationalized origins, discarding some unprofitable activities and investing abroad or in Austria in other areas of activity.

The ten largest Austrian enterprises in the early 1990s, based on turnover, were Austrian Industries, Österreichische Post/ Telegrafenverwaltung (national postal service), VÖEST-Alpine (steel), Österreichische Mineralölverwaltung (ÖMV) (petroleum and other mineral resources), Konsum Österreich (KÖ) (retail trade), Österreichische Bundesbahnen (Austrian Federal Railroad), Porsche Holding (vehicles), AL Technologies (diversified), Billa (trade), and Austria Tabakwerke (national tobacco monopoly). Of these enterprises, three are subsidiaries of Austrian Industries, two are state public-service monopolies, and the remainder are owned either by foreigners or by small share holder-members (such as the retail trade firm KÖ). None of these businesses except Austrian Industries has played a significant international role.

With the exception of Austrian Industries, even Austria's largest companies are small on an international scale. Only four Austrian companies were listed in the *Financial Times* "European 500" for 1992. Two were banks, the Creditanstalt-Bankverein (number 215 on the list) and Bank Austria (275). The third was ÖMV (288), the mineral and oil exploration and exploitation arm of Austrian Industries. The fourth was a construction company, Wienerberger Baustoffindustrie (318). Austrian Industries was not listed because it is not a private company. If it had been listed, it would probably have been among the top fifty.

Austria has never had a great entrepreneur-capitalist tradition. Many firms function within the Austrian market or within regions. In part because of the bitter experiences of inflation and the depression between the world wars, most Austrians do not attempt risky ventures but instead concentrate on geographic areas or on specific products where success is fairly certain. One of the challenges facing Austrian enterprises as they move into the European Economic Area (EEA) and into the European Union (EU) Single Market will be competing effectively against the giant firms that operate throughout Europe and have many more resources than virtually any Austrian firm could hope to command.

The Agricultural Sector

Although agriculture's share of the economy declined steadily after World War II, agriculture continues to represent an important element of the economy because of its social and political significance. The Chamber of Agriculture remains on an equal level with the chambers of commerce and labor, although its members produce only a fraction of the GDP that industrial and commercial workers produce.

The Government Role

In Austria, as in most other Western countries, the government has played an important role in agriculture since the end of War World II. The government has concentrated on mitigating social, regional, economic, and even environmental consequences of the sector's decline, as well as delaying the decline itself.

Agricultural policy has been carried out with different objectives and with different laws and policies depending on the times. In the early postwar years, the most important objectives were survival and self-sufficiency. As a poor country, Austria needed to be able to feed itself if its population was to survive.

By the 1950s, however, the policy was changing to a more global perspective, while keeping intact the traditional farm economy. The government wanted to protect domestic production, stabilize agricultural markets, protect farmers' incomes, and improve the sector's ability to compete in Austria and abroad. Increasingly, the government began to believe in the importance of maintaining rural society as an objective in its own right, for social reasons, and to protect the environment and encourage tourism. Because of these aims, agricultural policy, more than any other economic policy, reflects a mixture of economic and noneconomic objectives and concerns. The principal aim, however, is to preserve the existing number of farms as much as possible.

Within the structure of the social partnership, various organizations work to maintain farm incomes and thus farm existence, among them the Grain Board, the Dairy Board, and the Livestock and Meat Commission. These organizations set basic support prices, taking into account domestic costs and local supply and demand, with only weak linkages to world market prices.

The boards and commission use a variety of measures to achieve their broad purposes. Among these measures are import restrictions, such as border controls and entry controls—some of which may be bilaterally negotiated—and variable import duties.

If import restrictions are not sufficient to maintain prices because of excess production, the surplus is exported at subsidized prices (with the subsidies usually coming from federal or provincial authorities). Authorities also apply production controls, such as sales quotas or limits, on the size and density of livestock holdings. Quotas exist for many different products, with the quotas usually fixed on the basis of past production. Price and quality controls and limits also exist, especially with respect to different prices for different grades of wheat or milk. The government can also pay direct income supplements, but these payments are generally restricted to certain mountain farming zones and other equally disadvantaged areas. Subsidies are mainly paid by the federal government but may in some instances be paid by provincial governments.

Because of the complex system of price supports and market access limitations, the exact share of subsidy costs to the government and to consumers is virtually impossible to calculate. Experts estimate that the total cost to the federal and other governments for agricultural and forestry support during the late 1980s was approximately S16 billion a year, a level that would have been roughly at the same level as that of many other Organisation for Economic Co-operation and Development (OECD) governments but slightly higher than the EC average.

The economic research institute Österreichisches Institut für Wirtschaftsforschung (WIFO) estimated after a major 1989 study that about 71 percent of the cost of agricultural support was borne by consumers in the form of higher prices, with the taxpayers carrying the remaining 29 percent through such different programs as direct and indirect federal and provincial subsidies or various kinds of market regulation.

Austria's decision to enter the EU will have certain effects on its agriculture and forestry. Support prices in Austria are higher than those set under the EU's Common Agricultural Policy (CAP), although the two systems are in many ways similar. Austrian government-borne subsidy costs are at about the same level as those in the EU, but consumer-borne subsidy costs are higher, so that food prices in Austria average about 30 percent higher than those in the EU. Full integration into the EU will thus compel a number of adjustments in Austria. These adjustments may be even more severe if they become effective at the same time that some East European countries with lower production costs enter the EU. Much depends, of course, on any reforms that may take place in the CAP.

The Structure of Agriculture

Despite the government's efforts to sustain agriculture, by 1991 not one province had as much as 10 percent of the population involved in agriculture and forestry. At the beginning of the 1970s, all but two provinces (Vienna and Vorarlberg) had more than 10 percent of their populations involved in farming. This contrasted markedly to the situation in 1934, when all but those same two provinces had more than 30 percent of their populations working in agriculture. Over this period of two generations, the decline in the Austrian farm population was as fast as any in the Western world.

Of Austria's total area of almost 84,000 square kilometers, about 67,000 square kilometers are used for farming and forestry. Roughly half of that area is forest, and the remainder is arable land and pasture.

Agriculture and forestry accounted for about 280,000 enterprises in 1986, with the average holding being about twenty-three hectares. There were about 4,500 corporate farms. Beyond those farms, however, only a third of all farmers were full-time farmers or farming companies. Over half the farming enterprises were smaller than ten hectares; nearly 40 percent were smaller than five hectares. Just as the number of farmers has long been in decline, so also has been the number of farms.

Family labor predominates, especially in mountainous areas and on smaller farms. Only a third of all farm and forestry enterprises were classified as full-time occupations in 1986. A full half of these enterprises are spare-time, that is, less than half of household labor is devoted to farming or forestry. The remainder are part-time.

Farms up to ten hectares are more often tended by part-time and spare-time farmers rather than by full-time farmers. For most farm owners and workers, nonfarm income is as important as, if not more important than, farm income.

Despite the decline in the number of farmers and agriculture's share of GDP since 1960, agricultural output has risen. As of the early 1990s, Austria was self-sufficient in all cereals and milk products as well as in red meat. This gain was achieved because of the considerable gains in agricultural labor productivity.

The value of agricultural and forestry output is heavily concentrated in field crops, meat, and dairy products, with most of it coming from animal husbandry. Because large parts of Austria are mountainous, only the lowland areas of eastern Austria and some smaller flat portions of western and northern Austria are suitable for crop production and more intensive forms of animal husbandry. The remainder of the land is used for forestry and less intensive animal husbandry, most of which takes advantage of mountain pasturage.

The Industrial Sector

Industry

Industry in Austria is diverse but consists mainly of traditional industries of the second industrial revolution. It is concentrated in various processing industries, each of which has long specialized in its particular sector and had often gained a global reputation for high standards of production and service.

Industry exists throughout the country. Textile production represents the principal industrial activity of the mountainous west, whereas machinery production occurs principally in the east, as does production of glass, electrical goods, and chemicals (see fig. 9). Heavy industry tends to be located around Vienna and in several central river corridors. Iron and steel production is concentrated around Linz and Leoben.

Although industrial production is an important component of GDP, most companies are small and privately owned. Almost half employ fewer than five workers. The larger companies are often state-owned, either directly or through Austrian Industries (see Structure of the Economy, this ch.).

The metals industries, both production and related manufacturing, accounted for 43.1 percent of industrial value added in 1991. Chemicals were the second most important segment with 12.6 percent, followed by foods and beverages with 11.8 percent; forest products and paper with 11.6 percent; textiles, leather, and clothing with 7.7 percent; glass, pottery, and quarrying with 5.3 percent; mining with 4.7 percent; and petrochemicals with 3.2 percent.

Iron and steel are largely produced by Vereinigte Österreichische Eisen- und Stahlwerke (United Austrian Iron and Steel Works), commonly known as VÖEST-Alpine, one of the major components of Austrian Industries. The company pioneered a worldwide steel production method named the LD process (after the Austrian cities of Linz and Donawitz, where it was developed). Iron and steel production in turn formed the basis for other industries, such as mechanical engineering, machine tools, vehicle production, powder metallurgy, factory engineering and construction, and automobile components.

Chemicals and petrochemicals constitute another major industry, producing such items as synthetic textile fibers, pesticides, pharmaceuticals, plastics, and a wide range of fuels. Electrical engineering is another important component of Austria's industry and specializes in the production of precision and optical equipment and generators. Food also constitutes an important industry, ranging from milk produced in the mountains of western Austria to Viennese pastries.

Efforts to Improve Competitiveness

Like many other countries that had concentrated on industrial production and where industrial value added constituted an important element of national production as well as of national exports, Austria had to reevaluate its performance during the 1980s. The government commissioned a special report on the need for structural adjustment, and a number of steps were taken to make Austria more competitive worldwide.

Steps to increase competitiveness include privatization, greater incentives for research, and greater readiness to make decisions about curtailing subsidies where they are not warranted (especially for nationalized industries) and could drain resources from other potentially more competitive industries. Although industrial subsidies are harder to calculate than agricultural subsidies because of their greater range (from direct payments to accelerated depreciation allowances and the like), the government during the 1980s made special efforts to reduce those subsidies and encourage competitiveness. Some of these measures appear to have been at least in part effective, although they were not always carried out as fast as originally planned.

Mining and Minerals

Austria has unusually diverse mineral resources for a small

147

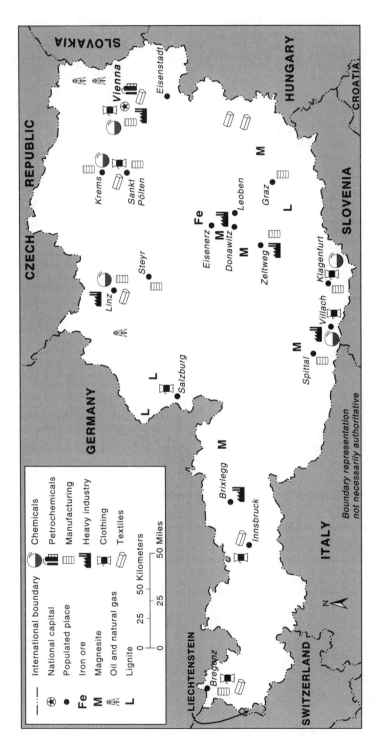

Figure 9. Economic Activity, 1993

country. It is the world's largest producer of magnesite. There are also significant deposits of lignite and iron ore and smaller deposits of wolfram, antimony, gypsum, graphite (lower grade), dolomite, talcum, kaolin, quartz, and salt. Minerals are found throughout the country, but most significant deposits are in Styria or in northeastern Austria.

Mineral production accounted for only about 2 percent of GDP in 1990, having declined steadily in economic importance since World War II. However, it remains a significant source of income and employment in certain mountainous areas and in 1991 consisted of 109 firms employing about 6,700 persons. The principal mineral products in 1990 were lignite (2.4 million tons), iron and manganese (2.3 million tons), magnesite (2.0 million tons), gypsum (753,000 tons), and kaolin (474,000 tons).

Energy

Austria is highly dependent on foreign sources for energy. In the early 1990s, it imported more than four-fifths of the petroleum and petroleum products it needed, four-fifths of the natural gas, and two-thirds of the coal, coke, and briquettes. About two-thirds of Austria's electricity is produced domestically from hydroelectric power plants, but most of the remainder is generated from imported fossil fuels. Despite extensive efforts to reduce power consumption after the first oil shock of 1973, Austrian reliance on foreign sources of power rose from 61 percent in 1970 to 70 percent in 1991. Nearly all imported natural gas comes from Eastern Europe, as does most imported coal.

Policies adopted during the 1970s and 1980s to conserve energy and to use it more efficiently were to some degree successful. Before 1973, for example, Austria's energy consumption exceeded the growth of its economy. In the 1973-90 period, however, the annual increase in energy consumption averaged only 0.8 percent while economic growth averaged about 2.4 percent a year.

Energy policies also aimed at decreasing the country's reliance on oil and coal and at moving more toward renewable and/or cleaner sources. Whereas petroleum, petroleum products, and coal had supplied 73 percent of Austria's energy sources in 1970, by 1990 their share had fallen to 57 percent, while the combined contribution of natural gas and hydroelectric power rose from 23 to 34 percent.

Although real consumption of petroleum and petroleum products has declined, Austria still relies heavily on fossil fuels for energy. In 1991, of the energy consumed, 42 percent came from petroleum and petroleum products, 20 percent from natural gas, and 16 percent from coal. Electricity supplied only 13 percent of the country's power, while wood, scrap, and other sources supplied the remaining 9 percent.

Austria has limited domestic reserves of oil and natural gas. Specialists believe that the entire region north of the Alps may be oil bearing. As of the early 1990s, however, proven deposits of oil and gas were found in Lower Austria, between Vienna and the northeastern border, and in Upper Austria between the Enns and Salzach rivers. Proven and probable oil reserves were estimated in 1992 at 15.0 million tons, while certain and probable gas reserves were put at 17.5 billion cubic meters. Certain and probable coal reserves were estimated at 69.9 million tons.

The county's largest refinery, at Schwechat near Vienna, is operated by the state-owned ÖMV and refines all the petroleum produced in Austria, as well as crude petroleum imported via a pipeline from Trieste, Italy. The state firm exploits deposits in eastern Austria, while a subsidiary of Mobil exploits deposits in western Austria.

By the early 1990s, Austria obtained two-thirds of its electrical energy from hydroelectric power plants. Nearly all the remainder came from thermal power plants fired with fossil fuel. Total electricity power production in 1991 was 45,000 gigawatt-hours, slightly less than the amount of electricity consumed. During the 1980s, Austria had consistently been an exporter of electricity. By the early 1990s, about two-thirds of Austria's hydroelectric power capacity had been harnessed. Austrians decided by referendum in 1978 not to generate power from nuclear fuels, although the country's certain and probable uranium reserves were estimated at about 500 tons (see Domestic Issues, ch. 1).

The Services Sector

Retail Trade

In 1991 wholesale and retail trade accounted for about 12 percent of GDP and provided employment for 435,000 persons, or 14.5 percent of the work force. Even in the early 1990s, retail trade was dominated by small shops, largely because of the many small towns and communities outside Vienna. In all, there were about 17,000 wholesale concerns throughout Austria and about 33,000 retail concerns.

Despite the very large number of small firms in the sector, several retail and wholesale firms are among the twenty largest Austrian companies. Two of these are the grocery store chains Billa and Spar Österreich. Another is Metro SB-Grosshandel, a wholesaler.

*View of the Limberg
Hydroelectric Power
Plant in the province
of Upper Austria
A Drau River power plant in
the province of Carinthia
Courtesy Embassy of Austria,
Washington*

Austria: A Country Study

The country's largest retailer is the cooperative Konsum Österreich (KÖ), formed in 1978 from a number of smaller cooperative
retailers. The company is the latest stage in the Austrian cooperative movement that dates from the mid-1800s. In addition to having hundreds of stores throughout Austria, some of them quite large
and selling many varieties of goods, KÖ is involved in manufacturing some of the products it sells. By the late 1980s, the company
employed about 20,000 persons, and more than 800,000 families
were KÖ members. They received dividends each year and voted
on KÖ's overall policies. In addition to KÖ, there are many other
cooperatives involved in wholesale trade and in purchasing and
marketing. In all, Austrians can shop at more than 1,000 cooperative retail stores.

Transportation and Telecommunications

Austria has a wide variety of transportation services and usage,
reflecting the diversity of its geography and its central location in
Europe (see fig. 10). Because of the mountainous topography, for
decades scheduled nonlocal bus service carried almost twice as many
passengers as rail service (288 million riders versus 168 million riders
in 1990). Air transport is becoming more commonly used and carried 9.1 million passengers in 1992, more than twice as many as
in 1982. Because of its central location, Austria is an important
segment of the European railroad network, and a number of high-
speed international trains pass through the country. The Brenner
Pass has long been the main north-south route from Germany to
Italy. The country's importance in east-west travel is also likely
to increase in the 1990s with the opening of Eastern Europe.

In the early 1990s, Austria's total railroad network amounted
to approximately 6,028 kilometers, of which 5,388 kilometers were
state owned. The standard-gauge (1.435 meter) network is 5,403
kilometers in length, of which 3,051 kilometers are electrified. The
number of electric trains increased during the 1980s, from 35,353
in 1980 to 47,803 in 1992. The number of train passengers remained
steady during the 1980s, amounting to 170 million in 1980 and
175 million in 1992.

The main railroad system is the state-owned and state-operated
Österreichische Bundesbahnen (Austrian Federal Railroad—ÖBB),
which accounts for 90 percent of the country's rail routes. The remainder is managed by nineteen small privately owned railroads
operating primarily narrow-gauge lines with a total length of about
550 kilometers. The ÖBB is pursuing an extensive investment in
modernization, the Neue Bahn (New Railroad) project. Major
projects include the construction of a tunnel under the Alps that

152

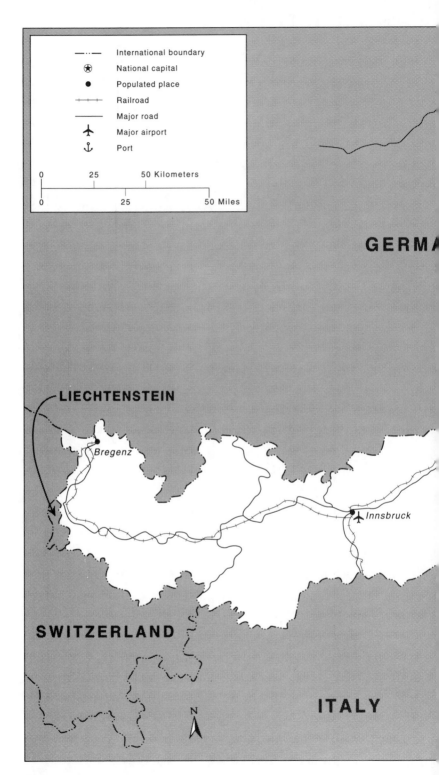

Figure 10. Transportation System, 1993

154

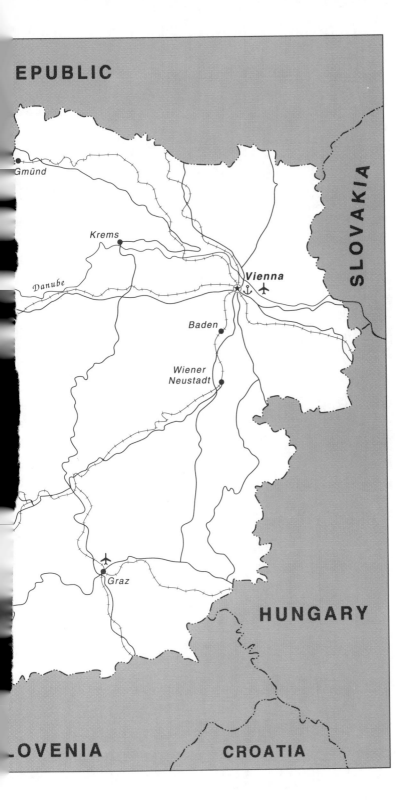

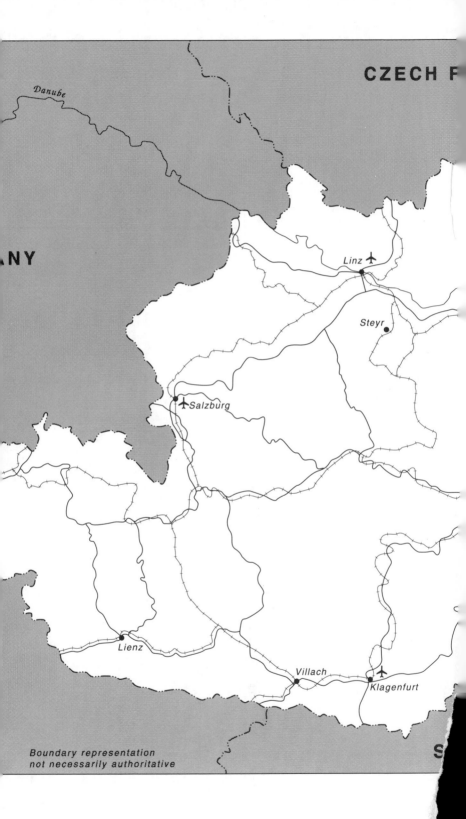

CZECH R

Danube

GERMANY

Linz ✈

Steyr ●

✈ Salzburg

Lienz ●

Villach ●

Klagenfurt ✈

S

would handle north-south traffic between Germany and Italy and greatly reduce the need to use the Brenner Pass. Freight operations have been steadily modernized, especially with the greater use of pallets and rail-container transport. Austria is part of the European Transfer Express Freight Train System.

As of the early 1990s, Austria had about 22,000 kilometers of paved roads. In 1992 there were 3.2 million private automobiles registered, compared with 2.3 million private automobiles in 1982. The increase in the number of trucks in Austria was not as great: 269,000 trucks in 1992, compared with 193,000 in 1982.

An increasing volume of freight is transported by truck. One-fourth of Austria's imports and one-half of its exports are carried by road. The growth of freight transported through Austria has increased greatly, going from 4 million tons in 1970 to 20 million tons in 1990. This traffic has begun to pose a threat to the country's natural environment. Government regulations to counter this threat include limiting the size of international trucks traversing the country, most importantly those traveling between Germany and Italy and the Balkans via Alpine passes, especially the Brenner Pass. The government, with widespread popular support, is also seeking to have freight shipped on the less noisy and less polluting railroad system. Government regulations also limit trucks using Alpine passes at night to 7.5 tons. This ban has been extended to other parts of country.

Transit road traffic poses such a great threat to the environment that part of the agreement with the European Economic Area (EEA) provides for separate negotiations with Austria on traffic volume. An agreement reached in 1992 limited the volume of traffic and also provided for rules protecting Alpine areas.

Austria's inland waterways total only about 350 kilometers. Of the country's rivers, only the Danube is navigable. Vienna has long been a major port on the Danube River. As of 1991, water transport brought in less than 10 percent of the amount of imports and exports transported by road or rail and accounted for only about 5 percent of domestic long-distance freight.

Water transport is likely to become more important in the future, with a related expansion of Vienna's role in river shipping because of the 1992 completion of the Rhine-Main-Danube Canal in Germany. The canal makes possible travel by boat from Rotterdam to the Black Sea. As a result, Europe's inland waterway traffic is expected to triple by the end of the 1990s. The main traffic will likely be in bulk commodities, some of which might be off-loaded in Vienna and transshipped elsewhere. The Vienna port already serves as a principal petroleum and petroleum products terminal because it is linked by an oil pipeline to Trieste. The port of Vienna is equipped with automobile transshipment facilities and a large grain terminal.

Austria has a small national airline. Austrian Airlines is 51 percent state owned and operates throughout Europe and the Middle East, as well as across the Atlantic. It also operates an air freight line, Austrian Airtransport. In addition, there are two smaller privately owned air carriers, Lauda Air and Tyrolean Airways. The latter airline operates from Innsbruck and largely ferries passengers to and from Alpine destinations. Austria's one important international airport is at Schwechat, located near Vienna. Of the smaller airports, Salzburg, Innsbruck, Graz, Klagenfurt, and Linz are the most important and receive international as well as domestic flights.

Telecommunications in Austria are excellent. In 1991 there were 3.3 million main telephone connections, or one for every two inhabitants. International facsimile (fax), data transmission, and telex services are also available. In 1992 there were 2.5 million television sets (black-and-white and color) and 4.7 million radios. The state-owned and state-controlled Austrian Radio and Television (Österreichischer Rundfunk—ORF) is responsible for all broadcasting. In 1992 there were six AM radio stations, twenty-one FM radio stations, and forty-seven television stations. The country's satellite ground stations are linked with International Telecommunications Satellite Organization (Intelsat) Atlantic Ocean and Indian Ocean satellites and with the European Telecommunications Satellite Organisation (Eutelsat) system.

Tourism

Tourism is an important part of Austria's services sector. In 1991 foreign tourists accounted for earnings of S192.4 billion, almost offsetting the negative trade balance and deficits in services or other accounts. Tourism is a principal industry and source of foreign exchange. In fact, Austria's per capita tourist revenue is the highest in the world. Foreign overnight stays in Austria have risen consistently since World War II, from 50 million in 1950, to 59 million in 1970, and to 95 million in 1990. With 20 million visitors in 1990, Austria was fifth in the world in tourist revenues, surpassed only by the United States, France, Italy, and Spain. Most tourists come from European countries. Almost two-thirds come from Germany, followed by the Netherlands (10 percent) and Britain (5 percent).

Austria's largest tourist attraction has long been the Alps—for skiing in the winter and for hiking and camping in the summer. For this reason, the mountainous provinces of Tirol, Carinthia, and Vorarlberg produce the greatest tourist revenues. Salzburg is

Vienna International Airport
Courtesy Luftreportagen Hausmann, Vienna, and ICD Austria, New York

an important tourist attraction in the summer. Vienna remains a tourist center all year but does not generate as much tourist revenue as the mountain areas.

Austria has 20,000 hotels and pensions, as well as an additional 50,000 private rooms available to house tourists. In addition, there are thousands of simpler accommodations, such as youth hostels, mountain huts, and campsites.

Austria has also made significant progress in becoming an international conference center. The so-called United Nations City, located outside Vienna, contains the headquarters of a number of major United Nations (UN) organizations. Vienna also has an international conference center. Taking advantage of Austria's neutral status, Vienna has hosted numerous East-West negotiations and is the permanent seat not only of such long-established organizations as the International Atomic Energy Agency but also of the newer Conference on Security and Cooperation in Europe. The

157

opening of Eastern Europe is likely to make Vienna an even more important center for East-West travel.

Money and Banking

The Austrian banking system is under the broad direction of the Nationalbank, the Austrian central bank, in coordination with the Austrian government. The bank is centralized, unlike the United States Federal Reserve System. It is the bank of issue and enjoys substantial autonomy, while consulting with the Austrian government.

Austria's currency, the schilling, is strong and stable. There was an attempt to float it in 1973, when various global currencies floated after the collapse of the Bretton Woods system, but in July 1976 the schilling was formally pegged to West Germany's currency, the deutsche mark. This policy was abandoned in December 1977, but the schilling remained stable in relation to the deutsche mark through management of short-term interest rates and through careful efforts to control the Austrian monetary supply. In practice, the policy meant that Austria was an informal member of the European Monetary System (EMS—see Glossary) and its exchange rate mechanism (ERM—see Glossary) since their establishment in 1979, and the country was expected to join the European Monetary Union (EMU) under whatever arrangement and timing might finally be agreed.

The principal banks are full-service banks, of which there were about fifty-five with approximately 850 branches at the end of 1991. They transact all kinds of business and also channel credit for all purposes. Many of them function only regionally, but the two largest—the Creditanstalt-Bankverein and Bank Austria—operate throughout Austria. The state owns majority shares in both those banks. Bank Austria, the country's largest bank, was created in 1991 by a merger of Österreichische Länderbank with Zentralsparkasse. This and other mergers could make Austrian banking more competitive within the larger European framework.

The banking system consists of a number of other kinds of institutions as well. These include the ten provincial mortgage banks (*Hypobanken*), with 124 branches in 1989; the savings banks (*Sparkassen*), of which there were about 126 with 1,278 branches in 1988 that function as regular local banks despite their name; the people's banks (*Volksbanken*), of which there were 103 with 323 branches in 1989 that serve small business as commercial credit cooperatives; the agricultural credit cooperatives (*Raffeisenkassen*), of which there were 863 in 1989 with over 1,600 branches; and a small number of private banks and specialized institutions.

The system is locally and regionally based, with savings and credit channeled at the district level; full-service banks serve large companies. The post office system, with over 2,000 branch offices throughout Austria, also plays an important role in household savings. Austria has one of the highest savings rates in the OECD, and most of the funds saved are deposited in the banking system.

Banks play the central role in the Austrian financial system, especially in corporate finance. They carry out not only regular deposit and lending activities but also such other functions as portfolio management and investment advice. Because most savings are deposited in banks, banks are the principal source of funds for business. Austrian banks tend to maintain close relations with industry, especially with the firms to which they have extended credit. Banks are often represented on supervisory boards or, at the very least, play prominent roles in advising firms with respect to business and investment decisions.

Austrian financial markets reflect this situation. There is an important bond market, largely for government and bank issues and for utilities, about eight times as large as the equity market. The debt-to-equity ratio for corporate financing is high, more like the German model than the British or United States model. In the early 1990s, the Vienna stock exchange was a very limited market, although it will probably become more important as the privatization of nationalized companies continues. The money market is also dominated by banks.

Foreign Economic Relations

Foreign Trade and the Balance of Payments

Like any small country, Austria depends heavily on foreign trade. Its central location in Europe reinforces that dependency and gives Austria a wide range of trading partners in both Eastern Europe and Western Europe. Austria also consistently seeks to avoid isolation and has joined international trading systems to ensure markets for its products and access to the goods it needs.

As the economy has evolved and produced a more sophisticated range of products, foreign trade has become more important. Foreign trade made up about one-fourth of GDP in 1955, one-third by 1975, and two-fifths by 1990. Austria's export structure has also evolved. One-half the country's exports were once raw materials, foods, and semifinished goods, but by the early 1990s two-thirds of its exports were finished products. Imports have came to reflect this change and consist mostly of industrial and semifinished goods that require further processing and finishing.

The largest category of exports in 1991 was machinery and equipment, accounting for almost one-third of all exports. Other major items included chemical products, paper and paper products, transportation equipment, metal manufactures, and textiles and clothing. The largest single import item was also machinery and equipment; other items were manufactured products, chemical products, and fuels and energy.

Austria's main trading partners are in continental Europe, especially Germany, Italy, and Switzerland (see table 11, Appendix). Because of a heavy dependence on imports, Austria usually has a negative trade balance, which is compensated for by positive services accounts and capital accounts (see table 12, Appendix). Income from tourism is especially important in reducing the negative trade balance. The trade balance deteriorated particularly during the 1970s because of increased oil prices, and Austria had to make special efforts during the 1980s to redress the balance.

Austria and European Integration

Given its dependence on international trade, Austria has always been interested in some form of customs union. Although it was recognized that there might be some competitive disadvantages in such associations, especially with countries that produced at more competitive prices, the Austrian government and Austrian manufacturers have always been even more afraid of being excluded. They feared that exclusion would prevent them from reaping any economies of scale and would ultimately consign them to an economic backwater.

The government, therefore, was anxious to join in some form of European economic association as several organizations were being shaped after World War II. It could not join the European Community (EC) as it was being formed, however, because of fear that this would violate the 1955 State Treaty prescription for neutrality. The member states of the EC called their organization the Common Market when they created it in 1958, but they made it clear from the beginning that it had a political as well as an economic purpose. Under those circumstances, Austria had to hold back as long as Europe was divided by the Cold War.

However, such considerations did not prevent Austria from joining the European Free Trade Association (EFTA—see Glossary) when it was formed in 1960. EFTA was a purely economic association, and its members included Finland, Sweden, and Switzerland, all neutral states that were not members of the North Atlantic Treaty Organization (NATO). Moreover, EFTA had no intention of becoming anything more than a trade association. EFTA was far from an ideal trading arena for Austria because most of its members were located on the periphery of Europe. EFTA countries came to account for less than 15 percent of Austria's trade, while 66 percent of its foreign trade was with the EC countries.

EFTA, however, did have a very important specific advantage from the Austrian standpoint because it did not require common tariffs. Thus, Austria could retain some control over the conditions under which its foreign trade operated, while expanding its close commercial links with a number of EC states (even as it remained formally outside the EC).

Austria attempted to obtain associate status in the EC despite the political barrier to full membership. As it became clear in the 1960s that some EFTA members, such as Britain, were beginning to edge toward EC membership, Austria began its own negotiations to obtain a special arrangement with the community. In 1972, after ten years of negotiations, Austria and the EC reached an agreement providing for a gradual lowering of tariffs to zero. Austria nonetheless remained outside the EC Common Agricultural Policy (CAP).

The Austrian government applied to join the EC in the summer of 1989, as the Soviet empire was crumbling and Moscow was no longer either disposed or able to use the neutrality restrictions of the State Treaty to bar Austria from membership. Like other EFTA states, Austrian officials agreed in 1991 to the formation of the European Economic Area (EEA) between EFTA and the EC as a preliminary step, but it also wanted to join the organization on its own.

Although Austria will probably not be able to join the European Union (EU)—as the EC came to be known in November 1993— until 1995, by which time the Single Market should be well advanced, the government has taken steps to begin adapting the economy to EC standards. Along with adopting many EC laws and regulations through the EEA in 1991, the government has adopted a number of additional EC rules, including those governing the freedom of capital flows. These measures have been taken to ensure that the social partners and the economy as a whole would not be at a disadvantage when Austria becomes an EU member.

Under the terms of the agreement reached at the EC summit at Maastricht in December 1991, Austria's membership in the EU will also lead to membership in the new European Monetary Union (EMU) if Austria can meet the convergence requirements by 1997. These requirements include a number of features: an inflation rate within 2.5 percent of the three lowest in the EU; long-term interest rates within 2 percent of the three lowest rates; a government deficit below 3 percent of GDP; and a public-sector debt of less than 60 percent of GDP. As of 1993, Austria was able to meet these requirements, but there is no guarantee that that will be the case in 1997.

Austria tied the schilling to the deutsche mark in the 1960s, largely because the country could not function without a predictable exchange rate with its largest trading partner, West Germany. In part to reinforce that linkage, Austria joined the EMS and its ERM in 1979. This membership has meant that Austrian interest rates have matched those of the Bundesbank and, as a result, to all intents and purposes have been set in Frankfurt. Therefore, Austrian adherence to the EMU would be a logical extension of long-established policies, and Austrian currency would become whatever the EMU adopted, whether it is called the European Currency Unit (ECU) or the Euro-Mark as some have proposed.

The link to the deutsche mark has had a major advantage for Austria in that it has given the country a long period of low inflation and the kind of monetary stability that those who suffered through the terrible inflation of 1921–23 well appreciate. It is, however, also a disadvantage for Austria's international competitive position. Goods denominated in schillings, like goods denominated in deutsche marks, cannot count on any sales increases because of devaluation of the currency. In fact, the schilling has consistently increased in value since the end of the Bretton Woods fixed exchange-rate era in 1971. It has generally moved with the deutsche mark vis-à-vis the United States dollar.

Openings Toward the East

Austria had maintained close trade relations with various states of Central and Eastern Europe under the Council for Mutual Economic Assistance (Comecon) arrangements. Those arrangements collapsed at the end of the 1980s and, as of the early 1990s, had not yet been renegotiated. Because of the turmoil in several East European states, for example in the former Yugoslavia, precise trade arrangements will likely require some time to be negotiated.

Nonetheless, Austrian firms have proceeded actively to strengthen their position in Eastern Europe. Austrian firms soon were a major part of the thousands of joint-venture agreements established with Hungary, the Czech Republic, and Slovakia. Austrian firms have also become involved in many joint ventures in the former Yugoslavia, but their fate remains uncertain as long as the region is unstable. Austrian firms have always been well placed in Slovenia and Croatia, both of which were once part of Austria-Hungary, and Austria resumed economic links with them as soon as they became independent in 1992.

Austrian foreign investment, which has always remained closely in balance with foreign investment in Austria, although both had risen over the years, suddenly doubled to $11.4 billion in 1989 and rose to a new high of $18.3 billion in 1990. Much of the new investment was destined for Eastern Europe.

One of the hopes of the government is that many companies wanting to expand their operations in Eastern Europe will establish offices in Vienna. The city offers office space with modern facilities, often at modest prices. As of the early 1990s, a number of companies had set up operations there for these reasons.

In a broader sense, many of Austria's domestic and international policies will need to be adjusted to take into account developments taking place around Austria. Such concerns have been expressed before, by Austrians and by others, but may be more urgent in the future than in the past. The opening toward Eastern Europe and the creation of the EEA and the Single Market have changed the foundations on which Austria has functioned since the 1950s and will present new competitive challenges for production, marketing, and services.

As of late 1993, however, there were no indications that Austria had changed its patterns of behavior and operations, largely because they have been successful. The pressures that might provoke such a revision have not risen to the level where change is imperative. Moreover, if Austria needs to make changes to adjust to new pressures, many arguments could be made that some form of social partnership or social consensus mechanism may be more necessary than ever.

*　　*　　*

As is the case with many small countries, few studies of Austria exist in English, and the economy receives even less attention than other areas. Except for one collection of essays dating back to 1982, *The Political Economy of Austria,* edited by Sven W. Arndt, nothing comprehensive is available on the economy. Even books in other languages are rare, in part because most German-language books are highly technical. Instead, those who want to read about the Austrian economy must look for economic chapters in general texts about Austria, many of which are unsatisfactory.

However, a number of publications exist that contain relatively good information. The most useful are the annual publications of the Organisation for Economic Co-operation and Development that not only contain statistical information but also essays on various basic aspects of the economy. The quarterly and annual surveys published by the Economist Intelligence Unit, *Country Report: Austria* and *Country Profile: Austria,* also offer useful statistical information as well as summary analyses.

A number of German-language periodicals are published in Austria, including some published by major banks and some that are published by the Österreichisches Institut für Wirtschaftsforschung. These periodicals offer some useful up-to-date analyses as well as complete statistics. Thus, although the Austrian economy does not receive the kind of bibliographic attention that larger economies attract, basic information is available and reliable. (For further information and complete citations, see Bibliography.)

Chapter 4. Government and Politics

Coat of arms of the province of Upper Austria

AUSTRIA'S POLITICAL SYSTEM has been a model of stability since democracy was restored in 1945. In contrast to the interwar period, when domestic political rivalries and foreign intervention brought the system of government set out by the constitution of 1920 to a standstill, after World War II this reestablished parliamentary democracy functioned smoothly in what came to be termed the Second Republic.

For most of the postwar period, Austrian politics appeared unique in many respects to outside observers. Between 1945 and 1966, the country was ruled by the so-called grand coalition of the two major parties, the Austrian People's Party (Österreichische Volkspartei—ÖVP) and the Socialist Party of Austria (Sozialistische Partei Österreichs—SPÖ). (In 1991 the name of the latter party was changed to the Social Democratic Party of Austria [Sozialdemokratische Partei Österreichs—SPÖ].) This arrangement appealed to Austria's politicians and people mainly because it symbolized the reconciliation between social groups that had fought a brief civil war before the absorption (Anschluss) of Austria by Nazi Germany in 1938. The coregency of the ÖVP and SPÖ led to the systematic dividing of political offices and civil service posts, known in Austria as *Proporz*. Also benefiting from this arrangement were key economic and professional organizations that were aligned with the two major parties.

At times, Austria's political system seemed impervious to change, but by the middle of the 1980s, it had become clear that far-reaching social and economic trends were beginning to affect the country's politics. The dominance of the ÖVP and SPÖ was challenged by the reemergence of the Freedom Party of Austria (Freiheitliche Partei Österreichs—FPÖ), led by Jörg Haider, a young right-wing populist who appealed to German nationalist sentiment. After the FPÖ's short-lived coalition with the SPÖ between 1983 and 1986, it continued to attract increasing numbers of voters. In the national election of 1990, the FPÖ won 16.6 percent of the vote, establishing itself as a new power in the Nationalrat (National Council), the lower house of parliament. In early 1993, however, some members of the FPÖ withdrew from it and formed their own party, The Liberal Forum (Das Liberale Forum), a potential threat to Haider's political future. Concern over environmental issues has also affected the Austrian political process, as evidenced by the entry of Green political parties into parliament in 1986. Previous patterns of government, which revolved almost exclusively around reaching agreement between the ÖVP and the SPÖ, were replaced by a more contentious, freewheeling atmosphere where more voices are heard.

While the political process underwent gradual but distinct changes, a variety of scandals during the 1980s brought Austria to the world's attention. The best-known involved Kurt Waldheim, elected president in 1986. Shortly after his election, a sharp international controversy erupted over whether he had been involved in Nazi atrocities in Yugoslavia during World War II. Although a thorough investigation found no evidence that Waldheim had participated in any atrocities, his method of handling the affair disappointed many Austrians and foreign observers. The strong emotions unleashed inside Austria by this matter showed that the older generation is still reluctant to discuss the country's role in the Nazi era.

Major changes in Austria's political landscape opened prospects of a new basis for its foreign policy. The bedrock of Austrian diplomacy in the postwar period has been its commitment to permanent neutrality. In order to achieve the removal of Soviet occupying forces, the Austrian government in 1955 pledged never to join a military alliance or to permit the stationing of foreign troops on its soil. Thereafter, Austria pursued a policy of active neutrality, which included participation in numerous United Nations peacekeeping operations. During the Cold War period, Austria was a consistent advocate of détente between the United States and the Soviet Union.

By the late 1980s, a growing number of politicians had concluded that the country should examine closely the question of whether or not to join the European Community. After a prolonged debate over the merits of membership, the Austrian government submitted a formal entry application in the summer of 1989. As of late 1993, a substantial number of Austrian citizens still had serious reservations about joining the organization, which as of November 1993 came to be known as the European Union. Membership would have to be approved in a popular referendum. Whatever the outcome of the vote, the disintegration of communism in Eastern Europe and the dissolution of the Soviet Union have raised the question of whether neutrality should—or could—remain the guiding principle of Austrian foreign policy.

Constitutional Framework

Austria is a parliamentary democracy of the kind that exists in most of Western Europe. The legal basis for the Austrian system of government is the constitution of 1920, which was amended in

Austria's parliament meets in this building in Vienna.
Courtesy Embassy of Austria, Washington

1929 and several times thereafter. The constitution of 1920 provided a transition from Austria-Hungary (also seen as the Austro-Hungarian Empire) to a democratic federal republic in which the law emanates from the people. The constitution was suspended from 1934 to 1938 during the authoritarian administrations of Engelbert Dollfuss and Kurt von Schuschnigg and again during the Anschluss that was forced on Austria by Adolf Hitler from 1938 to 1945. Since 1945, when the Second Republic was proclaimed, Austria has been governed by the 1920 constitution as amended.

Executive, legislative, and judicial branches of government were established by the 1920 constitution, with the executive branch subordinate to the legislative branch. The federal presidency as established by the 1920 constitution was a weak political office whose incumbent was elected by a joint session of the bicameral legislature, the Bundesversammlung (Federal Assembly). The constitutional amendments of 1929 increased the president's political role by granting him the formal power to appoint or dismiss the chancellor and, on the chancellor's recommendation, the cabinet. The 1929 amendments also provided that the right of electing the president be taken away from the legislature and given to the people.

Austria's political system is federal in nature, reflecting the fact that the country consists of nine provinces. Although Article 15 of the constitution states that the provinces shall have jurisdiction over all matters not explicitly reserved for the federal government, Austrian federalism is weak and underdeveloped. The areas of law reserved for the provinces are few in number and relatively unimportant. Among the areas where the federal government is almost exclusively responsible are foreign affairs, national security, justice, finance, civil and criminal law, police matters, and education. In other areas of law, the provinces are called on to pass implementing legislation for matters already decided at the federal level. This process, known as indirect federal administration, applies to areas such as elections, highway police, and housing affairs. Other laws are made and administered at the provincial level, but within federally established guidelines. These concern social welfare, land reform, and provincial administration. Areas where the provinces have primary authority include municipal affairs (for example, trash removal and major aspects of zoning), preschool and kindergarten, construction laws, fire control, and tourism.

The constitution does not include a bill of rights as such, but it does guarantee equality before the law and further guarantees that there shall be no discrimination because of birth, gender, civil status, class, or religion. Individual rights are further defined by inclusion in the constitution of the final article, which raises certain older Austrian laws to the rank of constitutional law. Among them is the Basic Law of December 1867, which establishes equality before the law, inviolability of property, and freedom of assembly, expression, and worship. Laws promulgated in 1862 set forth individual rights regarding personal liberty and one's home. These rights include not being held without a warrant and, except in unusual circumstances, not allowing homes to be searched without a warrant.

Some restrictions are placed on freedom of expression and association. Proper authorities must be informed when a new association is formed. Officials then have six weeks to object to its formation if the group is thought to be illegal or a potential threat to the republic. Since the Second Republic was established in 1945, care has been taken to ensure that laws concerning individuals are in accord with the United Nations Universal Declaration of Human Rights of 1948.

Amendments to the constitution can be made through laws designated constitutional laws or through constitutional provisions if the amendment is part of another law. Passage of an amendment requires a two-thirds majority vote in the presence of at least one-half the members of the Nationalrat (National Council), parliament's lower house. Constitutional laws or provisions are accompanied by a national referendum only if requested by one-third of the deputies of either the Nationalrat or the Bundesrat (Federal Council), parliament's upper house. In 1984 a constitutional amendment provided that amendments changing the division of responsibilities between the federal government and the provinces require the approval of two-thirds of the Bundesrat as well as two-thirds of the Nationalrat.

In addition to the amended constitution, two laws—a treaty and a constitutional law—are particularly important to the constitutional development of Austria because they concern the country's international status and reaffirm the people's basic rights. In April 1955, a stalemate over the restoration of full sovereignty to Austria was finally broken when the Soviet Union agreed to drop its insistence that a solution to the Austrian question be tied to the conclusion of a peace treaty with Germany. This paved the way for the signing of the State Treaty in May 1955 by the Four Powers (Britain, France, the Soviet Union, and the United States) and Austria. The treaty established Austria's frontiers as those existing on January 1, 1938, and forbade economic or political union with Germany. Rights to a democratic government and free elections were guaranteed, and the document reiterated guarantees of fundamental rights and freedoms, including equal rights for minorities. Specifically mentioned in this category were Slovenes and Croats. The second law of constitutional importance is the federal constitutional Law of October 26, 1955, on the neutrality of Austria. The law declared the country's permanent neutrality and prohibited it from entering into military alliances or allowing foreign countries to establish military bases within the borders of Austria.

Government Institutions

The Austrian system provides for a president who is popularly elected. The president functions as head of state and has little authority over the actions of the government. Political power is in the hands of Austria's head of government, the chancellor (prime minister), who, as in parliamentary systems elsewhere, is usually the leader of the party with the most seats in the lower house of the country's bicameral parliament, the Nationalrat (National Council). The chancellor and his cabinet have extensive executive powers and also are the authors of most legislation. Yet, however great the powers of the executive are, it is politically responsible to the Nationalrat and can govern only with its approval. The upper chamber of parliament, the Bundesrat (Federal Council), represents the interests of Austria's nine provinces. Its limited powers reflect the underdeveloped nature of Austrian federalism. The

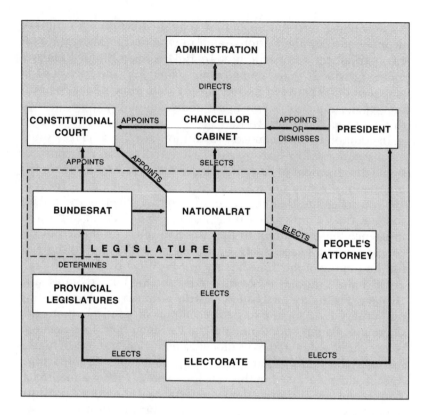

Source: Based on information from Kurt Richard Luther and Wolfgang C. Müller (eds.),
Politics in Austria, London, 1992, 101; and Melanie A. Sully, *A Contemporary History of Austria*, London, 1990, 155.

Figure 11. Structure of Government, 1993

chancellor and the cabinet, together with their party's representatives in the Nationalrat, are the main center of government activity and power (see fig. 11).

The Federal President

A 1929 amendment to the 1920 constitution introduced the concept of a popularly elected president. Because of the suspension of the constitution in 1934, however, the first popular election of a president did not take place until 1951. The president serves a six-year term and is limited to two consecutive terms. Candidates must be at least thirty-five years of age and eligible to vote in Nationalrat elections.

Political parties nominate presidential candidates, but it is customary, given the limited powers of the position, for the president to serve in a nonpartisan manner. To win an election, a candidate must receive more than 50 percent of the votes. If no candidate succeeds on the first ballot, a runoff election is held between the two candidates receiving the highest number of votes. The president serves as head of state. Presidential duties include convoking, adjourning, and, in rare cases, dissolving the Nationalrat. The president signs treaties, verifies that legal procedures for legislation have been carried out, and grants reprieves and pardons. Although he cannot veto legislation, the president is empowered to reject a cabinet proposal or delay enactment of a bill. Unless the constitution states otherwise, official acts of the president require the countersignature of the chancellor or the relevant minister.

The president plays an important, though largely formal, role in the political process of forming and dissolving governments. In the aftermath of a parliamentary election, the president invites the leader of the strongest party in the Nationalrat to form a government. This duty reflects the fact that both the government and parliament are responsible to the president in the sense that he can dismiss individual members of the government, including the chancellor, as well as dissolve the Nationalrat. The president, on the recommendation of the chancellor, also appoints individuals to cabinet positions and other important government positions, including that of vice chancellor. The president also can dismiss individual cabinet officials, but only on the recommendation of the chancellor. During the Second Republic (that is, since 1945), the president has dissolved the Nationalrat only twice, in 1971 and 1986, in both cases because the incumbent chancellor and his party wished to have a new election.

The president has emergency authority that gives him significant powers. Should an emergency arise when the Nationalrat is not in session, the cabinet can request that the president act on the basis of "provisional law-amending ordinances," as provided for in the constitution. Such ordinances require the countersignature of the cabinet. Emergency decrees must be sent to the Nationalrat. If it is not in session, the president must convoke a special session. The Nationalrat has four weeks either to enact a law to replace the decree or to void the decree.

Two procedures are outlined in the constitution for pressing charges against the president: one entails a referendum; the other entails a vote by a joint session of parliament, the Bundesversammlung (Federal Assembly). To set a referendum in motion, one-half of the Nationalrat deputies must be present and vote by a two-thirds majority to ask the chancellor to convoke the Bundesversammlung, which then must vote by a simple majority for a referendum. The referendum is carried if a simple majority of voters vote in favor of it. If the referendum is defeated, then the president is regarded as reelected, the Nationalrat is dissolved, and new elections are scheduled. Under no circumstances, however, shall a president serve more than twelve years in office.

The second procedure for bringing charges against the president results from his being responsible to the Bundesversammlung, which is authorized to vote on his actions. Either house of parliament can ask the chancellor to convoke the Bundesversammlung for such a purpose. One-half of the members of each house must be present, and the Bundesversammlung must cast a two-thirds vote to press charges against the president.

If the president dies or if the office is vacated for any other reason, a new election is held. In the interim, the chancellor carries out necessary presidential duties.

Chancellor and Cabinet

The chancellor (prime minister) is the head of government as well as chairman of the cabinet. Executive political power formally rests in the hands of the cabinet. The chancellor, the cabinet, and their working majority in the Nationalrat are the real focal point of executive power in the political system. The chancellor is appointed by the president and can also be dismissed by him. The chancellor is usually the leader of the party that has won the most seats in the latest parliamentary election. At the very least, he or she is the choice of a majority of the new deputies. The chancellor must be eligible to serve in the Nationalrat but need not be a member of it. The chancellor also serves as head of the Federal Chancellery, which is staffed with civil servants.

In most respects, the chancellor functions as first among equals in the cabinet. He coordinates the work of the cabinet but is not entitled to give orders to individual ministers. However, the chancellor's power varies depending on political circumstances and his own political gifts. In a coalition government, the chancellor shares coordinating duties with the vice chancellor, who is the leader of the junior party in the coalition. If the chancellor heads a one-party government, his or her leeway to make decisions is increased. During the long period of rule under Chancellor Bruno Kreisky (1970–83), the public visibility of the chancellor was enhanced through the increased use of television. From the standpoint of the public, the chancellor had become the dominant figure of government.

On the recommendation of the chancellor, the president appoints individuals to the various cabinet positions. Cabinet members do not have to be members of the Nationalrat, but they must be eligible to be elected to it. Persons chosen as cabinet ministers are usually leading members of a political party or interest group. Occasionally, however, a person has entered the cabinet from a high-level civil service position.

The number of ministries varies; in 1993 there were fourteen ministries. In a coalition government, the apportionment of the cabinet posts is roughly proportional to the parties' respective strengths in the Nationalrat. The awarding of particular posts is based on a coalition agreement reached between the two parties.

In keeping with the traditional Austrian principle of *Proporz* (the dividing of political offices according to the respective strengths and interests of the parties), parties name individuals to posts of particular concern to them. For example, if the SPÖ is a member of the coalition, at a minimum it names the minister for labor and social affairs, in keeping with the strong support it enjoys from the trade unions. By the same token, if the ÖVP is part of the coalition, it names the minister for agriculture and forestry because farmers are one of its main interest groups. The chancellor and vice chancellor do not have total control over the selection process for filling cabinet positions. For example, the SPÖ faction in the Austrian Trade Union Federation (Österreichischer Gewerkschaftsbund—ÖGB) usually chooses the minister for labor and social affairs, and the ÖVP is careful to allow its various auxiliary associations and provincial parties to make certain selections. Beginning in 1987, the ÖVP and SPÖ have followed a practice of selecting an independent to head the Ministry for Justice.

The cabinet is subject to dismissal by the president and the Nationalrat. The president can dismiss the entire cabinet without the concurrence of the chancellor, but removal of individual members requires the recommendation of the chancellor. If the Nationalrat passes a vote of no confidence—which requires that one-half of the deputies be present—concerning the entire cabinet or a minister, the cabinet or minister is removed from office.

State secretaries are appointed and leave office in the same manner as ministers, but each government ministry does not have a state secretary. State secretaries aid ministers in parliamentary business and are bound by their ministers' instructions. They are nonvoting participants in cabinet sessions. A state secretary is not necessarily a member of the same party as the minister he serves.

Nationalrat

The Nationalrat (National Council), the lower house of parliament, exercises all of the powers usually associated with a national legislature. It has the power to remove the entire cabinet or individual members of it by a vote of no confidence. All legislation and treaties must be approved by the Nationalrat. Before a vote can take place, at least one-third of the Nationalrat's members must be present. A simple majority suffices for the passage of legislation. Sessions are public unless the deputies determine otherwise.

Deputies elect a president and second and third presidents from among their members to serve during the four-year legislative term. Party leaders who are members of their party's executive and of a parliamentary faction that serves as a liaison between parliament and a political party are most likely to be presidential candidates. The president and the third president belong to the same party, usually the party holding the most seats in the Nationalrat. The second president belongs to the other major party. Presidential duties include nominating employees of the Federal Chancellery, whose staff serves the three presidents. The three presidents preside over plenary sessions in two-hour shifts. They also join with the chairmen of the parliamentary factions to form the Presidial Conference, which directs the Nationalrat's activities and decides the time and agenda of plenary sessions and, to a lesser extent, the time and agenda of the committees. The Presidial Conference is one of the rare groups not affected by the custom of proportional representation. All parties holding seats in the Nationalrat are represented on the conference.

In 1993 the Nationalrat contained roughly fifteen committees in which legislative proposals are both prepared and examined and the results of parliamentary investigations considered. Each committee has various numbers of subcommittees assigned to deal with specific kinds of legislation. In addition to the committees, there are also the Main Committee and the Permanent Subcommittee, the members of which are elected at the start of each new legislative period. The Main Committee has responsibility for overseeing aspects of the state-run industries and for dispatching Austrian troops on international peacekeeping missions. It also participates in deciding the date for Nationalrat elections and setting rates for postal and telephone services. The president of the Nationalrat serves as chairman of the Main Committee. The Permanent Subcommittee plays a limited role because its main function is to fulfill the duties of the Main Committee in the case of the dissolution of the Nationalrat by the president.

Equally as important as the committees are the *Klubs* (factions), which all parties in the Nationalrat maintain. The factions usually have a leader and an executive committee, and they provide deputies with a behind-the-scenes setting to discuss political strategy

Government and Politics

with like-minded colleagues. Individuals elected as deputies to the Nationalrat automatically become members of their party's faction. Faction leaders assign deputies to committees and decide on the questions that are to be asked during debates and the priority for legislative initiatives.

In addition to the work of the committees, another important function of the Nationalrat is to question the government regularly on its activities and legislative proposals. One device frequently employed is an "interpellation," which summons for questioning before the Nationalrat a particular cabinet minister or government official. A minimum of twenty deputies is required to set an interpellation in motion. Questioning a government official is the prelude to a parliamentary debate on the issue.

A 1970 amendment to the election laws increased the number of Nationalrat seats from 165 to 183. Seats in the Nationalrat are divided among the country's nine provinces according to population. Deputies serve a four-year term and are elected according to constitutional and other federal laws. Candidates must be at least twenty years old on January 1 of the election year and must also be eligible to vote.

The Nationalrat has only one session per year, beginning no earlier than September 15 and ending no later than July 15. An extraordinary session of the Nationalrat can be convoked either by order of the federal president, by request of the cabinet, or by request of one-third of the deputies. Once a request has been made, the extraordinary session must commence within two weeks. After a parliamentary election, the newly elected Nationalrat must be convened within thirty days.

The Nationalrat can be dissolved either by presidential action or by itself. The president can dissolve the Nationalrat at the chancellor's request, but he is limited to dismissing it only once for the same reason. New elections must be held soon enough to enable the new parliament to convene within 100 days of the dissolution. The Nationalrat is empowered to dissolve itself by a simple majority vote.

During the Second Republic, membership of the Nationalrat has been heavily weighted toward men who come from white-collar professions. Changes in the sociological profile of the deputies have occurred slowly. The Nationalrat elected in November 1990 contained a record 22 percent of female deputies. Prior to this election, female deputies had never accounted for more than 15 percent of the total number of deputies. The average age of the deputies elected in 1990 was forty-six. Almost 40 percent of the deputies elected in 1990 were university graduates, and 25 percent were employees of political parties, politically oriented interest groups, or social welfare organizations.

The majority of legislative proposals originate in the executive. Legislation occasionally starts in the Nationalrat, but the close cooperation between the executive and the majority party in parliament makes such initiation unnecessary most of the time. During the Second Republic, governmental legislative proposals have outnumbered Nationalrat initiatives by three to one. Parliament's role in the legislative process is focused more on bringing to public attention the background of the government's legislative proposals and exposing any mistakes the government may have made. Opposition parties have the right to force the government to answer any questions about pending legislation.

Before a bill is introduced in parliament, it has already passed through an intensive process of examination. The government solicits comments from the various interest groups affected by the bill, especially the chambers of agriculture, commerce, and labor (see Principal Economic Interest Groups, ch. 3). During this stage, a bill frequently is modified to meet the objections of key interest groups and opposition parties in parliament. Changes to legislative proposals may also be made after a bill has been introduced in the Nationalrat, but the majority of changes are made before the bill is introduced officially. Bills are amended significantly by the parliament only 10 to 15 percent of the time.

By West European standards, the percentage of bills passed unanimously by the Austrian parliament is high. Unanimity prevailed anywhere between 38 and 49 percent of the time during the parliaments of the 1970s and 1980s. In the late 1980s and early 1990s, with the advent of the Greens in parliament and the increased power of the FPÖ, unanimity was on the decline.

As the complexity of the issues facing government has increased, so too has the importance of committees to the parliament's work. After a bill reaches the Nationalrat, it is assigned to a committee and frequently also to a subcommittee. Deputies typically spend twice as much time in committee hearings as in plenary sessions. The subcommittees hold even more hours of hearings than the full committees. Because of the unwieldy nature of plenary sessions, 80 percent of changes to government legislation occur in committee.

In 1975 the Nationalrat amended its procedures to give the opposition and smaller parties a greater role in the legislative process. Under the 1975 amendments, one-third of the deputies can request the Constitutional Court to review a law for constitutionality. Further, one-third of the deputies can request the government's accounting agency to conduct an audit of a government agency. These

changes reflect the intensification of political competition that occurred in the Nationalrat after the long period of grand coalition
governments between the two major parties ended in 1966. The
ÖVP, as the major opposition party during the era of SPÖ rule
(1970–83), led the drive for greater rights for minority parties.

Bundesrat

The interests of Austria's nine provinces are represented at the
federal level in the Bundesrat (Federal Council), the upper house
of parliament. The Bundesrat has sixty-three seats, which are apportioned among the provinces on the basis of population. Each
province is guaranteed at least three seats. As of late 1993, the breakdown of seats was as follows: Vienna and Lower Austria had twelve
each; Styria and Upper Austria, ten each; Tirol, five; Carinthia
and Salzburg, four each; and Burgenland and Vorarlberg, three
each. The members of the Bundesrat are elected by the provincial
legislatures on the basis of proportional representation. At least one
seat must be given to the party having the second largest number
of seats in the provincial legislature. If several parties have the same
number of seats, the party that won the second largest number of
votes in the last provincial election is awarded a seat in the Bundesrat.

The main purpose of the Bundesrat is to protect provincial interests, but its powers are restricted because the government is not
answerable to it. All laws passed by the Nationalrat must be presented to the Bundesrat for review. However, the Bundesrat can at
most delay the passage of laws by means of a suspensive veto. In
such a case, the bill is sent back to the Nationalrat, which can override the Bundesrat's veto by reapproving the bill. Once this is done,
the bill becomes law. In 1984 the body's powers were increased
by a constitutional amendment that required approval by two-thirds
of the Bundesrat to any proposed constitutional change in the distribution of competencies between the federal government and the
provinces. Despite this change, the Bundesrat remains a weak in-
stitution.

Bundesversammlung

The two houses of parliament meet jointly as the Bundesversammlung (Federal Assembly) to witness the swearing in of the
president, to bring charges against him, or to declare war. Usually, the Bundesversammlung is convoked by the president. If charges
are brought against the president, the chancellor convokes the Bundesversammlung. Meetings are chaired alternately by the president of the Nationalrat and the chairman of the Bundesrat. If the

Bundesversammlung passes a resolution, its validity must be attested to by the chairman. The chancellor then countersigns and publishes the resolution.

Judicial System

The judicial system is independent of the executive and legislative branches. The constitution establishes that judges are independent when acting in their judicial function. They cannot be bound by instructions from a higher court (except in cases of appeal) or by another agency. In administrative matters, judges are subordinate to the Ministry for Justice. A judge can be transferred or dismissed only for specific reasons established by law and only after formal court action has been taken. The Austrian judiciary functions only at the federal level, and thus there is no separate court system at the provincial level.

The Constitutional Court

The Constitutional Court decides the legality of treaties and the constitutionality of laws and decrees passed at the federal, provincial, and local levels. Cases involving courts and administrative agencies or the Administrative Court and the Constitutional Court are heard in the Constitutional Court. Individuals can present cases to the court if they believe a decision of an administrative agency has violated their constitutional rights. Monetary claims against the state, provinces, administrative districts, or local communities that cannot be settled by a regular court or an administrative agency are brought to the Constitutional Court, as are claims regarding disputed elections. The court also decides questions of impeachment and hears cases charging the president with breaking a constitutional law or cases charging members of federal or provincial governments with breaking a law.

The court is composed of a president, vice president, twelve judges, and six alternates. The federal president, on recommendations from the cabinet, appoints the court's president, vice president, six judges, and three alternates. The federal president appoints six additional judges and three more alternates based on nominations from the Nationalrat (for three judges and two alternates) and the Bundesrat (for three judges and one alternate). The constitution requires that three judges and two alternates of the court, which sits in Vienna, live outside the city. The president of the court chairs its meetings and decides on the assignment of cases to individual judges, but he does not have voting rights. Cases are heard by five, nine, or all thirteen of the judges and are decided by majority vote.

The selection of judges for the Constitutional Court has been controlled by the ÖVP and the SPÖ. The two parties have applied
the principle of *Proporz* to filling vacancies on the court. Between
1945 and 1970, the ÖVP was the larger of the two parties in terms
of parliamentary strength, and it controlled seven of the judgeships
with voting rights; the SPÖ controlled six of the judgeships. Beginning in 1970, the ratio was reversed when the SPÖ gained more
seats in the parliament than the ÖVP.

The Administrative Court

The Administrative Court, located in Vienna, is the court of
final appeal for cases involving administrative agencies. The court's
specific purpose is to determine whether an individual's rights have
been violated by an administrative action or omission. Individuals can also appeal to this court if an administrative agency fails
to grant a decision in a case. The Administrative Court may not
rule on matters that come under the competence of the Constitutional Court.

The Administrative Court is presided over by a court president
who is assisted by a vice president and several other court officers.
Appointments to the court are made by the federal president on
the recommendation of the cabinet. Prerequisites for appointment
are completion of law and political science studies and ten years
of experience in a related field. At least one-third of the court's
members must be qualified judges, and at least one-fourth must
come from the provinces, preferably from civil service positions.
Panels of three, five, or nine judges sit in court at any one time,
depending on the importance of the case.

Ordinary Courts

The system of ordinary courts is headed by the Supreme Court
in Vienna. This court is the court of final instance for most civil
and criminal cases. It can also hear cases involving commercial,
labor, or patent decisions, but constitutional or administrative decisions are outside its purview. Justices hear cases in five-person
panels.

Four superior courts, which are appellate courts, are located in
Vienna, Graz, Linz, and Innsbruck. They are usually courts of
second instance for civil and criminal cases and are the final appellate courts for district court cases. Usually, a three-judge panel
hears cases.

On a lower level are seventeen regional courts having jurisdiction over provincial and district matters. Boundaries of judicial districts may or may not coincide with those of administrative districts.

Regional courts serve as courts of first instance for civil and criminal cases carrying penalties of up to ten years' imprisonment and as appellate courts for some cases from district courts. Justices usually sit as a three-person panel, but some cases can be heard by only one judge. Vienna and Graz have separate courts for civil, criminal, and juvenile cases, and Vienna also has a separate commercial court.

At the lowest level are about 200 district or local courts, which decide minor civil and criminal cases, that is, those involving small monetary value or minor misdemeanors. Questions involving such issues as guardianship, adoption, legitimacy, probate, registry of lands, and boundary disputes are also settled at this level. Depending on the population of the area, the number of judges varies, but one judge can decide a case. Civil and criminal matters are heard in separate courts in Vienna and Graz. Vienna further divides civil courts into one for commercial matters and one for other civil cases.

Ordinary court judges are chosen by the federal president or, if the president so decides, by the minister for justice on the basis of cabinet recommendations. The judiciary retains a potential voice in naming judges, inasmuch as it must submit the names of two candidates for each vacancy on the courts. The suggested candidates, however, need not be chosen by the cabinet. Lay people have an important role in the judicial system in cases involving crimes carrying severe penalties, political felonies, and misdemeanors. The public can participate in court proceedings as lay assessors or as jurors. Certain criminal cases are subject to a hearing by two lay assessors and two judges. The lay assessors and judges decide the guilt or innocence and punishment of a defendant. If a jury, usually eight lay people, is used, the jury decides the guilt of the defendant. Then jury and judges together determine the punishment.

Special Courts

Cases outside the jurisdiction of these courts are heard in special courts. For example, labor courts decide civil cases concerning employment. Employers and employees are represented in labor court hearings. Cases involving the Stock and Commodity Exchange and the Exchange for Agricultural Products are decided by the Court of Arbitration, which is composed of members of the exchanges. Social insurance cases are heard by the provincial commissions for social insurance. The Patent Court decides appeals of patent cases.

The People's Attorney

The Office of the People's Attorney, which was created in 1977 and granted constitutional recognition in 1981, functions in a manner similar to an ombudsman's office. It is designed to assist citizens who believe that they have been improperly treated by government administration. The office can also initiate its own investigations if it suspects that particular government offices are engaged in corruption or fraud. After concluding its investigations, the office has the authority to issue binding recommendations to government offices to rectify abuses.

Legal Training

Attaining the title of attorney-at-law requires eleven years of training. Four years of this period consist of prescribed studies in law and political science at a university. On completion of a doctoral program, the candidate undergoes a seven-year apprenticeship, during which one year must be spent in a civil or criminal court and three years in an attorney's office. Finally, it is necessary to pass the bar examination.

Civil Service

Civil servants have held a position of respect in Austrian society since the formation of the civil service in the eighteenth century, when it was considered to be "carrying out a mission for the state." The civil service is highly regulated. Public servants take an oath of office, promise obedience to their superiors, and pledge to keep official matters secret. A civil servant may neither join an association nor be employed in another job that could be interpreted as unworthy of his or her position.

Besides the high esteem in which the civil service is held, job security is also an attractive feature. Periodic raises are automatic, and promotions are scheduled at regular intervals. The retirement pension is adequate. A civil servant may be dismissed only for serious misconduct.

During the grand coalition of 1945–66, the ÖVP and SPÖ introduced the system of *Proporz* into the civil service. Prior to the founding of the Second Republic, the civil service had been dominated by ÖVP members, and thus after 1945 special steps were taken to recruit persons with ties to the SPÖ. The two parties came to exercise almost complete control of the personnel of the ministries that they controlled in the cabinet. During the period of single-party rule (1966–83), the importance of political allegiance came to play a lesser role in the selection process of the civil service.

Chancellor Kreisky made sure that a large number of persons without party affiliation were appointed to high-level positions in the civil service.

Reforms also were introduced in this period to make the civil service better able to attract highly qualified people. In 1975 a civil service training academy was established, and after 1980 some top positions were changed to fixed-term appointments. Further changes were made to give equal opportunity for career advancement to all members of the civil service, regardless of their specialty. Traditionally, people with legal training had a decided advantage in rising to the top of the system. As of 1993, the government was working on a comprehensive reform of the civil service system.

Provincial Government

Each of the nine provinces has its own constitution, which prescribes its governmental organization. Common to each province is an elected Landtag (provincial legislature), which is popularly elected on the basis of proportional representation. According to the federal constitution, the number of deputies can range from thirty-six to sixty-five, depending on the population of the province. Vienna, which is simultaneously a province and a city, is in a special category—its legislature has 100 deputies. A Landtag is subject to dissolution by the federal president at the cabinet's request. This process requires the consent of the Bundesrat. One-half of the Bundesrat's deputies must be present and cast a two-thirds vote in favor of the action.

The Landtag elects an executive composed of a governor and councilors. A deputy is elected to serve in the absence of the governor. Candidates for these positions must meet eligibility requirements of the Landtag, although they need not belong to it. Elections to the Landtag occur every five years, except in Upper Austria, where they are held every six years. Legislative periods can be shortened and elections held if the Landtag votes to dissolve itself.

Provincial constitutions can be amended, provided that changes do not conflict with the federal constitution. Passage of a constitutional amendment requires the presence of at least one-half of the Landtag's members and a two-thirds majority vote. Regulations for passage of other provincial laws vary, but generally the procedure requires a vote by the Landtag, verification that the proper procedure has been followed, the countersignature of the prescribed official, and publication in the provincial law gazette. Before a law is published, the federal minister whose jurisdiction covers the area of the proposed law has to be informed of the province's action. The cabinet then has eight weeks to notify the province if the bill interferes with federal interests. The Landtag can override the federal government's objections by voting again in favor of the bill with at least one-half of its members present. The federal government would probably appeal to the Constitutional Court if it strenuously objected to a provincial law.

The provinces have a restricted ability to raise taxes. They may not tax items already subject to federal taxation. Every four to six years, the federal government, the provinces, and the municipalities negotiate a Finance Equalization Law that determines how tax revenues raised at the federal and provincial levels are to be divided. This system ensures that the provinces are fully compensated for the many federal programs that they implement.

Article 15 (1) of the federal constitution states that matters not expressly reserved to the federal government come under the jurisdiction of the provinces. Matters in which the provinces have primary jurisdiction include local police, primary education, housing, health, and protection of the environment. If a provincial government believes that some federal action is infringing on its jurisdiction, it can appeal to the Constitutional Court for a ruling.

Provisions exist for interprovincial coordination of policies by means of compacts and treaties. Such coordination, however, is feasible only if the matters at hand are among the autonomous rights of the provinces. This manner of cooperation has rarely occurred. Instead, conferences of provincial officials are held to plan less formal methods of cooperation. The federal government must be notified of interprovincial action.

Local Government

Provinces are divided into districts and local communities. The primary function of district governments is to administer federal programs. They do not have the power of taxation. A district is headed by a district commissioner, usually a career civil servant, who is appointed by the provincial governor. Local communities are self-governing, having a popularly elected community council that is chosen by proportional representation on the basis of political party strength. The number of representatives ranges from seven to 100, depending on the population. Members serve a five- or six-year term as determined by provincial regulations. Community council meetings are presided over by a mayor, elected by and responsible to the community council.

The federal government or a province may delegate some functions to a local government. Otherwise, local communities deal with matters of local concern, such as safety, traffic, police, settlement of disputes that are not dealt with by the courts, public utilities, cultural institutions, public housing, and health care services.

Local actions, whether autonomous or delegated, are in the long run usually subject to provincial or federal supervision or controls. Administrative and legal regulations on the provincial and federal levels are so pervasive that even decisions that are considered the sole responsibility of local communities are actually limited. Local communities, however, have recourse to the Administrative Court and the Constitutional Court if they believe that their rights are being infringed upon.

Electoral System

The electoral system is based on the principle of proportional representation. The system's basic outline was established in the constitution of 1920, although significant changes were made in 1970 and 1992. Among other changes, the amendments of 1970 raised the number of seats in the Nationalrat from 165 to 183.

The 1992 reform of the election law, which went into effect in May 1993, alters the electoral system for the Nationalrat in a number of significant ways. It divides the country into nine provincial electoral districts that correspond to the country's nine provinces. These districts contain a further forty-three regional electoral districts. The creation of the small regional electoral districts is intended to foster a greater feeling of connection between voters and those who represent them in parliament. The law also aims to personalize elections by giving voters greater power than before of electing individual candidates of the party of their choice by voting directly for them rather than for the party list of candidates as a whole. This reform may reduce the power of party leaders to impose their preselected candidates on the electorate. The law also modifies vote-counting procedures to ensure that the number of parliamentary seats won by a party will conform more closely with votes cast. Lastly, the law attempts to prevent a proliferation of small parties sitting in the Nationalrat by barring a party from that body if it has not won at least 4 percent of votes cast nationwide. However, a party can be represented in parliament by winning at least one seat in a regional electoral district.

According to the 1992 law, votes in Nationalrat elections are counted in three stages, although a voter casts only one ballot. On this ballot, the voter indicates the party of his or her choice and then may choose two candidates from this party, one to be elected from the regional voting district and one from the provincial voting district. Votes going to a preferred candidate are called preferential votes. In the first stage of counting votes, the returns

Vienna's city hall
Courtesy Austrian National Tourist Office, New York

from regional voting districts are examined; in the second stage, those from provincial voting districts are examined. In these first two stages, the Hare system (see Glossary) is used to determine the proportional allocation of seats. In the third stage of counting votes, candidates on the national party list are allocated seats according to the d'Hondt method (see Glossary).

A party must win a parliamentary seat in the first stage of vote counting in order to win seats in the second and third stages. A candidate who receives preferential votes amounting to at least one-sixth of the votes his party receives wins a parliamentary seat. This is also the case for a candidate who receives preferential votes amounting to at least one-half the electoral quota (*Wahlzahl*), that is, the number of valid ballots in a voting district divided by the number of parliamentary seats allotted to it. The vote tallying procedures established by the new law mean that about ninety parliamentary seats come from regional voting districts, about sixty-five from provincial voting districts, and roughly twenty-five from the federal level. All persons aged nineteen and over by January 1 of the year in which the election is held are eligible to vote. Voter participation has traditionally been very high. In national elections, it has fallen below 90 percent only once (in 1990, when it stood at 86 percent). Voting always takes place on a Sunday.

Political Dynamics

Between the end of World War II and the late 1980s, when some new trends became evident, Austria's political system seemed stable and unchangeable. Most political scientists considered Austria a classic case of constitutional democracy, that is, a political system in which cohesive social groups are closely identified with political parties. According to this theory, Austrian politics, business, and society in general were decisively shaped by the influence of three major social camps, or subcultures (*Lager*)—the socialist, the Catholic-conservative, and the German-nationalist.

The most important factors in determining to which subculture a person belonged were geographic location (rural or urban), socioeconomic status, and professional occupation. The socialist camp had its basis in the urban working class of Vienna and other cities and in the intellectual class. The Catholic-conservative camp had its traditional base in the small towns and farming communities of Austria and was almost exclusively Roman Catholic. The German-nationalist camp was smaller than the other two subcultures and was founded on the enthusiasm for union with Germany that was prevalent during the years of the First Republic (1918–38). A high percentage of its members came from white-collar professions.

Austria's subcultures provided their members with a self-contained milieu in which to pursue their lives and a variety of occupations. In addition to the political parties aligned with the *Lager*, each camp featured professional and trade organizations that played an important role in party politics and in society as well.

This traditional system has continued into the 1990s. In 1993, in the socialist camp, the key organizations affiliated with the SPÖ were the Group of Socialist Trade Unionists (Fraktion Sozialistischer Gewerkschaftler—FSG), the Free Business Association of Austria (Freier Wirtschaftsverband Österreichs—FWB), and the SPÖ Farmers (SPÖ-Bauern). In the Catholic-conservative camp, the chief organizations of the ÖVP were the League of Austrian Workers and Salaried Employees (Österreichischer Arbeiter- und Angestelltenbund—ÖAAB), the League of Austrian Business (Österreichischer Wirtschaftsbund—ÖWB), and the League of Austrian

Farmers (Österreichischer Bauernbund—ÖBB). The German-nationalist camp, which is represented by the FPÖ, had only one auxiliary organization of note as of 1993, the Circle of Free Business Persons (Ring Freiheitlicher Wirtschaftstreibender—RFW).

A key source of influence for the professional and trade organizations is their control of the chambers of agriculture, commerce, and labor. In the Austrian corporatist system, the chambers are assigned responsibility for implementing certain aspects of economic laws and regulations. Moreover, membership in the chambers is obligatory for persons employed in a wide range of occupations. Thus, the professional and trade organizations and the chambers are assured a large amount of influence in the public realm. The ÖVP dominates the Chamber of Agriculture through the ÖAAB and the Chamber of Commerce through the ÖWB. The SPÖ has a controlling influence in the Chamber of Labor through the FSG.

The Austrian system of interests was dominated by the socialist and Catholic-conservative camps for virtually the entire postwar period. During the early years of the Second Republic, politicians of the SPÖ and ÖVP were adamant about the need for political consensus and compromise. One overriding reason for the emergence of a system designed to avoid conflict was the negative experience of the 1930s, when the political parties clashed so vehemently that they ended up fighting a short civil war in 1934. During the period of Nazi rule, many Austrian politicians found themselves imprisoned alongside their political opponents. This shared fate convinced the country's political elite of the imperative for consensus in postwar Austria. From 1945 to 1966, the country was ruled by the grand coalition formed by the ÖVP and the SPÖ, an astonishing duration of a series of governments composed of Austria's two main political competitors.

The cumulative effect of a variety of changes in Austrian society in the postwar era has led many political scientists to conclude that the strength of the political camps, or *Lager,* has weakened significantly. A major shift in the way people earn their livelihood—a decline in farming and manufacturing and a growth in the services sector—has weakened the hold of the *Lager* on voters. An increasingly secularized society has lessened the influence of the Roman Catholic Church. An increased sense of Austria's existence as a nation (up from less than 50 percent in the mid-1960s to 74 percent in one poll in 1990) has reduced the political potency of pan-Germanism. And the growth of the suburbs and the transformation of rural areas by tourism have reduced the homogeneity of traditional SPÖ and ÖVP enclaves.

The weakened hold of the *Lager* on Austrian society and politics has created opportunities for smaller parties. A 1990 poll showed that only 50 percent of respondents claimed some kind of identification with a political party; a mere 20 percent claimed strong identification. In the 1960s and 1970s, similar polls had shown that more than 30 percent of Austrians identified closely with a party. Services-sector, or white-collar, employees were often part of a block of so-called floating voters who did not identify with a particular party. This block can be the key to an electoral victory for the party that wins its votes.

The propensity toward what political scientists call electoral dealignment, that is, the breakdown of long-standing voter loyalties, was bound to have effects on Austrian voting behavior, and by 1986 the first signs of change were evident. In the parliamentary election of that year, the combined vote for the ÖVP and SPÖ fell to 84 percent, the first time since 1962 that it had dropped below 90 percent (see table 13, Appendix). The party benefiting the most from the losses by the major parties was the FPÖ, which doubled its vote. Moreover, for the first time ever, members of the Green political movement entered parliament.

The trend away from the dominance of the *Lager* system continued in the next parliamentary election in 1990, but this time it was the ÖVP alone that bore the brunt. Its share of the vote declined from 41.3 to 32.1 percent, a massive loss by the standard of Austria's ultrastable political system. The FPÖ had another striking success, and the environmentalists lost some votes but gained two seats in the Nationalrat.

Although the 1990 election did not lead to a change in government (because the ÖVP and SPÖ had renewed their grand coalition in 1987), it nevertheless marked a watershed in Austrian political history. For the first time in the Second Republic, the status of the ÖVP as a major party was placed in doubt. Whereas in the 1986 election the ÖVP received only 88,000 fewer votes than the SPÖ, in 1990 the difference ballooned to more than 500,000. Under its colorful leader, Jörg Haider, the FPÖ was changing the Austrian party system from one dominated by two parties to one with multiparty possibilities.

The Social Democratic Party of Austria

The Social Democratic Party of Austria (Sozialdemokratische Partei Österreichs—SPÖ), until 1991 known as the Socialist Party of Austria (Sozialistische Partei Österreichs—SPÖ), has its roots in the original Social Democratic Workers' Party (Sozialdemokratische Arbeiterpartei—SDAP), founded in 1889 by Viktor Adler, a young doctor. The SDAP supported revisionist Marxism and the use of democratic methods to establish working-class rule in a democratic government. The SDAP was responsible for pushing through universal voting rights for men in 1905 and for extending the same for women in 1919. From 1934 to 1945, during the regimes of Engelbert Dollfuss (1932–34) and Kurt von Schuschnigg (1934–38) and the takeover by the Nazis, the SDAP was outlawed. In 1945 it was reconstituted as the Socialist Party of Austria. In 1991 the party readopted the designation "Social Democratic."

Moderates such as Karl Renner and Adolf Schärf, each of whom eventually served as president of the Second Republic, led the postwar party (see table 14, Appendix). Their primary interests lay in increasing SPÖ power in the coalition government rather than in fostering Marxism. Between 1945 and 1957, the party supported democratic practices and intraparty cooperation, programs for higher wages and lower food prices, and increased government spending on social programs.

The election of Bruno Pittermann as party chairman in 1957 marked the beginning of major policy changes. The party had a strong following among industrial workers, but party officials wanted to expand SPÖ membership to the middle class and white-collar workers and to soften the party's anticlerical position in order to become acceptable to Roman Catholics. These changes were expressed in a new party program adopted in 1958. The program claimed that the SPÖ was "the party of all those who work for a living," and it stated the party's opposition to communism and fascism.

The late 1960s brought more changes in party doctrine. A new economic program in 1967 constituted a shift from concern for the distribution of wealth to concern for economic growth, including increasing foreign investment in Austria. Cultural and social reforms were demanded, and emphasis was placed on attending to the needs of young people. In line with its appeal to youth, the party supported a plan to shorten the term of military service.

Under Bruno Kreisky, who became chairman of the SPÖ in 1967, the party continued its move toward the center of the ideological spectrum. Although party platforms continued to refer to the classless society as an ideal, the SPÖ was careful to distinguish its brand of socialism from the centralized, inefficient version of Eastern Europe and the Soviet Union. The party program of 1978 stressed the four principles of freedom, equality, justice, and solidarity. Central to the SPÖ's philosophy was a guarantee for all Austrians of freedom from fear, hunger, exploitation, and unemployment.

The freedom to pursue wealth had to be balanced by the government's guarantee of equal opportunity and social justice. Under Kreisky the SPÖ triumphed at the polls in 1970, 1971, 1975, and 1979, and between 1971 and 1983 the party enjoyed an absolute majority in parliament. The Kreisky governments laid great emphasis on improving the social welfare system and achieving full employment. The Kreisky era also featured the flourishing of the technocrats—SPÖ politicians successful in business and banking whose lavish life-styles seemed incongruous in a party supposed to represent the interests of labor. In the parliamentary election of 1983, the SPÖ lost its absolute majority, and Kreisky decided to retire from politics rather than preside over a coalition government. Fred Sinowatz, Kreisky's minister for education, was chosen as chancellor in a coalition government with the FPÖ. The Sinowatz era, from 1983 to 1986, proved to be a short interregnum and was not distinguished by any great achievements (see Political Developments since 1983, this ch.).

Franz Vranitzky, born in 1937, became chancellor in June 1986 when Sinowatz resigned after the SPÖ lost the presidential election to Kurt Waldheim. Vranitzky replaced Sinowatz as party chairman in May 1988, becoming the first person from a working-class background to hold this position. Despite his working-class heritage, Vranitzky had had a successful career in banking before entering politics.

Under Vranitzky the SPÖ moved to restore its image among rank-and-file members by improving its methods of intraparty communication. Computers and direct mail technology were used to gauge the opinions of members in the provinces, and efforts were made to improve recruiting techniques by means of recreational groups. In the area of government policy, Vranitzky stressed that limits on state activity were necessary, although he noted that health care and education were fields where market forces had to be regulated.

Vranitzky displayed a more open attitude toward the question of privatizing government industries than Kreisky had. To a large extent, changes in this area were inevitable because of large losses in the state industrial sector that came to light in 1985. Vranitzky embraced the principle that privatization should be pursued if it would lead to greater operational efficiency. The press dubbed Vranitzky's approach "pinstripe socialism." The policy has proven to be a responsible one and has been fairly popular with Austrians.

In 1984 the SPÖ launched a program called Perspectives '90, designed to promote intraparty discussion on current issues. A major aim of the leadership was to show that the party was eager

Bruno Kreisky,
federal chancellor, 1970–83
Courtesy Austrian National
Tourist Office, New York

Franz Vranitzky,
federal chancellor, 1986–
Courtesy Austrian National
Tourist Office, New York

to listen to grass-roots concerns. A series of nationwide debates eventually led to the issuance of a draft document in 1986 that incorporated the views of party members on issues such as the environment, controls on the development of technology, and democratization of society. Events that had embarrassed the party, such as the conflict over the Hainburg power plant in 1984 and Minister for Defense Friedhelm Frischenschläger's reception of Walter Reder in 1985, were also discussed (see Political Developments since 1983, this ch.).

An estimated 30,000 party members participated in the Perspectives '90 meetings, which took place in 1,000 local groups. The success of this project led the SPÖ to stage the Congress for the Future in Vienna in the summer of 1987, where 400 of the party's top leaders and intellectual luminaries discussed the outlook for social democracy. It was agreed that the SPÖ needed to formulate an alternative to the neoconservatism of the 1980s that would allow for greater codetermination in the workplace but also avoid the pitfalls of too much state control. After the success of this conference, the SPÖ began planning another that would produce a Social Democratic Manifesto for the Year 2000.

Membership in the SPÖ is direct (unlike the ÖVP, where a person joins an organization affiliated with the party). SPÖ's membership grew rapidly in the postwar period—from 360,000 members in 1946 to its peak of nearly 720,000 members in 1979. With the loosening of the grip of the *Lager* on Austrian society, the SPÖ's membership has declined slightly. In the early 1990s, it was estimated at 700,000.

Party organization remained centralized as of the early 1990s. The main links between rank-and-file members and party leaders are the activists known as *Vertrauenspersonen,* who personally collect annual membership dues. At the local level, the SPÖ is represented by almost 4,000 groups in villages and towns. Every two years, the SPÖ holds a federal conference that elects the party executive, which has sixty-five members. Because of the executive's unwieldy size, a smaller group, known as the presidium, is selected from it and actually conducts most party business.

Delegates to the federal conference are drawn from the various suborganizations of the party. The party has two youth organizations, the Young Generation (Junge Generation—JG) and the Socialist Youth of Austria (Sozialistische Jugend Österreichs —SJÖ). The Group of Socialist Trade Unionists (Fraktion Sozialistischer Gewerkschaftler—FSG) sends fifty-two delegates to the conference. There is also a Women's Committee, which has representatives from each province. Over the years, women have consistently made up one-third of the SPÖ's membership. In 1985 the federal conference passed an amendment providing for greater representation of women in the party and larger numbers of female candidates. Progress toward this goal has been slow, however, and in 1989 only eleven of the SPÖ's deputies in the Nationalrat were female.

SPÖ candidates for parliamentary elections are determined by the Party Council, whose members come from the nine provincial party organizations. The party executive and the heads of the nine provincial parties have an input into the selection process. Roughly one-fifth of the places are reserved for high-ranking party officials, whose presence in the Nationalrat is considered imperative.

The Austrian People's Party

The Austrian People's Party (Österreichische Volkspartei— ÖVP) was created in Vienna in 1945 by leaders of the former Christian Social Party (Christlichsoziale Partei—CSP). The founders of the ÖVP made sure that the new party was only loosely tied to the Roman Catholic Church, unlike its predecessor. The ÖVP emerged as a conservative, democratic party based on Christian values that sought to include diverse interests. From 1945 to 1966, ÖVP politicians filled the post of chancellor in a series of grand coalition governments with the SPÖ (from 1945 to 1947, KPÖ members were also in the cabinet). From 1966 to 1970, the ÖVP ruled alone and thereafter entered a long period of opposition to the SPÖ, which ended in early 1987 when the two parties formed a new coalition government (see table 15, Appendix).

The ÖVP periodically has revised its party program. During the 1945–55 period, the party advocated low taxes, reduced government expenditures, a balanced budget, and low wage increases. The ÖVP favored a limited government role in the economy. After much debate, in 1965 the party adopted the Klagenfurt Manifesto, which referred to the ÖVP as an "open people's party" of the "new center." The manifesto laid less emphasis than previous ones on the priority of personal property in a democracy. It also stressed the importance of expanding economic welfare and educational opportunities for all social groups.

After suffering losses in the 1970 parliamentary election, the ÖVP entered the opposition for the first time. A wide-ranging discussion of principles took place at all levels of the party. The outcome of this process was the 1972 Salzburg Program, which described the ÖVP as a "progressive center party" dedicated to integrating Austria's different social groups. The program reaffirmed the party's commitment to a free and independent country, a multiparty democracy, and a social market economy combining free enterprise and some government intervention. As of 1993, the Salzburg Program had not been replaced as the basic statement of ÖVP ideology.

The ÖVP had a less centralized form of party organization than the SPÖ as of the early 1990s. At the top is the party presidium, composed of the party chairman, the chancellor and vice chancellor (if they are members of the ÖVP), the general secretary, up to six deputies to the chairman, the leader of the party's parliamentary faction, and eight additional members drawn from the provinces and interest groups affiliated with the party. The party holds a national conference at least once every three years. Roughly 600 delegates from the provinces and the party's auxiliary organizations attend the conference, which elects the party chairman, the deputies, and the general secretary.

The auxiliary organizations play important roles in the ÖVP's internal workings. The key organizations are the League of Austrian Workers and Salaried Employees (Österreichischer Arbeiter- und Angestelltenbund—ÖAAB), the League of Austrian Business

(Österreichischer Wirtschaftsbund—ÖWB), and the League of Austrian Farmers (Österreichischer Bauernbund—ÖBB). These organizations represent the ÖVP in the chambers of labor, commerce, and agriculture, respectively. Until 1980 the leaders of these three groups were automatically placed on the party presidium. However, this practice was abandoned after many party members complained about undue influence by interest groups over ÖVP affairs. This reform was yet another indication of the erosion in the influence of the traditional *Lager* over Austrian society.

The majority of ÖVP members acquire party membership indirectly via one of the auxiliary organizations. Because of indirect membership, it is difficult to arrive at a precise figure for total membership in the ÖVP. At the beginning of the 1990s, the combined membership of the three leagues was about 800,000. Adding to this figure members of the women's, youth, and senior organizations, a total membership of 1.2 million was attained. However, the ÖVP's actual membership was about one-third smaller than this because many individuals belonged to more than one league or subgroup.

The independence of auxiliary organizations affiliated with the ÖVP means that there is a fairly high degree of intraparty disagreement over policies compared with the SPÖ and other Austrian parties. One major cleavage exists between the ÖAAB, which represents the interests of working people in the ÖVP, and the ÖWB, which speaks for business interests. The farmers' group, the ÖBB, has clashed with the ÖWB over the issue of whether Austria should join the European Union (EU—see Glossary). Tensions between the wings of the party remained high even in the early 1990s, despite numerous partywide discussions of ideology designed to bring about consensus. Some experts believe that the cohesion of the Catholic-conservative *Lager* will be endangered if the ÖVP does not achieve a higher degree of party unity than that prevailing in 1993.

Alois Mock, who comes from Lower Austria, one of the party's strongholds, held the position of party chairman from 1979 to 1989. As the party struggled with declining vote totals, many in the ÖVP concluded that his uncharismatic leadership style was a hindrance to a recovery at the polls. Mock withstood pressure for his ouster after the party's poor performance in the national election of 1986, and his stature temporarily increased when he became vice chancellor and foreign minister in the coalition government formed in early 1987 with the SPÖ. Discontent with Mock resurfaced quickly, however, and there were also disturbing signs of party disunity.

After the heavy losses incurred by the ÖVP in the provincial elections in the spring of 1989, Mock's opponents pressed again for his resignation. At an emergency summit in April 1989, Mock was finally convinced to step down as party chairman. He also relinquished the post of vice chancellor. His replacement in both positions was Josef Riegler, a member of the ÖBB from Styria.

Riegler had served as agriculture minister between 1987 and 1989 and was known as a consensus seeker who would be able to get along well with the SPÖ. Riegler was also interested in developing new approaches to environmental problems, and many in the party hoped this would help the ÖVP regain some of the voters who had deserted it for the environmental, or Green, parties.

However, the devastating results of the October 1990 national election, in which the ÖVP's share of the vote declined by 9 percent, proved that the party's problems went much deeper than who held the post of party chairman. In May 1991, Riegler decided not to run again for the party chairmanship. Erhard Busek, a well-known ÖVP politician who had headed the party's Vienna branch between 1976 and 1989, won the election to succeed Riegler. At the same time, the party conference voted to reduce the number of the chairman's deputies from six to two, a sign that party members wanted to curb the influence of the interest groups.

The Freedom Party of Austria

The Freedom Party of Austria (Freiheitliche Partei Österreichs— FPÖ) was founded in 1956 by Anton Reinthaller, who had served in the national socialist government of Arthur Seyss-Inquart formed in collaboration with Hitler after the Anschluss in 1938. Anticlerical and pro-German, the FPÖ was the party of persons who were uncomfortable with the domination of Austrian politics by the "red-black" (socialist-clerical) coalition governments of the SPÖ and ÖVP. The party had liberal and nationalist wings, which frequently disagreed over strategy. Although the FPÖ was not an extremist party, it attracted many former Nazis with its philosophy that Austrians should think of themselves as belonging to a greater German cultural community.

The FPÖ's stress on nationalism made it an atypical liberal party. Nevertheless, in 1979 the FPÖ was admitted to Liberal International, the worldwide group of liberal parties. The FPÖ's ideology emphasized the preservation of individual liberties in the face of the growth of the state's power. The party enthusiastically endorsed free enterprise and individual initiative and opposed a larger role for the state in the ownership of enterprises. The FPÖ was also against the socialist idea of striving for greater equality among socioeconomic groups.

After Reinthaller's death in 1958, Friedrich Peter became the head of the FPÖ. Under his leadership, the liberal wing increased its influence, and ties to the SPÖ were developed. However, the FPÖ remained a minor party with a limited opposition role in the parliament. Between 1956 and 1983, the FPÖ's share of the vote stagnated between 5.0 and 7.7 percent. After the election of 1970, the FPÖ struck a deal with the SPÖ, which promised electoral reform in exchange for the FPÖ's support of Kreisky's minority government. The ensuing changes in the electoral laws helped the FPÖ increase its representation in parliament in subsequent elections, despite the fact that its vote totals did not rise at the same time. Peter's hope that he could make the FPÖ attractive to the SPÖ as a coalition partner was dashed by Kreisky's success in obtaining absolute majorities in the elections of 1971, 1975, and 1979. It was only in 1983, when the SPÖ lost its majority, that it turned to the FPÖ to form a government. The FPÖ's brief three-year experience in power in the SPÖ-FPÖ coalition of 1983–86 was mostly frustrating, as the government stumbled from one crisis to the next.

Norbert Steger was FPÖ party chairman between 1980 and 1986. A member of the party's liberal wing, Steger served as vice chancellor and minister for trade in the SPÖ-FPÖ coalition. He was not a charismatic politician, and, as the coalition's troubles mounted, he began to lose support among the party's rank and file. At an FPÖ convention in the spring of 1986, Jörg Haider, leader of the Carinthian branch of the party, launched a successful coup against Steger and became the new chairman.

Haider, born in 1950, is a handsome, dashing figure whose self-confidence strikes many observers as verging on arrogance. He comes from the nationalist wing of the party and has stirred controversy on many occasions by his remarks about Austria's proper place in the German cultural community. On one occasion in 1988, Haider referred to Austria as "an ideological deformity."

Since Haider took control of the FPÖ in 1986, the party has achieved dramatic gains at the polls in both national and provincial elections. In the March 1989 provincial election in Carinthia, the FPÖ displaced the ÖVP as the second strongest party, and Haider was elected governor of the province with votes from the ÖVP. This election marked the first time that a provincial governor was not from either of the two major parties. Haider's term as governor was cut short in June 1991 by the controversy unleashed by his remark during a parliamentary debate that the Third Reich's employment policy was a positive model. The ÖVP and SPÖ joined together to pass a vote of no confidence against Haider, marking the first time in the history of the Second Republic that a governor was forced to step down. Haider did not allow this setback to create challenges to his leadership of the party. In three provincial elections in the fall of 1991, Haider led the FPÖ to outstanding showings, proving that Austrian voters were increasingly ready to vote for alternatives to the two major parties.

A less charitable interpretation of the FPÖ's rise under Haider is that Austrian politics has taken a turn to the right. At times in his career, Haider has given his critics ample reason for accusing him of neo-Nazi tendencies. He has frequently pandered to the sentiments of the far right, but his everyday political discourse is more moderate. Haider tailors his remarks to his audiences, and he resorts to the rhetoric of right-wing populism in order to inspire the conservative nationalists in the FPÖ.

A major element in Haider's prescriptions for Austria is his desire to cut down drastically on the number of foreigners allowed to live in the country. Haider consistently argues that immigration is excessive and is causing serious problems for Austrian citizens in the areas of jobs and housing. Haider's campaign against foreigners was a major reason for the passage of a 1991 law that decreed that foreign workers could not make up more than 10 percent of the work force. In 1993 this ceiling was reduced to 9 percent when a new law, the Resident Alien Law, went into effect. Early in the same year, Haider sponsored a referendum to further tighten the control over the number of foreigners in Austria. Although he got only half of the 800,000 signatures he sought, the language Haider used in his campaign was extreme enough to cause large counterdemonstrations.

The tensions between Haider and the liberal wing of the party caused five FPÖ members of the Nationalrat to leave the party in early 1993 and form a new party, The Liberal Forum (Das Liberale Forum). Led by the FPÖ's 1992 presidential candidate, Heide Schmidt, the group won seats in the Upper Austria provincial elections of May 1993. The new party was also recognized by Liberal International, which was expected to expel Haider's FPÖ from its ranks in 1994 because it advocated policies incompatible with traditional European liberalism.

Despite these setbacks, Haider is expected to remain a formidable force in Austrian politics. His sense for the issues that trouble many voters and his ability to enunciate views too extreme for the larger parties will likely win him a substantial following during the rest of the 1990s as the country struggles to adapt to post-Cold War conditions.

Membership in the FPÖ is direct (there is no tradition of joining an organization affiliated with the party, as with the SPÖ). The party's membership grew from 22,000 in 1959 to 40,000 in 1990. The membership-voter ratio declined as the party made dramatic gains at the polls. The FPÖ's share of the vote in national elections tripled between 1983 and 1990, when it achieved 16.6 percent. The FPÖ has a strong base of support in the provinces of Carinthia and Salzburg. The party draws much of its support from the middle class, salaried employees, and the self-employed. More than 60 percent of its voters are under the age of forty-four, and many are well educated. The party has few auxiliary organizations, in comparison with the ÖVP and the SPÖ. In addition to an organization for people in business, it has groups for academics, students, and retired persons. The FPÖ's party structure is decentralized, and provincial organizations play an important role in party affairs. The party chairman, who is elected by the party conference, chooses the party manager and general secretary. The general secretary acts as a liaison between federal leaders and provincial organizations.

The Green Parties

Another clear sign that the Austrian party system is loosening up was the emergence during the early 1980s of organized environmental, or Green, parties. A major catalyst in the birth of the Green movement in Austria was the narrow defeat of the November 5, 1978, national referendum on nuclear energy. The Kreisky government, seeking to build a nuclear power plant in Zwentendorf near Vienna, decided to let the people decide on the question of nuclear energy (see Domestic Issues, ch. 1).

The victory of the antinuclear forces encouraged environmental activists to run in local elections, and in 1982 two national Green parties were formed. The more moderate of the two, the United Greens of Austria (Vereinigte Grüne Österreichs—VGÖ), had a strong commitment to working within the existing political system to change environmental policies. The Alternative List of Austria (Alternative Liste Österreichs—ALÖ), founded in 1982 on the fourth anniversary of the Zwentendorf referendum, was more willing to challenge the political status quo. In addition to championing radical changes in environmental policy, the ALÖ also advocated a guaranteed national income, a thirty-five-hour workweek, and greater government ownership in certain areas of the economy.

The prospects of the Green parties are limited by their frequent inability to form alliances for the purpose of contesting elections. When the ALÖ and VGÖ have campaigned on a common ticket, they usually have won seats in parliament. In 1983, the first national election in which the Green parties participated, the two groups ran on separate lists, and both failed to gain representation in the Nationalrat. The Green cause received a strong boost in 1984 from the confrontation between the SPÖ–FPÖ government and environmental activists opposed to the plan to build a hydroelectric plant in a wetland forest at Hainburg in eastern Austria. The government backed down from its plan, and the incident led to an increase in support for the Green parties from disillusioned SPÖ voters, intellectuals, and others with strong views on the environment.

Green activist Freda Meissner-Blau ran in the May 1986 presidential election, taking a surprising 5.5 percent of the vote, which necessitated a runoff between the ÖVP and SPÖ candidates. Encouraged by this showing, the ALÖ and VGÖ, after long negotiations, agreed to participate in the November 1986 national election on a single list, named the Green Alternative—Freda Meissner-Blau List. The Green Alternative took 4.8 percent of the vote and won eight seats in parliament. This marked only the second time in the history of the Second Republic that a fourth party had entered the Nationalrat. (The KPÖ had been in the parliament between 1945 and 1959.) The harmony between the two groups was short-lived, however, as they clashed over how to divide the federal financing that became available to the Green movement. In the 1990 national election, the VGÖ put up its own list of candidates, and the ALÖ ran as the Green Alternative/Greens in Parliament (Grüne Alternative/Grüne in Parlament—GAL). The VGÖ polled only 1.9 percent of the vote and failed to win any seats. The GAL took 4.5 percent of the vote and increased the number of Green deputies to ten.

As of the early 1990s, the future of Green politics in Austria remained uncertain because of the strong differences between the GAL and VGÖ over political strategy. The VGÖ was committed to developing a centralized party structure along the lines of the ÖVP and SPÖ, while the GAL preferred to allow complete autonomy for its affiliated organizations in the provinces. There were also questions about the longevity of the Greens' appeal to voters. Studies indicated that only 50 percent of Green voters had close ties to a Green party, and roughly 35 percent of Green votes came from floating voters who had abandoned the two major parties. However, many Austrians felt a lack of confidence in the abilities of the ÖVP and SPÖ to fashion constructive policies, and as long as this doubt persists, the Green parties will have opportunities to elect deputies to parliament.

Austria: A Country Study

Political Developments since 1983

In 1983 a thirteen-year period of single-party rule by the SPÖ came to an end. The period had been dominated by Bruno Kreisky, who served as chancellor for the entire time (see The Kreisky Years, 1970–83, ch. 1). With Kreisky as its leader, the SPÖ had emerged from the election in 1970 as the strongest party. This election marked a turning point in Austrian history because never before had a socialist party been given such a mandate by the voters. The outcome was conclusive proof that most Austrians had lost their fear of the SPÖ's being too leftist to govern alone.

SPÖ–FPÖ Coalition, 1983–86

In the election of 1983, the SPÖ lost its absolute majority in the Nationalrat, although it remained the largest party (see End of the Kreisky Era, ch. 1). Kreisky fulfilled his pledge to resign as chancellor if the SPÖ lost its undisputed position in parliament. Fred Sinowatz, a rather colorless figure who had been minister for education under Kreisky, was selected as the new chancellor. The SPÖ decided to form a coalition with the FPÖ, marking the first time ever that the FPÖ had joined the government. Norbert Steger, the moderate chairman of the FPÖ, was named vice chancellor and minister for economic affairs, and other members of his party became minister for defense and minister for justice.

The SPÖ–FPÖ coalition lasted only three years and was not very productive. It faced a series of crises that never allowed it to become firmly established. Although the coalition had made progress on environmental protection a high priority, its decision to build a hydroelectric plant at Hainburg in a wetland forest east of Vienna provoked a storm of opposition from environmental activists. In the end, the government decided to cancel the project (see The Green Parties, this ch.).

The coalition's image received another black mark in 1985 when FPÖ Minister for Defense Friedhelm Frischenschläger staged a welcoming ceremony at the airport for Walter Reder, a former Waffen SS member who had been serving a life sentence for executing civilians during World War II before being pardoned by the Italians. Some SPÖ members of the cabinet threatened to resign over this affair, but Frischenschläger was allowed to remain in his post. This incident hurt the SPÖ's standing among its own members, as well as among independent voters.

Austria received further unpleasant jolts in 1985. First came the news that diethylene glycol, a chemical used in antifreeze, had been

202

added to Austrian wines in potentially lethal amounts. The wines affected came from Burgenland, the home province of Chancellor Sinowatz. Even more damaging to the country's self-image, however, was the crisis in the state-run industrial sector that came to light at roughly the same time. The government announced that it had uncovered a financial scandal at the United Austrian Iron and Steel Works (Vereinigte Österreichische Eisen- und Stahlwerke—VÖEST; commonly known as VÖEST-Alpine) in Linz. Public funds were required to cover large losses incurred through risky and unauthorized speculation in oil ventures. Moreover, the entire state industrial sector required streamlining, and jobs had to be cut.

The method of staffing these industries was a prime example of the ÖVP and SPÖ's *Proporz* system, which created fiefdoms in which political affiliations were the main criteria for filling high-level management positions. The crisis in this sector of the economy revealed that the Kreisky governments had been guilty of serious mismanagement. The confidence of the SPÖ in particular was shaken as it faced the need for privatization and layoffs. The government abolished the *Proporz* system at VÖEST-Alpine and appointed new management to rectify the problems.

Election of Kurt Waldheim as President

In 1986 Austrians prepared to elect a new president. The race featured two major candidates, Kurt Waldheim for the ÖVP and Kurt Steyrer for the SPÖ, plus two less well-known candidates, a Green party activist and a former member of the FPÖ. Waldheim was one of Austria's best known citizens by virtue of his having served two terms as secretary general of the United Nations in the 1970s. Waldheim had joined the ÖVP only in early 1985 when the party decided to offer him its presidential candidate's spot. He was presented to the voters as "the man the world trusts." Steyrer was the minister for health and the environment in the SPÖ–FPÖ government. His campaign stressed his role as a family man and a humanitarian.

The 1986 presidential campaign would have taken place without many people outside Austria taking note of it, except that it focused on an issue that proved extremely sensitive for audiences inside and outside of the country. In March 1986, *Profil*, a Vienna-based magazine specializing in investigative reporting, began to publish a series of articles claiming that Waldheim had left out crucial details about his service in the army, the German Wehrmacht, during World War II. In an autobiography published a few months before, Waldheim had glossed over most of his wartime service, alleging that he had spent much of the war in Vienna studying law while recuperating from wounds he had received. *Profil,* foreign newspapers, and the World Jewish Council in New York unearthed evidence that Waldheim had spent considerable time on duty in the Balkans and in Salonika, Greece. The German army had carried out brutal occupations of these areas, murdering thousands of Yugoslav partisans and deporting Greek Jews to the concentration camps in Central Europe. Waldheim, while not accused of personally participating in any atrocities, made the unbelievable claim that he had not heard of any misdeeds by the German armed forces in the Balkans or Greece until he had read the current newspaper accounts. He stuck by his account that he had been on leave when atrocities were committed, and he defended himself by saying he "had only done his duty as a soldier."

As the scrutiny of Waldheim intensified, Austrians became polarized over whether to defend or criticize him. Many older Austrians, particularly those who had served in the German army, agreed with his self-defense that he had merely done his duty in a war that Austria had not wished for. Others became more suspicious of Waldheim when documentary evidence was produced suggesting that he may have joined the Nazi Party to further his chances for a diplomatic career. The presidential campaign degenerated into a mudslinging affair, and the ÖVP launched attacks against the character of the SPÖ candidate.

Despite the furor surrounding him, on May 4, 1986, Waldheim outpolled Steyrer by 49.7 to 43.7 percent. He fell only 16,000 votes short of the absolute majority required for victory, and thus a runoff between the two top candidates was scheduled for June 8. Waldheim won the runoff handily, garnering 54 percent of the vote. Steyrer's candidacy had been handicapped by his membership in a government burdened by financial mismanagement of state industries and other scandals. Waldheim benefited from a wave of sympathy from certain segments of the Austrian electorate, who viewed him as a victim of unfair attacks.

The Waldheim presidency proved to be a major burden for Austria. In April 1987, after a one-year study of the matter by the United States Department of Justice, the United States placed Waldheim on its "watch list" of undesirable aliens. The department had concluded that there was "a prima facie case that Kurt Waldheim assisted or otherwise participated in the persecution of persons because of race, religion, national origin, or political opinion." Waldheim became the first active chief of state ever to be placed on the list of 40,000 subversives, terrorists, and criminals. Waldheim became isolated internationally and found support only from the Soviet

Union, some of the communist governments of Eastern Europe, and Arab states such as Jordan, one of the few countries he was to visit during his presidency.

In June 1987, the Viennese branch of the SPÖ passed a resolution calling for Waldheim to resign. Chancellor Vranitzky and Sinowatz, the chairman of the SPÖ, defended Waldheim, arguing that he had been elected democratically. Strains were beginning to appear within the ÖVP–SPÖ coalition over the affair, and somehow a resolution needed to be brought about. In an effort to achieve this resolution, the Austrian government announced that it would appoint an international panel of historians and human rights experts to examine the whole matter.

The panel presented its findings in February 1988. The panel found no direct evidence that Waldheim had participated in war crimes during his military service in the Balkans and Greece. However, it concluded that he must have had some knowledge that atrocities were taking place. Predictably, Waldheim took the panel's report as his exoneration, as did most ÖVP leaders. The president gave a speech in which he said he believed it to be in the best interests of Austria that he remain in office.

The release of the panel's report came one month before the fiftieth anniversary of the Anschluss of March 1938. At a public commemoration of this event in Vienna, Vranitzky solemnly informed the Austrian people that it was time for all of them to face up to the fact that their country had been not only the first victim of Nazi aggression but also a participant in Hitler's military conquests. Waldheim gave a television address in which he described the Holocaust as one of the greatest tragedies of history and admitted that Austrians had played a role in it. He condemned fanaticism and intolerance and expounded on Austria's dual role as victim and culprit. For Waldheim's critics, it was a respectable performance, but woefully late. Austrian emotions had been rubbed raw by the Waldheim affair, but at least it presented Austrians with an opportunity to discuss openly issues that had effectively been taboo for fifty years.

The National Election of 1986 and the Grand Coalition of 1987–90

The election of Waldheim had a large impact on Austrian domestic politics as well. After Waldheim's victory, Sinowatz, the SPÖ chancellor who had been perceived as ineffective, resigned, and the SPÖ turned to Franz Vranitzky to fill the top position. Vranitzky decided to dissolve the SPÖ–FPÖ coalition when the leadership of the junior party was usurped in September 1986 by Jörg Haider. Haider was prone to making controversial remarks about Austria's place in the greater German cultural identity, and Vranitzky had little hesitation in cutting the SPÖ's ties to the FPÖ under its new leader. This action led to a premature parliamentary election in November 1986. Pressures for an early election also came from the financial failures in the state industrial sector that had embarrassed the SPÖ–FPÖ government.

The outcome of the election was a shock to both major parties, as the FPÖ attained its highest vote total since 1953, receiving 9.7 percent. The SPÖ lost ten seats in the Nationalrat, dropping to eighty, and the ÖVP lost four, declining to seventy-seven. After lengthy negotiations, in early 1987 the two major parties decided to form a grand coalition for the first time since 1966. Vranitzky remained chancellor, and Alois Mock, leader of the ÖVP, became vice chancellor and foreign minister. The two parties agreed to split the remaining cabinet posts, with the Ministry for Justice going to a person with no party affiliation. Former Chancellor Kreisky complained loudly about Vranitzky's giving the foreign ministry portfolio to the ÖVP, and he resigned as honorary chairman of the SPÖ in protest.

The new grand coalition was not able to function in the cozy way the old grand coalition had because media scrutiny was much greater in the 1980s than it had been between 1945 and 1966. Further, one of the coalition's top priorities was to address the problems in the state industrial sector and the budget deficit in general. The government carried out job cutbacks and early retirement programs at VÖEST-Alpine, the state-run iron and steel conglomerate, and also reduced subsidies to farmers. These policies hurt key interests of both parties' core constituencies, but ÖVP and SPÖ leaders saw little alternative to tackling these problems head on. Austrian politics had entered a new stage that was short on the optimism of the Kreisky era and focused on pragmatic and hard-headed solutions to economic problems.

The ÖVP–SPÖ government benefited from improving economic conditions, especially from 1988 onward. Economic growth for the years 1988–90 averaged around 4 percent annually. Other economic indicators were also positive, with unemployment averaging around 5 percent and inflation running at 2.5 percent. In the political realm, however, the coalition was plagued by numerous scandals involving primarily high-ranking officials of the SPÖ. In late 1988 and early 1989, two of these officials were forced to resign for large-scale tax evasion. Chancellor Vranitzky, who had replaced Sinowatz as party chairman in May 1988, initially was hesitant to fire his friend Günther Sallaberger, who had failed to pay taxes on S1.8 million (for value of the schilling—see Glossary). Pressure to remove

Sallaberger became intense after party members were shocked to learn that he was an example of a trend in which holders of multiple posts within the SPÖ were actually earning more money than the chancellor.

An even larger scandal emerged when the SPÖ became embroiled in an insurance scandal centering on Udo Proksch, the notorious former owner of Demel's, Vienna's most famous coffee house and meetingplace for SPÖ bigwigs. A ship commissioned by Proksch, the *Lucona,* had sunk in 1977 with the loss of six crew members. Proksch claimed that the ship had been carrying a uranium processing plant, but documents describing the ship's cargo were found to have been forged, and Proksch was accused of deliberately sinking the vessel. The investigation into the affair moved at a snail's pace. By early 1989, a parliamentary committee that had been formed to look into the case began to focus on two leading SPÖ officials, Minister for Interior Karl Blecha and Leopold Gratz, the first president of the Nationalrat.

The committee's investigations provided some of the most dramatic political theater ever seen in the Second Republic. After tough cross-examinations of subordinate officials, the committee and the public began to suspect that Blecha had deliberately slowed up the *Lucona* investigation in the early 1980s. Blecha's denials of any wrongdoing were unconvincing, and Vranitzky forced him to resign.

Gratz, who had been foreign minister at the time the forged documents relating to the *Lucona*'s cargo had arrived in Vienna, was suspected of even greater complicity in the affair. As the committee did its work, it appeared increasingly clear that Gratz had covered up important details of the affair to protect Proksch. Gratz resigned his position when, like Blecha, he had lost all support within the SPÖ. In the face of a very bleak ethical situation, Vranitzky could at least claim that he had acted relatively quickly to clean house.

The Parliamentary Election of 1990

The ÖVP and SPÖ approached the parliamentary election of 1990 with trepidation. In 1989 the political landscape had been shaken by Haider's FPÖ, which had racked up impressive gains in provincial elections in Carinthia, Salzburg, and Tirol. Even though questions had been raised about Haider's honesty, he continued to entice voters to leave the major parties. The FPÖ scored a spectacular success in Carinthia, where it displaced the ÖVP as the second largest party, and it caused the ÖVP to lose its absolute majority in Salzburg.

In the October 1990 national election, the FPÖ again shocked the political establishment by increasing its share of the vote from 9.7 to 16.6 percent. This gain came almost completely at the expense of the ÖVP, whose share of the vote declined from 41.3 to 32.1 percent. The SPÖ's share of the vote remained essentially the same, which surprised everyone. The party, realizing that its strong suit was the popularity of Vranitzky, employed a new electoral strategy that probably explains its ability to avoid the ÖVP's fate. With Vranitzky as the top candidate in all nine electoral districts, the SPÖ urged voters to cast preference votes for Vranitzky, which could be done without selecting the SPÖ box on the ballot (these votes would count toward the SPÖ's total number of seats in the Nationalrat, however). A nonpartisan committee was organized to carry out this campaign, and it succeeded in attracting support from sources that otherwise might not have voted for the SPÖ in the regular manner. Because of disagreements between the two Green parties, they did not run on a united ticket as they had in 1986. The Green Alternative/Greens in Parliament (Grüne Alternative/Grüne in Parlament—GAL), formerly known as the Alternative List of Austria, received 4.5 percent and increased its seats in the parliament from eight to ten. The United Greens of Austria (Vereinigte Grüne Österreichs—VGÖ) received only 1.9 percent and won no seats.

Given the antipathy that Vranitzky felt for Haider, there was no chance of a revival of an SPÖ–FPÖ coalition. After a period of negotiations, the SPÖ and ÖVP agreed to continue the grand coalition. Because economic conditions were much improved in comparison with 1986, the new coalition planned to focus on issues such as social welfare, health care, science, and research. Attention would also be given to reforming the country's electoral system and its chambers of commerce and labor. Increasing numbers of Austrians regarded the former as unrepresentative and resented the latter's requirement of compulsory membership. The coalition partners decided to upgrade the position of state secretary for women's affairs to full cabinet rank, and the new Ministry for Women's Affairs was created to oversee these matters.

Events of 1991–93

The trend toward the dissolution of the two-party system was confirmed by the outcomes in four provincial elections held in 1991. The FPÖ increased its share of the vote in all four elections, and in Styria and Upper Austria it tripled its vote to 15.4 and 17.7 percent, respectively. In Vienna the FPÖ displaced the ÖVP as the second most powerful party in the provincial legislature, a particularly embarrassing result for the ÖVP. The ÖVP lost ground in all four elections, while the SPÖ lost seats in three elections. With its showing in Vienna, the FPÖ became the second strongest party in two of Austria's nine provinces, having achieved the same status in Carinthia in 1989, also displacing the ÖVP.

In June 1991, President Kurt Waldheim announced that he would not seek reelection in 1992. ÖVP leaders were relieved that Waldheim had decided to retire from politics because they feared the eruption of another bitter controversy over his wartime record if he had chosen to run. Waldheim became the first incumbent Austrian president not to seek reelection. Initially, the ÖVP and SPÖ looked into the possibility of nominating a joint candidate for the 1992 election. However, the two parties were unable to agree on a candidate, and in November 1991 they and the FPÖ each announced separate candidates. The ÖVP selected Thomas Klestil, a career diplomat and former ambassador to the United States. The SPÖ candidate was Rudolf Streicher, head of the Ministry for National Industry and Transportation. The FPÖ candidate was Heide Schmidt, who was also third president of the Nationalrat. The Green candidate was the scientist Robert Jungk.

No candidate was able to win an absolute majority in the first balloting on April 26, 1992. Streicher polled 41 percent, compared with Klestil's 37 percent, but far ahead of Schmidt's 16 percent and Jungk's 6 percent. In the run-off elections four weeks later, when only the top two candidates were on the ballots, Klestil scored an easy victory over Streicher with 57 percent of the total vote. Controversy about his opponent's war record, a series of scandals connected to the SPÖ, and Klestil's skill in dealing with the media contributed to his easy victory in the second round of voting. Perhaps most important, however, was his career as a diplomat abroad, which had kept him out of politics (although he was an ÖVP member) and made him seem well suited for leading the country into the post-Cold War era.

The collapse of the Soviet empire and the former Yugoslavia increased the number of foreigners coming to Austria. The influx of asylum seekers and illegal immigrants posed a challenge to Austrian authorities. In 1992 and 1993, new laws went into effect that sought to reduce the number of those coming to the country for asylum and to more strictly control the large foreign community already present in Austria. The laws resulted both from serious practical problems of caring for foreigners in need of food and fears of many Austrians that their country was in danger of *Überfremdung*, that is, being submerged by ever-increasing waves of foreign immigrants. Some politicians, most notably Haider, sought to profit politically from these fears.

In early 1993, a referendum sponsored by Haider was held to determine popular support for further tightening the laws regulating foreigners. More than 400,000 signatures were collected, half of what Haider had sought but still a significant response. Large counterdemonstrations were held to protest Haider's suggested policies, but it was clear that Haider had tapped into widespread fears and resentments. Haider's extremism resulted in some FPÖ members leaving the party and forming their own party, The Liberal Forum (Das Liberale Forum). Led by Heide Schmidt, the FPÖ presidential candidate in 1992, the group won three seats in the May 1993 Landtag election in Upper Austria. Additional successes for the new party were its being recognized both by the Nationalrat as a political party and by Liberal International.

Apprehension about joining—or not joining—the European Union (EU—see Glossary) was another force driving Austrian politics. As the economy slumped and headed to an overall negative growth rate for 1993, Haider modified his previous endorsement of EU membership, sensing a chance to profit from fears about what Austria's participation in a larger Europe might bring. The ÖVP and SPÖ remained strongly in favor. After much delay, Austria will join the European Economic Area (EEA—see Glossary) on January 1, 1994. The EEA will then consist of EU and European Free Trade Association (EFTA—see Glossary) countries, with the exception of Switzerland, and will form a free-market economy of sixteen nations and 380 million inhabitants.

Mass Media

The Austrian press operates freely under the constitution of 1920, which guarantees all citizens freedom of expression in speech, writing, and print. The constitution also forbids any government censorship of the press or electronic media. Austria has a well-developed system of print and electronic media that provides its citizens with a wide variety of news sources and entertainment.

Newspapers and Periodicals

The Austrian newspaper market is one of the most concentrated in Europe. Three dailies, the *Neue Kronen-Zeitung, Täglich Alles,* and *Kurier,* account for more than half of the newspapers sold in the country. By 1993 their daily circulations were 1.1 million, 500,000, and 390,000, respectively, with higher circulations on Sundays. All three specialize in tabloid-style journalism, with a tendency toward sensationalism. Better educated Austrians, especially in the larger cities, read either *Die Presse* or *Der Standard,* both high-quality newspapers published in Vienna with circulations of less than 100,000.

As of the early 1990s, a total of seventeen daily newspapers were published in Austria, and thirteen regional editions of some of these papers were published. Since the early 1970s, the importance of political party newspapers has declined precipitously. The SPÖ publishes one newspaper and the ÖVP two, all of which have circulations of less than 100,000. The SPÖ's venerable newspaper, *Arbeiterzeitung,* established in 1895, was sold to private interests in the late 1980s when the party decided it no longer wished to cover the newspaper's massive losses.

Austria also has many periodicals and magazines. Among the weekly periodicals, *Profil,* with a circulation of more than 100,000 in 1993, has emerged as one of the best practitioners of investigative journalism in the country. Another weekly magazine, *News,* has a circulation of more than 200,000, although it was only founded in October 1992. Other periodicals of note include *Wochenpresse,* a weekly; *Trend,* a monthly journal devoted to economic news; and *Wiener,* a monthly.

Rising concern over financial difficulties faced by small publishers led the Austrian government to decide in 1975 that subsidies should be made available to newspapers and magazines meeting certain criteria. For a daily newspaper to receive government funds, it must have a minimum circulation of 10,000 and regional distribution. Weekly newspapers are required to have a minimum circulation of 5,000. Magazines are eligible for funds if they publish between four and forty issues a year. To be considered for funding, a newspaper or magazine must file a formal application with the government. Specific allocations are decided on a case-by-case basis, and various formulas are used to spread the funds among a large number of publications. No single newspaper can receive more than 5 percent of the total budget earmarked for support of the daily press.

In 1982 Austria brought its press laws up to date with the passage of the Federal Law on the Press and Other Journalistic Media, which clarifies the rights of individuals to sue for damages when they believe they have been slandered or defamed by the press. The law establishes maximum amounts of S50,000 for defamation of character and S100,000 for slander. The law stipulates that damages are not to be awarded if it can be shown that the public interest was served by the publication of the material or of allegations in dispute. The law also grants individuals and corporations the right to respond in print to published reports they regard as defamatory. However, a newspaper can refuse to publish a rejoinder if it can prove that the report is not factual. Individuals and corporations may respond only to factual reporting; articles containing editorial opinions and value judgments are not covered by this provision of the press law.

Other provisions of the 1982 law strengthened the rights of journalists. Journalists are guaranteed the right to refuse to collaborate in assignments they regard as incompatible with their ethical convictions. The law also affirms the right of journalists not to divulge their sources in a court of law. The law further states that the government may not place the communications facilities of an organ of the press under surveillance unless it has reason to believe that a crime carrying a sentence of at least ten years may have been committed.

Radio and Television

As of late 1993, radio and television programming in Austria was provided exclusively by Austrian Radio and Television (Österreichischer Rundfunk—ORF). This state monopoly is expected to end in the mid-1990s because such monopolies are no longer seen by many European jurists as compatible with the free exchange of information and ideas. ORF was formed as a public corporation in 1945 and reorganized in 1967 for greater political and financial independence. In 1974 a constitutional law was passed giving ORF complete financial autonomy from the government and guaranteeing it freedom from attempts by the government or any state body to exert influence on programming. Additional laws passed in that year required ORF to present objective reporting, a variety of opinions, and balanced programming.

As of 1993, ORF had two television channels and three radio channels. FS 1 and FS 2, the two television channels, feature a wide variety of programs, including news, entertainment, education, and music. In 1988 the nine regional ORF studios began broadcasting local programs. Various groups attempted to make the case for allowing independent television in Austria, but, as of 1993, they had not persuaded the government to lift the monopoly enjoyed by ORF. During the 1980s, cable television became available, and by 1990 roughly 15 percent of Austrian homes received cable programming. One of the major cable programs, 3 Sat, is a joint venture of ORF, the Swiss Broadcasting Corporation, and one of Germany's television networks.

ORF has four radio channels. The first channel, Österreich 1, features culturally oriented programs devoted to music, literature, science, and news. The second channel, Österreich Regional, carries programming produced by the nine regional ORF stations, with an emphasis on popular entertainment and local events. Österreich 3 is an entertainment channel, which also carries hourly news broadcasts. The fourth network, Blue Danube Radio, is also an entertainment channel but differs in that it broadcasts mainly in English. Its news programs are in German, English, and French.

Foreign Relations

Since 1955 the guiding principle of Austrian foreign policy has been neutrality. As part of an agreement reached that year with the Four Powers (Britain, France, the Soviet Union, and the United States), Austria passed an amendment to its constitution declaring that it would forever remain neutral. Specifically, Austria pledged that it would never join any military alliances or allow foreign troops to be stationed on its soil. The commitment to neutrality was seen by virtually all political groups as a sensible step to achieve the complete removal of occupying forces from the country.

However, Austria chose to pursue a looser model of neutrality than that followed by other states, such as Switzerland. Austria joined the United Nations (UN) in 1955, shortly after making its neutrality pledge. Austria did not take neutrality to mean that it should occupy a moral middle ground between the democratic countries of the West and the totalitarian states of the East during the Cold War period. In terms of political and social ideology, Austria was firmly within the community of democratic nations.

A second important principle of Austrian foreign policy is internationalism. Austria is active in many international organizations, such as the UN and its subsidiary agencies. The country is a long-time participant in UN peacekeeping operations. An Austrian medical team served in the Congo (present-day Zaire) between 1960 and 1963, and medical teams and soldiers have served continuously in Cyprus since 1964 and at various times in Egypt and Israel since 1968. Vienna is the home of two UN entities, the International Atomic Energy Agency and the United Nations Industrial Development Organization. During the Cold War period, Austria consistently supported all attempts at fostering détente between the United States and the Soviet Union. Austria's leaders pursued this policy because they realized that heightened tensions between the superpowers would make the maintenance of their country's neutrality more difficult.

Foreign Policy During the Kreisky Era

Bruno Kreisky, who had served as foreign minister between 1959

213

The Vienna International Center is also known as United Nations City because numerous United Nations offices are located there.
Courtesy Embassy of Austria, Washington

and 1966, laid great emphasis on an active, internationalist foreign policy during his tenure as chancellor (1970–83). Kreisky's vision of foreign policy was based on the notion that Austria, as a neutral country, should seek to mediate conflicts between countries and stake out independent and innovative policies on various issues. He offered Vienna as a site for many series of negotiations on nuclear arms reductions and other international matters.

Among Kreisky's more controversial policies was his decision to grant informal diplomatic recognition to the Palestine Liberation Organization (PLO) in 1980. This was an outgrowth of Kreisky's conviction that Israel was stubbornly refusing to recognize the legitimate interests of the Palestinian people. The fact that Kreisky was Jewish gave him a certain credibility in becoming so involved in trying to solve the Arab-Israeli conflict. Kreisky further surprised the world by receiving Libyan leader Muammar al Qadhafi in Vienna. He also showed his independent approach with his decision that Austria should participate in the 1980 Summer Olympics in Moscow, despite the boycott of the games orchestrated by United States president Jimmy Carter in response to the Soviet invasion of Afghanistan in 1979. Austria also did not adhere to the economic boycott of Iran organized by the United States after the seizure of its embassy in Tehran in 1979.

During the 1970s, Austria collaborated extensively with other neutral and nonaligned countries in the UN. Austria developed an independent voting profile, frequently joining with other neutrals such as Sweden to press for action on issues ignored by countries belonging to military alliances. Austria also pursued this kind of diplomacy with the nonaligned countries belonging to the Conference on Security and Cooperation in Europe.

New Focus on Europe

After Kreisky's departure from the political scene in 1983, Austrian foreign policy became more focused on European matters and less on global issues. This shift was caused partly by the increase in tensions between the United States and the Soviet Union, as United States diplomacy under President Ronald Reagan became more confrontational. In this climate, Austria's room to pursue a foreign policy of mediation was more constricted. Concern that the country faced exclusion from the increasing political and economic integration of Europe being pursued by the European Community (EC) was another factor that came to exert strong influence on Austrian diplomacy. The traditional concept of Austrian neutrality had held that membership in the EC was not possible or desirable, even though the EC was not a military alliance. The idea of ceding even limited areas of political and economic sovereignty to a supranational organization was seen as incompatible with neutrality.

As an alternative to the EC, Austria had joined with Britain, Denmark, Norway, Portugal, Sweden, and Switzerland to form the European Free Trade Association (EFTA) in 1960. EFTA was restricted to facilitating trade among its members and did not involve the ceding of sovereign powers. Austria also negotiated a special economic arrangement with the EC in 1972 that allowed for the duty-free exchange of industrial manufactured goods.

By the mid-1980s, the opinion of Austria's political elites had changed in favor of seriously considering the advantages and disadvantages of EC membership. Many argued that Austria could not expect to guarantee its economic future if it remained outside the EC. Two-thirds of Austria's trade was with members of the EC, with the Federal Republic of Germany (West Germany) by far its largest trading partner. There was also a fear that the country could become isolated within Europe as ideological barriers between East and West were lowered.

A long period of debate among the major parties over EC membership began in 1987, and the cabinet established a working group to examine the issue. It gradually became clear that, despite some misgivings over the expected impact of EC membership in certain areas, the two major parties, the ÖVP and SPÖ, favored applying for entry. The trade unions had some concerns about EC membership's diminishing their strong bargaining powers in the Austrian system of social partnership, but they, too, generally favored joining (see Social Partnership, ch. 3). There was also widespread concern that the high volume of highway traffic passing through Austria en route to West Germany and Italy was damaging the country's environment (see Ecological Concerns, ch. 2). Many Austrians believed that their country's environmental laws were stricter than those of the EC. The priority of protecting the environment led the Green deputies in parliament to oppose joining the EC.

Within the two major parties, there was little concern over the neutrality issue, and government leaders pointed out that although the EC might someday add a military dimension to its structure, for the foreseeable future it would remain primarily an economic union with aspirations of developing greater political unity. The new climate of *glasnost* in the Soviet Union ushered in by Mikhail Gorbachev led Austrian leaders to expect no objection from Moscow to an Austrian decision to seek EC membership, and this expectation proved true.

The government reached an internal consensus in favor of applying for membership in June 1989, and the following month, Foreign Minister Alois Mock delivered the application to the EC Commission in Brussels. Chancellor Vranitzky emphasized to his countrymen that during the upcoming negotiations with Brussels his government would seek clear understandings on the maintenance of environmental standards and the preservation of Austria's advanced social welfare system. Vranitzky also asserted that the issue of limiting the volume of motor vehicle traffic passing through Austrian territory would be handled separately from the application to join the EC. Austria's application met with a chilly reception from some quarters in Europe, especially from a few politicians who argued that the admission of a neutral country could hinder efforts at coordinating the foreign policies of the EC's members. However, the momentous events of late 1989 and 1990—the freeing of Czechoslovakia, Hungary, and Poland from Soviet domination and the unification of Germany—made it clear to all observers that Austrian neutrality would take on a new dimension and might even be jettisoned altogether. The disintegration of the communist system in the Soviet Union in late 1991 further reinforced the impression that neutrality was of little relevance in the new Europe.

In August 1991, after an examination of the Austrian application, the EC issued an initial assessment that was predominantly favorable. By late 1993, negotiations between Austria and the European Union (EU), the organization's name as of November 1993, were continuing over the terms of membership. Most observers expected that the EU and Austria would be able to reach an agreement on Austrian entry and that the country would join the EU in January 1995. The main issues involved limiting international road traffic through Alpine regions because of environmental concerns, subsidies for Alpine farming, and foreign ownership of residences in some parts of Austria. A less certain matter was whether the Austrian government could convince a majority of Austrians to support EU membership. The question of joining the EU will be voted on in a popular referendum because any governmental action that changes the constitution must pass this test. Many opinion polls taken in the early 1990s showed Austrians evenly divided over the merits of joining the EU. In order to ensure approval by the electorate, the Austrian government will have to gain significant concessions from the EU in the negotiations and mount an effective public relations campaign in favor of a yes vote.

Regional Issues

Austria has generally enjoyed good relations with its neighbors, although there have been exceptions. The most notable exception has been its relationship with Italy, which was strained by the issue over South Tirol during the 1960s. This largely German-speaking region, which belonged to Austria-Hungary prior to World War I, was ceded to Italy in 1919 as a result of the peace negotiations. Until 1992 ethnic Germans in South Tirol, in the present-day region of Trentino-Alto Adige, had to struggle to maintain the measure of autonomy promised to them by the Italian government. Acts of terrorism directed against Italian targets became a serious problem in the 1960s, and Italy accused Austria of not doing enough to capture terrorists whom it claimed were using Austrian territory as a sanctuary. Austria and Italy eventually reached an agreement in 1969 on a timetable for satisfying the demands of the German-speaking South Tiroleans for cultural autonomy. Progress was slow, but in June 1992 an agreement was finally realized that granted the German speakers a greater degree of autonomy. Although not allowed the right to secede from Italy, the cultural rights of German speakers in Trentino-Alto Adige were enhanced with guarantees of education in their own language, greater representation in the civil service, and the right to go to the International Court of Justice in The Hague without permission from the government in Rome. Both Italian and Austrian authorities have declared themselves satisfied with the agreement.

Austria became concerned as the political stability of its neighbor to the south, Yugoslavia, began to unravel in 1991. As it became clear that the republics of Slovenia and Croatia were preparing to break away from the Yugoslav federation, a disagreement arose within the ÖVP–SPÖ coalition over when to grant diplomatic recognition to the new states. In September 1991, Foreign Minister Mock advocated immediate recognition, but Chancellor Vranitzky preferred that Austria wait until other European governments were ready to take the same step. In the end, Vranitzky prevailed in this debate, and recognition was delayed until January 1992, after the EC recognized the newly independent states.

On other important aspects of policy toward the breakup of Yugoslavia, greater unanimity existed between the ÖVP and SPÖ. Foreign Minister Mock was an early advocate of sending a UN peacekeeping force to prevent bloodshed as the various Yugoslav republics sought to establish their independence. In August 1991, Austria became the first UN member to bring to the attention of the Security Council the fact that large numbers of civilians in

Bosnia and Hercegovina and in Croatia were being killed by Serbian forces. Despite their deep concern about the tragedy unfolding in the former Yugoslavia, both Mock and Vranitzky are in agreement that Austria's neutrality and its proximity to the fighting preclude the inclusion of Austrian troops in any UN peacekeeping force.

* * *

During the 1980s and early 1990s, the literature on Austrian politics in English grew considerably. *Austria: A Study in Modern Achievement,* edited by Jim Sweeney and Josef Weidenholzer, contains a useful collection of articles on Austria's political system and political parties. *Modern Austria,* edited by Kurt Steiner, covers roughly the same ground, in some cases in more detail, but is somewhat dated because it was published in 1981. Melanie A. Sully's *A Contemporary History of Austria* is an excellent treatment of Austrian politics during the 1980s. It is particularly good on the interaction between the parties and their internal problems. John Fitzmaurice's *Austrian Politics and Society Today* covers roughly the same ground as Sully's book and is a readable introduction to Austrian politics. *Politics in Austria,* edited by Kurt Richard Luther and Wolfgang C. Müller, contains a collection of essays by Austrian political scientists examining the sociological changes in Austria during the postwar era and their impact on the political system. Readers with a knowledge of German should consult *Handbuch des politischen Systems Österreichs,* edited by Herbert Dachs et al., which contains a wealth of articles on political parties, political institutions, trade unions, foreign policy, and many areas of government policy. Also in German is the very useful *Österreichisches Jahrbuch für Politik,* which contains articles by noted specialists and politicians about recent political developments. (For further information and complete citations, see Bibliography.)

Chapter 5. National Security

Coat of arms of the province of Vienna

IN 1993 THE AUSTRIAN DEFENSE ESTABLISHMENT was in the process of restructuring, from a force intended to defend Austria's territory against threats arising from hostilities between North Atlantic Treaty Organization and Warsaw Pact countries to a force that could react rapidly to local crises. Under the restructuring plan, both the standing army and reserves are to be scaled back but are to maintain individual units in a rapid-response status, enabling the army to intervene quickly with appropriate forces to prevent instability in Austria's border areas. In view of the civil warfare in the former Yugoslavia and the breakup of Czechoslovakia into two states, the Czech Republic and Slovakia, as well as the possibility of overwhelming movements of refugees fleeing violence in nearby states, Austria considers itself to be in a highly exposed position in spite of the end of East-West confrontation in Europe. The intervention of the Yugoslav army in Slovenia and Croatia in 1991 prompted the largest mobilization of the Austrian army since it was reconstituted in 1956.

The Austrian armed forces consist of only one branch, the Bundesheer (Federal Army), of which the air force (Fliegerdivision) is a component. There is no navy. Ground forces consist of 46,000 men on active duty, 19,500 of whom are conscripts who serve for six months, followed by sixty days of refresher training with their mobilization units spread over a ten-year period. There are 6,000 men in the air force, 2,400 of whom are conscripts. (There are no women in the Austrian armed forces.) The main active combat units are three mechanized brigades equipped with M-60 main battle tanks and Saurer armored personnel carriers. Two squadrons (twenty-four aircraft) of Draken fighter aircraft acquired from Sweden defend Austrian air space. Including activated reserve infantry brigades and regiments, total mobilized strength is about 200,000, but the mobilization level will decline to 120,000 under the reorganization plan, the New Army Structure, announced in late 1991 and to be completed in 1995.

Weapons of mass destruction and guided missiles were prohibited under the State Treaty of 1955. Also in 1955, parliament enacted a constitutional law prohibiting participation in any military alliance and specifying that the armed forces were to be used only for the defense of the country. However, neutrality, according to the Austrian interpretation, did not preclude contributing to peacekeeping operations under United Nations (UN) auspices. As of 1993,

Austria had battalion units serving the UN in Cyprus and on the Golan Heights in Syria. Austria did not, however, participate in the UN-supported coalition against Iraq after the Iraqi invasion of Kuwait in 1990.

Austria's Federal Police function in fourteen of the largest cities; the federal Gendarmerie functions in the remainder of the cities and towns and in most rural areas except for a few that maintain their own police forces. The Criminal Investigative Service, the Administrative Police, and the State Police (secret service) are also nationally organized under the federal Ministry for Interior.

Austrians are generally peaceful people; domestic politics are rarely violent, and the level of crime is moderate. Criminal codes and criminal procedure codes are enlightened. Practices relating to criminal justice and the penal system are considered fair by European standards, although questionable conduct by the police and the secret service has been investigated and reforms have been instituted.

Historical Background
The Habsburg Military

From the time the Habsburgs established hereditary rule over Austrian lands in the thirteenth century until the fall of the Habsburgs at the end of World War I, their armies were among the largest and most significant in Europe. For 200 years, Habsburg forces formed a bastion defending the continent against repeated Ottoman campaigns to overrun Europe. In 1529 and again in 1683, the Turks were turned back only after reaching the gates of Vienna. Count Ernst Rüdiger von Starhemberg, who commanded the imperial troops in the city, broke the siege in 1683 with the aid of German and Polish forces under the Polish king, Jan Sobieski, then drove the Turks back into the Balkans, finally ending the Ottoman threat.

One of Austria's greatest military commanders, Prince Eugene of Savoy, in concerted operations with Britain's Duke of Marlborough, won a series of victories over the France of Louis XIV in the War of the Spanish Succession (1701–14). Wars fought with the Prussia of Frederick the Great over Silesia in 1740–48 (the War of the Austrian Succession) and 1756–63 were less successful. The monarchy's military potential during the eighteenth century was limited by the emperor's dependence on provincial diets for recruits and tax receipts. The nobles of the imperial lands who controlled the enserfed peasantry had no fixed obligation to provide soldiers to the Habsburgs.

Austria was prominent in the coalitions that tried to check Napoleon Bonaparte's ambitions but was forced to accept humiliating peace conditions after being decisively defeated in 1800, again in 1805 when Napoleon occupied Vienna after the Battle of Austerlitz, and finally after the Battle of Wagram in 1809. Yet Austria joined with the other great powers in the final campaign resulting in Napoleon's downfall in 1814.

Habsburg armies displayed their loyalty to the monarchy in 1848 and 1849, suppressing the revolutionary regimes that had swept into power in Vienna, Budapest, Milan, and Prague. In 1859 Austria was provoked into war with Piedmont and its supporter, the France of Napoleon III. The Austro-Piedmontese War lasted only three months, but both sides mobilized large armies. The Austrians were defeated after bitter fighting at Magenta and Solferino, the young emperor, Franz Joseph, assuming personal command during the battle at Solferino.

Prussia established its domination over other German states by its victory over Austria in the Seven Weeks' War in 1866. The critical battle was waged at Königgrätz (Hradec Králové in the present-day Czech Republic). The Austrians, armed with muzzle-loading rifles, suffered 20,000 casualties and 20,000 prisoners. The battle overshadowed Austria's victories over Prussia's Italian allies at Custozza and in the naval Battle of Lissa (Vis) off the Dalmatian coast in which a smaller Austrian fleet of ironclads overcame the Italians by bold use of ramming tactics. Following the end of the Seven Weeks' War, Austria experienced fifty years of peace until World War I broke out in 1914.

In spite of their size and distinction in individual engagements, Habsburg armies of the nineteenth century had known little but defeat in encounters with other major powers of Europe. The armed forces were often handicapped by uninspired or timid battlefield leaders. The principal cause of their failure, however, was the fact that, among the five great powers, which also included Britain, France, Prussia, and Russia, Austria allocated the lowest proportion of its revenue to its military establishment. Various political groups blocked adequate expenditures on the army. For example, the Prussian infantry, using breech-loading rifles in 1866, had four to five times the effective firepower of the Austrian infantry. The constant economizing was also reflected in the poor training of conscripts and in the quality of the notoriously underpaid company-grade officers. Their tactics, based on frontal assault with fixed bayonets, were outdated. The quartermaster corps had a reputation for inefficiency and corruption.

The standing army of twelve corps had 240,000 men as of 1854. At its mobilized strength of 800,000, it was the largest in Europe, but the speed of mobilization and the capacity to move troops to the scene of battle were much inferior to those of the Prussians, who made full use of their growing rail system. As a matter of policy, conscripts were assigned to regiments far from their homes. A call-up involved slow train journeys for reservists; mobilization required eight weeks, nearly twice as long as mobilization of the Prussian army, which was organized by region.

The creation of Austria-Hungary (also seen as the Austro-Hungarian Empire) under the Compromise (Ausgleich) of 1867 separated the Hapsburg Empire into independent Austrian and Hungarian governments. Only the army, foreign affairs, and related budgetary matters remained joined under the emperor, who held supreme command of all forces in time of war. A new army law decreed universal three-year conscription followed by a ten-year reserve obligation. In practice, only about one in five of those liable to service were called up, and many were sent on leave after two years. The army of Austria-Hungary has been described as a state within a state. In an empire of ten nationalities and five religions, marked by ethnic conflict and sharp political and economic divisions, the army formed the only real bond among the emperor's subjects and the sole instrument through which loyalty to him could find expression.

Nevertheless, Austria-Hungary gave the impression of being a highly militarized nation. British historian Edward Crankshaw noted that not only the emperor but most males in high society never wore civilian clothes except when hunting. Select regiments of the army were splendidly outfitted, but, with a few dedicated exceptions, the officers, so magnificent on the parade ground, "shrank . . . from the arbitrament of arms as from an unholy abyss."

Regiments were organized along linguistic lines, although German was the language of command. Ethnic factors did not prevent recruitment of non-German speakers to the officer corps or their regular promotion. Hungarians, Croats, Serbs, Poles, Italians, Czechs, Slovenes, and Romanians could be found in senior positions. In the more prestigious units, most field-grade officers owed their ranks to birth or wealth. As of 1900, a majority of the officer corps in the Austro-Hungarian army were native German speakers, although only one-fourth of the empire's total population was German speaking.

Two World Wars, 1914–18 and 1939–45

Although Austria-Hungary's aim in 1914 was to fight a limited war to punish Serbia after the assassination of the heir to the Habsburg crown, Franz Ferdinand, the crisis quickly flared out of control as European powers mobilized their mass armies in accordance with their treaty commitments. Although poorly prepared for conflict and lacking essential weapons and unit cohesiveness, the Austro-Hungarians were immediately faced with a two-front war against Serbia and Russia. Their fifty-nine divisions (which included hastily raised reserve units) had to secure a front running from the Adriatic Sea to central Poland. The superior Russian army drove the Austro-Hungarians back with immense losses in Polish Galicia. The Russian front was stabilized only after German officers assumed command. Although Austria-Hungary had expected to conquer Serbia quickly, Serbia was not defeated until late 1915 after terrible fighting in Bosnia. The campaigns against Italy, which had entered on the side of the Allies in May 1915, were somewhat more successful, the Habsburg armies fighting with stubbornness and at times with great skill. In spite of rebellious secession movements among some non-Germans, the bulk of the army remained loyal, holding together until the last months of the war. Only among Czech soldiers affected by Slavic nationalism were there serious defections to the Russians. At the last, however, front-line troops in Italy abandoned their guns, and the revolt spread as even German-speaking troops refused to obey orders. Austro-Hungarian military casualties of 1.4 million killed or died in captivity and 3.6 million wounded were greater than those of Germany on a proportional basis.

Truncated Austria, reduced to some 6.5 million primarily German speakers after the war, was to some degree divided even against itself between a conservative population in the rural western areas of the nation and the urban socialists of Vienna and other industrial centers of the east. A regular Austrian army of 30,000 men was established in 1922, and, although free from political involvement, it had conservative leanings in the imperial tradition. Both police and army were weak; they could not prevent the formation of paramilitary groups by rival political blocs. The Social Democratic Workers' Party (Sozialdemokratische Arbeiterpartei—SDAP) formed the Republican Defense League (Republikanischer Schutzbund), and the right-wing Christian Social Party (Christlichsoziale Partei—CSP) had links with the various rightist militias that sprang up after the war. Both groups had impressive arsenals. In 1934, reacting to pressures by the CSP chancellor, Engelbert Dollfuss, and to provocations by rightist militias, the SDAP called a general strike and the Republikanischer Schutzbund rose in a number of cities. The uprising was put down in four days after the army used artillery against workers' apartment blocks in Vienna where the socialist revolt was centered. Although the army's actions were approved by Dollfuss, the episode seemed to attest to the army's alignment with rightist elements and its antagonism to the interests of the urban industrial workers.

Germany's annexation (Anschluss) of Austria in 1938 was accomplished without resistance under orders of the government. The armed forces suffered from low morale and were infused with pro-Nazi sentiment. Austrian troops in Salzburg and Innsbruck reportedly put themselves immediately under German command and participated in joint victory parades. The troops were dispersed throughout the army, the German Wehrmacht; no purely Austrian units were retained. Most of the generals and many field-grade officers were purged or were shifted to administrative posts. The thirty-five divisions raised on Austrian territory following the outbreak of World War II were composed mainly of Austrians. For the most part, they were assigned to the Russian front.

Austria suffered tremendous losses in the war, yet its 247,000 military deaths were fewer proportionately than German losses. A further 750,000 were made prisoners of war, the last of these returning from the Soviet Union as late as 1955.

During the postwar occupation (1945–55) by the Four Powers (Britain, France, the Soviet Union, and the United States), the three Western occupying powers permitted the Austrian government to equip a mobile regiment of the Gendarmerie, organized into "shock battalions." Their primary mission was to control communist-inspired disturbances. Headquartered in Linz, the First Battalion was responsible for the provinces of Salzburg and Upper Austria south of the Danube (the American Zone), the Second Battalion for Styria (the British Zone), and the Third Battalion for Tirol and Vorarlberg (the French Zone). (The Russian Zone consisted of Lower Austria, Burgenland, and Upper Austria north of the Danube. Vienna was occupied by the Four Powers.) Surplus equipment and vehicles were transferred to the Austrian battalions by the Western powers. In 1956 when the Austrian army, the Bundesheer (Federal Army) was reconstituted, 6,500 officers and enlisted men of these special units formed its nucleus.

Strategic Concepts and Missions of the Austrian Armed Forces

The withdrawal of the Allied forces as a result of the State Treaty of 1955 dramatically affected the general strategic situation in Central Europe. The presence of two neutral countries—Switzerland and Austria—in effect split the defenses of the North Atlantic Treaty

A noncommissioned officer armed with a 5.56mm Steyr assault rifle
Courtesy United States Department of Defense

Trainees in a tactical field exercise
Courtesy United States Department of Defense

Organization (NATO) into northern and southern tiers. Links between NATO forces in southern Germany and northern Italy had to be routed through France. Moreover, if Warsaw Pact forces had chosen to violate Austrian neutrality by driving westward through the Danube Basin, they would have been able to outflank strong NATO defenses on the central front and avoid a contested Danube River crossing in Bavaria. A second line of potential Warsaw Pact attack ran across the southern flanks of the main Alpine range from the Hungarian Plain leading into northern Italy.

The early years of the Bundesheer were directed by military leaders whose experience reflected their service as mid-level officers in the German army, the Wehrmacht. The army's structure resembled that of European NATO powers but on a smaller scale. Its combat units were filled with permanent cadre and nine-month conscripts. It lacked sufficient manpower and air cover.

In 1956 the Bundesheer was called on to handle the first of two border crises. It was in that year that the Hungarian uprising was crushed by the Soviet Union and 170,000 Hungarians fled into Austria. The second was in 1968 when Warsaw Pact troops invaded Czechoslovakia. Austria's experiences during the Hungarian and Czechoslovak crises helped clarify the nature of the potential threat to the nation's neutrality and led to a reorientation of defense policy and a revised definition of the military's mission.

After 1970, under the influence of a majority of the Socialist Party of Austria (Sozialistische Partei Österreichs—SPÖ) in parliament, military service was deemphasized and conscription reduced to six months. However, with the system of refresher training for former conscripts, the basis for a large militia program was established, and there was more total manpower available. The example of Switzerland's reliance on mobilization units to uphold its neutrality provided a useful lesson. However, strict budgetary limits continued to delay the acquisition of modern supersonic combat aircraft until the late 1980s.

Until the early 1990s, Austria's security policy centered on a strategy of *Abhaltestrategie* (deterrence or dissuasion). Its aim was to convince a prospective invader that any possible advantages derived from an attack on or across Austria would easily be offset by a loss in time, personnel, and equipment. The Austrian version of deterrence flowed from the philosophy of Comprehensive National Defense, also embraced by such other European neutrals as Switzerland, Sweden, and Finland. This concept encompasses the psychological, civil, economic, and military defense of the homeland. Military defense is based on an area defense combat doctrine that uses Austria's geography—its mountains and forests—to the utmost. Austrian forces would use hit-and-run tactics to slow and wear down the aggressor, while avoiding pitched battles. Defense of preselected key zones and strong points along or near primary areas of approach would be used to channel the enemy's advance to make it more susceptible to both commando and limited armor counterattacks.

Austrian military planners concluded that the least likely threat scenario was one in which Austria would be involved in an all-out nuclear war, a role that in any event was beyond the capability of such a small country. Rather, the problem was how Austria could best use its limited military capacity to deal with the range of threats with which the country might realistically be faced. Three levels of threat were identified. The first was a localized political crisis near Austria's borders, such as the case of Czechoslovakia in 1968 or the Slovenian assertion of independence from Yugoslavia in 1991. These situations could be faced by rapidly shifting armored and mechanized standing forces to the border area where trouble could break out. Austrian military leaders stressed that their purpose would be to avoid hostilities and to give credence to their determination to prevent, as one former army commander expressed, "wanton or negligent disregard of Austria's neutrality."

A second level of threat might arise in the case of hostilities between neighboring states. In such an event, Austria might have to deny right of passage, prevent Austrian territory from being used as a base or refuge, or defend the integrity of its air space. In this situation, reserves would have to be partially or fully deployed. In the other situation contemplated, defense against clear aggression threatening the state, the nation's entire military potential would be deployed.

In the third level of threat, it was assumed that the aggressor would consider Austrian territory useful only as a base of operations against a primary enemy. Thus, the purpose of an Austrian military buildup would be to compel a potential aggressor to conclude that the advantages of mounting an attack against Austria were out of proportion to the price that would have to be paid and the delay encountered.

To deal with these contingencies, Austria developed the area defense (*Raumverteidigung*) concept in the mid-1970s. Under this plan, all of Austrian territory was denoted as either a key zone (*Schlüsselzone*) or an area security zone. The key zones were those having prime value as military routes of advance, such as the Danube and Inn river valleys and the mountain passes of southern Austria. Austria's combat strength was to be concentrated in the key zones, where enemy forces could be funneled and then destroyed by armored and mechanized units. Main lines of communication were to be defended by static defenses consisting of fortified gun positions and prepared demolitions positioned around or near natural obstacles. Rear-echelon units of the enemy were to be simultaneously harried by reserve light infantry forces. In the area security zones (*Raumsicherungszonen*), the objective would be to deny unchallenged use of the terrain by the use of prepared artillery positions, antitank obstacles, and guerrilla-type actions (*Jagdkämpfe*) on the enemy's flanks and rear, forcing the invader to deploy combat troops to protect service and support operations.

The breakup of the Warsaw Pact and the subsiding of East-West tensions in 1990 and 1991 necessitated a fundamental reappraisal of Austrian security policy. Austrian planners no longer expected a large-scale invasion requiring defense of the entire territory. Therefore, changes in the security policy were undertaken in 1993 with the New Army Structure (Heeresgliederung Neu). This policy, to be completed in 1995, is intended to meet local crises arising from internal instability in countries on Austria's borders that would precipitate large refugee flows and spillover violence. Contemplated structural changes emphasize the immediate availability of reaction forces that could deal with particular situations without the need for mobilization.

Commenting in 1992, Defense Minister Werner Fasslabend said that although the collapse of the Soviet empire had put an end to East-West confrontation, the dramatic changes had contributed to new risks in the form of local and ethnic conflicts. Although the danger of world conflagration had diminished, Austria was in one of the regions where instability had actually increased.

Austria's miliary leadership saw a continuing mission to defend the country's border to prevent the Yugoslav civil war from spilling into Austrian territory. The breakup of Czechoslovakia into two states in 1993 also raised threats of instability on the nation's northern flank. Control over refugees attempting to flee fighting or economic hardship could also necessitate intervention of the armed forces.

Neutrality and the Armed Forces

Under the State Treaty of 1955, a number of restrictions were imposed that affected the buildup of the Bundesheer. Under Article 13 of the treaty, Austria was prohibited from possessing "any self-propelled or guided missiles or guns with a range of more than thirty kilometers." On October 26, 1955, the government passed a law in which Austria declared of its own free will its permanent neutrality. The law further specified that "Austria will never in the future accede to any military alliances nor permit the establishment of military bases by foreign states on her territory." The Austrian government asserted that it alone was competent to define Austrian neutrality.

Austria has interpreted its posture as a neutral state in Europe in somewhat the same terms as Switzerland. It has deliberately adopted a more active policy of involvement in international peace-keeping and humanitarian matters, in particular those it could perform in conjunction with other members of the UN or at the behest of the UN. In 1960 the army sent a medical team to the Congo (present-day Zaire) and has provided other medical units, military police, and observers to Cyprus and other areas in the Middle East since 1964. By the early 1990s, some 30,000 Austrians had served in UN missions. As of 1993, one battalion of 350 troops was deployed with the United Nations Peacekeeping Force in Cyprus (UNFICYP) patrolling the buffer zone between the Greek Cypriot and Turkish forces. Another battalion of 450 troops was on the Golan Heights in Syria as part of the United Nations Disengagement Observer Force (UNDOF). Seven observers were with the United Nations Iraq-Kuwait Observer Mission (UNIKOM), and seventeen observers were attached to the United Nations Truce Supervision Organization (UNTSO) in Cambodia.

Austria did not participate directly in the UN-backed action in 1991 to drive the Iraqi invasion forces out of Kuwait. It did, however, provide financial assistance to states suffering from dislocation caused by the invasion. In addition, the United States was granted expanded overflight authority for troops and supplies in connection with Operation Desert Shield and Operation Desert Storm. This action, a departure from Austria's former posture of strict neutrality, was interpreted as a gesture to help demonstrate that Austria's neutral status need not be a barrier to future membership in the European Union (EU—see Glossary). In the same vein, Austria announced that it would grant NATO permission to use its airspace for airborne warning and control system (AWACS) aircraft as "an expression of solidarity within the framework of pan-European security."

With the exception of the prohibition on guided missile systems, restrictions in the State Treaty on the acquisition of particular weapons have not prevented Austria's defense buildup. Austria refrained for many years from the purchase of modern antiaircraft and antitank guided missiles in spite of the fact that such weapons have been accepted as essential elements of defense in all modern armies. Short-range weapons of this type had not been developed when the treaty was concluded. Nevertheless, in 1988 when Austria sought a reinterpretation of Article 13 by the other signatories to justify purchasing such weapons, its attempt was not successful.

In 1989, however, Austrian authorities reached a decision to acquire surface-to-air missiles (SAMs) and antitank missiles on the understanding that they were intended solely for defensive purposes. The changed security situation in Europe made it possible for Austria to take such a step without fear of provoking countries that belonged to the Warsaw Pact. As of 1993, Austria was accepting delivery of BILL (Bofors, Infantry, Light and Lethal) antitank missiles from Sweden and was also planning to purchase larger antitank missiles from France or the United States. Its Draken interceptor aircraft will be armed with Sidewinder air-to-air missiles, and its ground-based antiaircraft missile defense will be equipped with French Mistral missiles.

National Defense

Under the constitution, the president is the nominal commander in chief of the armed forces. In reality, the chancellor has operational authority, exercised through the minister for national defense. The chancellor also chairs the National Defense Council, which has as its members a vice chairman, the minister for national defense, an appointee of this minister, the general troop inspector of the armed forces, and a parliamentary representative. The minister for national defense, acting in cooperation with the minister for interior, coordinates the work of the four major committees under the National Defense Council: the Military Defense Committee; the Civil Defense Committee; the Economic Defense Committee; and the Psychological Defense Committee. The general troop inspector acts as the senior military adviser to the minister for national defense, assists the minister in the exercise of his authority, and, as head of the general staff, is responsible for planning. However, the army commander exercises direct operational control of the Bundesheer in both peacetime and wartime.

Article 79 of the constitution, as amended in 1985, states that the army is entrusted with the military defense of the country. Insofar as the legally constituted civil authority requests its cooperation, the army is further charged with protecting constitutional institutions and their capacity to act, as well as the democratic freedoms of the inhabitants; maintaining order and security in the interior; and rendering aid in disasters and mishaps of extraordinary scope. In administering the armed forces, the Ministry for National Defense is organized into four principal sections and the inspectorate general: Section I deals with legal and legislative matters; Section II handles personnel and recruitment matters, including discipline and grievances; Section III is concerned with troop command, schools, and other facilities, and it also comprises departments G–1 through G–5 as well as a separate department for air operations; and Section IV deals with procurement and supply, quartermaster matters, armaments, and ordnance (see fig. 12).

The general troop inspectorate is a separate section of the ministry with responsibility for coordination and fulfillment of the missions of the armed forces. It encompasses a general staff department, an attaché department, and planning and inspection groups.

The armed forces consist solely of the army, of which the air force is considered a constituent part. As of 1993, the total active complement of the armed forces was 52,000, of whom 20,000 to 30,000 were conscripts undergoing training of six to eight months. The army had 46,000 personnel on active duty (including an estimated 19,500 conscripts), and the air force had 6,000 personnel (2,400 conscripts).

Army

Under the area defense strategy, which had determined the army's organizational structure until 1993, the army was divided into three principal elements: the standing alert force (Bereitschaftstruppe) of active units, including the air division; the mobile militia (Mobile Landwehr), organized as eight mechanized reserve brigades to be deployed to key danger spots in the event of mobilization; and the stationary militia (Raumgebundene Landwehr) of twenty-six reserve infantry regiments organized for territorial defense. Both the mobile militia and the stationary militia were brought up to strength only in times of mobilization or during periods allotted for refresher training, usually three weeks in June. Training of conscripts was conducted by twenty-eight training and equipment-holding regiments (*Landwehrstammregimenten*). On mobilization, these regiments would disband, with their cadre reassigned to lead reserve units or form replacement regiments and battalions.

At the army level were a headquarters, guard, and special forces battalions and an artillery battalion at cadre strength. Two corps headquarters, one in the east at Graz and one in the west at Salzburg, would, on mobilization, command the provincially organized units in their respective zones. Each corps included artillery, antitank, antiaircraft, and engineering battalions and a logistics regiment, all on a cadre basis.

Each of the nine provincial military commands supervised the training and maintenance activities of its training and equipment-holding regiments. On mobilization, these nine commands would convert to a divisional headquarters commanding mobile militia, stationary militia, and other independent units.

The only active units immediately available in an emergency were those of the standing alert force of some 15,000 career soldiers supplemented by conscripts. The force was organized as a mechanized division consisting of three armored infantry brigades. Each brigade was composed of one tank battalion, one mechanized infantry battalion, and one self-propelled artillery battalion. Two of the brigades had antitank battalions equipped with self-propelled weapons. The divisional headquarters was at Baden near Vienna; the three brigades were based in separate locations, also in the northeast of the country.

The New Army Structure—the reorganization plan announced in late 1991 and scheduled to be in place sometime in 1995—replaces the previous two-corps structure with one of three corps. The new corps is headquartered at Baden, with responsibility for the two northeastern provinces of Lower Austria and Upper Austria

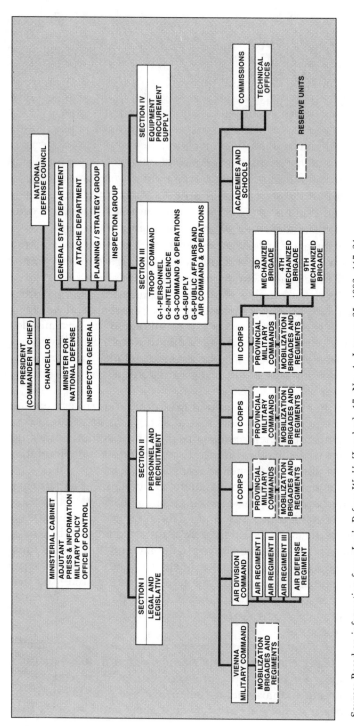

Source: Based on information from *Jane's Defence Weekly* [London], 17, No. 4, January 25, 1992, 117–24.

Figure 12. Organization of National Defense, Planned 1995

(see fig. 13). Army headquarters will be eliminated, as will the divisional structure for the three standing brigades. The three corps—in effect, regional commands—will be directly subordinate to the general troop inspector. The three mechanized brigades will be placed directly under the new Third Corps at Baden, although in the future one brigade may be assigned to each of the three corps. The mobile militia will be reduced from eight to six mechanized brigades. Each of the nine provincial commands will have at least one militia regiment of two to six battalions as well as local defense companies.

Total personnel strength—both standing forces and reserves—is to be materially contracted under the new plan. The fully mobilized army will decline in strength from 200,000 to 120,000. The standing alert force will be reduced from 15,000 to 10,000. Reaction time is to be radically shortened so that part of the standing alert force can be deployed within hours to a crisis zone (for example, one adjacent to the border with Slovenia). A task force ready for immediate deployment will be maintained by one of the mechanized brigades on a rotational basis. Separate militia training companies to which all conscripts are assigned will be dismantled; in the future, conscripts will undergo basic training within their mobilization companies. Conscripts in the final stages of their training could supplement the standing forces by being poised for operational deployment at short notice.

Personnel, Conscription, Training, and Reserves

Until 1971 Austrian males were obligated to serve nine months in the armed forces, followed by four days of active service every two years for training and inspection. In 1971 the period of initial service was reduced to six months, followed by a total of sixty days of refresher training in the reserves. In the early 1990s, about 45,000 conscripts completed their initial military training every year, and 80,000 reservists participated in some form of exercises each year.

Reducing the mobilization strength of the army to 120,000 under the New Army Structure plan is to be accomplished in part by limiting initial training of recruits to six months, followed by reducing the period allotted for refresher training from twenty years to ten years. Each reservist is to receive training over a twelve-day period every second year during his first ten years of reserve duty, generally not extending beyond the time he reaches his mid-thirties. The reduced need for conscripts corresponds to a lower pool of young men because of a declining birth rate. The existing availability of about 40,000 fit trainees annually as of 1993 is expected to fall to barely 30,000 by the year 2000 and to 26,000 by 2015.

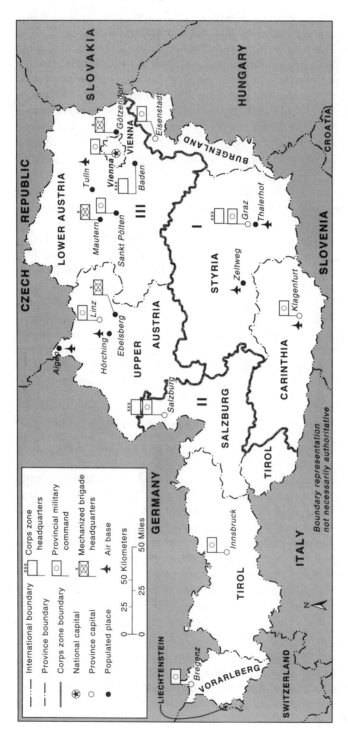

Figure 13. Major Military Installations, Planned 1995

Source: Based on information from *Jane's Defence Weekly* [London], 17, No. 4, January 25, 1992, 117–24.

Conscripts can choose to serve seven months instead of six, and they have a shorter reserve obligation. Some may serve their full obligation of eight months at one time and have no reserve obligations, but this may occur only at the army's discretion. Under a 1974 law, conscientious objectors can be assigned work as farm laborers, medical orderlies, or other occupations in lieu of military service. Exemptions from service are liberally granted—in 1992 about 12,000 persons were exempted, a great increase over the 1991 total of 4,500. The increase occurred after a new law, valid only for 1992 and 1993, no longer required young men to present their objections to the military in a credible way. Previously, that had not been the case. In 1990, for example, two young men rejected by the alternate service commission on the grounds that they did not present their beliefs in a credible manner were sentenced to prison terms of three months and one month, respectively.

Conscripts usually attain the rank of private first class by the completion of initial training. Those with leadership potential may serve a longer period to obtain noncommissioned officer (NCO) status in the militia. Those volunteering for the career service can, after three to four years, apply to attend the NCO academy and later a senior NCO course to qualify as warrant officers. Both regular and militia officer candidates undergo a one-year program of basic training. After a further three years, regular officer candidates attending the military academy at Wiener Neustadt and militia officer candidates undergoing periodic intensified refresher training qualify as second lieutenants. The reserve obligation of conscripts generally ends by the time they reach their mid-thirties; NCOs and officers usually end their reserve status at a later age depending on their rank and specialization. By the early 1990s, some 1.3 million men had completed their initial service and refresher training obligations and had no further active-duty commitment.

The military personnel system is an integral part of a comprehensive civil service system. The nine officer ranks from officer candidate through general correspond to grades I through IX of the civil service system. The highest grade, IX, may be occupied by a section chief (undersecretary), a career ambassador, or a three-star general. A grade VIII position may be held by a departmental counselor, a career minister, or a brigadier general. Salary levels are the same for both civil and military personnel in the equivalent grades, although various allowances may be added, such as flight pay or hazardous-duty pay.

Promotion is not based solely on merit but on position attained, level of education, and seniority. Officers with advanced degrees (for which study at the National Defense Academy qualifies) can expect to attain grade VIII before reaching the retirement age of sixty to sixty-five. Those with a baccalaureate degree can expect to reach grade VII (colonel), and those without university training will retire as captains or majors. Career NCOs form part of the same comprehensive personnel structure. It is common for NCOs to transfer at some stage in their careers to civilian status at the equivalent grade, either in the Ministry for National Defense or in the police or prison services after further training.

The system of promotion in the Austrian military, which offers no incentive for early retirement, means that the military is top-heavy with senior officers. The New Army Structure, which is intended to result in many fewer active-duty and reserve commands, compounds the difficulty. Personnel changes can be implemented only gradually, as the surplus of officers shrinks by attrition. As of 1991, the army had four officers of general rank, fifty-nine at the rank of brigadier general (one star), 155 colonels, and 254 lieutenant colonels. The education of career officers is conducted at the Maria Theresa Military Academy at Wiener Neustadt, thirty kilometers south of Vienna, which was founded in 1752. Young men who have completed their university entrance requirements are eligible to compete for places. The three-year course graduated 212 students in 1990. At the National Defense Academy in Vienna, which has a curriculum comparable to those of the National Defense University and the Army War College in the United States, operational and troop commanders of field-grade rank study for three years in preparation for general staff and command positions. The NCO school is located at Enns near Linz. Troop schools provide continuous specialized courses for officers and NCOs in artillery, air defense, armor, combat engineering, communications, and the like.

Women have never been accepted for service in the Austrian armed forces. In a public opinion survey in 1988, about 66 percent of those polled approved of opening the military to voluntary service by women; only 9 percent favored obligatory service. Although consideration had been given to opening certain specialties to female volunteers, the question is apparently in abeyance in an army already facing retrenchment.

According to data published by the United States Arms Control and Disarmament Agency, Austria had 5.6 persons in uniform in 1991 per 1,000 population. Two other neutral countries of Europe, Sweden and Switzerland, with populations comparable to that of Austria, had 7.3 and 3.2 persons in the standing military, respectively, per 1,000 population. However, the mobilization strengths of both countries were far higher than that of Austria: 700,000 for Sweden, and 625,000 for Switzerland.

Army Equipment

The principal armored weapons in 1993 were 169 M–60 main battle tanks of United States manufacture in service with the tank battalions of the three readiness brigades. Beginning in 1986, the M–60s were upgraded to A3 standard by the installation of new engines, fire-control systems with laser-range finders, and a stabilization system. The modernization was carried out by the Austrian firm of Steyr-Daimler-Puch, often referred to as Steyr. A light tank, the Kürassier SK–105, was developed by Steyr in the late 1960s. It carries a French-made 105mm gun that has been modified to fire more powerful fin-stabilized ammunition. The SK–105 serves in effect as an armored tank destroyer. The army's armored personnel carrier (APC) is the Saurer 4K–4E/F, an early version of a Steyr design that has been exported to a number of countries. Considered obsolete, the Saurer is expected to be replaced by a newly developed Steyr APC in the late 1990s.

The most modern artillery weapons are fifty-four 155mm self-propelled howitzers purchased from the United States in 1988. The army is planning to upgrade all fifty-four to A5 standards, and it has placed an order to purchase twenty-four additional howitzers. The remaining guns in the artillery inventory are forty-year-old towed 105mm and 155mm howitzers, considered to be obsolete in terms of range and accuracy. A 130mm truck-mounted rocket launcher of Czechoslovak manufacture, in the inventory since the 1960s, is of limited range and rate of fire.

Austria relies heavily on fixed artillery installations for defense of key points. In addition to twenty-four SFK 155mm guns in "fortress" configuration, Austria purchased 200 obsolete Centurion tanks from the Netherlands and converted their turrets into fixed-gun emplacements.

The army's most serious shortcomings are in air defense and antitank weaponry. Without improved protection against enemy tactical aircraft and attack helicopters, Austrian armored units are highly vulnerable. The primary air defense weapon is the 40mm self-propelled antiaircraft gun. A radar-directed 35mm system, with limited mobility and range, is used principally for static defense. Optically sighted 20mm guns, some mounted on all-terrain vehicles, are the only form of air defense for infantry forces but give little protection against modern combat aircraft. Austria is evaluating various low-level air defense missile systems with the intention of purchasing one battery of twelve launchers for each brigade beginning about 1994.

The announcement in 1989 that Austria considered the State Treaty limitation on short-range defensive missiles outdated and void has cleared the way for the army to acquire its first antitank missile system to replace obsolete guns, recoilless rifles, and rocket launchers. After trials of several weapons, Austria purchased the Bofors RBS-56 BILL, a man-portable system, from Sweden. The army is reportedly also considering purchase of either the United States TOW (tube-launched, optically tracked, wire-guided) or the French HOT (high-subsonic, optically guided, tube-launched) system as longer-range antitank missiles to be mounted on a wheeled armored vehicle. As many as 200 systems are expected to be purchased initially, enough for twelve launchers for each mechanized or infantry brigade.

Air Force

Austria's air force (Fliegerdivision) is headquartered at Tulln-Langenlebarn Air Base twenty-five kilometers northwest of Vienna. The air force has as its missions the defense of Austrian air space, tactical support of Austrian ground forces, reconnaissance and military transport, and search-and-rescue support when requested by civil authorities.

Until 1985, when the first of twenty-four Saab J-350e Drakens were delivered, the country had remained essentially without the capacity to contest violations of its airspace. The Drakens, reconditioned after having served the Swedish air force since the early 1960s, are armed only with a cannon, in accordance with the restrictions on missiles in the State Treaty of 1955. However, following Austria's revised interpretation of its obligations under the treaty, a decision was made in 1993 to procure Sidewinder air-to-air missiles. The first of these missiles will be purchased used from the Swedish air force. A higher performance model of the Sidewinder will be purchased directly from the United States; deliveries may begin in 1995. French Mistral surface-to-air missiles (SAMs) were purchased to add ground-based protection against air attack. The first of the French missiles arrived in Austria in 1993; deliveries are to be concluded in 1996.

Phaseout of the Drakens is scheduled to begin about 1995, and studies are under way to select a replacement, probably one that can be configured for both air defense and ground support missions. Possible replacements for the Draken are the United States F-16 and F-18. In addition to the two squadrons of Drakens, the air force has thirty-one Saab 105Oe fighters available for reconnaissance and close air support of ground troops; however, eight Saabs, borrowed from the combat squadrons, are regularly employed as

Over rugged, snowy terrain, horses still provide mobility.
An officer briefs two noncommissioned officers on the next phase of a
tactical field problem.
Courtesy United States Department of Defense

243

jet conversion trainers. Acquired in 1970–72 after service in the Swedish air force, the subsonic Saabs are of limited value in a combat role. The helicopter fleet includes Agusta-Bell (AB) 204s (mainly medical evacuation), AB–206s (training and liaison), and AB–212s (used by air-mobile troops and for light transport). French Alouettes are available for search-and-rescue tasks, including high mountain operations. The Bell OH–58 Kiowa, a scout helicopter, is mounted with a rapid-firing machine gun, but the air force lacks a true attack helicopter. Most of the helicopters, except the AB–212s, are becoming obsolete (see table 16, Appendix).

The air transport fleet is seriously deficient, a fact underscored by its inability to support the armed forces in their UN peacekeeping and humanitarian activities. The air force has at its disposal two Short Skyvans and twelve Pilatus PC–6s that can handle only light cargoes. Among air force priorities—unfulfilled because of budgetary constraints—is the procurement of three to six medium-transport aircraft.

The air force is organized into a division of three flying regiments and one radar (air defense) regiment. Air Regiment I at Tulln-Langenlebarn consists of the light transport squadron plus one helicopter wing of AB–206s and OH–58s. Air Regiment II at Graz-Thalerhof, Aigen in Ennstal, and Zeltweg consists of the air interceptor wing of Drakens and a wing of two Alouette helicopter squadrons. Air Regiment III at Linz-Hörsching consists of the fighter-bomber wing of Saab 105Oes and a helicopter wing of AB–204s and AB–212s. An air defense battalion equipped with 20mm and 35mm antiaircraft guns and a variety of radar systems is attached to each air regiment.

The Central Flying School at Zeltweg is equipped with Saab 91D Safirs and Saab 105Oes, while transport pilots train on PC–7s. Austrian pilots are sent to northern Sweden for training in operation of the Drakens.

Uniforms, Ranks, and Insignia

The service and dress uniform of the Austrian army is gray; for formal occasions, a white uniform may be worn. The air force uniform is identical, with the addition of wings worn on the right jacket breast—gold for officers and silver for enlisted personnel. Branches of service are identified by beret colors: scarlet for artillery; green for infantry; black for armor; cherry for air force; and dark blue for quartermaster. Insignia of rank are worn on the jacket lapel of the dress uniform (silver stars on a green or gold shield) and on the epaulets of the field uniform (silver or gold stars on a gray field).

Of the eight enlisted ranks, only a sergeant (Wachtmeister) or above is considered an NCO. There are two warrant officer ranks—Offiziersstellvertreter and Vizeleutnant. The lowest commissioned rank of officer candidate (Fähnrich)—is held by cadets at the military academy and by reserve officers in training for the rank of second lieutenant. To maintain conformity with grade levels in the civil service, there are only two ranks of general in the personnel system—brigadier general (one star) and lieutenant general (three stars). However, the ranks of major general (two stars) and full general (equivalent to four stars) are accorded to officers holding particular military commands (see fig. 14).

Military Justice

Sections 533 to 684 of the national criminal code deal with military offenses; there is no separate military code of justice, and there is no legal (judge advocate) organization in the armed forces. All actions in serious criminal cases involving military personnel, except those related to breaches of military discipline, are remanded to civil courts. The same holds true in wartime, although specific courts would be designated for military cases. Although no military person can be tried twice on the same charge, he can appear before an all-military disciplinary commission to be judged on purely military aspects of a crime.

For example, if a military person is accused of murder on an army base, military authorities notify the civil police, and the accused is taken into civil custody and tried before a civil court. The investigation, court, judges, and legal personnel are the same as those involved had the incident occurred among civilians. If the court finds the defendant guilty, it may sentence him to life imprisonment. The defendant is then called before a military disciplinary commission made up of military personnel. Commission members include, among others, servicemen of the same rank and from the same branch as the accused. The commission does not reconsider evidence relating to the crime, but it divests the defendant of his military rank, dishonorably discharges him from the service, and forfeits his pay and allowances up to the time of the action. Disciplinary commissions at the level of the Ministry for National Defense have professional lawyers on, or acting as advisers to, the commission; those at lower organizational levels ordinarily do not.

Unit discipline complies with accepted practice in nearly all armed forces. Infractions of the code of military discipline (military-specific offenses such as absence without leave or insubordination) are taken care of by company commanders if the appropriate punishment

OFFICERS

AUSTRIAN RANK	LEUTNANT	OBER-LEUTNANT	HAUPTMANN	MAJOR	OBERST-LEUTNANT	OBERST	BRIGADIER	DIVISIONÄR	KORPS-KOMMANDANT	GENERAL
ARMY	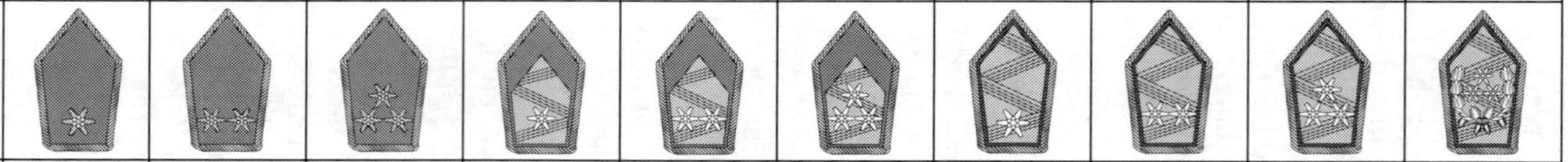									
U.S. RANK TITLE	2D LIEUTENANT	1ST LIEUTENANT	CAPTAIN	MAJOR	LIEUTENANT COLONEL	COLONEL	BRIGADIER GENERAL	MAJOR GENERAL	LIEUTENANT GENERAL	GENERAL

ENLISTED PERSONNEL

AUSTRIAN RANK	JÄGER	GEFREITER	KORPORAL	ZUGSFÜHRER	WACHTMEISTER	OBER-WACHTMEISTER	STABS-WACHTMEISTER	OBERSTABS-WACHTMEISTER	OFFIZIERSSTELL-VERTRETER	VIZELEUTNANT
ARMY 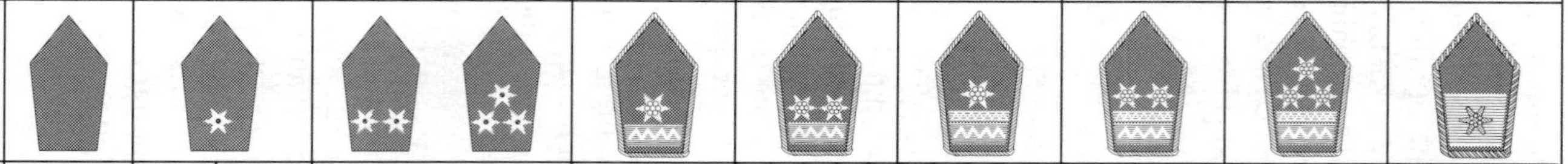										
U.S. RANK TITLE	BASIC PRIVATE	PRIVATE / PRIVATE 1ST CLASS	CORPORAL / SPECIALIST		SERGEANT	STAFF SERGEANT	SERGEANT 1ST CLASS	MASTER SERGEANT / FIRST SERGEANT		SERGEANT MAJOR/ COMMAND SERGEANT MAJOR

NOTE - Officer insignia have gold piping; enlisted insignia have silver piping.

Figure 14. Military Ranks and Insignia, 1993

is a reprimand, extra duty, confinement to quarters, or the like. Battalion and brigade commanders can hand down somewhat more severe punishments, such as reduction in grade or confinement to base guardhouses for short periods.

The Defense Budget

Austrians traditionally have been reluctant to allocate significant sums for improving the nation's defense. This attitude, combined with a sluggish economy and uncertainties over the shape of the armed forces in the post-Cold War era, has forced the military to postpone equipment acquisitions and to accept compromises in performance levels, operational readiness, and maintenance standards.

Set at S18.3 billion (for value of the schilling—see Glossary) in 1992, and climbing to S19.0 billion in 1993, the defense budget was higher than in 1989 (S17.2 billion) and 1990 (S17.5 billion) but was roughly the same in terms of real growth. Having reached a peak in 1986, the defense budget declined between 1987 and 1989 to level off at approximately the 1982 spending rate in real terms.

The government expects to maintain a relatively constant defense budget during the remainder of the 1990s. However, anticipated lower expenditures on personnel will permit some expansion in equipment procurement and improvement of facilities and infrastructure. In 1986 personnel costs absorbed 51 percent of the budget; operations, 32 percent; and investment, 17 percent. A downward trend in the investment budget has since been reversed. In 1992 new procurements were expected to reach S6.5 billion, or more than one-third of the entire budget. Part of these funds was to be allocated to renovating housing and barracks, much of which dates from the occupation period after World War II. Some S1.3 billion was earmarked for SAMs and air-to-air missiles.

Austria's defense spending as a proportion of the gross national product (GNP—Glossary) is the lowest in Europe, except for Luxembourg. During the 1981–91 decade, annual defense outlays were in the range of 1.0 to 1.3 percent of GNP, with the lowest percentage occurring recorded in 1991. Sweden and Switzerland, neutral countries often compared with Austria, had defense spending in 1991 that amounted to 2.8 and 1.9 percent of GNP, respectively. The Austrian defense budget in 1991 was 2.9 percent of total central government expenditure. The corresponding levels for Sweden and Switzerland were 6.4 and 19.4 percent, respectively. Military expenditures per capita amounted to US$213 in Austria in 1991, compared with US$751 in Sweden and US$667 in Switzerland in the same year. In defending the level of defense spending, an Austrian defense minister asserted that although it was not generous, it was sufficient to achieve high standards for the ground forces, although air defense remained inadequate. He rejected the comparison with Switzerland, because the Swiss have adopted the more ambitious goal of the absolute capability of defending their country against attack from any source.

Domestic and Foreign Sources of Military Equipment

Austria-Hungary was one of the world's major manufacturers of arms. The Skoda company in Bohemia was the largest single arms producer, fully meeting the empire's requirements with considerable output available for export. Under the Second Republic, from 1945 to the present, the largely privately owned firm of Steyr-Daimler-Puch has accounted for the bulk of Austria's production. Its manufacturing facilities are divided among three divisions. The first, Steyr-Mannlicher, produces small arms, notably the 5.56mm assault rifle, the standard weapon for both readiness and militia forces and a popular export item to military and police forces in many countries of the world. It is also available in carbine and light machine gun versions. The second, Steyr-Allradtechnik in Graz, is a producer of all-wheel-drive vehicles and trucks. The third Steyr division, Spezialfahrzeuge AG, has developed the Austrian Spanish Cooperative Development (ASCOD) family of mechanized infantry combat vehicles in conjunction with a Spanish firm. The basic version is equipped with a 30mm machine gun and carries eight infantry soldiers in addition to a three-man crew. The firm has also designed the Pandur armored vehicle for the Austrian army as an antitank-missile-launcher platform.

Noricum, previously a subsidiary of the state-owned United Austrian Iron and Steel Works (Vereinigte Österreichische Eisen- und Stahlwerke—VÖEST; commonly known as VÖEST-Alpine), manufactures artillery ordnance as well as the GHN–45 155mm gun. In 1991 fourteen defendants, including leading executives of Noricum and VÖEST-Alpine, were sentenced to prison terms for violating Austrian neutrality laws by selling 200 GHN–45 howitzers and large quantities of munitions to Iran during the Iran-Iraq War of 1980–88. Noricum is also reported to have marketed the guns illegally to Iraq. Noricum and Hirtenberger Patronenfabrik, another state-owned company implicated in the transactions, were later sold to the private firm of Emmerich Assmann, ending the government's involvement in arms manufacture.

The Austrian armaments industry is heavily dependent on export markets because the requirements of the country's forces are limited, and domestic procurement is open to competition from foreign suppliers. Production has to be set at far higher levels than can be absorbed domestically in order for manufacture to be economically feasible. Shrinking world demand and mounting sophistication of weaponry impose serious pressures on the industry. The United States Arms Control and Disarmament Agency has estimated that during the 1981–91 period, arms exports peaked in 1981 at US$430 million. They declined minimally until 1987, when they dropped sharply to US$60 million and later declined further to US$10 million. In only one year, 1981, did arms exports amount to as much as 2 percent of total exports. In 1987 and 1988, they amounted to 0.2 percent of total exports and to even less in the next three years.

During the first years after its formation in 1955, the Austrian army depended heavily on the United States for light weapons, trucks, uniforms, and even helmets, with some additional equipment transferred from the former British occupation forces as well. The first aircraft were older Soviet models. The army was initially supplied with American M–24 light tanks, which were replaced by the M–47. Since the 1970s, the main battle tank has been the M–60, which Steyr modernized to the A3 standard beginning in 1986, using engines and other equipment from the United States. Austria also made a major purchase of self-propelled howitzers from the United States. Nevertheless, the importance of the United States as an arms supplier declined in the 1980s. During the 1985–89 period, estimates suggested that Austria imported military equipment valued at US$240 million. The United States was the source of US$70 million worth of equipment, and Western Europe accounted for US$160 million worth of equipment. Very little came from France and Britain, and restrictions in the State Treaty precluded arms imports from Germany. Sweden—the primary source of aircraft and missiles—was believed to be the predominant supplier. Austria's purchases of Saab and Draken fighters from Sweden were largely offset by Swedish orders for Austrian munitions.

Internal Security

Respect for the law and devotion to social tranquillity are engrained in the Austrian character. Domestic groups committed to violence or terrorism play no significant political role. No major strikes, unruly demonstrations, or public unrest have threatened the stability of the Second Republic. Because of a high standard of living and minimal unemployment, crime remains relatively low. Assaults and other crimes involving violence are particularly uncommon, although crimes against property have risen more than

10 percent in some years. Law enforcement agencies are efficient and are regarded with respect. Since the late 1980s, however, instances of mistreatment of arrested persons and improper activities of the organs of security have made necessary measures to restore the public's confidence in the police.

Austria has been the country of first asylum for 2 million refugees from Eastern Europe since the end of World War II. Austria's hospitality toward refugees underwent a change in the early 1990s as political refugees were outnumbered by economically motivated immigrants seeking work. Feeling it necessary to stem the flow, Austrian authorities tightened entry requirements and reinforced regular border guards with armed forces, mainly to prevent illegal Romanian immigrants from entering the country through Hungary. Beginning in mid-1991, thousands of Yugoslavs were allowed into Austria as a result of civil war in their country, although more than 100,000 were turned back at the point of entry. As of May 1993, about 65,000 refugees had been admitted from the former Yugoslavia.

Austria is a frequent setting for international negotiation and conciliation, and individuals representing a wide spectrum of beliefs are permitted to carry out political activities without interference within its borders. In addition to being the headquarters of the International Atomic Energy Agency (IAEA) and the Organization of the Petroleum Exporting Countries (OPEC), Vienna is the site of major East-West negotiations. Austria has traditionally maintained good relations with many Middle Eastern states, and various Arab groups are allowed to operate freely in Austrian territory.

There is perhaps a price to be paid for this tolerance, however. Several terrorist incidents have been linked to situations in the Middle East, one of the worst occurring at an OPEC meeting in Vienna in 1975 when three men were killed, many were wounded, and thirty-three hostages were taken from among the Arab leaders attending. Attacks against Jewish targets in 1981 and among passengers awaiting a flight on El Al, the Israeli airline, at the Vienna airport in 1975 led to the imprisonment of several Arab terrorists. In 1987 the former Libyan ambassador to Austria, who was an opponent of Muammar al Qadhafi's regime in Libya, was wounded in an assassination attempt. In 1989 three Kurdish activists, including the leader of the Iranian Kurdish Democratic Party, were assassinated during a meeting with three Iranian officials. Criticism was leveled against Austrian authorities for their failure to curb the activities of the Libyan and Iranian diplomatic missions, whose personnel were implicated in the attacks.

*An Austrian-manned United Nations checkpoint
on the Golan Heights
Courtesy United States Department of Defense*

Prior to the adoption of an autonomy agreement in 1969, agitation among German-speaking residents of South Tirol (in the region of Trentino-Alto Adige) for its return to Austrian control from Italy was accompanied by a campaign of terrorist bombings. In 1967 army units were moved to the border area to support the Gendarmerie and border police in preventing Austrian territory from being used as a sanctuary and source of explosives. Terrorist incidents dropped off sharply thereafter, although, after an unsuccessful attempt to derail a train in 1988, a South Tirolean was sentenced by an Austrian court to a five-and-one-half-year prison term (see Regional Issues, ch. 4).

According to public opinion surveys, anti-Semitism continues to exist in Austria to some extent, and some Austrians remain pro-Nazi (see Attitudes Toward Minorities, ch. 2). Although freedom of assembly and association are provided for in the constitution, the State Treaty of 1955 and previous legislation made an exception in the case of Nazi organizations and activities. In early 1992, the security authorities cracked down on the neo-Nazi network after one group, the Trenck Military Sports Group, was found to have handguns and automatic weapons and to engage in paramilitary training. Police intelligence discovered that the groups had received funds and propaganda material from the United States and Canada. Moreover, thousands of names of sympathizers had reportedly been found in the files of Gottfried Küssel, a central figure in the neo-Nazi movement.

Penal Codes

Early criminal codes merely listed crimes—their definitions were considered self-evident or unnecessary—and provided for the extreme punishments characteristic of the Middle Ages. The codes did not presume to list all possible crimes, and a judge was authorized to determine the criminality of other acts and to fix sentences at his discretion. The first unified crime code was enacted in 1768, during the reign of Empress Maria Theresa. Investigation, prosecution, and defense were all in the hands of a judge. The code contained illustrated directions for the application of "painful interrogation"; that is, torture, if the judge entertained suspicions regarding a defendant. Torture was outlawed a few years later, however. The Josephine Code of 1787, enacted by Joseph II, declared that there was "no crime without a law"; thus, an act not defined as a crime was not a crime. Although it was a humanitarian document, the code had shortcomings that were remedied to a considerable extent by the codes of 1803 and 1852. A modern code of criminal procedure adopted in 1873 provided that ordinary court proceedings had to be oral and open. Capital punishment, which was prohibited for a time after 1783, was reinstituted and remained a possible punishment until 1950. Imprisonment in chains and corporal punishment were abolished in the mid-1800s.

The Austrian criminal code and code of criminal procedure were riddled with Nazi amendments between 1938 and 1945 after the Anschluss, but each code was restored to its 1938 status when the country regained independence. Revisions of the criminal code in the mid-1960s, based on ten years of work by a legal commission, give strong emphasis to the principle of government by law and allow unusual latitude in determining appropriate punishment and its implementation. Austria attempts to distinguish among lawbreakers whose crimes are committed on impulse, those who are susceptible to rehabilitation, and those who are addicted to crime and are incorrigible. Further reforms of the criminal code in 1974 emphasized the importance of avoiding jail sentences whenever possible because of the potentially antisocial effects of even a short prison term. Vagrancy, begging, and prostitution are specifically decriminalized. In large communities, prostitution is regulated by health authorities, and prostitutes and brothels are registered. Individual local jurisdictions retain the authority to prohibit prostitution, however. Provisions in the 1974 law modified the punishment for business theft and shoplifting and restricted the definitions of riotous assembly and insurrection.

Criminal Court Proceedings

Persons suspected of committing a crime can be held in investigative or pretrial detention for no more than forty-eight hours. Persons held on charges of "aggressive behavior" can be held for up to seven days before appearing before a magistrate. With the agreement of a magistrate, an accused may be held for up to a maximum of two years pending completion of an investigation. Domestic critics of the provisions concerning pretrial detention have pointed out that of those detained in Vienna, only 57 percent were eventually found guilty of crimes justifying prison sentences. The basis for investigative detention is set forth in law, as are conditions for release on bail.

Criminal offenses are categorized either as crimes—those cases in which the possible sentence is from three years to life imprisonment—or misdemeanors, covering all other cases. Misdemeanor cases for which the jail sentence cannot exceed six months are heard by one judge in district courts. Cases where the possible sentence is no more than three years (five years for burglaries) are heard in courts of first instance before one judge; if the punishment is in excess of three years, the case is heard before two judges and two lay assessors. Assize courts consist of three judges and eight lay assessors and hear cases where the potential sentence is of five years to life imprisonment. They also rule on such special crimes as high treason.

Members of the judiciary are appointed for life and are independent of the other branches of government. Trials are open to the public. The accused are provided with a written statement of the charges against them and have the right to be represented by counsel.

Police

The earliest urban police force was Vienna's City Guard of 1569, consisting of 150 men. By the beginning of the Thirty Years' War (1618–48), the City Guard consisted of 1,000 men organized as a regiment, individual companies of which took part in military campaigns. The soldiers of the guard were subject to the authority of the Imperial War Council, and the city was required to pay for their services. In 1646 the city set up its own Public Order Watch; serious frictions between the two bodies resulted in their replacement by a new service under a commissioner of police in 1776.

Its personnel were still made up of soldiers, either volunteers or assigned, but they failed to meet the city's needs because of a lack of training and continuity of service. Police functions were organized in a similar form in other large cities of the empire. It was not until a series of reforms between 1850 and 1869 that military influence over the police force was finally ended with the introduction of an independent command structure, a permanent corps of police professionals, training of officers in police skills, and distinctive uniforms and symbols of rank.

The Gendarmerie was created by Emperor Franz Joseph I in 1850 after the disorder and looting that accompanied the uprising of 1848. Initially composed of eighteen regiments and part of the army, its operational command was transferred to the Ministry for Interior in 1860 and wholly severed from the armed forces in 1867. Nevertheless, training, uniforms, ranks, and even pay remained patterned after the army. A special Alpine branch was formed in 1906, mainly to protect the part of Tirol that bordered Italy. Alpine rescue operations and border patrols have remained an important Gendarmerie function.

As of 1993, the more important law enforcement and security agencies were organized under the General Directorate for Public Security of the federal Ministry for Interior. The directorate is divided into five units: the Federal Police; the Gendarmerie central command; the State Police (secret service); the Criminal Investigation Service; and the Administrative Police. Security directorates in each of the nine provinces are also under supervision of the General Directorate for Public Security. Each of these is organized into a headquarters division, a state police division, a criminal investigation division, and an administrative police division.

Contingents of the Federal Police (Bundespolizei) are stationed in Vienna and thirteen of the larger cities. As of 1990, approximately one-third of the population of Austria lived in areas receiving Federal Police protection. The Gendarmerie accounts for nearly all of the remaining areas. A few small Austrian localities still have their own police forces separate from the Federal Police or the Gendarmerie. The Federal Police are responsible for maintaining peace, order, and security; controlling weapons and explosives; protecting constitutional rights of free expression and assembly; controlling traffic; enforcing environmental and commercial regulations; enforcing building safety and fire prevention rules; policing public events; and preventing crime. A mobile commando group is organized in each city directorate, in addition to a four-platoon "alarm group" in Vienna and a special force to maintain security at the international airport. In early 1992, it was announced that 150 officials would be assigned to special units reporting directly to the Ministry for Interior to fight organized crime.

As of 1990, the Federal Police had a personnel complement of 10,000 in the regular uniformed service (Sicherheitswache— Security Watch) and 2,400 plainclothes police in the Criminal Investigation Service. Federal Police contingents are armed with Glock 17 9mm pistol and truncheons. These can be supplemented with the standard army weapon, the Steyr 5.56mm automatic rifle, as well as various kinds of riot-control equipment. A separate women's police corps serves in the cities, principally to oversee school crossings and to assist with traffic control. As of 1990, about twenty-four women served in the Gendarmerie and sixty-six in the Federal Police, mostly to deal with cases involving women, youth, and children.

The secret service branch of the Federal Police, the State Police (Staatspolizei; commonly known as Stapo) specializes in counter-terrorism and counterintelligence. It also pursues right-wing extremism, drug trafficking, illicit arms dealing, and illegal technology transfers. It performs security investigations for other government agencies and is responsible for measures to protect national leaders and prominent visiting officials. Members of the State Police are chosen from volunteers who have served for at least three years in one of the other security agencies.

Numbering 11,600 in 1990, the Gendarmerie has responsibilities similar to the Federal Police but operates in rural areas and in towns without a contingent of Federal Police or local police. There is one member of the Gendarmerie for each 397 inhabitants in the areas subject to its jurisdiction and one member of the Federal Police for each 316 residents in the cities it patrols.

The Gendarmerie is organized into eight provincial commands (every province, except Vienna), ninety district commands, and 1,077 posts. A post can have from as few as three to as many as thirty gendarmes; most have fewer than ten. The provincial headquarters is composed of a staff department, criminal investigation department, training department, and area departments comprising two or three district commands. Basic Gendarmerie training is the responsibility of the individual provincial commands, each of which has a school for new recruits. Leadership and specialized courses are given at the central Gendarmerie school in Mödling near Vienna. The basic course for NCOs is one year; that for Gendarmerie officers lasts two years.

The Gendarmerie has its own commando unit, nicknamed *Kobra,* as do the separate provincial commands employing gendarmes with previous experience in *Kobra*. Alpine posts and high Alpine posts are served by 750 Gendarmerie Alpinists and guides. In 1988 more than 1,300 rescue missions were conducted, many with the aid of Agusta-Bell helicopters in the Gendarmerie inventory. Members of the Gendarmerie are armed with 9mm Browning-type semi-automatic pistols. They also have available American M–1 carbines and Uzi machine pistols.

The Administrative Police, in addition to maintaining the bulk of routine police records and statistics, work on import-export violations, illegal shipments of such items as firearms and pornographic materials, and alien and refugee affairs. Customs officials are ordinarily in uniform; other Administrative Police dress according to the needs of their assignments.

The late 1980s witnessed a growing incidence of complaints alleging police misconduct and unnecessary use of force. The minister for interior reported that there had been 2,622 allegations of ill-treatment by the police between 1984 and 1989, of which 1,142 resulted in criminal complaints leading to thirty-three convictions against police officers. In addition, 120 disciplinary investigations were carried out, and disciplinary measures were taken against twenty-six police officers. However, victims of police misbehavior were liable to be deterred from pressing their complaints because of the risk of being charged with slander by the accused officers. A new police law that went into effect in May 1993 stipulates more clearly the limitations on police conduct and imposes restrictions on holding persons on charges of aggressive behavior without an appearance before a magistrate. In addition, leaflets are to be given to detained or arrested persons setting out their rights, including the right to call a lawyer and to have their own doctors if medical examinations are required.

In 1990 it was disclosed that the State Police had extensively monitored the activities of private citizens without sufficient justification. Security checks had been carried out for private companies on request. Of some 11,000 citizens who inquired whether they had been monitored, some 20 percent were found to have State Police files. These actions appeared to be in violation of laws protecting personal data collected by the government, public institutions, and private entities, as well as constitutional protection of the secrecy of the mail and telephone. These revelations gave rise to a restructuring of the State Police, including the reduction of its staff from 800 to 440. The new police law that came into effect in 1993 also introduces parliamentary control over the State Police and the military secret police, with oversight to be exercised by separate parliamentary subcommittees.

Incidence of Crime

The Austrian police recorded 400,000 cases of criminal conduct during 1988; some 79,000 were defined as crimes, an increase of nearly 10 percent over 1987. The number of misdemeanors— 21,000—represented an increase of less than 1 percent. By far the largest category of crimes consisted of offenses involving property (74,343). Only 283 crimes against life and limb were recorded, and 1,167 moral offenses of a criminal nature were recorded. Among misdemeanors, offenses against property totaled over 202,000, and offenses against life and limb totaled nearly 80,000. The police reported that 4,963 persons were accused of narcotic offenses and that fifty kilograms of heroin, 215 kilograms of marijuana, and fourteen kilograms of cocaine had been seized. In the battle against the drug trade, Austria maintains contact with drug authorities in the United States and Canada as well as with authorities in other European countries and coordinates its enforcement efforts through the International Criminal Police Organization (Interpol). There is considerable evidence that international drug dealers are taking advantage of Austria's laws on banking anonymity to launder drug receipts. New restrictions were announced in early 1992 that require the identity of customers for all transactions above S200,000 and for all currencies, not just for dollars as had previously been the case.

Responding to an Interpol questionnaire on the kinds of infractions recorded, Austria reported the following offenses in 1988: homicides, 139; sexual crimes, 2,834, of which 336 were rapes; serious assaults, 120; all categories of theft, 189,794; armed or violent robbery, 2,317; and fraud, 19,904. Of those arrested, 11.0 percent were women, and 4.5 percent were juveniles between the ages of fourteen and seventeen. Noncitizens accounted for 15 to 20 percent of most criminal acts but were responsible for 23.5 percent of armed or violent robberies and 36 percent of counterfeiting cases.

The police reported that nearly 95 percent of crimes and misdemeanors involving threats to life and limb had been successfully resolved. Only 25 percent of thefts of all categories were solved; arrests occurred in 71 percent of sex offenses.

Penal System

All prisons from local jails to maximum security institutions are regulated by the Ministry for Interior. Revisions to penal statutes adopted in 1967 emphasize rehabilitation, education, work, prison wages, and assistance to prisoners on their return to society. Programs stress the humane treatment and rehabilitation of inmates, but program implementation is often inhibited by restricted prison budgets and lack of facilities.

Regulations stipulate that all able-bodied prisoners will be put to useful work. If proceeds from an individual's work exceed the cost to the state of his maintenance, the prisoner is paid a wage. Part can be used for pocket money, and the remainder is paid to the offender after release. Where facilities are inadequate or the situation justifies work or education beyond what is available on the prison grounds, those not considered dangerous or likely to attempt to escape can work or attend classes in the nearby area.

The penal system in Austria includes seven penitentiaries (Garsten, Graz, Hertenberg, Schwarzau, Stein, Suben, and Vienna-Simmering); three institutions of justice; two special institutions; and eighteen jails at the seats of courts of first instance. In spite of the rising crime rate, the prison population fell steadily from 7,795 in 1987 to 5,975 at the end of 1989. The average prison population of 6,318 in 1988 was composed of 6,054 males and 264 females. The rate of incarceration was seventy-seven per 100,000 population, typical for Europe as a whole but higher than some Scandinavian countries. Those on supervised probation numbered 4,930—2,762 adults and 2,168 juveniles.

The number held in investigative detention also declined, from 1,666 in 1987 to 1,466 in late 1989. This reduction was attributed to implementation in 1988 of the law easing the requirements for conditional release. According to Austrian authorities, the number of detainees had been reduced to a level corresponding to the European average.

* * *

Much of the information in the foregoing chapter on the Austrian army's strength and equipment is based on *The Military Balance, 1993-1994*. Under the heading ''JDW Country Survey: Austria'' in *Jane's Defence Weekly*, several articles describe the New Army Structure plan of the defense establishment, with charts showing the proposed organizational pattern. The concepts underlying Austria's defense policies prior to the New Army Structure are set forth in ''Defense Policy from the Austrian Point of View'' by Emil Spannocchi. Detail on the army's structure, weaponry, and strategic plans as of 1986 is included in Friedrich Wiener's *Die Armeen der neutralen und blockfreien Staaten Europas*.

The annual *Country Reports on Human Rights Practices* produced by the United States Department of State summarizes the operation of the criminal justice system and the internal security agencies. *Das grosse Buch der Polizei und Gendarmerie in Österreich* by Friedrich Jäger gives an account of the functioning of the various police organizations from the Middle Ages to the present day. (For further information and complete citations, see Bibliography.)

Appendix

Table

1 Metric Conversion Coefficients and Factors
2 Population, Selected Years, 1600-1991
3 Population by Province, 1951, 1981, and 1991
4 Population of Official Ethnic Groups, Selected Years, 1910-81
5 Overview of Education System, Academic Year 1990-91
6 Enrollment of Students Aged Ten to Fourteen, Selected Academic Years, 1960-61 to 1990-91
7 University Attendance, Selected Academic Years, 1955-56 to 1991-92
8 Principal Causes of Death by Gender, 1989 and 1990
9 Gross Domestic Product by Sector, Selected Years, 1960-90
10 Labor Force by Sector, 1970, 1980, and 1990
11 Distribution of Trade, 1970, 1980, and 1990
12 Balance of Payments, 1989 and 1991
13 Selected Nationalrat Election Results, 1945-90
14 Presidents of Austria, 1945-
15 Governments of Austria, 1945-
16 Major Military Equipment, 1993

Appendix

Table 1. Metric Conversion Coefficients and Factors

When you know	Multiply by	To find
Millimeters	0.04	inches
Centimeters	0.39	inches
Meters	3.3	feet
Kilometers	0.62	miles
Hectares (10,000 m²)	2.47	acres
Square kilometers	0.39	square miles
Cubic meters	35.3	cubic feet
Liters	0.26	gallons
Kilograms	2.2	pounds
Metric tons	0.98	long tons
....	1.1	short tons
....	2,204	pounds
Degrees Celsius	1.8	degrees Fahrenheit
(Centigrade)	and add 32	

Table 2. Population, Selected Years, 1600-1991
(in thousands)

Year	Population	Year	Population
1600	1,800	1960	7,047
1700	2,100	1970	7,467
1800	3,064	1980	7,549
1850	3,650	1985	7,558
1900	6,004	1990	7,718
1930	6,684	1991	7,796

Source: Based on information from Austria, Österreichisches Statistisches Zentralamt, *Statistisches Jahrbuch für die Republik Österreich, 1993*, Vienna, 1993, 13.

Table 3. *Population by Province, 1951, 1981, and 1991*
(in thousands)

Province	1951	1981	1991
Burgenland	276	270	271
Carinthia	475	536	548
Lower Austria	1,400	1,428	1,474
Salzburg	327	442	482
Styria	1,109	1,187	1,185
Tirol	427	587	631
Upper Austria	1,109	1,270	1,333
Vorarlberg	194	305	331
Vienna	1,616	1,531	1,540
TOTAL *	6,934	7,555	7,796

* Figures may not add to totals because of rounding.

Source: Based on information from Austria, Österreichisches Statistisches Zentralamt, *Statistisches Jahrbuch für die Republik Österreich, 1993,* Vienna, 1993, 13.

Table 4. *Population of Official Ethnic Groups, Selected Years, 1910–81*

Year	Croats	Slovenes	Czechs and Slovaks	Hungarians
1910	44,243	74,210	119,447	26,570
1951	34,427	42,095	4,118	5,566
1971	28,084	23,579	7,967 [1]	14,815 [2]
1981	22,371	18,371	5,168	12,415

[1] Increase caused by naturalization of Czech and Slovak asylum seekers after Warsaw Pact invasion of Czechoslovakia in 1968.
[2] Increase caused by naturalization of Hungarian asylum seekers after failed Hungarian Revolution of 1956.

Source: Based on information from Jim Sweeney and Josef Weidenholzer (eds.), *Austria: A Study in Modern Achievement,* Aldershot, United Kingdom, 1988, 252.

Table 5. Overview of Education System, Academic Year 1990-91

Type of Institution	Number of Schools	Number of Teachers	Number of Students
Preschool and kindergarten	4,715	16,794	217,414
Elementary and middle schools	5,074	68,953	648,719
Basic vocational school	238	4,530	149,806
Middle vocational school	747	—	67,207
Vocational high school	299	18,292 *	99,109
Teacher-training high school	44	7,121	10,227
Academic high school	325	17,999	83,801
Vocational college	44	155	2,863
Teacher-training college	27	1,715	6,281
University	18	11,511	192,928

* Includes teachers at middle vocational schools.

Source: Based on information from Austria, Österreichisches Statistisches Zentralamt, *Statistisches Jahrbuch für die Republik Österreich, 1992*, Vienna, 1992, 75.

Table 6. Enrollment of Students Aged Ten to Fourteen, Selected Academic Years, 1960-61 to 1990-91

Year	AHS [1]	HS [2]	Ratio AHS:HS
1960–61	50,773	205,965	1:4.1
1970–71	81,232	308,935	1:3.8
1980–81	102,743	367,611	1:3.6
1990–91	92,818	238,953	1:2.6

[1] *Allgemeinbildende Höhere Schule* (higher school of general education). Provides schooling leading to university study or advanced technical training.
[2] *Hauptschule* (middle school). Provides compulsory general education.

Source: Based on information from Austria, Österreichisches Statistisches Zentralamt, *Statistisches Handbuch für die Republik Österreich, 1991*, Vienna, 1991, 80.

Table 7. University Attendance, Selected Academic Years,
1955–56 to 1991–92

Year	Students Enrolled	Percentage of Males	Percentage of Females	Degrees Awarded
1955–56	19,124	80	20	2,970
1960–61	38,533	77	23	3,257
1970–71	53,152	75	25	6,025
1980–81	115,616	60	40	8,047
1990–91	192,928	56	44	9,694
1991–92	201,615	56	44	n.a.

n.a.—not available.

Source: Based on information from Austria, Österreichisches Statistisches Zentralamt, *Statistisches Jahrbuch für die Republik Österreich, 1992*, Vienna, 1992, 80.

Table 8. Principal Causes of Death by Gender, 1989 and 1990
(per 100,000 of the same gender)

Cause	1989 Males	1989 Females	1990 Males	1990 Females
Cardiovascular diseases	505.4	329.7	477.9	317.2
Cancer	263.5	160.9	262.7	159.5
Accidents	99.5	37.9	94.8	35.2
Respiratory diseases	58.2	25.2	58.7	26.3
Cirrhosis of the liver	42.7	13.1	41.9	13.2
Suicide	35.6	12.5	33.8	11.5
Other	69.4	68.6	70.4	69.7
TOTAL	1,074.3	647.9	1,040.2	632.6

Source: Based on information from Austria, Österreichisches Statistisches Zentralamt, *Statistisches Handbuch für die Republik Österreich, 1991*, Vienna, 1991, 441; and Austria, Österreichisches Statistisches Zentralamt, *Statistisches Jahrbuch für die Republik Österreich, 1992*, Vienna, 1992, 453.

Table 9. Gross Domestic Product by Sector, Selected Years, 1960–90 (in percentages)

Sector	1960	1970	1980	1990
Agriculture and forestry	11.1	6.9	4.4	3.1
Mining and manufacturing	36.6	34.4	28.3	26.6
Power and water supply	2.8	2.8	3.1	2.5
Construction	7.6	8.2	8.2	7.0
Trade and tourism	15.5	18.1	16.8	16.4
Transportation and communications	6.0	5.9	5.8	6.2
Property administration	6.2	8.4	12.0	16.7
Other services	2.9	3.0	3.2	4.0
Less imputed bank service charges	– 2.3	– 3.1	– 4.5	– 5.8
Other	10.9	11.9	13.7	13.8
Import levies	2.7	3.5	0.6	0.7
Value-added tax	n.a.	n.a.	8.5	8.8
TOTAL *	100.0	100.0	100.0	100.0

n.a.—not available.
* Figures may not add to totals because of rounding.

Source: Based on information from Austria, Österreichisches Statistisches Zentralamt, *Statistisches Handbuch für die Republik Österreich, 1991*, Vienna, 1991, 210.

Table 10. Labor Force by Sector, 1970, 1980, and 1990 (in percentages of total work force)

Sector	1970	1980	1990
Agriculture and forestry	18.8	10.5	7.9
Mining and quarrying	1.0	0.6	0.4
Manufacturing	30.0	29.5	27.0
Electricity, gas, and water	1.1	1.3	1.2
Construction	8.2	8.8	8.4
Wholesale and retail trade, restaurants, and hotels	14.2	17.1	18.6
Transportation, storage, and commerce	6.3	6.3	6.4
Finance, insurance, and business services	3.4	5.0	6.5
Communal, social, and personal services	16.5	20.8	23.7
Activities not adequately defined	0.3	0.1	—
TOTAL *	100.0	100.0	100.0

— means negligible.
* Figures may not add to totals because of rounding.

Source: Based on information from Austria, Österreichisches Statistisches Zentralamt, *Statistisches Handbuch für die Republik Österreich, 1991*, Vienna, 1991, 108; and Organisation for Economic Co-operation and Development, *OECD Economic Surveys, 1991–1992: Austria*, Paris, 1992, 160–61.

Table 11. *Distribution of Trade, 1970, 1980, and 1990*
(in percentages)

	1970	1980	1990
Exports			
EC [1]	39.4	55.2	64.5
EFTA [2]	25.3	12.4	10.1
Eastern Europe [3]	12.9	12.1	8.5
OPEC [4]	n.a.	5.6	2.7
West Germany	23.4	30.8	36.7
Switzerland	10.4	7.5	6.9
Italy	9.7	11.0	9.8
Britain	6.1	3.7	3.9
United States	4.1	2.2	3.2
Netherlands	2.9	2.6	2.9
Soviet Union	2.9	2.7	2.2
France	2.2	3.5	4.8
Japan	0.5	0.8	1.6
Imports			
EC	56.0	62.4	68.3
EFTA	19.1	7.9	7.1
Eastern Europe	9.3	9.7	6.0
OPEC	n.a.	7.1	2.1
West Germany	41.2	40.8	43.7
Switzerland	7.4	5.0	4.3
Britain	6.8	2.7	2.6
Italy	6.5	9.1	9.1
France	3.5	3.9	4.2
United States	3.4	3.4	3.6
Netherlands	2.9	2.7	2.8
Soviet Union	2.2	4.2	1.8
Japan	1.0	2.4	4.5

n.a.—not available.
[1] European Community. In November 1993, it became known as the European Union.
[2] European Free Trade Association.
[3] Does not include the Soviet Union.
[4] Organization of the Petroleum Exporting Countries.

Source: Based on information from Austria, Österreichisches Statistisches Zentralamt, *Statistisches Handbuch für die Republik Österreich, 1972,* Vienna, 1972, 196–97; Austria, Österreichisches Statistisches Zentralamt, *Statistisches Handbuch für die Republik Österreich, 1982,* Vienna, 1982, 369; and Austria, Österreichisches Statistisches Zentralamt, *Statistisches Handbuch für die Republik Österreich, 1991,* Vienna, 1991, 310.

Table 12. Balance of Payments, 1989 and 1991
(in millions of United States dollars)

	1989	1991
Merchandise exports, f.o.b. *	31,832	40,136
Merchandise imports, f.o.b.	− 38,437	− 52,186
Trade balance	− 6,605	− 12,050
Exports of services	18,814	26,064
Imports of services	− 10,931	− 12,524
Other income received	6,876	9,893
Other income paid	− 7,965	− 11,693
Private unrequited transfers (net)	− 57	166
Official unrequited transfers (net)	− 72	− 108
Current account balance	59	− 252
Direct investment (net)	− 66	− 768
Portfolio investment (net)	1,197	574
Other capital (net)	− 300	211
Capital account balance	831	17
Errors and ommissions (net)	106	1,107
Overall balance	996	872

* f.o.b.—free on board.

Source: Based on information from *The Europa World Year Book, 1993,* 1, London, 1993, 412.

Table 13. Selected Nationalrat Election Results, 1945–90
(in percentages of valid votes and number of seats)

Year	SPÖ[1] Percentage	SPÖ[1] Seats	ÖVP[2] Percentage	ÖVP[2] Seats	FPÖ[3] Percentage	FPÖ[3] Seats	KPÖ[4] Percentage	KPÖ[4] Seats	Greens[5] Percentage	Greens[5] Seats
1945	45	76	50	85	—	—	5	4	—	—
1949	39	67	44	77	12	16	5	5	—	—
1953	42	73	41	74	11	14	5	4	—	—
1956	43	74	46	82	7	6	4	3	—	—
1959	45	78	44	79	8	8	3	0	—	—
1962	44	76	45	81	7	8	3	0	—	—
1966	43	74	48	85	5	6	1	0	—	—
1970	48	81	45	78	6	6	1	0	—	—
1971	50	93	43	80	6	10	1	0	—	—
1975	51	93	43	80	5	10	1	0	—	—
1979	51	95	42	77	6	11	1	0	—	—
1983	48	90	43	81	5	12	0	0	0	0
1986	43	80	41	77	10	18	0	0	5	8
1990	43	80	32	60	17	33	0	0	5	10

— means not applicable.
[1] Sozialistische Partei Österreichs (Socialist Party of Austria).
[2] Österreichische Volkspartei (Austrian People's Party).
[3] Freiheitliche Partei Österreichs (Freedom Party of Austria).
[4] Kommunistische Partei Österreichs (Communist Party of Austria).
[5] Greens are those environmentalist groups elected to the Nationalrat. The various groups that make up the Greens were formed in the 1980s. They gained their first seats in 1986.

Source: Based on information from Austria, Österreichisches Statistisches Zentralamt, *Statistisches Handbuch für die Republik Österreich, 1991*, Vienna, 1991, 424.

Appendix

Table 14. Presidents of Austria, 1945–

Name	Years in Office	Party Allegiance
Karl Renner	1945–50	SPÖ [1]
Theodor Körner	1951–57	-do-
Adolf Schärf	1957–65	-do-
Franz Jonas	1965–74	-do-
Rudolf Kirchschläger	1974–86	-do-
Kurt Waldheim	1986–92	ÖVP [2]
Thomas Klestil	1992–	-do-

[1] Sozialistische Partei Österreichs (Socialist Party of Austria). In 1991 the name changed to Social Democratic Party of Austria (Sozialdemokratische Partei Österreichs—SPÖ).
[2] Österreichische Volkspartei (Austrian People's Party).

Table 15. Governments of Austria, 1945–

Period in Power	Chancellor and Party Affiliation	Parties in Government
1945	Karl Renner (SPÖ) [1]	SPÖ, ÖVP [2], KPÖ [3]
1945–49	Leopold Figl (ÖVP)	-do-
1949–53	-do-	SPÖ, ÖVP
1953–56	Julius Raab (ÖVP)	-do-
1956–59	-do-	-do-
1959–61	-do-	-do-
1961–64	Alphons Gorbach (ÖVP)	-do-
1964–66	Josef Klaus (ÖVP)	-do-
1966–70	-do-	ÖVP
1970–83	Bruno Kreisky (SPÖ)	SPÖ
1983–86	Fred Sinowatz (SPÖ)	SPÖ, FPÖ [4]
1986–	Franz Vranitzky (SPÖ)	SPÖ, ÖVP

[1] SPÖ—Sozialistische Partei Österreichs (Socialist Party of Austria). In 1991 the name changed to Social Democratic Party of Austria (Sozialdemoktatische Partei Österreichs—SPÖ).
[2] ÖVP—Österreichische Volkspartei (Austrian People's Party).
[3] KPÖ—Kommunistische Partei Österreichs (Communist Party of Austria).
[4] FPÖ—Freiheitliche Partei Österreichs (Freedom Party of Austria).

Source: Based on information from Jim Sweeney and Josef Weidenholzer (eds.), *Austria: A Study in Modern Achievement*, Aldershot, United Kingdom, 1988, 278–79.

Table 16. *Major Military Equipment, 1993*

Type and Description	Country of Origin	In Inventory
Army		
Main battle tanks		
M-60A3	United States	169
Armored personnel carriers		
Saurer 4K-4E/F	Austria	465
Tank destroyers		
Kürassier SK-105	-do-	285
Self-propelled artillery		
M-109A2 155mm howitzers	United States	54
Towed artillery		
IFH (M-2A1), 105mm	-do-	108
M-114, 155mm	-do-	24
Fortress artillery		
SFK M-2, 155mm	Sweden	24
Mortars		
M-2, 107mm	United States	102
M-43, 120mm	Austria	274
Multiple rocket launchers		
M-51, 130mm	Czechoslovakia	18
Antitank guided missiles		
RBS-56 BILL	Sweden	118
Antitank guns		
M-52/-55, 85mm	Czechoslovakia	240
M-47 tank turrets, 90mm	United States	60
Centurion tank turrets, 105mm ...	Britain	200
Air defense guns		
M-58 Oerlikon, 20mm	Switzerland	560
Oerlikon twin, towed, 35mm	-do-	74
M-42 twin, self-propelled, 40mm ..	United States	38
Air force		
Fighter/ground attack aircraft		
Saab 1050	Sweden	30
Fighter aircraft		
Draken J-350e	-do-	24
Helicopters		
Agusta-Bell AB-212, medium,		
transport	Italy	23
Agusta-Bell AB-204, light,		
transport	-do-	8
Bell OH-58B Kiowa,		
reconnaissance	United States	12
A-316B Alouette III, search and air		
rescue	France	24
Light transport/liaison		
Short Skyvan 3M	Britain	2
Pilatus PC-6B Turbo Porter	Switzerland	11
Air defense weapons		
M-65 twin Oerlikon, 35mm guns ..	-do-	18

Source: Based on information from *The Military Balance, 1993–1994*, London, 1993, 72.

Bibliography

Chapter 1

Barker, Elisabeth. *Austria, 1918-1972.* Coral Gables, Florida: University of Miami Press, 1973.

Bridge, F.R. *The Habsburg Monarchy among the Great Powers, 1815-1918.* New York: Berg, 1990.

Evans, Robert John Weston. *The Making of the Habsburg Monarchy, 1550-1700: An Interpretation.* Oxford: Clarendon Press, 1984.

Gellott, Laura S. *The Catholic Church and the Authoritarian Regime in Austria, 1933-1938.* New York: Garland, 1987.

Jelavich, Barbara. *The Habsburg Empire in European Affairs, 1814-1918.* Chicago: Rand McNally, 1969.

_____. *Modern Austria: Empire and Republic, 1815-1986.* Cambridge: Cambridge University Press, 1987.

Johnson, Lonnie. *Introducing Austria: A Short History.* Riverside, California: Ariadne Press, 1989.

Kann, Robert A. *A History of the Habsburg Empire, 1526-1918.* Berkeley: University of California Press, 1977.

Leeper, Alexander Wigram Allen. *A History of Medieval Austria.* London: Oxford University Press, 1941.

Low, Alfred D. *The Anschluss Movement, 1918-1938: Background and Aftermath—An Annotated Bibliography of German and Austrian Nationalism.* New York: Garland, 1984.

Luza, Radomir. *Austro-German Relations in the Anschluss Era.* Princeton: Princeton University Press, 1975.

_____. *The Resistance in Austria, 1938-1945.* Minneapolis: University of Minnesota Press, 1984.

Macartney, Carlile Aylmer. *The Habsburg Empire, 1790-1918.* London: Weidenfeld and Nicolson, 1968.

Reinerman, Alan J. *Austria and the Papacy in the Age of Metternich.* (2 vols.) Washington: Catholic University of America Press, 1979.

Sully, Melanie A. *A Contemporary History of Austria.* London: Routlege, 1990.

_____. *Continuity and Change in Austrian Socialism: The Eternal Quest for the Third Way.* Boulder, Colorado: East European Monographs, 1982.

Tapié, Victor Lucien. *The Rise and Fall of the Habsburg Monarchy.* New York: Praeger, 1971.

Vexler, Robert I. *Austria: A Chronology and Fact Book, 1437–1973.* Dobbs Ferry, New York: Oceana, 1977.
Ward, David. *1848: The Fall of Metternich and the Year of Revolution.* New York: Weybright and Talley, 1970.
Williamson, Samuel R. *Austria–Hungary and the Origins of the First World War.* New York: St. Martin's Press, 1991.
Zöllner, Erich. *Geschichte Österreichs: Von den Anfängen bis zur Gegenwart.* Vienna: Verlag für Geschichte und Politik, 1970.

Chapter 2

Austria. Austrian Museum for Economic and Social Affairs. *Survey of the Austrian Economy, 92–93: The Austrian Economy and Its International Position in Data, Diagrams, and Tables.* Vienna: 1992.

———. Austrian Museum for Economic and Social Affairs. *Survey of the Austrian Economy, 93–94: The Austrian Economy and Its International Position in Data, Diagrams, and Tables.* Vienna: 1993.

———. Austrian Museum for Economic and Social Affairs. *Survey of the Austrian Economy, 94–95: The Austrian Economy and Its International Position in Data, Diagrams, and Tables.* Vienna: 1994.

———. Bundeskammer für Arbeiter und Angestellte. *Wirtschafts- und Sozialstatistisches Taschenbuch, 1992.* Vienna: 1992.

———. Dokumentationsarchiv des Österreichischen Widerstandes und Ministerium für Erziehung, Kunst, und Sport. *Österreicher und der Zweite Weltkrieg.* Vienna: Österreichischer Bundesverlag, 1989.

———. Federal Press Service. *Austria: Facts and Figures.* Vienna: 1990.

———. Federal Press Service. *Austria and the New Emigration.* Vienna: 1990.

———. Federal Press Service. *The Austrian Educational System.* Vienna: 1990.

———. Federal Press Service. *Burden Sharing: Austria's Contribution to International Solidarity.* Vienna: 1991.

———. Federal Press Service. *The First Republic, 1918–1938.* Vienna: 1988.

———. Federal Press Service. *Jewish Life in Austria.* Vienna: 1992.

———. Federal Press Service. *The Rational Approach to Labour and Industry.* Vienna: 1990.

———. Federal Press Service. *Religions in Austria.* Vienna: 1990.

———. Federal Press Service. *Social Security in Austria.* Vienna: 1988.

_____. Ministerium für Wissenschaft und Forschung. *Hochschulbericht, 1990.* Vienna: 1990.

_____. Ministerium für Wissenschaft und Forschung. *Statistisches Taschenbuch.* Vienna: 1991.

_____. Ministerium für Wissenschaft und Forschung. *Zur Sozialen Lage der Studierenden, 1990.* Vienna: 1990.

_____. Ministry for Foreign Affairs. *Austrian Foreign Policy Yearbook, 1991.* Vienna: 1991.

_____. Österreichisches Statistisches Zentralamt. *Sozialstatistische Daten, 1990.* (Beiträge zur Österreichischen Statistik, No. 967.) Vienna: 1990.

_____. Österreichisches Statistisches Zentralamt. *Statistisches Handbuch für die Republik Österreich, 1991.* Vienna: 1991.

_____. Österreichisches Statistisches Zentralamt. *Statistisches Jahrbuch für die Republik Österreich, 1992.* Vienna: 1992.

_____. Österreichisches Statistisches Zentralamt. *Statistisches Jahrbuch für die Republik Österreich, 1993.* Vienna: 1993.

_____. Staatssekretariat für allgemeine Frauenfragen, Bundeskanzleramt. *Frauen in Österreich, 1975–85.* Vienna: 1985.

_____. Staatssekretariat für allgemeine Frauenfragen, Bundeskanzleramt. *Frauen in Österreich, 1985–90.* Vienna: 1990.

Baratta, Mario von (ed.). *Der Fischer Weltalmanach, 1994.* Frankfurt: Fischer Taschenbuch Verlag, 1993.

Bartunek, Ewald. "Erwerbstätigkeit, Arbeitsmarkt." Pages 133–86 in Austria, Österreichisches Statistisches Zentralamt, *Sozialstatistische Daten, 1990.* (Beiträge zur Österreichischen Statistik, No. 967.) Vienna: 1990.

Dallinger, Alfred. "Social Security in Austria." Pages 197–204 in Jim Sweeney and Josef Weidenholzer (eds.), *Austria: A Study in Modern Achievement.* Aldershot, United Kingdom: Avebury, 1988.

Dungler, Herta, and Wilhelm Janik. "Wohnen." Pages 323–50 in Austria, Österreichisches Statistisches Zentralamt, *Sozialstatistische Daten, 1990.* (Beiträge zur Österreichischen Statistik, No. 967.) Vienna: 1990.

Fassmann, Heinz. "Einwanderung, Auswanderung, und Binnenwanderung in Österreich-Ungarn um 1910." Pages 92–101 in Heinz Fassmann et al. (eds.), *Demographische Informationen, 1990–91.* Vienna: Institut für Demographie, Österreichische Akademie der Wissenschaften, 1991.

Fassmann, Heinz, and Rainer Münz. "Einwanderungsland Österreich?" Pages 85–91 in Heinz Fassmann et al. (eds.), *Demographische Informationen, 1990–91.* Vienna: Institut für Demographie, Österreichische Akademie der Wissenschaften, 1991.

Filla, Wilhelm. "National Minorities in Austria." Pages 250–55 in Jim Sweeney and Josef Weidenholzer (eds.), *Austria: A Study in Modern Achievement.* Aldershot, United Kingdom: Avebury, 1988.

Findl, Peter. "Ehe, Familie, Haushalt." Pages 43–76 in Austria, Österreichisches Statistisches Zentralamt, *Sozialstatistische Daten, 1990.* (Beiträge zur Österreichischen Statistik, No. 967.) Vienna: 1990.

Fitzmaurice, John. *Austrian Politics and Society Today: In Defence of Austria.* New York: St. Martin's Press, 1990.

Fraser, Angus. *The Gypsies.* Oxford: Blackwell, 1992.

Hainka, Alexander. "Bevölkerung." Pages 9–42 in Austria, Österreichisches Statistisches Zentralamt, *Sozialstatistische Daten, 1990.* (Beiträge zur Österreichischen Statistik, No. 967.) Vienna: 1990.

Heiler, Bernhard, and Friedrich Nitsch. "Schulwesen, Bildung." Pages 101–33 in Austria, Österreichisches Statistisches Zentralamt, *Sozialstatistische Daten, 1990.* (Beiträge zur Österreichischen Statistik, No. 967.) Vienna: 1990.

Johnson, Lonnie. *Introducing Austria: A Short History.* Riverside, California: Ariadne Press, 1989.

Karmasin, Fritz. *Austrian Attitudes Toward Jews, Israel, and the Holocaust.* (Working Papers on Contemporary Anti-Semitism.) New York: American Jewish Committee, 1992.

Leitner, Helga. "Demography and Population Problems." Pages 75–98 in Kurt Steiner (ed.), *Modern Austria.* Palo Alto, California: Society for the Promotion of Science and Scholarship, 1981.

März, Eduard. "Austria's Economic Development: 1945–85." Pages 27–46 in Jim Sweeney and Josef Weidenholzer (eds.), *Austria: A Study in Modern Achievement.* Aldershot, United Kingdom: Avebury, 1988.

Mayerhofer, Claudia. *Dorfzigeuner: Kultur und Geschichte der Burgenland-Roma von der Ersten Republik bis sur Gegenwart.* Vienna: Picus Verlag, 1987.

Moritz, Herbert. "Education in Austria." Pages 217–25 in Jim Sweeney and Josef Weidenholzer (eds.), *Austria: A Study in Modern Achievement.* Aldershot, United Kingdom: Avebury, 1988.

Neyer, Gerda. "Alleinerziehende in Österreich." Pages 68–73 in Heinz Fassmann et al. (eds.), *Demographische Informationen, 1990–91.* Vienna: Institut für Demographie, Österreichische Akademie der Wissenschaften, 1991.

Pauley, Bruce. *From Prejudice to Persecution: A History of Austrian Anti-Semitism.* Chapel Hill: University of North Carolina Press, 1992.

Population Crisis Committee. "The International Human Suffering Index." Washington: 1992.

Stadler, Karl. *Austria.* (Nations of the Modern World Series.) New York: Praeger, 1971.

Steger, Gerhard. "The Churches and Politics." Pages 250–54 in Jim Sweeney and Josef Weidenholzer (eds.), *Austria: A Study in Modern Achievement.* Aldershot, United Kingdom: Avebury, 1988.

Steiner, Kurt. "Education and Educational Policy." Pages 321–34 in Kurt Steiner (ed.), *Modern Austria.* Palo Alto, California: Society for the Promotion of Science and Scholarship, 1981.

———. "Higher Education." Pages 335–44 in Kurt Steiner (ed.), *Modern Austria.* Palo Alto, California: Society for the Promotion of Science and Scholarship, 1981.

Steiner, Kurt (ed.). *Modern Austria.* Palo Alto, California: Society for the Promotion of Science and Scholarship, 1981.

Stojka, Ceija. *Wir leben im Verborgenen: Erinnerungen einer Rom-Zigeunerin.* Vienna: Picus Verlag, 1989.

Stourzh, Gerald. *Vom Reich zur Republik: Studien zum Österreichisch-bewusstsein im 20. Jahrhundert.* Vienna: Edition Atelier, 1990.

Strasser, Rudolf. "Social Policy Since 1945: Democracy and the Welfare State." Pages 301–20 in Kurt Steiner (ed.), *Modern Austria.* Palo Alto, California: Society for the Promotion of Science and Scholarship, 1981.

Sweeney, Jim, and Josef Weidenholzer (eds.). *Austria: A Study in Modern Achievement.* Aldershot, United Kingdom: Avebury, 1988.

Tomašević, Nebojša. *Gypsies of the World.* New York: H. Holt, 1988.

United States. Department of State. *Country Reports on Human Rights Practices for 1993.* (Report submitted to United States Congress, 103d, 2d Session, House of Representatives, Committee on Foreign Affairs, and Senate, Committee on Foreign Relations.) Washington: GPO, 1994.

Vollman, Kurt, and Eva Dragosits. "Einkommen, materieller Lebensstandard." Pages 187–234 in Austria, Österreichisches Statistisches Zentralamt, *Sozialstatistische Daten, 1990.* (Beiträge zur Österreichischen Statistik, No. 967.) Vienna: 1990.

Weinzierl, Erika. "Religions and Their Relations to State and Parties." Pages 99–122 in Kurt Steiner (ed.), *Modern Austria.* Palo Alto, California: Society for the Promotion of Science and Scholarship, 1981.

Welpton, Eric. *The Austrians: How They Live and Work.* London: David and Charles, 1970.

Wohlschlägl, Helmut. "Austria: Landscape and Regional Structure." Pages 23–74 in Kurt Steiner (ed.), *Modern Austria.* Palo

Alto, California: Society for the Promotion of Science and Scholarship, 1981.

Wright, William E. (ed.). *Austria since 1945*. Minneapolis: Center for Austrian Studies, University of Minnesota, 1982.

Chapter 3

Arndt, Sven W. *Political Economy of Austria*. Washington: American Enterprise Institute, 1982.

Austria. Austria Documentation. *Austria for Investors: General Information*. Vienna: Federal Press Service, 1990.

———. Austria Documentation. *The Rational Approach to Labor and Industry*. Vienna: Federal Press Service, 1990.

———. Austrian Information Service. *Austria: Selected Economic Data*. Vienna: Bundeswirtschaftskammer, 1992.

———. Austrian Museum for Economic and Social Affairs. *Survey of the Austrian Economy, 91–92: The Austrian Economy and Its International Position in Data, Diagrams, and Tables*. Vienna: 1991.

———. Austrian Museum for Economic and Social Affairs. *Survey of the Austrian Economy, 92–93: The Austrian Economy and Its International Position in Data, Diagrams, and Tables*. Vienna: 1992.

———. Austrian Museum for Economic and Social Affairs. *Survey of the Austrian Economy, 93–94: The Austrian Economy and Its International Position in Data, Diagrams, and Tables*. Vienna: 1993.

———. Austrian Museum for Economic and Social Affairs. *Survey of the Austrian Economy, 94–95: The Austrian Economy and Its International Position in Data, Diagrams, and Tables*. Vienna: 1994.

———. Bundeskammer der Gewerblichen Wirtschaft. ''Bundessektion Geld-, Kredit-, und Versicherungswesen.'' Pages 61–73, 235–51 in *Jahrbuch der Österreichischen Wirtschaft, 1990*. Vienna: Ungar, 1991.

———. Bundeskammer der Gewerblichen Wirtschaft. ''Bundessektion Handel.'' Pages 225–34 in *Jahrbuch der Österreichischen Wirtschaft, 1990*. Vienna: Ungar, 1991.

———. Österreichisches Statistisches Zentralamt. *Statistisches Handbuch für die Republik Österreich, 1972*. Vienna: 1972.

———. Österreichisches Statistisches Zentralamt. *Statistisches Handbuch für die Republik Österreich, 1982*. Vienna: 1982.

———. Österreichisches Statistisches Zentralamt. *Statistisches Handbuch für die Republik Österreich, 1991*. Vienna: 1991.

———. Österreichisches Statistisches Zentralamt. *Statistisches Jahrbuch für die Republik Österreich, 1992*. Vienna: 1992.

Baratta, Mario von (ed.). *Der Fischer Weltalmanach, 1994.* Frankfurt: Fischer Taschenbuch Verlag, 1993.

Butschek, Felix. "EC Membership and the 'Velvet' Revolution: The Impact of Recent Political Changes on Austria's Economic Position in Europe." Pages 62–80 in Günter Bischof and Anton Pelinka (eds.), *Austria in the New Europe.* (Contemporary Austrian Studies, No. 1.) New Brunswick, New Jersey: Transaction Books, 1993.

The Europa World Year Book, 1993, 1. London: Europa, 1993.

Gruenwald, Oskar. "The Political Economy of Austria." Pages 150–55 in Sven W. Arndt (ed.), *Austrian Industrial Structure and Industrial Policy.* Washington: American Enterprise Institute, 1982.

Haschek, Helmut H. "Trade, Trade Finance, and the Austrian Economy." Pages 176–98 in Sven W. Arndt (ed.), *Austrian Industrial Structure and Industrial Policy.* Washington: American Enterprise Institute, 1982.

Organisation for Economic Co-operation and Development. *OECD Economic Surveys: Austria* (annuals 1972 and 1981–1982 through 1992–1993). Paris: 1972 and 1982–93.

Österreichisches Institut für Wirtschaftsforschung. "Kennzahlen zur Konjunkturlage der Industriebranchen," *WIFO Monatsbericht* [Vienna], April 1992, 5, 25, 164–70, 178, 180–81.

Stankovsky, Jan. *Der Aussenhandel Österreichs: Entwicklung und Struktur.* Vienna: Bundeswirtschaftsakademie, 1990.

Starik, W. "Die Österreichische Energieversorgung—Bisherige Entwicklung und Perspektiven," *Österreichische Zeitschrift für Elektrizitätswirtschaft* [Vienna], August, 1991, 281–88.

Sweeney, Jim, and Josef Weidenholzer (eds.). *Austria: A Study in Modern Achievement.* Aldershot, United Kingdom: Avebury, 1988.

Traxler, Franz. "Austria: Still the Country of Corporatism." Pages 270–97 in Anthony Ferner and Richard Hyman (eds.), *Industrial Relations in the New Europe.* Oxford: Blackwell, 1992.

(Various issues of the following periodicals were also used in the preparation of this chapter: *Austria Today* [Vienna]; *Economist* [London]; Economist Intelligence Unit, *Country Profile: Austria* [London] and *Country Report: Austria* [London]; *Financial Times* [London]; Foreign Broadcast Information Service, *Daily Report: West Europe; Handelsblatt* [Düsseldorf]; Österreichisches Institut für Wirtschaftsforschung, *Statistische Berichten* [Vienna]; and *Trend* [Vienna].)

Chapter 4

Austria. Federal Press Service. *The Mass Media in Austria.* Vienna: 1990.

_____. Federal Press Service. *The Political System in Austria.* Vienna: 1987.

Bischof, Günter, and Anton Pelinka (eds.). *Austria in the New Europe.* (Contemporary Austrian Studies, No. 1.) New Brunswick, New Jersey: Transaction Books, 1993.

Dyk, Irene. "The Austrian People's Party." Pages 67–81 in Jim Sweeney and Josef Weidenholzer (eds.), *Austria: A Study in Modern Achievement.* Aldershot, United Kingdom: Avebury, 1988.

The Europa World Year Book, 1993, 1. London: Europa, 1993.

Fabris, Heinz. "The Media." Pages 236–44 in Jim Sweeney and Josef Weidenholzer (eds.), *Austria: A Study in Modern Achievement.* Aldershot, United Kingdom: Avebury, 1988.

Feichtlbauer, Hubert. "The Media." Pages 279–300 in Kurt Steiner (ed.), *Modern Austria.* Palo Alto, California: Society for the Promotion of Science and Scholarship, 1981.

Fellner, Fritz. "The Genesis of the Austrian Republic." Pages 1–22 in Kurt Steiner (ed.), *Modern Austria.* Palo Alto, California: Society for the Promotion of Science and Scholarship, 1981.

Fischer, Heinz. "Das Parlament." Pages 96–117 in *Handbuch des politischen Systems Österreichs,* eds., Herbert Dachs et al. Vienna: Manz, 1991.

_____. "Die Reform der Nationalratswahlordnung, 1992." Pages 341–60, in *Österreichisches Jahrbuch für Politik, 1992,* eds., Andreas Khol, Günther Ofner, and Alfred Stirnemann. Vienna: Verlag für Geschichte und Politik, 1993.

Fitzmaurice, John. *Austrian Politics and Society Today: In Defence of Austria.* New York: St. Martin's Press, 1990.

Flanz, Gisbert H., and Peter Knize. "Austria." Pages 1–133 in Albert P. Blaustein and Gisbert H. Flanz (eds.), *Constitutions of the Countries of the World.* Dobbs Ferry, New York: Oceana, 1985.

Frischenschlager, Friedhelm. "Zur Praxis der parlamentarischen Arbeit im Österreichischen Nationalrat." Pages 723–56 in Herbert Schambeck (ed.), *Österreichs Parlamentarismus: Werden und System.* Berlin: Duncker und Humblot, 1986.

Gerlich, Peter. "Government Structure: The Principles of Government." Pages 209–22 in Kurt Steiner (ed.), *Modern Austria.* Palo Alto, California: Society for the Promotion of Science and Scholarship, 1981.

Haerpfer, Christian. "Austria: The 'United Greens' and the 'Alternative List/Green Alternative'." Pages 23–38 in Ferdinand

Müller-Rommel (ed.), *New Politics in Western Europe: The Rise and Success of Green Parties and Alternative Lists*. Boulder, Colorado: Westview Press, 1989.

Handbuch des politischen Systems Österreichs. (Eds., Herbert Dachs et al.) Vienna: Manz, 1991.

Klose, Alfred. *Machtstrukturen in Österreich*. Vienna: Signum, 1987.

Kneucker, Raoul F. "Public Administration: The Business of Government." Pages 261–78 in Kurt Steiner (ed.), *Modern Austria*. Palo Alto, California: Society for the Promotion of Science and Scholarship, 1981.

Kostelka, Peter, and Ralf Unkart. "Vom Stellenwert des Federalismus in Österreich." Pages 337–60 in Heinz Fischer (ed.), *Das politische System Österreichs*. Vienna: Manz, 1991.

Kramer, Helmut. "Strukturentwicklung der Aussenpolitik: 1945–1990." Pages 637–57 in *Handbuch des politischen Systems Österreichs*, eds., Herbert Dachs et al. Vienna: Manz, 1991.

Luif, Paul. "Austrian Neutrality and the Europe of 1992." Pages 19–41 in Günter Bischof and Anton Pelinka (eds.), *Austria in the New Europe*. (Contemporary Austrian Studies, No. 1.) New Brunswick, New Jersey: Transaction Books, 1993.

Luther, Kurt Richard. "Consociationalism, Parties, and the Party System." Pages 45–98 in Kurt Richard Luther and Wolfgang C. Müller (eds.), *Politics in Austria: Still a Case of Consociationalism?* London: Frank Cass, 1992.

Luther, Kurt Richard, and Wolfgang C. Müller. "Consociationalism and the Austrian Political System." Pages 1–15 in Kurt Richard Luther and Wolfgang C. Müller (eds.), *Politics in Austria: Still a Case of Consociationalism?* London: Frank Cass, 1992.

Luther, Kurt Richard, and Wolfgang C. Müller (eds.). *Politics in Austria: Still a Case of Consociationalism?* London: Frank Cass, 1977.

Mitten, Richard. *The Politics of Antisemitic Prejudice: The Waldheim Phenomenon in Austria*. Boulder, Colorado: Westview Press, 1992.

Müller, Wolfgang C. "Austrian Governmental Institutions: Do They Matter?" Pages 99–131 in Kurt Richard Luther and Wolfgang C. Müller (eds.), *Politics in Austria: Still a Case of Consociationalism?* London: Frank Cass, 1992.

Neisser, Heinrich. "Die Reform der Nationalratswahlordnung." Pages 361–85 in *Österreichisches Jahrbuch für Politik, 1992*, eds., Andreas Khol, Günther Ofner, and Alfred Stirnemann. Vienna: Verlag für Geschichte und Politik, 1993.

Neuhofer, Hans. "Gemeinden." Pages 774–84 in *Handbuch des politischen Systems Österreichs*, eds., Herbert Dachs et al. Vienna: Manz, 1991.

Nick, Rainer, and Anton Pelinka. *Österreichs politische Landschaft.* Innsbruck: Haymon Verlag, 1993.

_____. *Parlamentarismus in Österreich.* Vienna: Jugend und Volk, 1984.

Nick, Rainer, and Sieghard Viertler. "Survey of Austrian Politics." Pages 193–210 in Günter Bischof and Anton Pelinka (eds.), *Austria in the New Europe.* (Contemporary Austrian Studies, No. 1.) New Brunswick, New Jersey: Transaction Books, 1993.

Österreichisches Jahrbuch für Politik, 1992. (Eds., Andreas Kohl, Günther Ofner, and Alfred Stirnemann.) Vienna: Verlag für Geschichte und Politik, 1993.

Pelinka, Anton. "The Peculiarities of Politics in Austria: The Constitution, Federalism, Parliamentary and Social Democracy." Pages 47–54 in Jim Sweeney and Josef Weidenholzer (eds.), *Austria: A Study in Modern Achievement.* Aldershot, United Kingdom: Avebury, 1988.

Prisching, Manfred. "The Transformation of Austria in the Context of New Europe." Pages 81–106 in Günter Bischof and Anton Pelinka (eds.), *Austria in the New Europe.* (Contemporary Austrian Studies, No. 1.) New Brunswick, New Jersey: Transaction Books, 1993.

Quendler, Franz. "Österreich in internationalen Organisationen." Pages 705–18 in *Handbuch des politischen Systems Österreichs,* eds., Herbert Dachs et al. Vienna: Manz, 1991.

Steiner, Kurt (ed.). *Modern Austria.* Palo Alto, California: Society for the Promotion of Science and Scholarship, 1981.

Stuhlpfarrer, Karl. *Austria: Permanently Neutral—Austrian Foreign Policy since 1945.* Vienna: Federal Press Service, 1987.

Sully, Melanie A. *A Contemporary History of Austria.* London: Routledge, 1990.

_____. *Political Parties and Elections in Austria.* London: C. Hurst, 1981.

Sweeney, Jim, and Josef Weidenholzer (eds.). *Austria: A Study in Modern Achievement.* Aldershot, United Kingdom: Avebury, 1988.

Weidenholzer, Josef. *Der österreichische Weg: Einsichten und Aussichten.* Vienna: Zimmermann und Karrer, 1989.

Wicha, Barbara. "Parteienfinanzierung in Österreich." Pages 489–526 in Anton Pelinka and Fritz Plasser (eds.), *Das österreichische Parteiensystem.* Vienna: Bohlau, 1988.

Widder, Helmut. "Der Nationalrat." Pages 261–336 in Herbert Schambeck (ed.), *Österreichs Parlamentarismus: Werden und System.* Berlin: Duncker und Humblot, 1986.

(Various issues of the following periodicals were also used in the preparation of this chapter: *Austria Today* [Vienna]; *Der Spiegel* [Hamburg]; *Economist* [London]; Economist Intelligence Unit, *Country Report: Austria* [London]; Foreign Broadcast Information Service, *Daily Report: West Europe;* New York Times; *Profil* [Vienna]; and *Washington Post.*)

Chapter 5

Amnesty International. *Amnesty International Report, 1991.* New York: 1991.

————. *Amnesty International Report, 1993.* New York: 1993.

Austria. Österreichischer Bundesverlag. *Ein Heer für jede Jahreszeit: Das österreichische Bundesheer.* Vienna: 1985.

————. Österreichisches Statistisches Zentralamt. *Statistisches Handbuch für die Republik Österreich, 1990.* Vienna: 1990.

Bauer, Robert A. (ed.). *The Austrian Solution: International Conflict and Cooperation.* Charlottesville: University Press of Virginia, 1982.

Bell, Raymond E., Jr. "Austria and Conflict in Central Europe," *Military Review,* 70, No. 2, February 1990, 48–54.

Clarke, John L. "Austria's Raumverteidigung: Central Front Solution?" *Armed Forces Journal,* 123, No. 2, September 1985, 46–48.

Crankshaw, Edward. *The Fall of the House of Habsburg.* New York: Viking, 1963.

Danspeckgruber, Wolfgang F. "Neutrality and the Emerging Europe." Pages 265–88 in Wolfgang F. Danspeckgruber (ed.), *Emerging Dimensions of European Security Policy.* Boulder, Colorado: Westview Press, 1991.

————. "Security in Europe 1992." Pages 107–36 in Günter Bischof and Anton Pelinka (eds.), *Austria in the New Europe.* (Contemporary Austrian Studies, No. 1.) New Brunswick, New Jersey: Transaction Books, 1993.

Defense and Foreign Affairs Handbook. (Ed., Gregory R. Copley.) Alexandria, Virginia: International Media, 1990.

Dupuy, R. Ernest, and Trevor N. Dupuy. *The Encyclopedia of Military History: From 3500 B.C. to the Present.* New York: Harper and Row, 1986.

Fernau, Heribert, Johann Maurer, and Franz Stierschneider. *Daten, Trends, und Interpretationen zum Budget der österreichischen Landesverteidigung.* Vienna: Institut für Militärische Sicherheitspolitik an der Landesverteidigungsakademie, 1990.

Hacksey, Kenneth, and William Woodhouse. *Penguin Encyclopedia of Modern Warfare: 1850 to the Present Day.* London: Viking, 1991.

Hagelin, Björn. *Neutrality and Foreign Military Sales.* Boulder, Colorado: Westview Press, 1990.

Harnischmacher, Robert. "The Federal Gendarmerie in Austria," *International Journal of Comparative and Applied Criminal Justice*, 13, No. 1, Winter 1989, 123-34.

International Crime Statistics, 1987-1988. St. Cloud, France: International Criminal Police Organization, n.d.

Jäger, Friedrich. *Das grosse Buch der Polizei und Gendarmerie in Österreich.* Graz: H. Weishaupt Verlag, 1990.

Jelavich, Barbara. *Modern Austria: Empire and Republic, 1815-1986.* Cambridge: Cambridge University Press, 1987.

Katzenstein, Peter J. *Disjoined Partners: Austria and Germany since 1815.* Berkeley: University of California Press, 1976.

Keegan, John. *World Armies.* Detroit: Gale, 1983.

Kurian, George Thomas. *World Encyclopedia of Police Forces and Penal Systems.* New York: Facts on File, 1989.

Luchak, John M. "Austria and U.S. Security," *Parameters*, 18, No. 3, September 1988, 87-93.

Luif, Paul. "Austrian Neutrality and the Europe of 1992." Pages 19-41 in Günter Bischof and Anton Pelinka (eds.), *Austria in the New Europe.* (Contemporary Austrian Studies, No. 1.) New Brunswick, New Jersey: Transaction Books, 1993.

The Military Balance, 1991-1992. London: International Institute for Strategic Studies, 1991.

The Military Balance, 1992-1993. London: International Institute for Strategic Studies, 1992.

The Military Balance, 1993-1994. London: International Institute for Strategic Studies, 1993.

The Military Balance, 1994-1995. London: International Institute for Strategic Studies, 1994.

Miller, Charles (ed.). "Republic of Austria." Pages 37-41 in Charles Miller (ed.), *Air Forces of the World, 1988-89.* Geneva: Interavia, 1988.

Pleiner, Horst. "Das Bundesheer: In einem veränderten Umfeld—neue Aufgaben, Strukturen, Wege in die Zukunft," *Österreichische Militärische Zeitschrift* [Vienna], 31, No. 2, May-June 1993, 197-206.

Pochhacker, Christian. "Austria: Equipped to Defend Neutrality?" *Defence* [London], 20, No. 10, October 1989, 777-81.

Sauerwein, Brigitte. "Current Issues of Austrian Defense," *International Defense Review* [London], 22, No. 2, March 1989, 299-301.

Skuhra, Anselm. "Austria and the New Cold War." Pages 117–47 in Bengt Sundelius (ed.), *The Neutral Democracies and the New Cold War*. Boulder, Colorado: Westview Press, 1987.

Spannocchi, Emil. "Defense Policy from the Austrian Point of View." Pages 381–91 in Kurt Steiner (ed.), *Modern Austria*. Palo Alto, California: Society for the Promotion of Science and Scholarship, 1981.

Stone, Norman. *The Eastern Front, 1914–1917*. New York: Scribner's, 1975.

Thompson, Wayne C. *Western Europe, 1990*. Washington: Stryker-Post, 1990.

United States. Arms Control and Disarmament Agency. *World Military Expenditures and Arms Transfers: 1990*. Washington: GPO, 1991.

———. Department of State. *Background Notes: Austria*. (Department of State Publication No. 7955.) Washington: GPO, December 1992.

———. Department of State. *Country Reports on Human Rights Practices for 1990*. (Report submitted to United States Congress, 102d, 1st Session, Senate, Committee on Foreign Relations, and House of Representatives, Committee on Foreign Affairs.) Washington: GPO, 1991.

———. Department of State. *Country Reports on Human Rights Practices for 1991*. (Report submitted to United States Congress, 102d, 2d Session, House of Representatives, Committee on Foreign Affairs, and Senate, Committee on Foreign Relations.) Washington: GPO, 1992.

———. Department of State. *Country Reports on Human Rights Practices for 1992*. (Report submitted to United States Congress, 103d, 1st Session, Senate, Committee on Foreign Relations, and House of Representatives, Committee on Foreign Affairs.) Washington: GPO, 1993.

———. Department of State. *Country Reports on Human Rights Practices for 1993*. (Report submitted to United States Congress, 103d, 2d Session, House of Representatives, Committee on Foreign Affairs, and Senate, Committee on Foreign Relations.) Washington: GPO, 1994.

———. Department of State. *Patterns of Global Terrorism, 1989*. Washington: 1990.

Vetschera, Heinz. "Austria." Pages 59–77 in Richard E. Bissell and Curt Gasteyger (eds.), *The Missing Link: West European Neutrals and Regional Security*. Durham: Duke University Press, 1990.

Wiener, Friedrich. *Die Armeen der neutralen und blockfreien Staaten Europas: Organisation, Kriegsbild, Waffen, und Gerät*. Vienna: Ueberreuter, 1986.

Zeger, Hans G., et al. *Alpen-Stasi: die II. Republik in Zerrspiegel der Staatspolizei.* Linz: Edition Sandkorn, 1990.

(Various issues of the following periodicals were also used in the preparation of this chapter: *DMS Market Intelligence Report;* Economist Intelligence Unit, *Country Report: Austria* [London]; Foreign Broadcast Information Service, *Daily Report: West Europe; Jane's Defence Weekly* [London]; *New York Times;* and *Washington Post.*)

Glossary

Bretton Woods system—Established in 1944, the system aimed at stabilizing exchange rates by fixing the price of gold at US$35 per troy ounce. Other currencies were linked to the system according to their exchange rates with the United States dollar. The system was replaced by one of floating exchange rates in the early 1970s. *See also* European Monetary System (EMS).

d'Hondt method—Also known as the highest-average method of determining the allocation of seats to political parties after an election. The d'Hondt method was devised by a Belgian, Victor d'Hondt, to be used in electoral systems based on proportional representation. In addition to Belgium, the method has been adopted by Austria, Finland, Portugal, and Switzerland. Under this method, voters do not choose a candidate but vote for a party, each of which has a published list of candidates. The party winning the most votes in a constituency is awarded the area's first seat, which goes to the candidate at the top of the winning party's list. The total vote of this party is then divided by two, and this amount is compared with the totals of the other parties. The party with the greatest number of votes at this point receives the next seat to be awarded. Each time a party wins a seat, its total is divided by the number of seats it has won plus one. The process continues until all the seats in a constituency are awarded. The d'Hondt method slightly favors large parties.

European Community (EC)—*See* European Union (EU).

European Economic Area (EEA)—An economic area encompassing all the members of the European Union (EU—*q.v.*) and the European Free Trade Association (EFTA—*q.v.*), with the exception of Switzerland. Created in May 1992, the EEA went into effect on January 1, 1994. The EEA is a single market for the free movement of labor, services, capital (with some restrictions on investments), and most products. EFTA members have agreed to accept EU regulations in many areas, including company law, education, environmental protection, mergers, and social policy.

European Economic Community (EEC)—*See* European Union (EU).

European Free Trade Association (EFTA)—Founded in 1960, EFTA aims at supporting free trade among its members and increasing the liberalization of trade on a global basis, particularly

287

within Western Europe. In 1993 the organization's member states were Austria, Finland, Iceland, Liechtenstein, Norway, Sweden, and Switzerland.

European Monetary System (EMS)—Established in 1979 by the European Economic Community (EEC—*q.v.*), the EMS was created to stabilize currency values because the Bretton Woods system (*q.v.*) proved not fully satisfactory.

European Monetary Union (EMU)—The EMU is a plan for a single European central bank and for a single European currency to replace national banks and currencies for those European states that qualify.

European Union (EU)—Until November 1993, the EU was known as the European Community (EC). The EU comprises three communities: the European Coal and Steel Community (ECSC), the European Economic Community (EEC), and the European Atomic Energy Community (Euratom). Each community is a legally distinct body, but since 1967 they have shared common governing institutions. The EU forms more than a framework for free trade and economic cooperation: the signatories to the treaties governing the communities have agreed in principle to integrate their economies and ultimately to form a political union. Belgium, France, Italy, Luxembourg, the Netherlands, and the Federal Republic of Germany (West Germany) were charter members of the EU; Britain, Denmark, and Ireland joined on January 1, 1973; Greece became a member on January 1, 1981; and Portugal and Spain entered on January 1, 1986.

exchange rate mechanism (ERM)—Mechanism established in 1979 to regulate currency exchange rates in the European Monetary System (EMS—*q.v.*). Member currencies are permitted to fluctuate in value only within a narrow margin (the so-called snake).

gross domestic product (GDP)—The total value of goods and services produced by the domestic economy during a given period, usually one year. Obtained by adding the value contributed by each sector of the economy in the form of profits, compensation to employees, and depreciation (consumption of capital). Most GDP figures in this book are based on GDP at factor cost. Real GDP is the value of GDP when inflation has been taken into account.

gross national product (GNP)—Obtained by adding the gross domestic product (GDP—*q.v.*) and the income received from abroad by residents, less payments remitted abroad to nonresidents. Real GNP is the value of GNP when inflation has been taken into account.

Hare system—Also known as the single transferable vote formula. The Hare system was developed in the nineteenth century by Thomas Hare, a British political reformer, to create constituencies with multiple representatives in electoral systems based on proportional representation. Ballots are used on which a voter may rank his or her choices in order of preference. Any candidate who has received enough first-preference votes to meet a quota wins a seat. Votes above this quota are transferred to the candidates with second-preference votes, and each of those who meet the quota is awarded a seat. The process continues until all seats in a constituency are filled.

Organisation for Economic Co-operation and Development (OECD)—Established in 1961 to replace the Organisation for European Economic Co-operation (OEEC), the OECD is an international organization composed of the industrialized market economy countries (twenty-four full members as of 1993). The OECD seeks to promote economic and social welfare in member countries, as well as in developing countries, by providing a forum in which to establish and coordinate policies.

Organisation for European Economic Co-operation (OEEC)— *See* Organisation for Economic Co-operation Development (OECD).

schilling (S)—National currency. Consists of 100 groschen. In relation to the United States dollar, the average annual exchange rate was S13.2 in 1989, S11.4 in 1990, S11.7 in 1991, S11.0 in 1992, and S11.4 in 1993.

Western European Union (WEU)—Founded in 1948 to facilitate West European cooperation in economic, social, cultural, and defense matters. Reactivated in 1984 to concentrate on the defense and disarmament concerns of its members, the WEU is headed by a council consisting of its members' ministers of foreign affairs and defense. The council meets twice a year; lower-level WEU entities meet with greater frequency. In late 1993, WEU members included Belgium, Britain, France, Germany, Greece, Italy, Luxembourg, the Netherlands, Portugal, and Spain.

Index

abortion, 83, 103; church opposition to, xxvii, 102; as controversial issue, 61; legalized, 62, 81

acquired immune deficiency syndrome (AIDS), 112

Adler, Viktor, 190

Administrative Court, 180, 181, 186

Administrative Police, 224, 254, 256

Advisory Committee for Economic and Social Questions, 139

Afghanistan: immigrants from, 84; Soviet invasion of, 216

Agrarian League (Landbund), 36

agricultural: credit cooperatives, 158; policy, 143–44; production, 146

agriculture, 143–46; in the Alps, 73; decline in, xxvi, 140, 143; employment in, 68, 136, 141, 145; government role in, 143–45; as percentage of gross domestic product, xxvi, 141, 143; price controls for, 144; quotas for, 144; in social partnership, xxxvi, 138, 144; structure of, 145–46; subsidies for, xxx, 132, 144–45

AIDS. See acquired immune deficiency syndrome

air force, 223, 242–44; aircraft of, 230; insignia, 244; matériel, 241; mission of, 242; number of personnel, 234; organization of, 244; ranks, 245; training, 244; uniforms, 244

Alemanni. See Swabians

Alexander I, 20

Allied Council, 51

Allied occupation, 48–56, 228; distribution of power in, 50–51; economy under, 122–26; end of, 4, 56; legacy of, 4; national identity under, 79; nationalization under, xxvi, 52, 124–25; zones in, 50–51

Allies: economic support by, 54, 121, 122; position of, on Austria, 48

ALÖ. See Alternative List of Austria

Alps, 70–73; agriculture in, 73; climate in, 75; tourism in, 156; transit through, 75

AL Technologies, 142

Alternative Liste Österreichs. See Alternative List of Austria

Alternative List of Austria (Alternative Liste Österreichs—ALÖ): in elections of 1983, 63, 201; in elections of 1986, 201; platform of, 200

Amnesty Act (1948), 53

Anabaptists, 9–10

Andrássy, Gyula, 29

Anschluss (see also Nazi occupation), xxiv, 3, 44–47, 228; constitution suspended under, 169; debate over, 94, 206; desire for, 22, 24, 29, 36, 38, 39, 121; economy under, 121; end of, 50; impact of, on national identity, 79; international reactions to, 44; support for, 37, 45

anti-Semitism, xxiv, 32, 37, 93, 251; debate over, 94; under Nazi occupation, 46

Arab-Israeli conflict, 216

Arbeiterzeitung, 211

Arbeitsbeirat. *See* Labor Advisory Council

Arbeitskammertag. *See* Chamber of Labor Conference

Argentina: immigrants from, 84

aristocracy, 95; political power of, 32

armed forces (*see also* air force; army): commander in chief, 233–34; conscientious objectors, 239; conscription in, 226, 230, 234; exemptions from service in, 239; in Habsburg Empire, 224–26; matériel of, 223; missions of, 230; mobilization of, 226; morale of, 228; and neutrality, 232–33; number of personnel in, 223, 226, 234, 240; organization of, 223; reserves, 226, 231; restructuring of, 223; women in, 240

army (*see also* air force), 223, 235–37; active units of, 235; conscripts in, 237–40; demobilization of, 237; deployment of, 237; insignia, 244; matériel, 241–42; mission of, 234; number of personnel in, 228, 234, 237; organization of, 229, 235; ranks, 245; reconstituted, 228; term of service in, 239; training of, 235; uniforms, 244

attorneys, 183

Augustinians, 13

Ausgleich (Compromise) of 1867, 26, 226; implemented, 27

Austria: in Dual Monarchy, 27; establishment of, after World War I, 35, 38–39; etymology of, 6, 7; in Quadruple Alliance, 20
Austria, Duchy of, 6–7
Austria, Margravate of, 6
Austria-Hungary (*see also* Dual Monarchy), xxi–xxiii, 26–35, 226; Balkans partitioned by, 29; Bosnia and Hercegovina acquired by, 29–30, 33; in Dual Alliance, 30; foreign relations of, 27–28; government of, 27; matériel produced by, 248; migration within, 86; in Triple Alliance, 30, 34; war declared on Serbia by, 34; in World War I, 34
Austrian Airlines, 156; privatized, 128, 132, 156
Austrian Airtransport, 156
Austrian Federal Railroad (Österreichische Bundesbahnen—ÖBB), 142, 152
Austrian Industries (*see also* nationalization): branches of, 142, 147; number of employees in, 142; restructured, 127, 128
Austrian People's Party (Österreichische Volkspartei—ÖVP) (*see also* Christian Social Party), xxviii–xxxii, 4, 50, 194–97, 217; auxiliary organizations of, 195–96; economy under, 127; in election of 1945, 51; in election of 1949, 54; in election of 1971, 61; in election of 1983, 63; in election of 1986, 190, 206; in election of 1990, 190, 207, 208; in election of 1991, 209; in election of 1992, 209; in election of 1994, xxxi–xxxii; in grand coalition, xxviii, 56–60, 167, 190, 195; in single-party government, 56–60; modifications in, 52–53; national conferences of, 195; newspaper of, 211; organization of, 195; platform of, 195; popularity of, 58; special interests of, 189
Austrian Radio and Television (Österreichischer Rundfunk—ORF), 156, 212
Austrian Spanish Cooperative Development, 248
Austrian Trade Union Federation (Österreichischer Gewerkschaftsbund—ÖGB), 136; membership in, 136; political role of, 175; in social partnership, 125, 134, 138, 139
Austria Tabakwerke, 142

Austro-Hungarian Empire. *See* Austria-Hungary
Austro-Piedmontese War (1859), 225
Avars, 5

Babenberg family, 6
Badeni, Kasimir, 31
balance of payments, 159–60
balance of trade, 160
Balkan League, 33
Balkan Peninsula: foreigners from, 94; partition of, 29; rivalries in, 29
Balkan War, First (1912), 33
Balkan War, Second (1913), 33
Bank Austria, 143, 158
banking, 158–59; regulation of, 136; savings, 159
banks, 158; agricultural credit cooperatives, 158; mortgage, 158; people's, 158; savings, 158
Baroque era, 13–15
Basic Law (1867), 170
Battle of Austerlitz (1805), 225
Battle of Custozza (1866), 225
Battle of Königgrätz (1866), 26, 225
Battle of Lechfeld (955), 6
Battle of Lissa (1866), 225
Battle of Magenta (1859), 225
Battle of Mohács (1526), 9
Battle of Solferino (1859), 225
Battle of Wagram (1809), 225
Battle of White Mountain (1620), 12
Bauer, Otto, 38, 40
Bavarians, 3, 5
Benedictines, 13
Berlin blockade (1948), 55
Beust, Friedrich Ferdinand von, 26
Billa grocery stores, 150
birth control, 83; effect of, on population, 81
Blecha, Karl, 207
Bohemia, 9, 12; ethnic tensions in, 31; German speakers in, xxii; immigrants from, 88; Maria Theresa as queen of, 15; religious restrictions in, 12; riots in, 31
Bohemian Granite Massif, 73
Bonaparte, Napoleon: marriage of Marie Louise to, 19; opposition to, 18, 225
borders, 69; set by Congress of Vienna, 19; set by Treaty of St. Germain, 38–39, 86

Bosnia and Hercegovina: annexation of, by Austria-Hungary, 29, 30–31, 33
Bosnians: as refugees, 85
Brandt, Willy, 60
Bregenz, 74
Brenner Pass, 75; pollution in, 76; transit through, 76, 152
Bretton Woods system, 126, 158, 162
Britain: in Crimean War, 25; in European Free Trade Association, 217; matériel from, 249; occupation of Austria by, xxiv–xxv, 48–56; in Quadruple Alliance, 20; reaction of, to Anschluss, 44; relations with, 15, 21; in World War I, xxiii, 34
budget: structure of, 128
budget deficit: efforts to limit, 127; in magic pentagon, 130; in 1970s, 126; as percentage of gross domestic product, 126, 127; servicing, 127
Bulgarian Orthodox Church: official recognition of, 102
Bundesbank (Germany), 129, 130, 162; stability policy of, 140
Bundesheer (Federal Army). *See* army
Bundespolizei. *See* Federal Police
Bundesrat (Federal Council), 171, 179; established, 39; number of seats in, 179; powers of, 179
Bundesversammlung (Federal Assembly), 169, 179–80
Bundeswirtschaftskammer. *See* Federal Economic Chamber
Burgenland, 69; emigration from, 80; ethnic composition of, 87–88, 90; seats in Bundesrat for, 179
Busek, Erhard, 197

cabinet, 171–72, 174–75; appointments to, 174–75; dismissal of, 175; members of, 174–75; powers of, 174
Calvinists, 102, 103
Cambodia: United Nations observer missions in, 233
Canada, 252
CAP. *See* Common Agricultural Policy
Carinthia, 69; ethnic composition of, 62, 87, 88; ethnic tensions in, 88; Haider as governor of, 198–99; political affiliation in, 200; seats in Bundesrat for,

179; tourism in, 156; Yugoslavia's desire for, 88
Carinthia, Duchy of, 6
Carolingian Empire, 5–6
Carter, Jimmy, 216
Catholic Church, Old: official recognition of, 102
Catholic Church, Roman: concordat of 1855, 25, 32; concordat of 1934, 43, 47; concordat of 1960, 59; government relations with, 25, 42–43, 102; members of, xxvii, 102, 103; under Nazi occupation, 47, 102; official recognition of, 102; political power of, xxvii, 32, 36, 102, 103, 189, 191, 194; reestablishment of, 13; schools run by, 104
Catholic League: formed, 12
Catholics, Roman: conflicts of, with Protestants, 11–12
Celtic era, 4–5
central bank. *See* Nationalbank
Central Flying School, 244
Central Office for Jewish Emigration (Zentralamt jüdischer Auswanderung—ZjA), 46
Chamber of Labor Conference (Arbeitskammertag), 135
chambers of agriculture, 134–35, 143, 189, 196; functions of, 134, 135, 137; membership in, 133–34; organization of, 134; in social partnership, 120, 125, 138
chambers of commerce, 134, 189, 196; established, 134; functions of, 134, 137; membership in, 133–34; organization of, 134; reform of, 208; in social partnership, 120, 125, 138
chambers of labor, 135, 189, 196; established, 135; functions of, 134, 135, 137; membership in, 133–34; organization of, 134; reform of, 208; in social partnership, 120, 125, 138
chancellor, 171–72, 174–75; powers of, 174, 234; role of, 174
Charlemagne, 5
Charles II, 14
Charles V: territories of, 8–9
Charles VI, 14
Charles Albert, 15
Chile: immigrants from, 84
Christian Corporatist State, 102
Christianity (*see also under individual denominations*): conversion to, 6; evangelization in, 5–6

Christian Social Party (Christlichsoziale Partei—CSP) (*see also* Austrian People's Party), xxiii–xxiv, xxviii, 32, 35, 36–37, 42, 102, 194; in elections of 1920, 40; in elections of 1930, 41; militias of, 227; platform of, 36–37, 39
Christlichsoziale Partei. *See* Christian Social Party
Church of Jesus Christ of Latter-Day Saints. *See* Mormon Church
church taxes, 104
Circle of Free Business Persons (Ring Freiheitlicher Wirtschaftstreibender—RFW), 189
Cis-Leithania (*see also* Austria), 27
Cistercians, 13
City Guard of Vienna, 253
civil code of 1811, 21
civil service, 183–84; military personnel in, 239; popular view of, 183; *Proporz* system in, xxviii–xxix, 183; reform of, 184; training academy for, 184
climate: Atlantic maritime, 75, 76–77; characteristics of, 75–76; continental, 75; Mediterranean, 75, 76, 77; and pollution, 76–77
coal: consumption of, 150; imports of, 149; sources of, 39
Columban, Saint, 5
Comecon. *See* Council for Mutual Economic Assistance
Common Agricultural Policy (CAP), 145, 161
Common Market. *See* European Community
communications. *See* telecommunications
Communist Party of Austria (Kommunistische Partei Österreichs—KPÖ), 38, 50; in election of 1945, 51; in election of 1949, 54; outlawed, 42; popularity of, 59
Comprehensive National Defense strategy, 230
Compromise of 1867. *See* Ausgleich of 1867
concentration camps: deaths in, 80, 90, 91; prisoners in, xxv, 52, 90
Conference of Presidents of the Chambers of Agriculture, 134
Conference on Security and Co-operation in Europe (CSCE), 157, 216
Congo: United Nations peacekeeping forces in, 232

Congress for the Future, 193
Congress of Vienna (1814-15), 19–21
Congress System, 20
constituent assembly, 22, 23
Constitutional Court, 178, 180–81, 186; members of, 180–81; president of, 180
constitutional framework, 168–71
constitution of 1849, 24
constitution of 1867 ("December Constitution"), 27; religious freedom under, 102
constitution of 1918, 35
constitution of 1920: amendments to, xxv, 168–69, 170–71; freedom of expression under, 210; individual rights under, 170; neutrality under, 213; suspended, 169, 172
constitution of 1934, 42–43
corporatist system, 189
Council for Mutual Economic Assistance (Comecon): trade with, 162
Council of the Austrian Chambers of Labor, 139
Council of Trent (1545-63), 10
Counter-Reformation, 3, 11–13, 101; origins of, 10; policies, 13
coup d'état, attempted: of 1934, xxiv, 43
Court of Arbitration, 182
courts: administrative, 180, 181; of arbitration, 182; constitutional, 178, 180–81; criminal, 253; district, 182; labor, 182; patent, 182; *Proporz* system in, 181; regional, 181–82; superior, 181; supreme, 181
Crankshaw, Edward, 226
Creditanstalt: collapse of, 41
Creditanstalt-Bankverein, 143, 158; privatized, 132
credit institutions: nationalized, 124–25
crime: categories of, 253; investigative detention for, 253; military, 245; rate, 249–50, 257; trials for, 253
Crimean War (1853-56), 25
crimes, war, 4, 53
Criminal Investigative Service, 224, 254
Croatia, 223; economic relations with, 162–63; recognition of, 219
Croats, xxii, 56; as ethnic minority, 87, 88, 89; immigration by, 5; under Nazi occupation, 46; rights for, 62, 171
CSCE. *See* Conference on Security and Co-operation in Europe
CSP. *See* Christian Social Party

currency (*see also* schilling): common European, 120; policies, 120
current account: balance, 119; in magic pentagon, 130; in 1970s, 126
customs union, 160
Cyprus: United Nations peacekeeping forces in, 213, 224, 232
Czech language, 31
Czechoslovakia: creation of, 35; German-speaking minorities in, 86; population of, 39; refugees from, 81; in revolution of 1989, 218; Warsaw Pact invasion of, 58, 83, 230
Czech Republic, 223; border with, 69; joint venture agreements with, 162
Czechs: in Austria-Hungary, xxii, 27, 86, 88; as ethnic minority, 87, 89; government of, in exile, 35; as guest workers, 92; immigration by, 5, 83, 88; under Nazi occupation, 46; parliament boycotted by, 30; political participation by, 23, 31; as refugees, 83

Dachau: politicians imprisoned at, 52
Dairy Board, 144
Danube Confederation, 78–79
Danube River, 70; transportation on, 155
Danube River Basin, 73; climate in, 75; as defense zone, 231
Das Liberale Forum. *See* Liberal Forum, The
deaths: causes of, 111; in concentration camps, 80; in World War I, 80; in World War II, 80
debt servicing, 120, 127
December Constitution. *See* constitution of 1867
defense, national, 233–49
defense industry, domestic, 241, 248; exports, 248–49
defense spending: budget, 247–48; in Habsburg Empire, 225; as percentage of gross national product, 247; reluctance regarding, 247
de Gaulle, Charles, 57
demography, 80–86
denazification, 53
Denmark: in European Free Trade Association, 217; military intervention by, 12

Deutsche Arbeiterpartei. *See* German Workers' Party
deutsche mark (*see also* currency; schilling): schilling tied to, 120, 130, 158, 162
divorce, 98; causes of, 99; rate, xxvii, 98–99, 103
Dollfuss, Engelbert, xxiv, 41, 227; killed, 43
Dollfuss government, xxiv, 41–43; fascist support for, 41; political parties under, 42, 191; state of emergency under, 42, 169
Drau River, 70
Drau River Valley: transit through, 75
Dual Alliance, 30
Dual Monarchy (*see also* Austria-Hungary): founded, 26–27; nationalities in, 27; negotiations for, 25; organization of, 26–27

East Germany. *See* Germany
EC. *See* European Community
economic collapse of 1873, 31
Economic Commission: established, 125
economic infrastructure: under Nazi occupation, 46
economic reform, 127–30
economic stabilization plan, 40, 121, 125
economy: adapting to European Community standards, 161; Allied support for, 54–55, 121, 125–26; and decline in agriculture, xxvi, 143; interwar, xxv, 39; under Metternich, 22; modernization of, xxvi, 46; under Nazi occupation, 45–46; structure of, xxvi, 140–43
Edict of Tolerance (1781), 16
education (*see also* schools), 104–9; access to, xxvii, 68, 95; foreign children in, 106–7; government responsibility for, 192; higher, xxvii, 107–9; policy, 109; reform of, 106, 107; rigidity of, 105–6; technical, 106; two-track, 105; vocational, xxvii, 101, 106; of women, 101; of working class, 107
EEA. *See* European Economic Area
EEC. *See* European Economic Community
EFTA. *See* European Free Trade Association

Egypt: United Nations peacekeeping forces in, 213

elections: of 1919, 38; of 1920, 40; of 1930, 41; of 1938 (Nazi plebiscite), 44–45; of 1945, 51–52; of 1949, 54; of 1970, 61, 192, 198; of 1971, 61, 192; of 1975, 61, 192; of 1979, 61, 192; of 1983, 63, 198, 200, 201; of 1986, 190, 201, 205–7; of 1990, 200, 207–8; of 1991, 208–9; of 1992, 209; of 1993, 210; of 1994, xxxi–xxxii

electoral system, 186–88; districts in, 186; reform of, 61, 186, 208; vote-counting procedures in, 186–88

electric power: consumption of, 150; distribution of, 150; generation of, 119, 150; hydroelectric power, 119, 149, 150

emigration, 46, 68, 80–81, 86, 91; from Eastern Europe, 83–84; from East Germany, 84

Emmerich Assmann, 248

employment: benefits, 61, 110; distribution of, 124; in magic pentagon, 130; policies, 192; in retail trade, 150; of women, 83

Employment of Foreigners Law (1991), 92

EMS. *See* European Monetary System

EMU. *See* European Monetary Union

energy: consumption of, 149–50; policies, 149

energy installations: nationalized, 124–25

energy sector, 149–50; imports by, 149; regulation of, 136

Enlightenment: influence of, 16

Enns River, 70

environmental damage: as controversial issue, xxx, 61, 76–78, 167, 200–201, 217, 218; and decline in agriculture, 143, 144; to forests, 77; from northwestern Europe, 76–77, 217, 218; from road traffic, 76, 155; from tourism, 77–78

equal rights law of 1976, 100

Equal Treatment Law (1979), xxviii, 100

ethnic groups (*see also under ethnic minorities and individual groups*): in Austria-Hungary, xxii, 27, 86

Ethnic Groups Law (1976), 89

ethnic minorities, 86–94; attitudes toward, 93–94; criteria of identification, 88–89; in Czechoslovakia, 86; in Italy, 86–87; population of, 87, 89; rights

for, 61, 62

Eugene of Savoy (prince), 14, 224

Europe: balance of power in, 21, 25, 27–28, 29; borders of, redrawn, 19; common currency for, 120; liberal uprisings of 1830s in, 21; system of alliances in, 34

Europe, Eastern: energy imports from, 149; immigrants from, 83–84, 94; joint ventures in, 120, 129, 162; refugees from, xxxii, 68, 81, 85, 94, 250; trade with, 162

Europe, Western: exports to, 119

European Community (EC) (*see also* European Union): attempts to join, xxx, 119, 160, 161, 168, 216–18; trade with, 217

European Economic Area (EEA), 163; formed, 119, 161; membership in, xxvi, xxx, 127, 143, 210; negotiations on, 155

European Economic Community (EEC): formed, 57; trade with, 63

European Free Trade Association (EFTA), xxvi, 57, 160–61; formed, 57; members of, 119, 160, 210, 217; trade with, 161

European Monetary System (EMS), 156; membership in, 162

European Monetary Union (EMU), 156, 161–62; convergence requirements for, 161–62; membership in, 161

European Recovery Program. *See* Marshall Plan

European Telecommunications Satellite Organisation (Eutelsat), 156

European Transfer Express Freight Train System, 155

European Union (EU) (*see also* European Community), 73; membership in, xxvi, xxx–xxxi, xxxiii, 168, 196, 210, 218, 233; trade in, 121

Eutelsat. *See* European Telecommunications Satellite Organisation

Evangelical Union: attempts to join, 119; formed, 12

Exchange for Agricultural Products, 182

exchange rate, 158

exports (*see also under individual products*), 127, 159, 160; decline in, 129; of electricity, 150; to Germany, 119, 129; of machinery and equipment, 160; of military matériel, 248–49; subsidies for, 144; to Western Europe, 119

families, 96–101; benefits, 113–14; changes in, 68; division of labor in, 100; illegitimacy in, 99; single-parent, 98; single-person, 98; size of, 96
farms: labor devoted to, 145–46; number of, 145; size of, 145
Fasslabend, Werner, 232
Fatherland Front (Vaterländische Front), 42
Federal Army. *See* army
Federal Assembly. *See* Bundesversammlung
Federal Chamber of Trade and Commerce, 134, 137, 139
Federal Chancellery, 174, 176
Federal Council. *See* Bundesrat
Federal Economic Chamber (Bundeswirtschaftskammer). *See* Federal Chamber of Trade and Commerce
Federal Law on the Press and Other Journalistic Media (1982), 211–12
Federal Police (Bundespolizei), 224, 254–55; deployment of, 254; duties of, 254; matériel of, 255; number of personnel in, 255; organization of, 254–55; women in, 255
Federal Republic of Germany. *See* Germany
Federation of Austrian Industrialists (Vereinigung Österreichischer Industrieller—VÖI), 134, 137–38; functions of, 137–38; membership of, 137
Ferdinand I: career of, 9; death of, 11; peace agreement of, with Turks, 11; religion under, 10
Ferdinand I of Austria, 21; abdication of, 23
Ferdinand II, 12
Ferdinand III, 13
Figl, Leopold, 56; as chancellor, 51, 54
Finance Equalization Law, 185
financial markets, 159
Financial Times "European 500," 143
First Republic (1918–38), 35–44; founded, 38; political factions in, xxv, 35–38
Fligerdivision. *See* air force
food: prices, 145, 191; production, 119; sources of, 39
foreigners: political campaign against, xxix–xx, xxi, 199, 209–10
foreign exchange: controls on, 128
foreign investment, 163

foreign loans, 40
foreign policy: under Franz Joseph, 26; under Kreisky, 62–63, 213–16; in 1950s, 56–58; in 1960s, 57–58; in 1980s and 1990s, xxx–xxxi, xxxii–xxxiii, 216–20
foreign relations, 213–20
foreign workers. *See* guest workers
forestry: employment in, 68, 145; subsidies for, 144–45; workers in, 136
forests, 73; environmental damage to, 77; land area of, 145
Four Power Control Agreement (1946), 51–52; veto powers under, 51–52
Fourteen Points (Wilson), 35
FPÖ. *See* Freedom Party of Austria
Fraktion Sozialistischer Gewerkschaftler. *See* Group of Socialist Trade Unionists
France: in Crimean War, 25; matériel from, 233, 241, 242, 244, 249; military intervention by, 12; occupation of Austria by, xxiv–xxv, 48–56; reaction of, to Anschluss, 44; relations with, 15, 27–28; retaliation by, 41; Second Republic of, 22; in World War I, xxiii, 34
Franche-Comté: in Habsburg Empire, 8
Franco-Prussian War (1870–71), 28
Franks, 5
Franz (husband of Maria Theresa), 15
Franz I (of Austria), 18; domestic policies of, 21–22
Franz II (of Holy Roman Empire), 18
Franz Ferdinand (archduke): assassination of, xxiii, 33–34, 227
Franz Joseph I: armed forces under, 225, 254; crowned, 24; death of, 34; foreign policy of, xxi, 26
Frederick III, 8; as Holy Roman Emperor, 8
Frederick V, 12
Frederick the Great, 224
Free Business Association of Austria (Freier Wirtschaftsverband Österreichs—FWB), 188
Freedom Party of Austria (Freiheitliche Partei Österreichs—FPÖ) (*see also* League of Independents), xxix–xxxii, 58–59, 197–200; auxiliary organizations, 200; in election of 1970, 198; in election of 1971, 61; in election of 1983, 63, 198, 200; in election of 1986, 190, 206; in election of 1990, 190, 200, 207,

208; in election of 1991, 208–9; in election of 1992, 209; in election of 1994, xxxi–xxxii; founded, 197; members of, 59, 197, 200; platform of, 197–98; popularity of, 167, 190; structure of, 200

Freier Wirtschaftsverband Österreichs. *See* Free Business Association of Austria

Freiheitliche Partei Österreichs. *See* Freedom Party of Austria

French Revolution, 18–19

Frischenschläger, Friedhelm, 193, 202

FSG. *See* Group of Socialist Trade Unionists

FWB. *See* Free Business Association of Austria

Gail River, 70

GAL. *See* Green Alternative/Greens in Parliament

Gall, Saint, 5

gas, natural: consumption of, 149; import of, 149; reserves, 150

Gastarbeiter. See guest workers

GDP. *See* gross domestic product

Gendarmerie, 224, 251, 254, 255; in Allied occupation, 228; created, 254; functions of, 254, 255–56; matériel of, 256; misconduct among, 256; number of personnel in, 255; organization of, 255; training of, 255; women in, 255

General Directorate for Public Security, 254

General Law for University Education (1966), 104

General Social Insurance Act of 1955, 109

geography, 69–78

geostrategic situation, 228–29

German Austrians: desire of, for union with Germany, 29, 36, 78–80, 188; in independent Austria, 35; politics of, xxii, xxiii–xxiv, 31, 36, 188

German Confederation, 19; dissolved, 26; restored, 24; revolutions of 1848 in, 22

German Democratic Republic. *See* Germany

German Front, 33; platform of, 33

Germanic tribes, 3, 4–5

German People's Party (Grossdeutsche Volkspartei—Nationals), 36, 40; desire of, for unification, 39; in elections of 1919, 38

German Workers' Party (Deutsche Arbeiterpartei), 36

Germany: border with, 69; division of, 55; in Dual Alliance, 30; economic relations with, 41, 120, 126, 129, 217; emigration from, 84; emigration to, 86; exports to, 119, 129, 217; influence in, 25–26, 27–28; relations with, 25, 29; trade with, 160; in Triple Alliance, xxi, 30, 34; in World War I, 34; in World War II, xxiv, 47–48

Gewerbeordnung. *See* Regulation of the Professions

glasnost, 217

GNP. *See* gross national product

Gorbach, Alphons, 58

Gorbachev, Mikhail, 217

government: administrative organization of, 69; branches of, 169; liberals in, 30–31; Nazi Party in, 38; *Proporz* system in, 54, 167, 175; reduction of, 128; relations of, with Catholic Church, 25, 42–43, 102; reorganization of, in 1848, 23–24; responsibilities of, 170; role of, in agriculture, 143–44

government, local, 185–86; federal controls on, 186; powers of, 185; purview of, 185–86; role of, 185

government, provincial, 169–70, 184–85; constitution of, 184; dissolution of, 184; elections for, 184; executive of, 184; legislation of, 184–85; members of, 184; purview of, 185

government, provisional, 48–50; recognition of, 50–51

government spending: as percentage of gross domestic product, 127, 128

Grain Board, 144

grand coalition, xxviii, 56–60, 167, 189, 190, 205–7, 208; scandals in, 206–7; social partnership under, 59–60, 189

Gratz, Leopold, 207

Graz: immigrants to, 88; riots in, 31

Greek Orthodox Church: official recognition of, 102

Green Alternative—Freda Meissner-Blau List, 201

Green Alternative/Greens in Parliament (Grüne Alternative/Grüne in Parlament—GAL), 201; in election of 1990, 208

Green parties, xxx, 77, 167, 200-201; in election of 1983, 201; in election of 1986, 190; in election of 1992, 209; in election of 1994, xxx, xxxi; future of, 201; origins of, 200; platforms of, 200, 217

Greens, The (Die Grünen), xxx-xxxi

Grossdeutsche Volkspartei. *See* German People's Party

gross domestic product (GDP): under Allied occupation, 125; growth, xxvi, 129; in magic pentagon, 130

gross domestic product fractions: agriculture, xxvi, 141, 143; budget deficit, 126, 127, 128; government services, 127, 128; industry, xxvi, 141, 146; mining, 149; retail trade, 150; services sector, xxvi, 141; subsidies, 128-29, 130; trade, xxvi, 159

Grossglockner Mountain, 70

Group of Socialist Trade Unionists (Fraktion Sozialistischer Gewerkschaftler—FSG), 188, 194

Grüne Alternative/Grüne in Parlament. *See* Green Alternative/Greens in Parliament

Grünen, Die. *See* Greens, The

guest workers, xxvii, 75, 87, 89, 91-93, 95, 119, 132-33; assimilation of, 93; entitlements for, 106-7; naturalization of, 92; number of, 83, 85, 133; popular opinion toward, 93; as percentage of work force, xxvii, 133; population growth caused by, 81, 92; religious affiliations of, 103; unemployment among, 129

Gypsies, 90-91; as ethnic minority, 87, 90; geographic distribution of, 90; under Nazi occupation, 90; popular opinion toward, 90, 91, 94; population of, 90; social organization of, 90

Habsburg, Rudolf von, 7

Habsburg Dynasty, xxi; branches of, 9; inheritable succession in, 8; privileges of, 8; rebellions against, 11-12; support for, 12-13, 36-37

Habsburg Empire, xxi-xxiii, 7-11; armed forces in, 224-26; borders of, redrawn, 19; collapse of, 3, 35; division of, 11; ethnic groups in, 18; extent of, 3; Hungary under, 14; organization of, 8; religious tolerance in, 101-2; territories of, 8-9

Haider, Jörg, xxix-xxx, xxxi-xxxii, 167, 190, 198-99, 205-6, 207; background of, 198; as governor of Carinthia, 198-99; ideology of, 198, 199; xenophobia of, 199, 210

Hainburg power plant, 193, 202

health, 111-12; habits, 111

health benefits, 68

health care, 112; regulation of, 192

health care professionals, 112

health insurance, 112

Heer, Friedrich, 78

Heeresgliederung Neu. *See* New Army Structure

Heimatbloc (Homeland Bloc), 41

Heimatschutz (Homeland Defense), 40-41

Heimwehr (Home Guard), 40-41; under Dollfuss, 41, 42

Hercegovina. *See* Bosnia and Hercegovina

Hereditary Lands, 8-9, 12; created, 8

High Tauern Range, 75

Hirtenberger Patronenfabrik, 248

Hitler, Adolf, xxiv, 36; meeting of, with Schuschnigg, 43-44; plebiscite of 1938 under, 44-45

Holstein: control of, 26

Holy Alliance, 20

Holy Roman Empire, 6-8; dissolved, 19; emperors in, 7-8, 11, 12, 15; organization of, 8; origins of, 6

Home Guard. *See* Heimwehr

Homeland Bloc. *See* Heimatbloc

Homeland Defense. *See* Heimatschutz

hotels, 157

housing, 114-15; amount of, 114; expenditures for, 115; ownership of, 114-15; standards, 114; vacation, 115

Hungarian Plain, 73

Hungarian Revolution (1956), 83

Hungarians: as ethnic minority, xxii, 87, 88, 89; government of, in exile, 35; as guest workers, 92

Hungary, 12; border with, 69; captured by Habsburg Empire, 14; division of, 9; independence declared by, 24; joint venture agreements with, 162; under Maria Theresa, 17; negotiations with, 25; Protestant rebellion in, 11; reconciliation with, 26; resistance of, to

Austrian government, 25; in revolution of 1989, 218; Soviet invasion of, 58, 229-30

immigration, xxvii, xxxi, 68, 80-81, 83-86; illegal, 85, 94, 209-10, 250; rate of, 83; waves of, xxix, 83
imports, 159, 160; of energy, 149; of machinery and equipment, 160; restrictions on, 144
industrialization, 31-32, 124
industry, 146-50; under Allied occupation, 125; competitiveness of, 147; decline in, 140; employment, 141-42; geographic distribution of, 146; growth of, 68; kinds of firms in, 146-47; nationalization of, 124; under Nazi occupation, 45; as percentage of gross domestic product, 141, 146; production costs in, 132; *Proporz* system in, 203; size of firms in, 142-43, 146; in social partnership, 138; subsidies for, 132
inflation: under Allied occupation, 125; interwar, 121; in magic pentagon, 130; in 1970s, 126; policies, 130
inland waterways, 70, 155
Innovation and Technology Fund, 132
Inn River, 70
Inn River Valley, 75; as defense zone, 231
Innsbruck, 74
insurance services: regulation of, 136
Intelsat. *See* International Telecommunications Satellite Organization
internal security, 249-58
International Atomic Energy Agency, 157, 213, 250
International Criminal Police Organization (Interpol), 257
International Telecommunications Satellite Opanization (Intelsat), 156
Interpol. *See* International Criminal Police Organization
investment, 127
Iran: boycott of, 216; immigrants from, 84; matériel sold to, 248
Iranian Kurdish Democratic Party, 250
Iraq: United Nations observer missions on Iraq-Kuwait border, 233
Iron Ring government, 31
Islam: official recognition of, 102

Israel, 216; immigration to, 84; United Nations peacekeeping forces in, 213
Italianization campaign, 87
Italy, xxi, xxii, 26; border with, 69, 86; emigration to, 86; German-speaking minorities in, 86; reaction of, to Anschluss, 44; relations with, 25, 219; South Tirol ceded to, 39, 86-87; support of, for Dollfuss, 41; trade with, 160; in Triple Alliance, 30, 34; in World War I, 227

Jagiellon family, 9
Jesuits, 13
Jews, 18, 84, 91; in Austria-Hungary, 86; emigration of, 46, 80, 91; as ethnic minority, 87, 89; extermination of, 46, 80, 91; immigration of, 80; political participation of, 30, 32; population of, 46, 91, 93, 103; restrictions on, 16, 91
JG. *See* Young Generation
Jonas, Franz, 58, 61
Joseph II: death of, 18; penal code under, 252; reforms under, 16-18, 91
journalists, 212
Judaism: official recognition of, 102
judges, 180, 182, 253; appointment of, 253; selection of, 181, 182
judicial system, 180-83
Junge Generation. *See* Young Generation
Jungk, Robert, 209

Karl (emperor), 34; abdication of, 35
Kirchschläger, Rudolf, 61
Klagenfurt, 74
Klagenfurt Manifesto (1965), 195
Klaus, Josef, 58, 59
Klestil, Thomas, 209
KÖ. *See* Konsum Österreich
Kommunistische Partei Österreichs. *See* Communist Party of Austria
Konsum Österreich (KÖ), 142, 152
Körner, Theodor, 58
KPÖ. *See* Communist Party of Austria
Kreisky, Bruno, xxviii, 56; background of, 60; as chancellor, 202, 216; as party chairman, 191-92, 206; use of television by, 174
Kreisky government, 60-63; civil service

under, 184; domestic policy under, 61–62; foreign policy under, 62–63, 213–16

Küssel, Gottfried, 252

Kuwait: United Nations observer missions on Iraq-Kuwait border, 233

Labor Advisory Council (Arbeitsbeirat), 138

labor unions (*see also* Austrian Trade Union Federation), 188, 217; functions of, 136, 137, 139; membership in, 136; in social partnership, 120, 125, 138, 140

Lager (social camps), xxiii–xxiv, 35, 95–96, 188–90; decline in, xxvii, xxix, 194, 196; strength of, 189

land: arable, 73, 74, 145; area, 69

Landbund. *See* Agrarian League

Landtag. *See* government, provincial

land use, 73

Lauda Air, 156

Law of October 26, 1955, 56, 171, 232

League of Austrian Business (Österreichischer Wirtschaftsbund—ÖWB), 188, 195–96

League of Austrian Farmers (Österreichischer Bauernbund—ÖBB), 188–89, 196

League of Austrian Workers and Salaried Employees (Österreichischer Arbeiter- und Angestelltenbund—ÖAAB), 188, 195

League of Independents (Verband der Unabhängigen—VdU) (*see also* Freedom Party of Austria; Nazi Party), 53–54; in election of 1949, 54; formation of, 53

League of Nations: financial support by, 121

legal system. *See* courts

legislation: preparation of, 176, 178

Leitha Range, 73

Leitha River, 27

Leopold I, 14

Leopold II, 18

Liberal Forum, The (Das Liberale Forum), xxxi, 167; formed, xxix, 199, 210

Liberal International, 197, 199, 210

liberalism: conflict of, with nationalism, 22–23

liberals: in government, 30–31

Liechtenstein: border with, 69

Linz: immigrants to, 88

livestock, 73

Livestock and Meat Commission, 144

living standards, 68, 120; improvements in, 95

Louis (king), 9

Louis XIV, 14

Louis XVI: marriage of, 15

Lower Austria, 69; seats in Bundesrat for, 179

Low Tauern Range, 75

Lutherans, 9, 102; number of, 102–3

Maastricht Treaty, 120

magic pentagon, 130

Magyars, 6

Maria Theresa: accession of, 15; Hungary under, 17; penal code under, 252; as queen of Bohemia, 15; reforms under, 16–18

Maria Theresa Military Academy, 239, 240

Marie Antoinette: marriage of, to Louis XVI, 15

Marie Louise: marriage of, to Napoleon, 19

Marlborough, Duke of, 224

marriage: age for, 98; frequency of, 96, 98; prerequisites for, 96

Marshall Plan (European Recovery Program), 54–55; aid under, 122; end of, 57; industry under, 125

matériel: acquisition of, 230, 233; air force, 230, 241; from Britain, 249; configuration of, 241; domestic, 241, 248–49; exports of, 248–49; from France, 233, 241, 242, 244, 249; from Netherlands, 241; from Soviet Union, 249; from Sweden, 233, 242–44, 249; from United States, 233, 241, 242, 244, 249

maternity benefits, 113

Matthias (king), 11

Maximilian I, 8

Maximilian III, 11

media, 210–13

medieval era, 5–7

Meissner-Blau, Freda, 201

Methodist Church: official recognition of, 102

Metro SB-Grosshandel, 150
Metternich, Clemens von, 19, 21–22; at Congress of Vienna, 19; domestic policies of, 21–22; economy under, 22; international developments under, 21
middle class, 95; political power of, 32
migration, 83, 124; within Austria-Hungary, 86
military: discipline, 245–47; justice, 245–47; policy, 230
military officers: commissioned, 239; in Habsburg Empire, 226; noncommissioned, 239, 240; promotion of, 239–40; surplus of, 240; training of, 239, 240
military strategy: area defense concept, 231, 235; deterrence, 230; in Habsburg Empire, 225; levels of threat in, 230–31; in World War I, 227
militias, 227
minerals, 147–49; production of, 149
mining, 147–49; employment in, 149; as percentage of gross domestic product, 149
ministries: distribution of, 175; number of, 175
Ministry for Education, 104
Ministry for Interior, 224, 254, 257
Ministry for Justice, 175, 206
Ministry for National Defense, 234
Ministry for Science and Research, 104
Ministry for Women's Affairs, 208
minorities. *See* ethnic minorities
Mobil Oil, 150
Mock, Alois, xxx, 196–97, 206, 218, 219
monasteries, 5
Moravia, xxii, immigrants from, 88
Mormon Church (Church of Jesus Christ of Latter-Day Saints): official recognition of, 102
Moscow Declaration (1943), 48
Mur River, 70
Mur River Valley, 75
Mürz River, 70
Mürz River Valley, 75
Muslims (*see also* Islam), 103

Napoleon III, 225
Napoleonic Wars, 225
Nationalbank, 158; monetary policies of, 120, 132; privatized, 128

National Council. *See* Nationalrat
National Defense Academy, 239, 240
National Defense Council, 234; members of, 234
national identity, xxv, 3–4, 78–80; development of, xxv, 67, 68, 79–80; regional subcultures in, 74
nationalism, xxii, 3; conflict of, with liberalism, 22–23
nationalist movement: anti-Semitism in, xxiv, 32; growth of, xxii, 32–33
Nationalists/Liberals (*see also* German People's Party), xxix, 35, 36, 188
nationalization (*see also* Austrian Industries): under Allied occupation, xxvi, 52; of industry, 124
Nationalization Act (1946), 124
Nationalization Act (1947), 124
Nationalrat (National Council), 171–72, 175–79, 201, 210; candidates for, 177; committees in, 176, 178; competition in, 178–79; dissolution of, 177; established, 39; interpellation in, 177; *Klubs* (factions) in, 176–77; legislation in, 176; members of, 177–78; number of seats in, 177; powers of, 175–76; presidents of, 176; sessions in, 177; terms in, 177; women in, xxviii, 177
Nationals. *See* German People's Party
National Socialist Act (1947), 53
National Socialist German Workers' Party (National-Sozialistische Deutsche Arbeiterpartei—NSDAP). *See* Nazi Party
National Socialists. *See* Nazis
National-Sozialistische Deutsche Arbeiterpartei. *See* Nazi Party
NATO. *See* North Atlantic Treaty Organization
Nazi occupation (*see also* Anschluss), xxiv, 3; anti-Semitism under, 46; Austrian Nazis under, 45; Catholic Church under, 47, 102; economy under, 45–46, 121; political parties under, 191; population policies under, 81, 88, 89; repression under, 47; social policies under, 45–46
Nazi Party, 36, 204; influence of, 43–44; origins of, 36; outlawed, 42, 53; popularity of, 41; putsch by, 43
Nazis: as percentage of population, 53; political parties of, 197; registration of, 53

neoabsolutism, 22–26; failure of, 24–25
neo-Nazis, 251–52
Netherlands: in Habsburg Empire, xxi, 9; matériel from, 241
Neue Bahn (New Railroad), 152–54
Neue Kronen-Zeitung, 210
neutrality, xxx, xxxii–xxxiii, 55–56, 160, 168; and armed forces, 232–33; under constitution of 1920, 213; definition of, 57–58, 213; obstacles to, xxx, 55–56; under State Treaty of 1955, 223
New Army Structure (Heeresgliederung Neu), 223, 231–32, 235–37; personnel under, 240; reduction in strength under, 237
New Railroad. *See* Neue Bahn
News, 211
newspapers (*see also* journalists; media), 210–12; circulation of, 210, 211; number of, 211; party, 211; subsidies for, 211
Noricum (Celtic state), 4
Noricum (arms manufacturer), 248
North Atlantic Treaty Organization (NATO), 228–29, 233; founded, 55
Northern Alpine Foreland, 70–73; climate in, 75
North German Confederation, 26
Norway: in European Free Trade Association, 217
NSDAP. *See* National Socialist German Workers' Party
nuclear power: as controversial issue, 61, 77; plans for, 62

ÖAAB. *See* League of Austrian Workers and Salaried Employees
ÖBB. *See* Austrian Federal Railroad
ÖBB. *See* League of Austrian Farmers
OECD. *See* Organisation for Economic Co-operation and Development
OEEC. *See* Organisation for European Economic Co-operation
Office of the People's Attorney, 183
ÖGB. *See* Austrian Trade Union Federation
oil (*see also* petroleum): embargo of 1970s, 62, 120, 126, 133; refining of, 150; reserves of, 150
Olympic Games, 1980 Summer, 216

ÖMV. *See* Österreichische Mineralölverwaltung
OPEC. *See* Organization of the Petroleum Exporting Countries
Operation Desert Shield, 233
Operation Desert Storm, 233
ORF. *See* Austrian Radio and Television
Organisation for Economic Co-operation and Development (OECD), xxvi, 127
Organisation for European Economic Co-operation (OEEC), 54, 57
Organization of the Petroleum Exporting Countries (OPEC), 62, 250
Österreichische Bundesbahnen. *See* Austrian Federal Railroad
Österreichische Länderbank, 158; privatized, 132
Österreichische Mineralölverwaltung (ÖMV), 142, 143; petroleum refining by, 150
Österreichische Post/Telegrafenverwaltung (national postal service), 142; savings in, 159
Österreichischer Arbeiter- und Angestelltenbund. *See* League of Austrian Workers and Salaried Employees
Österreichischer Bauernbund. *See* League of Austrian Farmers
Österreichischer Gewerkschaftsbund. *See* Austrian Trade Union Federation
Österreichischer Rundfunk. *See* Austrian Radio and Television
Österreichischer Wirtschaftsbund. *See* League of Austrian Business
Österreichisches Institut für Wirtschaftsforschung (WIFO), 144
Österreichische Volkspartei. *See* Austrian People's Party
Ostrogoths, 5
Otakar II, 6–7
Ottoman Empire: Hungary in, 9
Otto the Great, 6
ÖVP. *See* Austrian People's Party
ÖWB. *See* League of Austrian Business

Palestine Liberation Organization (PLO): recognition of, 63, 216
Parity Commission for Prices and Wages, 59, 137, 139–40; established, xxvi, 59, 139; functions of, 139; members of, 139; subcommittees of, 139

parliament. *See* Bundesrat; Bundesversammlung; Nationalrat
Patent Court, 182
patronage, political (*see also Proporz* system): xxviii–xxix
Peace of Aix-la-Chapelle (1748), 15
Peace of Westphalia (1648), 12–13
peasants, 94, 95; families of, 96, 98
penal codes, 21, 252–53; capital punishment under, 252; torture under, 252
People's Defense. *See* Volkswehr
periodicals, 211–12; subsidies for, 211
Perot, Ross, xxxii
Perspectives '90, 192–93
Peter, Friedrich, 198
petroleum (*see also* oil): consumption of, 149; imports of, 149, 150; refining of, 150
Phryn Pass, 75
Pitterman, Bruno, 191
PLO. *See* Palestine Liberation Organization
Poland: emigration from, 83–84; independence of, 35; military support from, 14; partitions of, 17; in revolution of 1989, 218
Poles: as guest workers, 92; in Habsburg Empire, xxii, 18; immigration by, 83–84; politics of, 31; popular opinion of, 94; as refugees, 83–84
police. *See* Administrative Police; Criminal Investigative Service; Federal Police; Gendarmerie; State Police
political: affiliation, 103–4; asylum, 83–85, 209–10; system, diversity in, 167–68; unrest, 42
political parties (*see also under individual parties*): cooperation among, xxv, xxviii, 52; identification with, 190; outlawed by Dollfuss, 42
population, 80; age distribution in, 83; of Czechoslovakia, 39; density, 74; distribution of, 73–75, 81–82, 124; in 1843, 22; ethnic distribution in, 87, 89; growth, 80, 81; of guest workers, 83, 85, 92; of Gypsies, 90; of Jews, 46, 80, 91, 103; Nazi policies on, 81, 89; Nazis as percentage of, 53; in 1900, 80; in 1919, 39; in 1991, 80; projected, 81; urban, 22; of Vienna, 22
population fractions: engaged in agriculture, xxvi, 68, 145; engaged in forestry, 68, 145; engaged in mining, 149; of ethnic minorities, 87, 89; working in services sector, xxvi, 60
population statistics: birth rate, xxvii, 80, 81, 85–86, 92, 96–98; death rate, 80; fertility rate, 81, 83, 96; growth rate, 22, 81; infant mortality rate, 81; life expectancy, 82, 111; mortality rate, 80
Porsche Holding, 142
Portugal: in European Free Trade Association, 217
postal service, 142
poverty, 96
Pragmatic Sanction, 15
president, 172–74; candidates for, 172; as commander in chief, 233; election of, 172–73; powers of, 173; pressing charges against, 173–74, 179; role of, 169, 173; succession to, 174; term for, 172
Presidential Conference of the Austrian Chambers of Agriculture, 139
Presidial Conference, 176
press (*see also* journalists; media; newspapers): under constitution of 1920, 210; slander by, 211–12
Presse, Die, 211
prices, 132; controls on, 144, 191; food, 145, 191
prisoners, 258
prison system, 257–58; population of, 258; sentences in, 252
privatization, 128, 132, 147, 192
professional associations, 188
professions, 136; regulation of, 135–36
Profil, 203, 204, 211
Proksch, Udo, 207
Proporz system, 54, 175, 181, 183, 203
prostitution, 252–53
Protestantism (*see also under individual denominations*): official recognition of, 102
Protestant Reformation, 9–10
Protestants: conflicts of, with Catholics, 11–12; number of, 102–3; rebellion by, in Hungary, 11; rights of, 16
provinces, 169–70
Prussia: military relations with, xxi, 224, 225; occupation of Poland by, 17; in Quadruple Alliance, 20; relations with, 21; unification of Germany by, 3, 28
Public Order Watch, 253

Qadhafi, Muammar al, 216, 250
Quadruple Alliance, 20

Raab, Julius, 56; as chancellor, 55, 58
Radetzky, Joseph, 23
radio, 156, 212–13; languages of broadcast, 213; programming, 212–13; stations, 212–13
railroad system, 152–54; construction of, 152–54; network, 152; passengers, 152
Reder, Walter, 193, 202
reform: under Joseph II, 16–18; under Maria Theresa, 16–18; under revolution of 1848, 22
Reformation. *See* Protestant Reformation
refugees, 83; from Eastern Europe, xxxii, 68, 81, 85, 94, 132, 223, 250; illegal, 94; as security threat, 232
Regulation of the Professions (Gewerbeordnung), 135–36
Reinthaller, Anton, 197
religion (*see also under individual denominations*), 101–4; distribution of, in population, 103; of guest workers, 103; and political affiliation, 103–4; restrictions on, 12, 13; suppression of, 16
religious tensions, 11–12
religious tolerance, 16, 101–2
Renner, Karl, 37–38, 191; as chancellor, 38; as president, 51, 58; as head of provisional government, 48–50; plebiscite under, 45
Renner government, 38
Republican Defense League (Republikanischer Schutzbund), 40, 227; personnel strength of, 40; uprising of, 227–28
Republikanischer Schutzbund. *See* Republican Defense League
Rerum Novarum (1891), 32, 138
Resident Alien Law (1993), 92, 199
retirement, 110–11; age for, 110; benefits, 110–11
revolutions of 1848, 22–26, 225
RFW. *See* Circle of Free Business Persons
Rhine-Main-Danube Canal, 70; transportation on, 155
Riegler, Josef, 197
Ring Freiheitlicher Wirtschaftstreibender. *See* Circle of Free Business Persons

rivers, 70; drainage system, 70; transportation on, 155
roads, 155; environmental damage from traffic on, 76, 155; freight transport on, 155
Roma. *See* Gypsies
Roman Catholic Church. *See* Catholic Church, Roman
Roman era, 4–5
Romania: refugees from, 81, 250
Romanian Orthodox Church: official recognition of, 102
Romanians: as guest workers, 92; in Habsburg Empire, xxii, 18; popular opinion of, 94
rural areas: social importance of, 144
Russia (*see also* Soviet Union): colonial expansion by, 30; in Crimean War, 25; interests of, in Balkans, 29, 33; military support from, 14; occupation of Poland by, 17; in Quadruple Alliance, 20; relations with, 21; in World War I, 34
Russian Orthodox Church: official recognition of, 102
Russo-Turkish War (1877–78), 29
Ruthenians: in Habsburg Empire, 18

Sallaberger, Günther, 206–7
SALT. *See* Strategic Arms Limitation Talks
Salzach River, 70
Salzburg, 5–6, 18, 74; political affiliation in, 200; seats in Bundesrat for, 179; tourism in, 156–57
Salzburg Program (1972), 195
Salzburg Province, 69
SAP. *See* structural adjustment program
scandals, 202–7; in grand coalition, 206–7; *Lucona*, 207; Reder, 193, 202; Sallaberger, 206–7; VÖEST-Alpine, 203; Waldheim, 168, 203–5; wine, 202–3
Schärf, Adolf, 56, 58, 191
schilling (*see also* currency), 158; revalued, 126, 162; tied to deutsche mark, 120, 130, 162
Schleswig: control of, 26
Schmidt, Heide, 199, 209, 210
Schönerer, Georg von, 36
School Law (1962), 104, 106

schools: Catholic, 104; elementary, 105; enrollment patterns in, 105, 106; higher, 105-7, 109; middle, 105-7, 109; private, 109; technical, 106; vocational, 106

Schuschnigg, Kurt von: as chancellor, xxiv, 43; meeting of, with Hitler, 43-44

Schuschnigg government, 43-44; constitution suspended under, 169; Nazi influence in, 43-44; political parties under, 191

Schwechat, 150, 156

SDAP. *See* Social Democratic Workers' Party

Second Republic: founded, xxv, 48-50

security threats: levels of, 230-31; political instability as, 232; refugees as, 232; Serbia as, 33; Turkey as, 10-11; Warsaw Pact as, 229

Seipel, Ignaz, 36; as chancellor, 40

self-administration associations, 139-40

Semmering Pass, 75

Serbia: expansion of, 30; Russia's protection of, 33; as security threat, 33; war declared on, by Austria, 34; in World War I, 227

Serbian Orthodox Church, 103; official recognition of, 102

Serbs, xxii; as guest workers, 92; popular opinion toward, 94

services sector, 150-59; employment in, 60, 142; growth of, 68, 140; as percentage of gross domestic product, xxvi, 141

Seven Weeks' War (1866), 26, 225

Seven Years' War (1756-63), 17

Seyss-Inquart, Arthur, 197

Siege of Vienna (1529), 10

Siege of Vienna (1683), 14

Silesia, xxii

Single European Act, 127

Single Market, 143, 163

Sinowatz, Fred: as chancellor, 63, 192, 202

Sinti. *See* Gypsies

SJÖ. *See* Socialist Youth of Austria

skiing: environmental damage from, 77-78; and weather, 76

Skoda company, 248

Slavs: in Austria-Hungary, 27

Slovakia, 223; border with, 69; immigrants from, 88; joint venture agreements with, 162

Slovaks: as ethnic minority, xxii, 87, 89; government of, in exile, 35; as guest workers, 92; immigration by, 5, 83; under Nazi occupation, 46; as refugees, 83

Slovenes, xxii, 56; as ethnic minority, 87, 88, 89; immigration by, 5; under Nazi occupation, 46; rights for, 62, 171

Slovenia, 223; border with, 69; economic relations with, 162-63; recognition of, 219

Sobieski, Jan, 224

social class: importance of, 68, 94-95

Social Democratic Manifesto for the Year 2000, 194

Social Democratic Party of Austria (Sozialdemokratische Partei Österreichs—SPÖ) (*see also* Social Democratic Workers' Party; Socialist Party of Austria), 190-94; auxiliary organizations, 194; candidates for, 194; in election of 1992, 209; in election of 1994, xxxi-xxxii; federal conferences of, 194; membership in, 194; newspaper of, 211; organization of, 194; platform of, 191-92, 193-94; women in, 194

Social Democratic Party of Austria Women's Committee, 194

Social Democratic Workers' Party (Sozialdemokratische Arbeiterpartei—SDAP) (*see also* Socialist Party of Austria), xxii, xxviii, 32, 35, 37-45, 102, 190-91; in elections of 1920, 40; in elections of 1930, 41; founded, 32; militias of, 227; outlawed, 42; platform of, 32; popularity of, 40; role of, in government, 38; support of, for unification with Germany, 39

Social Insurance Act (1955), 109

Socialist Party of Austria (Sozialistische Partei Österreichs—SPÖ) (*see also* Social Democratic Party of Austria; Social Democratic Workers' Party), xxviii-xxix, 4, 50, 188, 217; accommodation of, to church, 102; coalition with Freedom Party of Austria, 202-3; communication within, 192-94; economy under, 127; education reform under, 107; in election of 1945, 51; in election of 1949, 54; in election of 1970, 61, 192; in election of 1971, 192; in election of 1975, 192; in election of 1979, 192; in election of 1986, 190, 206; in election of 1990, xxviii-xxx, 190, 208; in elections of 1991, 209; in grand coalition, xxviii, 56–60, 167, 190; under Kreisky, xxviii, 191–92; modifications in, 52, 192–94; platform of, 192; special interests of, 189

Socialist Youth of Austria (Sozialistische Jugend Österreichs—SJÖ), 194

social partnership, xxi, xxvi, 59, 67, 120, 124, 138–40; agriculture under, 138, 144; incentives for, 124, 140, 167, 189; institutions in, 120, 125, 138; principles of, 138–39

social security, xxvi–xxv, 68, 109–14, 191, 192, 218; organization of, 109–10; origins of, 109

social structure, xxvii, 94–96; and decline in agriculture, xxvi, 143

Society of Jesus. *See* Jesuits

Southeastern Alpine Foreland, 73; climate in, 75

South Tirol, 86–87, 219; autonomy for, 56–57, 87, 219; ceded to Italy, 39, 86–87; terrorism in, 219, 251

Soviet Union (*see also* Russia): confiscation of Austrian assets by, 52, 122, 124; and détente with United States, 168, 213; emigration from, 84; *glasnost* in, 217; invasion of Afghanistan by, 216; invasion of Hungary by, 58, 229–30; matériel from, 249; occupation of Austria by, xxiv–xxv, 48–56; reparation payments to, 122; role of, in occupation, xxv, 54, 56

Sozialdemokratische Arbeiterpartei. *See* Social Democratic Workers' Party

Sozialdemokratische Partei Österreichs. *See* Social Democratic Party of Austria

Sozialistische Jugend Österreichs. *See* Socialist Youth of Austria

Sozialistische Partei Österreichs. *See* Socialist Party of Austria

Spain: in Habsburg Empire, xxi, 9

Spar Österreich grocery stores, 150

Spezialfahrzeuge AG, 248

SPÖ. *See* Social Democratic Party of Austria

SPÖ. *See* Socialist Party of Austria

Staatspolizei. *See* State Police

Standard, Der, 211

Stapo. *See* State Police

Starhemberg, Ernst Rüdiger von (prince), 41, 224

State Police (Staatspolizei—Stapo), 224, 254, 255; illegal intelligence activities of, 256; restructuring of, 256

state secretaries, 175

State Treaty (1955), xxxii, 4, 55–56, 79, 160; borders under, 171; government under, 171; minority rights under, 62, 88, 171; neutrality under, 223, 232; reparation payments under, 122

Steger, Norbert, 198, 202

Stephen (king), 6

Steyr: immigrants to, 88

Steyr-Allradtechnik, 248

Steyr-Daimler-Puch, 241, 248, 249

Steyr-Mannlicher, 248

Stock and Commodity Exchange, 182

Stock Exchange Act (1989), 128

Strategic Arms Limitation Talks (SALT), 63

Streicher, Rudolf, 209

strikes, 140; general, 42, 227

structural adjustment program (SAP): need for, 147

Styria, 69; seats in Bundesrat for, 179; transit through, 75

Styria, Duchy of, 6

subsidies: for agriculture, xxx, 132, 144, 145, 218; attempts to reduce, 128–29, 147; for nationalized industry, 132; for newspapers and periodicals, 211; as percentage of gross domestic product, 128–29, 130; policies governing, 130–32

suffrage. *See* voting

suicide, 112

Supreme Court, 181

Swabians, 3, 5

Sweden: defense spending in, 247; in European Free Trade Association, 217; matériel from, 233, 242–44, 249; military intervention by, 12; military training by, 244; military troop strength of, 240

Switzerland: border with, 69; defense spending in, 247; emigration to, 86; in European Free Trade Association, 217; military troop strength of, 240; trade with, 160

Syria: United Nations peacekeeping missions in, 224, 233

Taaffe, Eduard, 31

Täglich Alles, 210

Tauern Pass, 75
taxes: church, 104; income, 110; reform of, 129; social security, 109-10
telecommunications, 156; regulation of, 136; workers in, 136
telephones, 156
television, 156; cable, 212; channels, 212; languages of broadcast, 213; programming, 212; use of, in politics, 174
terrorism, 219, 250
Third Reich: Austrian Nazis in, 45
Thirty Years' War (1618-48), 11-12; reconstruction following, 13
Tirol, 69; population density of, 74; seats in Bundesrat for, 179; tourism in, 156
Tito, Josip Broz, 88
topography, 70-73; drainage system, 70
tourism, 156-58; environmental damage from, 77-78; government support for, 144; revenues from, 156, 160; and weather, 76
trade, domestic: employment in, 150; as percentage of gross domestic product, 150; regulation of, 136; retail, 150-52
trade, foreign (*see also* balance of trade; exports; imports), 159-60, 161; deficit, 119; as percentage of gross domestic product, 169
transit, 74-75, 83; through Brenner Pass, 76, 152; by emigrants, 84
transportation, 152-56; air service, 152; barge service, 70; bus service, 152; railroads, 152; regulation of, 136; river, 70; workers in, 136
Treaty of St. Germain (1919), 38, 86
Treaty of Utrecht (1713), 14
Trenck Military Sports Group, 251
Trend, 211
Trentino-Alto Adige. *See* South Tirol
Triple Alliance (1882), 30, 34
Triple Entente, 33
Tulln-Langenlebarn Air Base, 242
Turkey: in Crimean War, 25; peace agreement of, with Ferdinand, 11; as security threat, 10-11; siege of Vienna by, 10, 224
Turkish wars, 14
Turks: as guest workers, 92, 103, 133; popular opinion toward, 94
Tyrolean Airways, 156

Überfremdung, xxix
Uganda: immigrants from, 84
unemployment, 41; benefits, 110; of college graduates, 109; insurance, 110; interwar, 121; under Nazi occupation, 45; rate, 125-26, 127, 129, 133
unification of Austria with Germany. *See* Anschluss
Union of Arts, Journalism, and the Professions, 136
Union of Commercial, Clerical, and Technical Employees, 136
United Austrian Iron and Steel Works (Vereinigte Österreichische Eisen- und Stahlwerke—VÖEST-Alpine), 142, 147; financial scandal in, 203, 248; matériel manufactured by, 248; restructuring of, 206
United Greens of Austria (Vereinigte Grüne Österreichs—VGÖ): in election of 1983, 63, 201; in election of 1986, 201; in election of 1990, 208; platform of, 200
United Nations: membership in, xxxii, 213; peacekeeping forces, 219-20 ; peacekeeping missions, 168, 213, 223-24, 232-33, 244; voting in, 216
United Nations City, 157
United Nations Industrial Development Organization, 213
United Nations Universal Declaration of Human Rights (1948), 170
United States, xxiii, xxiv-xxv, 252; aid from, 122, 124; and détente with Soviet Union, 168, 213; immigration to, 80; matériel from, 233, 241, 242, 244, 249; occupation of Austria by, xxiv-xxv, 48-56; in World War I, 34
United States Arms Control and Disarmament Agency, 249
United States Department of Justice, 204
universities, 107-9; attrition rate, 109; enrollment in, 107; overcrowding in, 107
University of Vienna, 104
University Organization Law (1975), 104
Upper Austria, 69; seats in Bundesrat for, 179; transit through, 75
urban areas: population in, 22
urbanization, 31-32
urban migration, 68

Vandals, 5
Vaterländische Front. *See* Fatherland Front
VdU. *See* League of Independents
Venice: military support from, 14
Verband der Unabhängigen. *See* League of Independents
Vereinigte Grüne Österreichs. *See* United Greens of Austria
Vereinigte Österreichische Eisen- und Stalhwerke. *See* United Austrian Iron and Steel Works
Vereinigung Österreichischer Industrieller. *See* Federation of Austrian Industrialists
VGÖ. *See* United Greens of Austria
Vienna: as center for international negotiations, xxxii, 63, 250; ethnic minorities in, 87, 88, 90; growth of, 17; guest workers in, 92; immigrants to, 88; occupied by Napoleon, 225; office space in, 163; politics in, xxiv, 40; population in, 22; port of, 155-56; as province, 69; riots in, 31; seats in Bundesrat for, 179; siege of (1529), 10, 224; siege of (1683), 14, 224; tourism in, 157
Vienna stock exchange, 159
Viennese Basin, 73, 75
Visigoths, 5
VÖEST-Alpine. *See* United Austrian Iron and Steel Works
VÖI. *See* Federation of Austrian Industrialists
Volkswehr (People's Defense): founded, 38; suppressed, 40
Vorarlberg, 69; seats in Bundesrat for, 179; tourism in, 156
voting: age for, 188; participation in, 188; reform, 31; rights, 191
Vranitzky, Franz, xxviii, xxxi, 205, 208; background of, 192; as chancellor, xxxi, 192, 205, 218, 219

wages, 129, 191; collective bargaining for, 110; in social partnership, 125; of women, 101
Waldheim, Kurt, xxxii, 4, 62, 93-94, 209; international disapproval of, 204-5; as president, 192, 203-5; pressure on, to resign, 205; scandal involving, 168, 203-5; wartime service of, 203-4
War of the Austrian Succession (1740-48), 15, 224
War of the Spanish Succession (1701-14), 14, 224
Warsaw Pact: breakup of, 231; invasion of Czechoslovakia by, 58, 83, 230; as security threat, 229
Wehrmacht, xxiv, 47, 228
welfare, xxvi-xxvii, 68, 109-14
West Germany. *See* Germany
Western European Union (WEU), xxxii
Wiener, 211
Wienerberger Baustoffindustrie, 143
WIFO. *See* Österreichisches Institut für Wirtschaftsforschung
Wilson, Woodrow, 35
Windischgrätz, Alfred, 23
wine scandal, 203
Wochenpresse, 211
women, 99-101; in armed forces, 240; education of, 101; employment of, xxviii, 83, 101; equality for, xxviii, 61, 100; income of, xxvii, 101; marriage of, xxvii, 96, 98; maternity benefits for, 113-14; in police force, 255; in politics, xxvii, 177, 194
Women's Omnibus Law (1993), xxviii, 100
workers: benefits for, 61, 110; in services sector, 60
workers, foreign. *See* guest workers
work force, 119; in agriculture, 141; guest workers as percentage of, 133; in industry, 141-42; percentage of, in labor unions, 136; in services sector, 142, 150
working class, 95; families of, 98; university education for, 107
works councils, 137
World Jewish Council, 204
World War I, xxi, xxiii, 33-34, 226-27; Austria's liabilities in, 38; deaths in, 80, 227; purpose of, 226-27; Russia's withdrawal from, 34; strategy in, 227; United States entry into, 34
World War II, xxiv, 47-48, 228; Austria in, 47-48; Austrian Nazis in, 45; deaths in, 80, 90, 228; German defeat in, 47-48

Young Generation (Junge Generation—JG), 194

Yugoslavia: civil war in, xxxii, 232; refugees from, xxxii, 81, 85, 103, 219, 250; territorial claims of, 55, 88

Zentralamt jüdischer Auswanderung. *See* Central Office for Jewish Emigration

Zentralsparkasse, 158

ZjA. *See* Central Office for Jewish Emigration

Zwentendorf nuclear power plant, 62, 77

Contributors

Steven R. Harper is a government affairs analyst for the Earth Observation Satellite Company.

Lonnie Johnson is coeditor of the quarterly *Higher Education Science & Research in Austria* for the Austrian Academic Exchange Service and is the author of *Introducing Austria: A Short History* and a forthcoming book on Central Europe for Oxford University Press.

David E. McClave, formerly a Soviet affairs analyst at the Federal Research Division, Library of Congress, is an independent researcher and writer on Central and East European politics and environmental issues.

John F. Schaettler is a foreign affairs analyst for the Department of the Army.

W.R. Smyser teaches and writes about European political economy and is the author of *The German Economy: Colossus at the Crossroads.*

Eric Solsten is Senior Research Specialist in West European Affairs, Federal Research Division, Library of Congress.

Jean R. Tartter is a retired Foreign Service Officer who has written extensively on Western Europe for the Country Studies series.

Published Country Studies

(Area Handbook Series)

550-65	Afghanistan		550-87	Greece
550-98	Albania		550-78	Guatemala
550-44	Algeria		550-174	Guinea
550-59	Angola		550-82	Guyana and Belize
550-73	Argentina		550-151	Honduras
550-169	Australia		550-165	Hungary
550-176	Austria		550-21	India
550-175	Bangladesh		550-154	Indian Ocean
550-170	Belgium		550-39	Indonesia
550-66	Bolivia		550-68	Iran
550-20	Brazil		550-31	Iraq
550-168	Bulgaria		550-25	Israel
550-61	Burma		550-182	Italy
550-50	Cambodia		550-30	Japan
550-166	Cameroon		550-34	Jordan
550-159	Chad		550-56	Kenya
550-77	Chile		550-81	Korea, North
550-60	China		550-41	Korea, South
550-26	Colombia		550-58	Laos
550-33	Commonwealth Caribbean, Islands of the		550-24	Lebanon
550-91	Congo		550-38	Liberia
550-90	Costa Rica		550-85	Libya
550-69	Côte d'Ivoire (Ivory Coast)		550-172	Malawi
550-152	Cuba		550-45	Malaysia
550-22	Cyprus		550-161	Mauritania
550-158	Czechoslovakia		550-79	Mexico
550-36	Dominican Republic and Haiti		550-76	Mongolia
550-52	Ecuador		550-49	Morocco
550-43	Egypt		550-64	Mozambique
550-150	El Salvador		550-35	Nepal and Bhutan
550-28	Ethiopia		550-88	Nicaragua
550-167	Finland		550-157	Nigeria
550-155	Germany, East		550-94	Oceania
550-173	Germany, Fed. Rep. of		550-48	Pakistan
550-153	Ghana		550-46	Panama

550-156	Paraguay	550-53	Thailand
550-185	Persian Gulf States	550-89	Tunisia
550-42	Peru	550-80	Turkey
550-72	Philippines	550-74	Uganda
550-162	Poland	550-97	Uruguay
550-181	Portugal	550-71	Venezuela
550-160	Romania	550-32	Vietnam
550-37	Rwanda and Burundi	550-183	Yemens, The
550-51	Saudi Arabia	550-99	Yugoslavia
550-70	Senegal	550-67	Zaire
550-180	Sierra Leone	550-75	Zambia
550-184	Singapore	550-171	Zimbabwe
550-86	Somalia		
550-93	South Africa		
550-95	Soviet Union		
550-179	Spain		
550-96	Sri Lanka		
550-27	Sudan		
550-47	Syria		
550-62	Tanzania		